MacArthur's
Amphibious
Navy

Seventh
Amphibious
Force
Operations
1943-1945

MacArthur's Amphibious Navy

by Daniel E. Barbey
Vice Admiral, USN (Ret.)

United States Naval Institute
Annapolis, Maryland

This story is compiled, in the main, from notes, memoranda, and official reports made at the time by the participants. It tells in small part of the courage, resourcefulness, and exploits of the men of the Seventh Amphibious Force who did so much, with so little, in so short a time.

I am tremendously proud of the performance of the officers and men of the Seventh Amphibious Force. To them I dedicate this book.

Foreword

A QUARTER CENTURY AFTER THE GREATEST WAR IN HISTORY, the name of Vice Admiral Daniel E. ("Uncle Dan") Barbey, who helped so materially to fashion U.S. victory in the Pacific, is but little known to the general public.

This, of course, is often the fate of good and gallant and modest leaders. But Admiral Barbey deserves—and, among his fellow professionals and naval historians will always have—an important place in the narrative of World War II. As commander of the Seventh Amphibious Force in the Southwest Pacific, he accomplished much with little—the true measure of a great commander. He demonstrated an extraordinary organizing capability. Through energy, force of personality, professional competence, and common sense, he was able to fashion a smoothly functioning amphibious force from the most heterogeneous collection of craft and men in history. And he got along with MacArthur—not by any means the easiest of his tasks.

Indeed, if it had not been for the Seventh Amphibious Force, MacArthur's victories would have been impossible. For the key to Pacific strategy is water, and Admiral Barbey's men and ships made the stepping-stone approach from New Guinea to Luzon feasible. The Seventh Amphibious Force was the real "workhorse" of the Southwest Pacific and probably accomplished a greater variety of landings than any similar group in the world. Yet its commander received but little attention in World War II and is little known today, for in the Southwest Pacific there was room for only one dramatic and public personality. MacArthur personalized and epitomized the men, the ships, the planes.

Admiral Barbey understood this at the time, and makes some matter-of-fact observations about it in this book. He shrewdly avoided the yen for publicity that marked the demise of so many promising careers under MacArthur. He stuck to his business—the business of teamwork for victory.

Admiral Barbey is as comfortable as an old shoe and inspires immediate liking. He is like his book—straightforward, honest, and frank. He offers opinions, but never offensively; he lets facts speak for themselves.

The general story that Admiral Barbey sketches in these pages is well known to historians, but it has never before been told from the vantage point of the admiral's cabin. This account supplies many new professional details and some important footnotes to history. Admiral Barbey has been at pains to see that credit is given where credit is due, and he has provided new insights and judgements of permanent value.

In the broadest sense, this book is a long-delayed tribute to the Navy's amphibious forces, so often in the past neglected or downgraded. It emphasizes, too, the importance to the nation's future security of the techniques, methods, and principles developed the hard way during World War II. One of the most mistaken forecasts of our time was the rash prediction of one high-ranking general, just a few months before Korea, that there would never again be an amphibious landing. The atomic bomb, he said, had made such old-fashioned methods of warfare obsolete.

Inchon was only a few months away, and as Admiral Barbey points out in his epilogue:

"Every important naval operation since World War II . . . has been amphibious in character. And it is likely to remain so as long as United States military might is projected into areas without adequate port facilities."

So Admiral Barbey's easy-reading, plain-spoken book is a guide to "Tomorrow," as well as an illumination of "Yesterday."

HANSON W. BALDWIN

Preface

LOOKING BACK AT WORLD WAR II AFTER TWENTY-FIVE YEARS, it is difficult to realize the fear that gripped the people of Australia in the early months of 1942. The Japanese had been successful everywhere. Southeast Asia had been over-run, most of New Guinea had been occupied, and it appeared that Australia would be next on the Japanese timetable. Inadequately trained Allied troops were hurried to New Guinea to stop the Japanese advance before they could seize and establish air and naval bases for the jump-off to Australia.

In desperate fighting in the mountains and through the jungles the Allies, foot by foot, pushed the invaders back from their threatening position. The losses were heavy and the progress was slow.

And then came the ships of the Seventh Amphibious Force. The first trickle of these ships with their landlubber crews arrived in Australia in the early part of 1943. Before the trickle became a stream and even before the landlubbers became seamen there was an urgent cry from MacArthur's weary troops in New Guinea for a helping hand from this new flat-bottomed Navy.

No longer would it be necessary for MacArthur's troops to make frontal assaults on skillfully prepared positions. From now on enemy strong points could be bypassed and Allied troops landed on lightly defended beaches of their own choosing. More territory would be gained in a few weeks than had been gained in the previous twelve months. All this was made possible by the new ships with the new men of the new amphibious Navy.

Its ships carried close to one million Allied troops and a million tons of supplies from Australia, along the New Guinea coast, and into the Philippines, and landed them in a series of lightning strokes on enemy-held beaches in a series of fabulously successful assault operations with a casualty list of but 272 men. Considering the numbers engaged, it was phenomenal in its smallness.

All the operations were of the hurry-up type that got bigger and bigger with larger but different groups of troops. The ships were always the same, only more of them, with the same commanders and the same crews, for the demand was always greater than the supply.

Preparations were being made for participation in the amphibious assault on Japan when the abrupt capitulation of the Japanese changed all plans. The Seventh Amphibious Force thereafter was employed in transporting Army troops to Korea, Marines to North China, Chinese forces from South China to ports in North China, and in the repatriation of two million Japanese from Korea and the China Coast.

How the Seventh Amphibious Force—initially known as the Amphibious Force, Southwest Pacific—came into being in January 1943, how it grew, what it accomplished, is told in this book.

DE Barbey

Vice Admiral, U.S. Navy (Retired)
Commander, Seventh Amphibious Force
during World War II

Olympia, Washington
22 August 1968

Table of Contents

List
of
Illustrations

ILLUSTRATIONS

Credit for illustrations is acknowledged to the following:

U.S. COAST GUARD: 41, 93, 113, 114(2), 116(2), 117(2), 118, 137, 139(2), 149, 171, 174, 180(2), 189, 200, 201(2), 208(2), 209(2), 212, 213, 246, 256, 257, 293, 294, 295, 296, 313. LIFE MAGAZINE: 23, 163. JAMES C. FAHEY: 41, 63. UNITED PRESS INTERNATIONAL: 14, 63. BUREAU OF AERONAUTICS: 289. U.S. ARMY: 99, 105, 129, 155(2), 163, 181, 189, 256, 267, 312, 313. ARMY AIR FORCE: 105, 115, 164(2), 165, 171, 188. U.S. MARINE CORPS: 114, 115, 118. *All other photographs not credited are official U.S. Navy.*

MacArthur's
Amphibious
Navy

1: Origin of the Seventh Amphibious Force

NOWHERE IN THE MILITARY WORLD WERE THE INTERSERVICE bickerings so bitter in the early days of World War II as around Allied Headquarters in Brisbane, Australia. The Air Force usually prefaced their references to the Navy as the "damn Navy." The Navy labeled the Air Force a bunch of publicity hounds who got lost whenever out of sight of land. The commander in chief of the Allied Forces in the Southwest Pacific, General Douglas MacArthur, was outspoken in his criticism of his senior naval commanders, whom he considered were timidly conserving their ships instead of boldly supporting his strategic objectives.

It was in this atmosphere of tension and strain that I reported to Vice Admiral A. S. Carpender, the commander of Allied Naval Forces in the Southwest Pacific, for duty as commander of the Southwest Pacific Amphibious Forces—later called the Seventh Amphibious Force. On my reporting on 10 January 1943, the Seventh Amphibious Force was born. At its birth it consisted of two members, Commander M. T. Farrar and myself, but little else.

Two days before, on a rainy, blustery day, the seaplane in which I was riding had set down in the choppy waters of the harbor of Brisbane, Australia. Aboard the plane was a full passenger load of civilian and military personnel who were headed for assorted wartime jobs in various parts of the Southwest Pacific. Farrar and myself were the only ones assigned to the Southwest Pacific Amphibious Force.

A few weeks previously I had been promoted to rear admiral and ordered to

Australia to bring into being an amphibious force from ships yet to be built and with men yet to be assigned.

The plane trip from San Francisco had taken ten days. During an overnight stop at Pearl Harbor, I was the house guest of Admiral C. W. Nimitz, the commander in chief of our naval forces in the Pacific. Around Nimitz's headquarters there was little interest in General MacArthur's New Guinea campaign. Such interest as there was regarding activities in the Southwest Pacific centered around the submarines that were working out of Australia, but under their operational control.

The atmosphere around the admiral's headquarters and his comfortable home, where he lived with his chief of staff, was one of informality. My plane was taking off at daybreak, so he arranged to have breakfast for me at 5 A.M. Then to my surprise and pleasure, he joined me at that early hour in his bathrobe for a cup of coffee.

He brought me up to date on recent happenings and mentioned in particular the successes of Allied submarines operating out of the Australian ports of Fremantle and Brisbane. They had ranged far and wide. Among their latest accomplishments was the laying of mines off the coast of Japan and the sinking of the Japanese cruiser *Tenryu* and a submarine in the waters off New Guinea—and then he casually mentioned that his son, and his chief of staff's son, were on submarines operating out of Australia.

There was a sense of optimism in his words. The bitter fighting for Guadalcanal was drawing to a close, and General MacArthur's troops were slowly closing in on the strategically important village of Buna on the north coast of New Guinea. The Japanese advance had been halted everywhere in the Pacific and as soon as more ships and troops became available the rollback would commence. Admiral Nimitz sent his greetings to my new boss, Vice Admiral A. S. Carpender, wished me luck in my new job, and then I was on my way.

The plane trip from Pearl Harbor onward was merely a series of daylight hops from one little island to another in the general direction of Australia. The trip was uneventful unless crossing both the Equator and the International Date Line on 31 December was noteworthy. We left a little island base on 31 December and arrived at another just before sundown on the same day, but on a different date, 1 January. We missed having a New Year's Eve celebration, but on our war-darkened atoll it would have been a pretty dreary affair.

What I remember most on this trip was the marked variation in the security regulations of the bases where we were housed overnight. The more remote from the combat area, the more stringent the regulations regarding "darkened lights" and the more complete the bomb shelters and trenches. In contrast was the activity at Nouméa, the combat headquarters of Admiral W. F. Halsey, commander of the South Pacific Force, which was fairly ablaze with lights as stevedoring crews were working around the clock. The urgency of nighttime work in the combat zone far outweighed security considerations.

Farrar and I were overnight guests of Admiral Halsey in his shore-based headquarters which was housed in a group of Quonset huts. The talk at the very simple dinner that night revolved around the past week's military activities and the plans for the future.

Halsey's words were very expressive and almost boastful. He seemed to take pride in minimizing the difficulties that lay ahead. What he said was in accord with his well-known aggressive optimism which had sometimes created concern among his more conservative associates in the Navy Department.

There was little discussion on what was taking place in the Southwest Pacific or in the other theaters of war. Those other activities seemed so distant and there was so much to be done near at hand. Interest in the broad picture was confined to the theater commander and to a few others, which I later found to be true not only in Nouméa but in the Southwest Pacific and presumably in other areas.

The next day I met with Rear Admiral Richmond Kelly Turner, commander, Amphibious Force, South Pacific, aboard his flagship the USS *McCawley,* which was anchored in the harbor. Kelly Turner was an able, explosive officer who had been in command of the amphibious landing at Guadalcanal the previous August. He reviewed the details of that landing and dwelt upon the difficulties in getting large quantities of stores from the ships to the shore even under ideal weather and beach conditions. He had to withdraw transports and cargo ships from the Guadalcanal area on the third day after the landing even though most of them were but half unloaded. This left the Marines ashore in a precarious position, but he felt he had no other alternative, as air protection had been withdrawn and amphibious shipping was being harassed by air attacks and threatened by naval forays. He said that hereafter he would take steps to reduce the unloading time and insist on continuous air coverage and better naval coverage of the landing area. I had good reason to remember his words in my own numerous landings in the ensuing months.

In my conversations with Halsey's staff, I noticed the frequent use of the word "Nipponese" in place of "Japanese" and "Nip" in place of "Jap," a phraseology in common usage throughout most of the Pacific, but not in Washington.

Inasmuch as January is midsummer for areas south of the Equator, I had expected to be greeted in Brisbane by warm weather and clear skies; instead, we found unseasonably strong winds and heavy rain. I was welcomed by Commander B. B. C. Lovett, my prospective aviation officer, who escorted us to the Canberra Hotel where we would be housed until a flagship became available for my use.

The Canberra, second largest hotel in the city, was a "temperance" hotel, strictly enforced. By American standards, it was somewhat old-fashioned, more like our western hotels at the turn of the century. The only modern hotel was Lennon's, where General Douglas MacArthur lived with his wife and young son in a top floor apartment. Most of his senior staff officers were living in the Lennon Hotel, as was Vice Admiral Carpender, and some of his staff, but it was not big enough to house all its would-be guests. For the next few days I had most of my meals with Carpender in his Lennon Hotel apartment.

It didn't take long to absorb the idea that living was a serious business to the residents of Brisbane. In marked contrast to Washington, which wasn't very much bigger and where living conditions were almost normal, I found little social life in Brisbane, very few streetcars, and fewer automobiles. Regardless of distance, all but the senior military walked to work. As a substitute for gasoline, civilian automobiles were equipped with charcoal burners which were carried above the trunk compartment. Mounted over the body of the occasional truck was a gas-filled balloon. Neither was very satisfactory because of the low power and short range. Only military cars and trucks operated under normal conditions. Uniforms were everywhere. Groups of women volunteers with long strides and stiff, swinging arms marched through the streets.

The Australians were warmly hospitable and seemed reassured by the presence of the Americans. Less than a year previously, invasion seemed imminent, morale was low, and the people felt abandoned. Then MacArthur had come and his arrival had been like a shot in the arm. The attitude of the people changed overnight. He spoke confidently of American help and his plans for an offensive against the Japanese. As a practical expression of Australian appreciation, office space and living quarters were often made available by the local residents at considerable personal sacrifice. In addition to my rooms in the Canberra Hotel, temporary office space was assigned me in the New Zealand Insurance Building, vintage 1900, on Queen Street.

The industrial facilities in Brisbane, as elsewhere in Australia, were woefully inadequate to meet the demands of a major military buildup. Piers, dockyards, and transportation systems were barely able to meet peacetime requirements, and by American or European standards were quite backward. Ships loaded with essential military cargo would often wait weeks for discharge. One of the worst instances occurred at Townsville, in northeast Australia, where 185 ships were simultaneously in port with just eight docks available. But there was little that could be done about it. The munitions output of mighty America was too great to be absorbed by small ports on distant shores.

Shortage of Australian facilities was matched by shortage of equipment and supplies. But this was not due to any slack spots in their war effort. With a population of a little over seven million, Australia had more than 600,000 men in uniform and 66,000 women in auxiliary services. In the early days of the war, it was the Australians

General Douglas MacArthur, U.S. Army, Commander in Chief, Allied Forces, Southwest Pacific.

Admiral Chester W. Nimitz, U.S. Navy, Commander in Chief, Pacific Fleet.

Admiral William F. Halsey, U.S. Navy, Commander, South Pacific Force.

Admiral Ernest J. King, U.S. Navy, Chief of Naval Operations.

who held the superior Japanese forces in check in the mountains of New Guinea and on the shores of Milne Bay. Not until the latter part of 1942 were American soldiers available to take over part of this burden and release some of the men to the civilian end of the war effort.

In our frequent get-togethers during my first few days, Vice Admiral Carpender and his staff gave me a good picture of the local situation, the conflicting personalities of the senior commanders, and the successful operations of the U.S. submarines based in Australia, as well as considerable information regarding the campaign for the capture of Buna which was then drawing to a close. That campaign had been almost solely a ground force operation with strong air force support. Except for a few PT boats, the Navy had not participated.

Allied submarines which operated out of Fremantle and Brisbane were only under Carpender's nominal command. The real control was exercised by Fleet Headquarters at Pearl Harbor. He felt the PT boats were the only units of his force that should operate in the waters of the western Solomon Sea until the Allies obtained control of the air and the area was better charted. In his opinion, the risks to large ships from air attack and uncharted shoals in the waters between New Guinea and New Britain far outweighed any possible gains, and it was essential to husband slender resources if he was to carry out the many projects on which he was then engaged.

The negligible part played by the Navy in the Buna campaign had led to a further straining of already strained relations between MacArthur and Carpender. MacArthur had asked for naval ships, particularly destroyers, to operate in the waters off the northeast coast of New Guinea to give gunfire support to his troops who were advancing along the coast toward Buna, as well as to protect the small Dutch freighters and miscellaneous craft that were attempting to run supplies to his hard-pressed men. Carpender felt it was foolhardy for his few cruisers and destroyers to enter these coral-studded and vaguely charted waters, where they would be subject to air attack from Japanese planes that roamed the skies at will. He pointed to the fact that nearly all the Dutch and native small craft that had taken part in the supply runs had either been sunk or badly damaged. He considered his few cruisers and destroyers were primarily a defensive force to be used to protect the Australian coast and the shipping in those waters against surface raids and submarines. He did not think such ships were suitable for the type of operations MacArthur had in mind until better charts were obtained and the Allied Air Force could provide adequate protection to his ships.

The divergent points of view regarding naval ships operating in the waters off the northeast coast of New Guinea were of particular interest to me as it was the area where I assumed I would be expected to operate with amphibious ships and accompanying destroyers.

Since MacArthur and his chief of staff, Lieutenant General R. K. Sutherland, were in New Guinea supervising the windup of the Buna campaign, I called on his able operations officer, Brigadier General Stephen J. Chamberlin. He briefly sketched MacArthur's immediate plans. They provided for a continuation of the move from Buna along the New Guinea coast in the direction of Lae. After Lae, it was proposed to jump across Vitiaz Strait to the western end of New Britain as part of the encirclement of Rabaul, the Japanese stronghold on the eastern end of that island. While these moves were under way, according to Chamberlin, it was expected that Admiral Halsey's South Pacific Forces would be advancing toward Rabaul through the Solomon Islands. All these activities were being undertaken as part of the Joint Chiefs of Staff directive for the reduction of Rabaul. Chamberlin also mentioned that the Navy would have to take a more active part in future moves along the New Guinea coast if the time schedule of the forces of the Southwest Pacific was to be kept, and that "the General expects you and your amphibious force to do just that."

In the Southwest Pacific, when anyone referred to "the General" he meant General MacArthur, although there were a great many other generals in the area. Even Mrs. MacArthur in her soft southern drawl referred to her husband, at least in public, as "the Gineral," with the accent on the "Gin."

Chamberlin felt that the hazards of naval operations in the waters between New Guinea and New Britain had been exaggerated. He told me that the PT boats seemed to be operating in that area satisfactorily, and that three small Australian survey ships had been able to buoy a channel through some of the worst places a few months before, and that three Australian corvettes had carried three battalions of Australian troops to Oro Bay—about twenty miles to the east of Buna—just one month earlier. If it had not been for the small Dutch freighters and even smaller miscellaneous craft moving supplies and even tanks for the Allied troops advancing toward Buna, he doubted if the campaign for its capture would have succeeded, as air transport could not meet all the supply requirements. It was evident that the manner in which U.S. naval ships were used was a touchy subject.

General Chamberlin spoke with an air of certainty when he said that after the capture of Rabaul it was the General's intention to move westward along the New Guinea coast and then northwestward into the Philippines. These were the military moves needed to carry out MacArthur's well-publicized statement, "I shall return (to the Philippines)." But I knew that these projected moves did not fit into the Navy Department's idea of how the war in the Pacific would be fought.

The Navy Department plans provided for an island-hopping approach through the Central Pacific in the general direction of the Marianas Islands, just southeast of Japan, and on to Formosa or China if necessary. The Philippines would be bypassed. These plans further provided for the establishment of naval bases en route, bringing the Japanese fleet into action if possible, cutting off Japan's supplies to Southeast Asia and constructing air bases on her defense perimeter, and eventually bombing her into submission. The Pacific Fleet was expected to play the dominant role in these operations. If these plans were carried out there appeared no need for MacArthur to go to the Philippines.

Although the Joint Chiefs of Staff in Washington would make the final decision regarding the strategic moves and the assignment of major forces in the Pacific, as they did elsewhere, it was well known that the views of the Navy member of the Joint Chiefs, Admiral E. J. King, were likely to prevail on all matters relating to operations in the Pacific, as did the views of General George C. Marshall, the Army member of the Joint Chiefs, on most matters relating to operations in the Atlantic.

I made no comment on Chamberlin's outline of MacArthur's future moves, but wondered if he was fully aware of Navy Department thinking on these matters. The farther MacArthur's troops advanced along the New Guinea coast, the more vulnerable they became to Japanese naval raids and the more they would require the protection of the Pacific Fleet. But Navy planners expected to keep the Pacific Fleet concentrated in the Central Pacific and ready for any major engagement with the Japanese main body, and it was a long way from the Marianas to New Guinea.

If the Navy's views prevailed, it was unlikely that any battleships or aircraft carriers would be ordered to the Southwest Pacific. Any buildup of MacArthur's forces would probably be limited to the troops and amphibious ships needed to meet the immediate objectives of the Joint Chiefs of Staff. Air and surface protection for these moves would have to be provided by shore-based aircraft in New Guinea and the few cruisers and destroyers under Admiral Carpender's control.

2:

U.S. Ship Design and Construction

AT THE TIME OF THE JAPANESE ATTACK ON PEARL HARBOR, THE U.S. Navy did not have a single oceangoing ship that could run its bow onto the beach and deliver a cargo of big tanks and other heavy equipment directly to the shore without benefit of piers or cranes. Less than a year later ships of this type were sliding down the building ways of small shipyards in a steady stream. Without these ships there would have been no Southwest Pacific Amphibious Force. Without these ships the major amphibious invasions of Europe and the Pacific could not have been undertaken.

After Pearl Harbor every major operation was amphibious in character. Why then were we, and the British, and the Germans, so unprepared for a type of warfare that dominated all other types?

Although World War II was destined to be an amphibious war, neither the military leaders of the Allies nor those of the Axis powers foresaw its direction. Had the Germans prepared for the over-water invasion of England with the same care they prepared for the land invasion of Europe, they would have had great numbers of landing craft available to carry their victorious troops across the English Channel in 1940 when the British Army was shattered from the disaster at Dunkirk and home defenses pitifully weak. Building an amphibious fleet takes time and it was too late for the Germans to do overnight what they had failed to do in the years before. They lost their chance, and it was never to be offered again.

As for the Allies, the weaknesses in their prewar preparations were largely over-

11

come because the industrial might of America was able to build an amphibious fleet, after Pearl Harbor, as fast as the invasion troops were ready to use it.

In the fall of 1939, however—even after the outbreak of the European war—the British gave no serious attention to the landing craft requirements for a major amphibious invasion. In April of that year, with war imminent, a study was made within the British Admiralty on future requirements for landing troops on hostile beaches. In his book, *Assault from the Sea,* Rear Admiral L. E. H. Maund, who headed the study group, has given us their conclusions:

> Raids might be undertaken from submarines in a matter of weeks: a raid by a brigade couldn't be staged under six months because of the lack of L.C.A. (landing craft assault—a lightly armed, shallow-draft boat of 41½ ft. length): we should need two years to prepare for a landing by a brigade with the object of occupying territory.

When war did come a few months later, Admiral Maund and his small group of co-workers—the only members of the British Navy who had been studying the amphibious problem—had a few prototype landing boats and considerable knowledge to show for their efforts. To their amazement, they were informed "there would be no combined [amphibious] operations in this war," and the group was disbanded. Apparently the Admiralty was convinced that the friendly ports and piers of France, and of other countries of Europe and Africa, would always be available to them to handle the overseas movement of troops and supplies.

It was not until after the fall of France in the following year that the Admiralty reversed itself regarding combined operations and turned its attention to the development of an oceangoing ship that could land cargo on an open beach. This first came about because of the failure of the expedition against Dakar in North Africa where the French garrison refused to cooperate and surrender. Since the Expeditionary Force could not land troops, tanks, and equipment across friendly piers and had no way of landing them on the beaches, the force shamefacedly returned to England. The beginnings of Britain's amphibious fleet may be said to have resulted from this failure. At the urging of Prime Minister Winston Churchill, plans were then drawn for the various types of ships that would be needed for the amphibious operations he had in mind, but limited British resources could provide only a very few of the great numbers that would be required.

Similarly, American prewar planners never gave serious consideration to the matter of large-scale amphibious operations, such as would be required for an invasion of Europe across its beaches. They had unbounded faith in the ability of the French to hold the Germans in check, and consequently believed that the ports and piers of Europe would be available, if required, as they were in World War I. Also, the unfortunate experience of the British in their landing at Gallipoli during World War I was fresh in the minds of military leaders of that day. The consensus was that modern armies with their complex equipment could not be successfully debarked in the face of superior air power on vigorously defended beaches. And Germany had the superior air power and could be counted upon to defend her shores.

American planners confidently believed that the approaching European war would be an updated version of World War I and that defense funds should not be diverted to costly experimentation with new types of weapons or new types of ships. As a result, our Army continued its development of tanks and planes, our Navy modernized its battleships and carriers, and the technique of hunting down submarines was improved.

American preparations in the event of war against Japan, however, were on a different basis. Such a war, it was assumed, would be predominantly naval in character, with the U.S. fleet moving westward from Hawaii across the Central Pacific, establishing naval and air bases as it advanced. Although little was known about Japanese island bases, such as Tarawa, Truk, Saipan, and Palau, their capture was not considered one that would greatly tax our military capabilities. Information regarding off-island coral reefs and tidal data was very sketchy and often inaccurate. The skill of the Japanese in erecting island defenses was as grossly underestimated as was U.S. bombardment capability overestimated. It was believed those islands could be captured by a small number of Marines landed after the defenses had been battered to helplessness by heavy ship gunfire and by bombing from U.S. aircraft carriers.

Since the Marines would be given the job of capturing the Japanese mandated islands, if a Pacific war should break out, they turned their attention to a series of amphibious training exercises to fit them for their wartime role of landing troops and tanks and equipment across open beaches where there would be no harbors or piers. I participated in these exercises. Fortunately, a previous tour of duty in the Navy Department had kept me abreast of naval planning for war.

From 1937 to 1940, I had been in charge of the section in the Navy Department which was concerned with the mobilization of personnel for war. This meant the preparation of plans for wartime crews for active duty ships, reactivated ships, and ships to be built; assigning retired and reserve personnel to duty; working with the selective service group; preparing plans for an expanded recruit training program; and many other matters relating to naval personnel requirements in an all-out war. These activities necessarily required that I be kept fully informed of the various war plans as they developed.

In 1940, I was assigned as chief of staff to the Commander, Training Force, Atlantic Fleet. In my new capacity I participated in all the amphibious training exercises in the Atlantic, which included those with the First Army Division as well as those with the 1st Division of Marines. This duty continued until shortly after

*By early 1942, thousands of amphibious craft were under construction by U.S. firms.
One of these ships, the LCT (Landing Craft, Tank), was 118 feet long, and was
designed primarily for short-range runs.*

*The LCI(L) (Landing Craft, Infantry, Large) was designed to carry troops and land
them directly onto the beach by means of two ramps located on either side of the bow.
The funnel-like structure is the combined pilothouse and conning tower.*

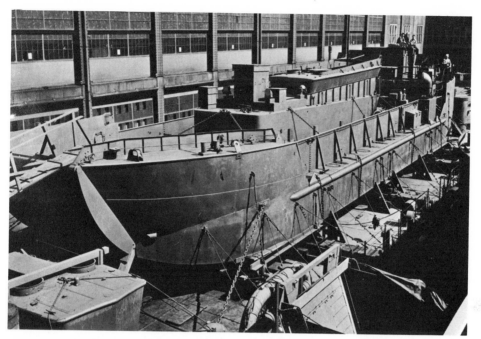

The LST (Landing Ship, Tank) was 328 feet long and could carry 4,000 tons. On the deck of this LST an LCT is firmly lashed. Inside the LCT is an LCM (Landing Craft, Mechanized). Topping off the "nestling" is an LCVP (Landing Craft, Vehicle, Personnel).

The LCM (Landing Craft, Mechanized) was the largest landing craft normally carried by transports and cargo ships. It was designed to carry about 30 tons of cargo. Note the shelving bow and ramp.

Pearl Harbor and was a rewarding experience. Much of what I learned then, however, was not applicable to the amphibious landings later undertaken in the Southwest Pacific because of the far different conditions under which they were carried out.

The doctrine developed by the Marines, in conjunction with the Navy, for use against the mandated islands called for the use of large troop transports, capable of carrying large numbers of small boats. The boats would be used to land assault troops with light equipment on a beach in accordance with a carefully rehearsed ship-to-shore technique, similar to that then in use by the Japanese. To provide the necessary transports on short notice, records were kept in the Navy Department of the day-to-day location of all U.S. passenger ships with a view to their conversion to troopships, if the need arose. No difficult conversion problems were expected. Since there was no expectation of immediate amphibious operations, there was no sense of urgency in any amphibious preparations. Landing exercises were expanded in scope in 1940 and 1941, and the conversion of a few passenger ships to transports was begun, but that was about all.

The fact that heavily laden troops would have to climb over the bows of conventional boats and jump onto the beach six to eight feet below was not considered of great moment, although a "landing boat development board" was looking into the matter and a few experimental ramp-type boats had been built which could off-load light tanks in sheltered waters.

The ramp-type boat was not a new concept; the Japanese had been using it for years. Their boat was self-propelled with a hinged ramp in the bow that could be lowered at will so that troops and light artillery could be landed dry-shod on the beach. More than four hundred of these boats were used in the Japanese assault on Tientsin, China, in 1937. The Navy Department was fully aware of this operation and the characteristics of the landing boats that were used.

Even as late as the spring of 1941, in amphibious exercises off the North Carolina coast, the Marines and Army troops were still going over the bows of ships' boats of conventional design. The only innovations in these exercises was the landing of light tanks and bulk cargo from the few experimental ramp boats which had become available. But these exercises proved one thing for certain—great numbers of ramp boats would be required before the Marines could carry out their war commitments in the Pacific.

Because the attention of U.S. military leaders was focused on the European struggle, and because of the probability of involvement there, where beach landings would not be required, a low priority was assigned to amphibious preparations for a Pacific war and particularly to the ramp boat program. Other slow-down factors resulted from a wrangle between the Navy Bureau of Ships and some private shipbuilders as to the types of boats that would best meet the requirements for landing troops and light tanks through the surf.

The craft finally adopted were designed and built by the Higgins Ship Building Company of New Orleans. Their principal features involved the hinged bow—borrowed from the Japanese—and the flat bottom with tunnel-shaped stern—borrowed from another enemy of the government, the rumrunner of prohibition days.

Particularly useful to the rumrunners was the tunnel-like stern which protected the propellers of fast boats when they jumped the log booms that had been stretched across the bayous of the Mississippi River to cut off their escape. Adaptation of this tunnel-like stern to landing boats would likewise be useful in protecting the propellers during beaching operations. Higgins boats came in two sizes, a 36-foot LCVP (Landing Craft—Vehicle, Personnel) designed to carry personnel or small vehicles, and a 50-foot LCM (Landing Craft—Mechanized) to carry a light tank or its equivalent.

While the Americans were experimenting with Higgins boats and similar types, the British turned their attention to the development of beaching ships of ocean-going size. When the threat of invasion of their own shores had evaporated, they began thinking less of Commando raids ("hit-and-run" operations) and more of amphibious operations in terms of major undertakings, including a cross-channel invasion of France, in which all the trappings of a modern army would accompany the troops. To secure American assistance for this program, the British Admiralty sent a delegation to Washington under the leadership of Captain T. A. Hussey, Royal Navy.

This group reached Washington about the middle of November 1941, and met with the Chief of Naval Operations and senior officers of the Navy Department. Captain Hussey acted as spokesman and presented the problem. In essence, he stated that the British were now thinking in terms of major landing operations, and that they needed ships of a type that could carry tanks and heavy equipment directly to the beaches. He had sketches of the types of ships required and he requested that these ships be furnished under the Lend-Lease program.

A specific request was made for two hundred of the type later known as "Landing Ship, Tank"; two hundred of a smaller type later known as "Landing Craft, Tank"; and seven "Landing Ship, Dock." To add point to his remarks, Hussey mentioned that a large number of armored tanks being built in America for British use could not be transported to the continent of Europe unless special ship types were provided to get them ashore.

The delegation was advised to return in two weeks for a decision. On 28 November, the second meeting was held. The Navy Department decision, in substance, disapproved the request because American yards were fully occupied with warship and merchant ship construction of types considered essential to the British war effort. The special types of ships that Captain Hussey proposed were not considered in an essential category; and furthermore, all Lend-Lease funds had already been obligated.

Through a mutual friend, Captain Hussey enlisted the support of Justice Felix Frankfurter, who in turn interested General George Marshall and Mr. Harry Hopkins, a close associate of President Roosevelt. Hussey hoped the President might reverse the Navy Department decision on the British proposal if the matter could be brought to his personal attention. A few days later, however, the entire situation changed. Pearl Harbor was attacked and the United States was at war.

Captain Hussey returned to England and reported the failure of his mission. But as he subsequently learned, it was not a complete failure. There had been changes in the top command of the U.S. Navy and a month later Hussey had the satisfaction of reading a dispatch stating that the American government had reversed its decision and would build the ships his delegation had recommended. In addition, the government was instituting a program of equal numbers and similar types for its own account.

After Pearl Harbor, events moved swiftly. Admiral Ernest J. King was made overall commander of the Pacific and the Atlantic Fleets with headquarters in Washington. Although he had been commander in chief of the Atlantic Fleet during the previous year, he had been limited in what he could do to promote the amphibious program, in which he was a firm believer. But now he was in a position to carry out his ideas.

I was ordered to his staff with instructions to establish, within the Navy Department, an amphibious warfare section whose functions would include the coordination of all training programs and the procurement of whatever was necessary for large-scale amphibious operations. By April 1942, more than one hundred million dollars had been made available for amphibious craft construction, and a few months later this amount was increased ten times. There was little time left for further experimentation. A few months after our entry into the war, hundreds of thousands of Higgins boats and thousands of beaching ships of the modified British types were under construction for an amphibious Navy that was destined to land millions of men and millions of tons of supplies across enemy beaches in Africa, Europe, and the far Pacific.

Since most large U.S. shipyards were concentrating on the construction of heavy ships, and on destroyers and destroyer escorts to combat the submarine menace, contracts for building amphibious ships, including Higgins boats, were awarded to an assortment of concerns. These included bridge builders, small boat yards, and newly organized construction firms—the main requirements being that they had the tools to do the job and were located on a waterway. The principal types were:

Landing Craft, Tank (*LCT*). This was a short-range craft, 118 feet long, with a ramp bow, that could carry medium-sized tanks or their equivalent. Its speed was five or six knots, depending on its load and the sea conditions. LCTs were so designed that they could be built in three sections, transported overseas on freighters, and readily assembled at their destination. There was no provision for crew accommodations, or for storage space for food, water or spare parts, as these craft were expected to be used only for short runs in the vicinity of shore bases.

Landing Craft, Infantry (*LCI*). Much faster, with an operating speed of about fourteen knots, and longer than the LCT, the LCI was designed solely to carry infantry. In addition to the crew, it could carry about 188 troops and land them directly on the beach by means of two ramps, lowered on either side of the bow. The original British design had no sleeping accommodations for the troops as the craft were to be used only in short-range operations, such as crossing the English Channel, and never far from a good shore base. Benches for the troops were considered adequate for the few hours they would be aboard. However, all American-built LCIs had bunks installed for the troops as well as the crew. Even so, these craft were not suitable for operations of more than one or two hundred miles at the most. As it turned out, in the Southwest Pacific, necessity required their almost continuous use in waters far distant from adequate shore or repair bases.

Landing Ship, Tank (*LST*). Perhaps the most important beaching ship was the LST—often called "large, slow target" because its bulk and unwieldiness made it an easy target for planes and submarines. It was designed for 11 knots, but usually good for only 8 or 9. It was a comparatively shallow draft ship considering its size—328 feet long and about 4,000 tons. It could carry about 20 medium-sized tanks on the tank deck in addition to miscellaneous cargo on an upper deck. Tanks could be landed directly on the beach by means of ramp doors in the bow. Although the troop accommodations were supposedly limited to troops accompanying tanks and cargo—about 160 officers and men—LSTs in the Southwest Pacific frequently carried as many as 1,000 men as part of a landing force. (For LSTs used in the postwar repatriation of Japanese, the usual load was 2,000 men, women, and children.)

Trying out each new type of amphibious craft and vehicle before it went on the production line was one of my jobs during the summer of 1942. Some of these try-out jobs had their interesting moments. One Sunday afternoon off the Cape Cod coast, on a trial run of a new LCI, we asked the builder's representative to run it up on a beach and not to be too cautious. He wasn't. The craft stopped only after it had crossed a scenic highway and disrupted traffic. But the test was useful. It gave us confidence in the ability of the ship to take heavy punishment.

On another occasion, I was one of a group assigned to test a contrivance called an "alligator," designed to travel on land, through water, and over reefs. It had a watertight steel hull and the cleated tracks of a tank. (A later armored model was called the "buffalo.") One bright afternoon, I was picked up at the Navy Department building by one of these strange craft and driven through the streets of Washington and across the Potomac to a nearby lake. The "alligator" entered the lake, executed a few maneuvers, and emerged quite happily. We were all promptly placed under arrest for having invaded a wild fowl sanctuary.

By November 1942 the amphibious building program was reaching full stride with ships being launched in a steady stream from nearly every inland waterway in the country. Owing to the magnificence of this construction effort and the postponement of the cross-channel invasion of France, many of these ships became surplus to the requirements in the Atlantic and so they became available for operations in the Pacific.

The Southwest Pacific was an area particularly suitable for landing craft operation because of the lack of man-made harbors in New Guinea, where General MacArthur's Southwest Pacific Force was operating. His offensive was being held up owing to inadequate sea transport and he urgently requested the immediate assignment of an amphibious force. His request was approved. A few weeks later, in December 1942, I was promoted to rear admiral and given this new command.

In Navy Department circles, assignment to duty in the Southwest Pacific was not a cause for congratulations. MacArthur had already fired one Allied naval commander and his present one was in trouble.

My last call in Washington was on my boss, Admiral Ernest J. King. He did not see eye to eye with General MacArthur on how the war in the Pacific should be fought and had a particular distaste for the remark, "I shall return." I think he felt that MacArthur's interest in the Philippines was unduly influencing his strategic recommendations. During the next several months, I had many occasions to think of his remarks in the light of future happenings. In his parting words, he wished me well and added, "You have the enviable opportunity to take into combat the ships you helped create."

3:   General
MacArthur
and His
Commanders

GENERAL MACARTHUR'S WORKING HOURS WERE A BIT UNUSUAL. He arrived at mid-morning, left for lunch quite late, and returned to his office at mid-afternoon, remaining there with some of his personal staff well along into the evening. "SoWesPac" headquarters were in the modern AMP Building in Brisbane, Australia. Occasionally the General would walk to work from his apartment a few blocks away, but usually he would arrive in a chauffeur-driven black Cadillac. Invariably, there would be a small group of Australians gathered at the building entrance to witness his arrival.

My first call on MacArthur was somewhat of an occasion. He was friendly but deadly serious. He never smiled. There was no light touch to his words nor the informality and camaraderie that was so evident around the Pacific Fleet headquarters of Admiral Nimitz. Because of my specialized background, I fully expected to be queried about the progress of the amphibious building program, what ships might be expected in the Southwest Pacific, and other matters relating to landing operations. But such was not the case. It was a one-way conversation in which the General spoke of the current military situation and his plans for the future. The only question he asked was a very curious one—"Are you a lucky officer?"

MacArthur's office was plainly furnished with a few straight-backed chairs, a black leather couch, and a desk that was devoid of papers. There was only one map in the room. He referred to the Joint Chiefs' of Staff instructions for the capture of Rabaul, the Japanese stronghold at the northeastern tip of New Britain. With pipe in hand he gestured toward the map, making his points as he strode back and forth. I remained seated on the couch.

MacArthur reiterated in somewhat more detail than had General Chamberlin his proposals regarding the future campaigns in the Southwest Pacific. In his opinion, the reconquest of the Philippines must be given priority over all other objectives in the Pacific. Not only did he feel that we had a moral commitment to throw the Japanese out of the Philippines, but also that a thrust in that direction would give heart to all the guerrilla forces then operating in Southeast Asia. "Your job," he said, "is to develop an amphibious force that can carry my troops in those campaigns." His voice took on a bitter tinge and he stopped his pacing when he spoke of the meagerness of the troops, planes, and ships which had been given him for the job he had to do.

During the preceding six months MacArthur had thrown inadequately trained and inadequately equipped troops into New Guinea to stop the deadly advance of jungle-trained Japanese soldiers. As a result, he said, the Allied casualties were terrifying, but it was vital that the Japanese be stopped in their tracks.

It was Japanese doctrine to take seaports from the rear, and they worshiped doctrine like a god. From the rear (or flank) in World War I, they had taken Tsingtao in China from the Germans and bypassed the great entrance forts. In the early months of World War II they similarly had taken Singapore and Manila.

At one time it looked as if the Japanese would scale the Owen Stanley Mountains and capture Port Moresby from the rear, the only semi-decent port on the south coast of New Guinea. If such an event had come to pass and Port Moresby had become a Japanese bomber and submarine base, the results could well have been disastrous for Australia.

MacArthur referred to the high priority given to the European effort in troops, ships, planes, and supplies and questioned whether the combined Chiefs of Staff had fully appreciated the Japanese threat to Australia.

As he talked, I recalled the lack of enthusiasm in Washington which greeted MacArthur's repeated and urgent requests through military and diplomatic channels for more ships, more planes, and more troops. There was a feeling that many of his requests were unreasonable and improper in view of the decision which had been reached in concert with the British that the Germans were the main threat to Allied security and that the first call on U.S. resources must be pointed to that end.

As a consequence, the Pacific war, in the initial stages, was relegated to a holding war. The threat of an invasion of Australia was not considered imminent by the Combined Chiefs of Staff as it was believed the Japanese were overextended and that they could be held in check in the Southwest Pacific by the assignment of a Marine Division to Guadalcanal and a couple of National Guard Divisions to New Guinea. And this had been done.

General Douglas MacArthur (left) and Lieutenant General Walter Krueger, U.S. Army, discuss the progress of the war in the Pacific aboard a Navy PT boat. General Krueger commanded the Sixth Army, which provided most of the American assault troops.

Lieutenant General R. L. Eichelberger, U.S. Army, the First Corps commander, successfully completed the Buna campaign.

Rear Admiral Daniel E. Barbey, U.S. Navy, Commander, Seventh Amphibious Force.

MacArthur spoke of his organization as a smoothly functioning team, but left no doubt as to who called the signals. As I was soon to learn, his team was not functioning as smoothly as he indicated. Within his own staff there was jealousy and friction between those who had served with him in the Philippines and the recent arrivals. Then there were the interservice rivalries which were so bitter in Washington and even more so in the headquarters in Brisbane. In the Southwest Pacific, however, as in other theaters of war, the nearer one got to the combat zone the closer became the cooperation and mutual support between the various fighting services.

MacArthur spoke with admiration of Halsey's audacity and mentioned several times that he wished he had him in his outfit. I sensed a touch of irritation at what he termed the cautious attitude of the naval forces in the Southwest Pacific. If the Navy had been a bit more aggressive, he felt, they could have given him a lot more assistance than they had in the six months' campaign for the capture of Buna. This small village of a few native huts on the northeast coast of New Guinea had been captured only a few days previously, and the casualties were still coming in.

If MacArthur appeared unenthusiastic about the support he received from most of the Navy, it was different when he spoke of the PT boats. A squadron of them were operating under the command of Lieutenant Commander M. C. Mumma in the western reaches of the Solomon Sea. They were manned by a bunch of brash youngsters who cruised at night off the shores of New Britain and New Guinea seeking out Japanese barge traffic carrying troop reinforcements and supplies. The hit and run tactics of these eggshell PT boats were outstandingly successful.

It was a pleasure to listen to MacArthur. He had the voice and manner of an orator and though I was but an audience of one, he spoke deliberately as if what he said would be recorded for posterity. He was convincing and exhilarating. The only jarring notes were his words of caution on my departure, "Since you were on Admiral King's staff, I assume you will write to him from time to time as well as to other friends in the Navy Department; but it is well to remember that echoes of what you say will come back to me." I was quite surprised, hurt, and a bit resentful. These parting words may have been due to his sensitiveness to criticism, or perhaps to his belief that some future historian might find in my letters some improper comment.

I left MacArthur's office in a disturbed frame of mind and wondered whether the job to which I had been assigned would be a happy one. I need not have had any misgivings on the subject, for General MacArthur proved to be the finest commander I had ever worked for. He delegated authority far more than do most commanders. He gave his subordinates a job and then left to them the details of how it was to be done. If the job was not being done to his satisfaction, he simply found another man to do it.

Like everyone else in the Southwest Pacific, I soon found myself falling into the habit of referring to "MacArthur's troops," "MacArthur's planes," and "MacArthur's ships." The habit was widespread. In the Navy Department in 1942, a friend heard I was going to the Southwest Pacific and wisecracked, "So you are leaving the U.S. Navy to join MacArthur's Navy. God help you. No one else will."

My immediate job was to get my staff and office functioning, become acquainted with the military leaders with whom I would be working, and learn what I could about the area of operations—New Guinea, New Britain, and the adjacent islands.

New Guinea, directly north of Australia, is one of the largest islands in the world. From its western end on the Equator it extends more than 1,300 miles in a southeasterly direction to Milne Bay at its eastern end, ten degrees south of the Equator. The western half of the island was administered by the Dutch and the eastern half by the Australians. This latter half was subdivided, for administrative purposes, into Papua and New Guinea. In this account, the whole territory will be referred to as New Guinea.

The island ranges from tropical coastal swampland to dense rain forests, then to jagged peaks. The peaks rise to about 15,000 feet in a range running parallel to the coast line throughout most of the length of the country.

The dusty black natives lived in small villages, constantly at war with each other. Many were headhunters, some practiced cannibalism, and nearly all were completely ignorant of what lay behind the next range of hills. The island was sparsely settled, with no national unity. More than seven hundred different languages were in use, the nearest thing to a common language being "pidgin" English. The villages, many of which were separated by steep ravines and deep valleys, had been loosely administered by hardy Australian patrol officers who had attempted to curb the villagers' warlike activities and to turn their attention to farming. Small patches of land were cultivated in the vicinity of the villages, but these areas produced barely enough food to raise the standard of living above the subsistence level.

Man-eating crocodiles could be found in all the coastal streams, poisonous snakes were plentiful, and malaria-carrying mosquitoes came out at sundown to take their toll. The average life span of the natives was but thirty years. In this area I would spend the next year and a half; but, fortunately, not ashore.

I learned at firsthand from Lieutenant General R. L. Eichelberger, U.S. Army, the First Corps commander, what it was like to live and fight in New Guinea. He had just returned from a successful campaign, the capture of Buna on New Guinea's north coast.

When the campaign in New Guinea bogged down during the latter part of

November 1942, Eichelberger had been flown into the combat area with instructions from MacArthur to take on-the-spot command. He was given a free hand to make any changes in leadership and operating procedures he felt necessary, and the final word was to "take Buna or not come back." I thought the Marines had a pretty rough time in the jungles of Guadalcanal until I heard Eichelberger's story of Buna.

He told me the 32nd National Guard Division had been rushed to New Guinea to push back the Nipponese who had been threatening to overrun the area. The U.S. troops had little or no jungle training and for most of them it was their first time in combat. When Eichelberger took over command at the front, conditions were deplorable: no will to fight, food scarce, medical supplies woefully inadequate. The sick and wounded were left unattended for days at a time. Leadership had broken down, and the new commander had to relieve almost every officer of field grade or above. The casualty rate from malaria and other tropical diseases was so great that at one time he doubted if he would have enough effectives to continue the fighting.

Eichelberger told me his activities had been greatly hampered because of supply difficulties. Allied planes could deliver only a bare minimum of logistic requirements. Although under frequent day and night attack from Japanese aircraft, a small group of Dutch freighters and native fishing craft had supplied more than half of his needs, as well as the equipment for the construction of a nearby air base at Dobodura. These small boats had followed a tortuous channel two hundred miles long and three miles wide, from Milne Bay to Oro Bay, the supply base for those U.S. troops fighting their way toward Buna. The channel had been buoyed a few months previously by three Australian survey ships who had done this marvelous bit of business while under almost daily bomber attack.

The Buna campaign was a pretty grim tale. Disease was a more potent enemy than the Japanese. The 32nd Division, with a combat strength of about 11,000, had suffered more than 9,500 casualties—7,000 due to tropical diseases and 2,500 due to Japanese bullets. Losses in the Australian sector were just as heavy, and in about the same ratio. Of 1,100 men in one of the U.S. battalions who fought with the Australians, less than 100 were able to walk out when finally relieved.

But the Allies had taken their toll of the enemy in the Buna area. Approximately 4,300 Nipponese dead were counted; the number of their casualties evacuated could only be guessed at. The small number of prisoners taken, considering the numbers engaged, was a ratio unprecedented in modern war. Eichelberger told me many other things about fighting in the low lands of New Guinea—tall razor-sharp Kunai grass, mangrove swamps, bugs, heat, and the deadening of the mind from the continual sound of falling rain.

If the Americans and Australians had found it difficult to obtain adequate supplies, the Japanese had found it even more so. I learned about the Japanese side of the campaign from Colonel Sid Mashbir, a fluent Japanese linguist, who commanded an outstandingly successful intelligence unit on the outskirts of Brisbane. Documents found on the Japanese dead and all prisoners were turned over to Colonel Mashbir's unit, and from them he was able to supply some startling facts about the ferocity of the Buna campaign and some gruesome tales of disease, filth, and hunger. One soldier's dairy bore mute evidence of the effectiveness of Allied bomber and PT boat attacks on the Japanese supply lines of ships and barges to their beleaguered garrisons in the Buna-Lae area. The soldier's diary told how his platoon, cut off from food, had turned to cannibalism. The final entry contained these horrifying words, "This is the first time I have ever tasted human flesh—and it is very tasty."

Eichelberger, an able officer with a warm personality, was well liked by the press and not averse to friendly publicity. He had strong friends in the War Department and was known to be a close associate of Colonel Edwin M. (Pa) Watson, the military aide to the President. With a successful campaign behind him, and with all these other attributes, it was assumed he would be in the forefront of the leaders of all upcoming operations. But it didn't turn out that way. There was no place in the Southwest Pacific for two glamorous officers. For almost a year he fretted his time away in comparatively unimportant training roles in northeast Australia.

An entirely different type of officer was Lieutenant General Walter Krueger who was assigned to command the Sixth Army, a job that Eichelberger had hoped to get. Krueger arrived from the States a few weeks after I did and set up his headquarters at Camp Columbia, a few miles outside of Brisbane. He was a taciturn Prussian type of officer of the no-nonsense sort who commenced his military career as a private. What his seniors wanted done, he wanted done—and well. He had an excellent military reputation. He shunned publicity, which was all to the good in the Southwest Pacific.

The Allied Air Force, which included the American Fifth Air Force, was under the command of Lieutenant General George Kenney. He was a short, cocky individual, thoroughly competent in his own field and highly regarded by his men, but not interested in any phase of warfare that was not centered around an airplane, particularly a bomber.

General Sir Thomas Blamey, an affable, rotund Australian, was the Allied Commander of Land Forces. He went out of his way to be helpful, including the assignment to my staff of some excellent liaison officers. One of those officers who remained with me throughout the entire campaign was Brigadier R. N. L. Hopkins. This able officer tactfully guided me over many rough spots in my dealings with Australian military and naval leaders.

Until I left Brisbane for New Guinea the latter part of June 1943, I was in touch with these officers almost every day. I came to know them and admire them for their distinctive characteristics. Each contributed, in his own sphere of activity, a major part in the winning of the war.

4: Amphibious Staff Personnel

THE LITTLE STAFF ASSEMBLED IN ITS TWO-ROOM OFFICE IN THE New Zealand Insurance Building in Brisbane was not much of a beginning for the tremendous job that lay ahead. First, we had to set up an organization to handle the hundreds of ships and thousands of men that were being assembled in the States for our Amphibious Force. Some were already en route and would arrive in a few days. Arrangements had to be made for docking, repair facilities, supplies, training, lodging, and feeding. Every port on the east coast of Australia was visited to determine which ones could best bear part of this load. Our skeleton staff was expanded as personnel became available.

A few of the officers and men were flown out from the States, but for the most part they came by ship. Although there were some career officers among them, by far most were Reserve officers, commissioned directly from civil life. They had been commissioned in the corps and in the rank to which their age and civilian experience seemed to qualify them. This was the group that formed more than ninety per cent of my staff of more than one hundred officers at its peak.

My most important job before leaving Washington should have been the selection of a staff. Its importance was emphasized by Vice Admiral R. L. Ghormley, an old friend and brilliant officer who had just returned to Washington after a short and difficult tour of duty in the South Pacific. He counseled, "Don't let them hurry you off to Australia without a competent staff of your own choosing or you'll pay for it later, as I did." But I was so anxious to be on my way that I wasn't making any conditions, and so my staff was picked by the Bureau of Personnel without any detailed assistance from me. My first meeting with most of them was on their arrival in Australia.

The original group included an assortment of scientists, salesmen, teachers, architects, lawyers, and representatives of other professions. A few had orders to a particular job, but mostly they were ordered to report for further assignment. Nearly all did an outstanding job. There were a few misfits who left after a short stay, but generally officers stayed on the job until they were physically and mentally exhausted by the strain of the conditions as operations moved along the humid, malarial coast of New Guinea. Some more fortunate officers were recalled to the States to act as instructors and to pass along their experiences to new groups being readied for overseas duty. Our first groups of officers, however, did not have this luxury of experienced instructors. They had to learn their jobs as they went along and the adjustment from civil to military life was not easy.

The first sea voyage for most of our Reserves was aboard the USS *Hermitage,* a transport converted from the Italian "luxury" liner *Biancamano.* The ship sailed from Norfolk to Brisbane, via the Panama Canal, Bora Bora, and Nouméa. The voyage was anything but comfortable for the more than one thousand Army troops and approximately one hundred naval passengers who were crowded aboard. During the thirty-eight-day voyage, only two meals a day could be served. The men ate off mess trays wherever they could find space. All passengers were ordered below decks from sunset till sunrise, and portholes were baffled against showing light and against allowing any fresh air whatsoever to seep in. Lights were switched off, except for blue bulbs in the passageways. The men sat in the pitch dark in sweltering heat. It was a foretaste of what they might expect in the war zone.

Among the passengers were my prospective training officer, Commander John W. Jamison, a career officer, and two Reserve officers, Lieutenant Commander John Mosher and Lieutenant William S. Mailliard. Mosher was ordered to report as intelligence officer and Mailliard as flag lieutenant and aide. A recent graduate of the Reserve Officers Training Corps at Yale University, Mailliard had had a few months of active duty. Compared with most of the other young officers who joined my staff, he had the right to consider himself a salty veteran. For the next three years, he was constantly at my side in combat, in frustration, and in recreation. And I suppose that he—like aides have done from time immemorial—took action in his boss's name on matters of which he had little knowledge and no authority.

Jamison and Mosher were the only prospective staff members with prior experience in amphibious operations. Jamison had worked with the Marines in the peacetime landing exercises on the East Coast and had been beachmaster at Fedhala during the North African landings a few months previously. Mosher had been an assistant intelligence officer in planning the North African affair. To utilize to the full their time on the *Hermitage,* both officers delivered daily lectures to their shipmates on those bits of warfare with which they were familiar.

As might be expected, there was a wider variation in the age, experience, and education of the hundreds of enlisted men assigned to the Amphibious Force than of the officer personnel. As I look back I marvel at the initiative, willingness, cooperative good nature, courage, and common sense of the average American far from home. Thrust into a strange environment, he was to risk his life in a war of which he had little knowledge and less understanding.

The *Hermitage* passengers were very thankful, at long last, to go up the Brisbane River to New Farm Wharf and see the welcoming public—for in those days Americans were exceedingly, almost excessively, welcome in any part of the British Empire.

The newly arrived officers and enlisted men were shuffled around until niches were found most suited to their capabilities. The few career officers who joined my staff in those early days carried the burden of learning their own amphibious job—usually in combat—and of breaking in the newcomers to the ways of the Navy.

Generally speaking, Reserve officers had no intention of making the Navy a career. They were in the Navy to do a job the best they knew how and when the war was over they wanted out, and fast. A few had come to the Seventh Amphibious Force by choice, as it promised to provide an active and exciting job in the combat area, but most had come by chance rather than choice.

First of these Reserve officers to deserve mention was Lieutenant Commander John S. Mosher, a quiet scholar with an analytical mind that stood us in good stead in the troublous times ahead. In prewar days, he had been a vice-consul in Peking. He spoke Chinese and had done some professional writing regarding the China scene. He had been an assistant intelligence officer for the North African invasion and, when the Amphibious Force was organized a few months later, he was ordered as the chief of my Intelligence Section. He had no nucleus of personnel to start with, but was given the pick of the new officers, and picked well. In going over his list I found a stockbroker, a couple of photographers, a mathematics instructor, an architect, and others from such varied professions that one wondered how they could be used in the Intelligence Section.

Among Mosher's group was Lieutenant Herbert Krueger, U.S. Naval Reserve, a mathematics teacher who found the sudden transition to a naval career more difficult than most and very painful. His head, which was six feet five inches above the deck, collided with every overhead steampipe, and he had the scars to prove it.

Krueger more than proved his military worth in the code room. One day, for instance, on duty during the slack spell in the communication traffic, he amused himself by toying with an intercepted message not in any of our cipher systems. Something of a genius at figures, in about an hour he had the message all "Englished," and the system in which it had been enciphered neatly set forth and

Lieutenant William S. Mailliard, U.S. Naval Reserve, served for three years as Admiral Barbey's flag lieutenant and aide.

The Seventh Amphibious Force planning staff. Left to right: Major J. S. Blais, U.S. Marine Corps, gunfire support plans; Lieutenant Commander Russell Schmidt, U.S. Naval Reserve, communications plans; Commander Sherman Betts, U.S. Navy, meteorological plans; Captain B. G. Lake, U.S. Navy, advice and assistance on all planning and support operations; Commander Charles Adair, U.S. Navy, organization of assault plans, direct assault, and resupply plans; Commander B. B. C. Lovett, U.S. Navy, aviation plans.

explained. It turned out to be a message sent by the Army to all holders of an elaborate little cipher machine, the Haglin, issued to the troops for use in the forward area. When we sent Krueger's copies of both message and decipherment to Army Headquarters in Washington, the instrument was promptly jettisoned before it ever had a chance to give away Army secrets. Krueger was a fine example of the unexpected mine of military values the United States found available in its young civilians when war came.

Before World War II, it was especially difficult for architects to obtain Naval Reserve commissions. The art of photographic interpretation changed all that, and just in time, for it was discovered that an architect could take an oblique aerial photograph and "rectify" it into a precisely accurate vertical drawing of the subject. In the miserably charted, coral-pinnacle-infested seas of the Southwest Pacific, this skill, so available in civilian life at home, suddenly became an absolutely essential need to our war effort. Lieutenant Nolan E. Barrick was such an architect and by the grace of God was commissioned, given a course in photo interpretation, and sent out to our force. He was shortly joined by Lieutenants George R. Frisby and Clark M. Pettit, both graduates of the Photo Interpreters' School, and at least partly trained in architecture or engineering drawing. This small force, with Lieutenant James B. Gratiot, a former news photographer and good organizer, operated Mosher's chart and map-making department. In the beginning, they used Australian army printing facilities; after the arrival of the flagship *Blue Ridge,* they used her complete photographic and printing laboratories, three decks below the Intelligence Office.

As amphibious operations progressed and practice increased, these young men proved that there was almost no scrap of useful, not to say vital, information they could not extract from well-taken aerial pictures. Cooperation from the Army Fifth Air Force, our only source of aerial photography in General MacArthur's area, was at first given most grudgingly; they could not (very humanly) see the point of risking trained flyers' lives for overlapping pictures of endless stretches of salt water adjacent to uninhabited beaches or jungles. But in the end, when the reasons for such demands were explained personally to General MacArthur, we began to get the pictures by which all the little seas were charted for safe navigation, at night without lights, and the future landing beaches charted and mapped with an unfailing accuracy and clarity which still amazes and gratifies my soul.

Among the photo interpreters' feats: At Cape Gloucester they prevented the Marines from committing a parachute landing upon an inviting-looking area of bare ground by proving that it was actually a deeply crevassed slope of impassable lava. At Lae, they showed that a strip of hard-looking sand across the mouth of the river delta could not be crossed by troops who had intended to join paratroops who were to be landed to the westward. At several places they correctly predicted the limit of heavy traffic that might be able to roll inland through dry-looking coconut groves before becoming hopelessly mired. They distinguished dummy guns and their emplacements from real ones and pinpointed the positions of the real guns, although hidden under heavy trees, by finding the faint tracks of the gun crews and ammunition wagons. By the gradual development of such tracks, they closely estimated the growth in numbers of enemy troops in the locality.

But it was not just the officers in Intelligence who did such an outstanding job in photo interpretation. The leading petty officers performed duties that were unprecedented in naval experience for men of their ratings. The same may be said for men of the photographic and printing laboratories whose high-speed turnouts of very large orders for beach maps, gunfire charts, navigational charts and other products made possible the issuance of operations plans on time, again and again. The quantities and accuracy required, and the brevity of time usually available, made their contributions the more striking in their efficiency.

Before leaving the subject of personnel, I want to mention a few Reserve officers who had seen service in World War I. The irreverent among the younger officers referred to them as "re-treads." But it was these middle-aged officers—volunteers all—who carried on in the combat zone and exercised a calming and mature influence, out of all proportion to their rank, on their impetuous and younger shipmates. Among them were J. Glen Sample, head of a successful advertising agency in Chicago; Morton Webster and W. R. Chappell, investment bankers from New York; James Van Zandt who resigned his seat in Congress to join our forces; and I. K. Stevenson who preferred duty on an LST to a desk job in the Navy Department.

When Stevenson reported for duty in the Southwest Pacific and gave his age as forty-six, I mentioned that forty-six was a bit old for amphibious work. His answer startled me: "You seem to be doing all right." He was assigned to an LST as a "make-you-learn" skipper because he knew something about navigation. In those early days anyone who could navigate was a real find. It wasn't long before Stevenson commanded his own LST, than a Division, and finally a Group of these unglamorous work horses of the amphibious force.

As might be expected, Reserve medical officers came from every age group. Our staff medical officer, Dr. James Barnard, was a budding allergist with considerable success in his chosen speciality when I met him in 1942 at the Naval Hospital in Washington. I had gone there for allergy treatment. Shellfish and I had never agreed and so one day when I had incautiously eaten some excellent lobster, the expected happened and my lips swelled up like a female Ubangi. Dr. Barnard gave me some injections or whatever they do to bring one's features back to normal. It was the start of a series of treatments. Before they were over he joined me in Australia and became a member of my staff, with an allergy patient for continuous experimental observation during the upcoming campaign in the Southwest Pacific. In addition to his medical skill, he proved to be a fine organizer and a cheerful shipmate.

5:

Training Activities in the Southwest Pacific

EVEN BEFORE THE NEW STAFF MEMBERS HAD FOUND THEIR WAY around, General MacArthur issued orders placing all amphibious training in the Southwest Pacific under my command and sent word he wanted all troops started on amphibious training as soon as possible. The 7th Australian Division was to start training on 1 March—three weeks hence. Also transferred to my command were some small Australian naval bases where the training could be held. MacArthur wanted a new division in training every month.

It was quite an order. Our staff training section was in the throes of organization; we had no training program; the 7th Australian Division needed a rehabilitation period after heavy jungle fighting in New Guinea; and I was not familiar with the bases I had inherited. To add to our problems, the various types of amphibious ships that were needed for training purposes would not be available for some weeks. The few ships that had arrived in Australia, in most cases, needed a major overhaul. Australian shipyards were overloaded with their own work and it was doubtful if American amphibious shipping could be given a priority rating.

As a first step, I made a hurried inspection of the Australian training bases assigned to the Seventh Amphibious Force. The one at Nelson's Bay, a hundred miles north of Sydney, was the best equipped. The Australian facilities in this area, generally referred to as Port Stephens, had been in use as a Joint Operations School for Australians and Americans, and for troop training in small boat operations. But activities had been on a very small scale. As an indication of the meagerness of their training equipment, they had but six small landing boats. Ship's cargo nets had been hung over cliffs and troops got their training in simulated debarking from big transports by clambering down the nets into the sand below. HMAS *Ping Wo*—a refugee ship from China—acted as stores ship and water barge.

Port Stephens was an area, however, that lent itself to major expansion. Temporary buildings and tents were available and there was plenty of water from artesian wells. Good campsites for the troops were nearby. Nelson's Bay, with its crooked channel entrance, offered an anchorage for surface vessels, safe from torpedoes that might be fired from Japanese submarines off the harbor entrance. The beaches within the Bay were excellent for smooth-water training in boat handling, and just outside was a fine sandy beach where more advanced surf training could be undertaken. The principal drawback to the use of Nelson's Bay was its considerable distance from the campsites of the ground troops who would need to be transported to the training area.

Except for the 1st Marines, encamped at Melbourne, all the troops to be trained were in campsites at Brisbane or further north—anywhere from six hundred to a thousand miles away. In the States, that distance would have been of no great concern. But in Australia, the rail system was overburdened, motor trucks were scarce, and the highways had been badly worn by heavy war traffic. Even long distance telephoning was a problem. A wait of four or five hours for a call between Port Stephens and troop campsites was not uncommon.

The base at Toorbul Point on Moreton Bay, about twenty miles northeast of Brisbane, was better located. The Australians had been doing some small-boat training at Toorbul Point but it was on an even less impressive scale than that at Port Stephens. There was plenty of available land in the immediate vicinity but the lack of adequate fresh water was a major handicap. Another disadvantage was the need to rely on water transportation to and from Brisbane because of the impossible road conditions during most of the year.

There was not enough time to be choosy so, balancing the good features with the bad, we decided to commence amphibious training activities at Port Stephens.

Commander Jamison was placed in charge of the training programs with his headquarters at Port Stephens. Instructors were drawn from United States and Australian combat veterans of Guadalcanal, North Africa, New Guinea, and Malaya. Ships were assigned to Jamison as they became available. (The training of the ship's officers and crews in ship handling remained in the hands of their own squadron and division commanders.)

Developing a smooth-functioning staff from a group of veterans with widely varying backgrounds of experience and procedures required tact and patience, and Jamison had both.

In order to standardize the training, General MacArthur directed that U.S. equip-

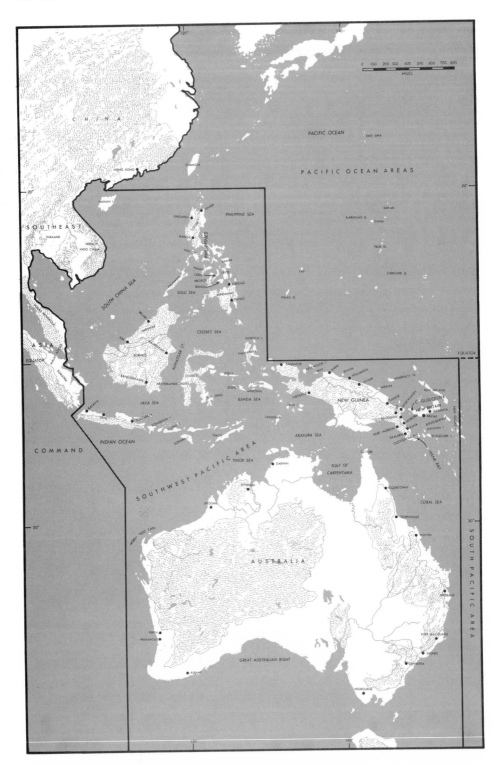

BOUNDARIES OF THE SOUTHWEST PACIFIC AREA

ment, communications procedures, and landing force techniques be used. Landing Operations Doctrine as contained in *U.S. Navy Fleet Training Publication 167* served as the guide.

The Marines from Guadalcanal felt they had all the answers regarding landing on hostile beaches and assumed future landings would follow the procedure with which they were familiar; that is, landings would be made from small boats carried over long distances by APAs; beach parties would be provided by the APAs; shore parties would be provided by the troops they carried; and protection at the landing area would be provided by heavy naval gunfire and shore-based or carrier-based planes.

Australians had been indoctrinated in the British type of "combined operations"— hit and run commando raids, and short-range operations of the cross-channel type. But there was little difference in the two techniques and they were readily integrated into a training program that was satisfactory to all. A few differences in communication procedures cropped up that created some minor problems.

A short classroom course was given to the officers before the arrival of their troops. The first group of enlisted trainees was from the 7th Australian Division, and they were typical of those that followed. They were a colorful, rough, tough and ready lot. Their choice of words was sub-standard. They didn't expect much in the line of equipment and they could get along without many of the creature comforts that U.S. troops seemed to consider a necessity.

The training program followed the procedures laid out in *FTP 167,* an amphibious technique based almost solely on the use of big transports. The technique had proven itself in the successful landings in North Africa and at Guadalcanal. Emphasis was placed on such matters as communications; loading transports with supplies and equipment for easy discharge and priority of need; troops disembarking via cargo nets with heavy knapsack and rifle into rolling boats; formation and timing of boat assault waves; and waterproofing vehicles. Waterproofing consisted of greasing engine parts affected by sea water and installing a three-foot-high carburetor breathing pipe which supposedly gave the vehicle ability to operate in water up to four or five feet deep. These precautions were seldom very effective.

One feature of the training program that was as new to the instructors as to the trainees were the beaching ships and craft that were on the way—the LSTs, LCIs, and LCTs. These ships and craft, able to run their bows onto the beach and discharge troops and cargo over ramps, were not designed to be part of the assault force, but rather to be used on reinforcement runs. Even so, their proper loading would present problems. Proper loading required trimming down by the stern so their keels conformed to the slope of the unloading beach, and this information was seldom available. If a short gap appeared between the ramps and the shoreline, it could be overcome by sand bags. A longer gap would require pontoons. Pontoons would be difficult to handle as they were about sixty feet long, heavy, cumbersome, awkward to load and carry on the side of an LST, and somewhat of a problem to launch in an open sea.

Instruction of U.S. "GIs" and Australian "Diggers" included a few bits of advice about conduct aboard ship. They were told not to whistle, or to run, except in an emergency. A whistle might indicate some engineering trouble, or a bomb falling, or the boatswain's pipe. In combat areas the sound of running feet echoing throughout a ship created tension as it meant trouble—usually a prelude to "battle stations." They were also instructed to keep their sleeves rolled down as a protection against flash burns in battle, as well as partial protection against mosquitoes and the blistering tropical sun on open decks.

Speech differences were more amusing than important. Australian English as spoken by the "Diggers" and their civilian counterparts, was almost unintelligible to the untutored ear. They talked with a clipped accent and mostly through their teeth, somewhat like an English Cockney, but they did not like the comparison. Their vocabulary and pronunciation had a meaning of its own.

Lieutenant Commander J. W. McLaughlin of my staff took a commercial plane to Sydney, and approached the ticket seller at the airport with his small bag in hand. The ticket seller said, "You lefta pie on the port." It took several repeats in a rising voice before a bystander stepped in and translated: "You'll have to pay on the portmanteau."

Although, initially, all amphibious training was centered at Port Stephens, sites were staked out for possible development at two other ports—Cairns and Mackay— quite a bit north of Brisbane and therefore much closer to the major billeting areas for both Australian and American troops. But we had to forego their use for the time being.

In regard to the use of Brisbane and points farther north for troop billeting areas, I remembered the "hassle" that had developed between General MacArthur and the 1st Marine Division as to where the Marines would be encamped for rest and rehabilitation when they arrived from Guadalcanal a few months before. MacArthur wanted to keep them in Northeast Australia where they would be closer to the combat area and closer to his other divisions. The Marines objected on the ground that the climatic conditions of North Australia were unsuitable for the rehabilitation of troops who had been through some tough jungle fighting and were recovering from heavy doses of malaria. The Marines won their point, after getting Navy Department support, and so they went south to Melbourne in Victoria, a lovely, cool, and hospitable city.

In addition to the search for training sites, the Amphibious Force had to find repair yards, big and small, that could put our limping amphibious shipping in operating condition. With some of my maintenance staff, I visited all the various areas where these facilities might be found. Because of the fine cooperation everywhere, from both civilians and the military, our ships were repaired far quicker than we had dared to anticipate.

Higgins boats, both the 36-foot and 50-foot types, and the crews to handle them were arriving on almost every freighter, and a number of the beaching type ships, the LSTs, LCIs, and LCTs, would soon be available. But the only large transport that had arrived was the USS *Henry T. Allen*—formerly the SS *President Jefferson*—which had been transferred to us from the forces of Rear Admiral Kelly Turner in the South Pacific as a result of an order from Admiral King.

Kelly Turner was in command of the amphibious forces in the South Pacific. I didn't expect him to give us one of his best ships, but I was hardly prepared for the *Henry T. Allen*. She leaked fuel so badly she could not be used in the combat zone because of the oil trail left behind that enemy submarines could follow. A major overhaul job on the *Allen* would be required, but Australian shipyards could not undertake it as they were fully engaged in round-the-clock repair work and new construction activities.

Pending the assignment of more and better APAs for amphibious operations, consideration was given to the partial conversion to amphibious transports of some American freighters available then in Australia. It didn't take long to conclude that even the partial conversion of the large number of freighters that would be required was not feasible. One Australian shipyard, with a working force of a thousand men, took six months to convert the Australian merchant cruiser *Manoora* to an APA, and an equal effort would be required on two more of their conversions, the *Westralia* and the *Kanimbla*.

Although the poor material condition of the *Henry T. Allen* made her unsuitable for use in the forward areas, she could be useful in other ways: as an administrative flagship in the rear areas, and in troop training exercises. We were still wedded to the idea that future landings would follow the pattern employed at Guadalcanal and North Africa—that is, big transports would carry the troops to the vicinity of the landing area and then the troops would be carried to the beach in the ships' boats to make the actual assault.

Prior to the full functioning of Port Stephens, an amphibious landing exercise was carried out on the beaches of Port Phillip Bay—the Bay on which Melbourne is located. The poor old *Henry T. Allen* and the Australian ship *Manoora* served as APAs and one regiment of Marines from nearby Melbourne was the demonstration team. A large group of Allied observers of all ranks were on hand to see the show. First there was the simulated bombardment of the beach by a Free French destroyer

Tough Australian troops complete a day of invasion rehearsal. They return from a "beach assault" to go up the landing nets and over the side to their quarters aboard the transport.

Australian and American troops unload artillery landing craft during training maneuvers in the South Pacific. The mock invasions start from assault transports lying offshore.

The transport USS Henry T. Allen (AP-30) was pressed into the service as the administrative ship in the rear area, and proved useful in troop training exercises. Her poor condition made her unsuitable for use in forward areas.

and an American destroyer, then a few Australian planes did a bit of simulated beach strafing. Next came the Marines who clambered down the sides of the *Allen* and *Manoora* via cargo nets into the small boats, and headed toward the shore. It was an international show, all done according to the technique authorized in the Navy's fleet training publication, *FTP 167*.

Among the observers aboard my flagship during the landing exercise was Vice Admiral Conrad Helfrich, Royal Netherlands Navy. Nearly all his ships had been lost in the battle of the Java Sea in the Dutch East Indies. He was a pathetic individual, a distinguished admiral whose country had been overrun by the Germans and whose fleet had been destroyed by the Japanese. He lived in a hotel in Melbourne and nightly received short wave radio broadcasts from the underground in Java and Sumatra. He dreamed of the day when the Japs would be driven out of the East Indies. At every opportunity he advocated his theory that the quickest way to defeat Japan was by a thrust along the north coast of Australia into Timor, Java, and Sumatra, finally joining up with the British in Southeast Asia. Neither the Joint Chiefs of Staff nor MacArthur had any interest in this route.

At the Port Phillip training exercise we assembled all the naval amphibious resources available in Australia, but it was still a rather shabby showing. There was a great gap between what we had and what we needed. I could see no immediate hopes of betterment. It was doubtful if Admiral Nimitz would release any of his carriers or heavy ships from the Pacific Fleet to operate under MacArthur and apparently Admiral Turner was not going to be open-handed with the South Pacific Amphibious Force's APAs.

The few conversations I had with Lieutenant General George Kenney did not evoke much interest in providing shore-based air cover from the Fifth Air Force for amphibious landings, and none at all for providing planes at Port Stephens to round out our training program. Kenney had a lot of jobs for his few planes and he insisted that concentration on the destruction of enemy air bases by his bombers would give our shipping better protection than they could get from any air cover.

Although Kenney's ideas caused us some misgivings, we knew his flyers were doing an outstanding job in their own way. The Bismarck Sea battle was an example. On 4 March, while we were at Port Phillip, General MacArthur's Brisbane Headquarters reported the destruction by Allied planes of a Japanese convoy of twenty-two ships, estimated to be carrying 15,000 reinforcements across the Solomon Sea to Lae in New Guinea. Some of our PT boats got in on the end of this action by torpedoing the remnants of the convoy at night. Later reports from Japanese prisoners and other sources indicated the figures in the communique were somewhat exaggerated—the exact number was eight transports and four destroyers—but even so it was a magnificent performance and had an important bearing on operations in an area in which I would soon be operating.

6:

Development of New Amphibious Techniques

AS IT BECAME APPARENT THE SOUTHWEST PACIFIC WAS NOT likely to get any more of the big amphibious transports, that is, the APAs, and only a few of the smaller fast transports, the APDs—converted from World War I destroyers for use by raiding parties—it became necessary to change our thinking regarding the conduct of future amphibious operations.

It was obvious the Seventh Amphibious Force[1] would have to rely mainly on beaching type ships, that is, the LSTs, LCIs, and the LCTs, not only for the reinforcement echelons but for the assault landings as well. We could not count on shore-based air cover over the landing area, and naval gun fire support would probably be limited to a few destroyers. A new technique based on the new conditions would need to be developed.

Amphibious Force resources showed four APAs—the USS *Henry T. Allen* and HMAS *Westralia, Kanimbla,* and *Manoora*—and a steadily increasing number of beaching craft. Not a very impressive group for the type of operations MacArthur had in mind.

The *Henry T. Allen,* after some temporary repairs to make her seaworthy, became the Amphibious Force administrative ship in the rear area. She carried personnel records and pay accounts, always remaining at a discreet three or four hundred miles in the rear as we advanced island by island toward the Philippines. The three Australian APAs were not enough in themselves to conduct an assault landing, and

[1] On 15 March 1943 the Southwest Pacific Amphibious Force became the Seventh Amphibious Force.

so they were initially assigned to training activities at Port Stephens and for the movement of troops from Australia to the occupied areas in New Guinea.

Our new technique would require a surprise landing of the troops at dawn about two hours before high tide, and a quick getaway about four hours later. It would be inadvisable for the ships to remain in the beach area for longer periods since no strong naval force would be available to protect them from enemy surface raids nor could they count on adequate air cover to protect them from bomber attack. Landing beaches would need to be selected with unusual care. Surf conditions that would present no problem to the small Higgins boats carried aboard APAs might be hazardous for the LSTs, LCIs, and LCTs. Also, the landing beaches would need to be free of enemy strong points so that a very short prelanding bombardment could take care of small pockets of enemy resistance.

The phase of the moon would be an important consideration. A surprise landing would require an approach to the beach during the dark of the moon, or during overcast weather, so that the convoy would not be sighted by enemy reconnaissance planes. The tidal conditions must be just right, and the ships lightly loaded and with just the right trim, so they could be unloaded and away before an enemy bomber attack found them high and dry on a receding tide.

Because of the limited amount of supplies that could be landed on the first day of the assault, there might result major differences with the ground forces who would want more ammunition and supplies than the Navy would consider practicable for a quick unloading and getaway. Understandably, the troops would not want to be left stranded in enemy territory without adequate supplies, which might happen if follow-up ships on succeeding days did not meet their schedule or were destroyed by bomber attack. As it turned out these matters were always ironed out without any serious disagreements, although I remember it was much easier to work with those generals and their staffs who had prior combat experience rather than with those who were fresh out of the States and imbued with certain textbook procedures that were not practicable in our type of warfare.

Inasmuch as these flat-bottomed LSTs, LCIs, and LCTs would have to spearhead the assault in landing operations, it seemed advisable to take another look at their capabilities. How skilled were their crews; how adequate their gunpower defense; how reliable their engines; and how long could they maintain themselves in food, water, fuel, and ammunition without outside assistance? These were but some of the questions that had to be answered before we could fit them into a new amphibious technique.

New ships mean new crews, but I was hardly prepared to find that the total sea experience aboard most of the beaching ships was just about zero. I do not mean combat experience. I mean enough experience to go aboard a ship and take her from here to there.

Lying at anchor side by side, two LST's present bow and stern, disclosing unusual features of the design. The bow doors, which open to receive or disgorge troops and cargo, can be seen in the ship at the right.

An APc was converted for use as a small planning ship by putting in some extra bunks, one typewriter, and a hand-operated mimeograph machine. Assault plans were written, reproduced, and assembled on this planning "ship."

Here are a couple of examples. In the log of the *LST-471* appears the following:

> The crew that came aboard shortly before the ship was waterborne in Vancouver, Washington, were all green hands. There were six officers and about seventy men. None of the officers and only one of the men had ever been to sea in the past.

The log of the *LST-462* carried this notation on its departure from San Francisco:

> We sailed hopefully to find it (Australia).

My sympathy went out to the few regular officers who had been assigned to these ships as squadron and group commanders. It will always be a mystery to me how those few regulars successfully chaperoned so much inexperience across the seas to far-away Australia.

If the LSTs had green crews, the LCIs had even greener ones. I went aboard a group of LCIs when they arrived in Sydney under the command of Commander Homer F. McGee. He had a pretty rough time in sailing his craft from the Chesapeake Bay through the Panama Canal and thence via a lot of small islands to the final destination in Australia. McGee tried to have his group looking shipshape on arrival in Sydney and they probably were, in comparison with the way they looked when they left Virginia. He told me that more than fifty percent of the officers and men had no personnel records or pay accounts when they reported to his ships. Some had not been paid for two months. There was even some uncertainty as to the names of the men who were aboard.

McGee said a storm scattered the ships soon after leaving the Virginia capes; some of them failed to get the word when to change course and never did rejoin the formation. Ninety percent of the crews were seasick. Many men worried as the ships' plates creaked and groaned and fervently wondered if the lady welders in the shipyards had done their jobs properly.

When the LCIs finally reached Panama, McGee undertook to give the officers of these little craft some elementary instruction in navigation, station keeping, and general onboard routine. They were told that a chronometer is not a watch and it must not be reset daily as some were doing, and that Venus and Jupiter are planets, not stars, which had been bothering some in their effort to navigate by them.

The group that left Panama included a total of forty-seven miscellaneous ships, made up of tugs, a couple of LSTs, some subchasers, and the LCIs. They headed hopefully for Bora Bora in the Society Islands. McGee had plenty of trouble en route. There were frequent engine breakdowns, two men fell overboard, and the subchasers required fresh water and fuel every four days from the two LSTs. There was no surplus water for the LCIs, so these unlucky ships were put on a strict ration.

Finally, after twenty-six days, a friendly patrol plane from Bora Bora guided them into the harbor. They confidently expected to fill up on fresh water, fresh provisions, and the other niceties of normal living, only to find that Bora Bora itself was on short rations. Bora Bora depended on rainfall for its water supply, and at the moment was in difficulty because of a drought. As for food, Bora Bora was on reduced rations while anxiously awaiting the supply ship due in two weeks. So McGee's convoy continued onward as before. One LCI hung up on a reef in Nouméa. Another was towed more than a thousand miles because the engineer thought the engines sounded "funny" only to find on inspection in Australia that the funny noises were normal noises, and that his engines were running satisfactorily.

On my visit to McGee and his ships I stopped in the tiny galley on one of them to thank the cook for the coffee and sandwiches he had supplied for our inspection party. I inquired about his prior experience and how he happened to become the cook. His answer emphasized the haphazard, but apparently workable assignment of personnel in these small craft. He said that when the crew reported aboard the ship at the building yard the skipper lined them all up and told them a cook was needed. Did anyone know anything about cooking? Since no one else stepped forward, he answered that he had helped his mother do a bit of cooking on the farm. From then on, he said, "I was the cook; and so that's why I'm here."

Adding to the personnel difficulties of the ships was the prevalent idea that the Amphibious Force was the disposal school for ensigns, and that assignment to an amphibious craft was merely a ticket to the battle zone with no return—that the crews and the craft on which they served were the expendables of the new war. LST, it was said, stood for "large, stationary target." The stories were apparently widespread in recruit training centers, for a number of incidents were reported that seemed to bear out this belief. Lieutenant E. F. Norwood, the medical officer aboard an LST during the transpacific crossing from San Francisco, had this to say about the matter:

Before sailing from San Francisco, the LSTs in his group had been so depleted by the hospitalization of the crews that there were not enough men remaining aboard to get them under way. As their doctor, he was sent to all hospitals in the area to round up those he felt were well enough to be released to their ships. Most of them had been hospitalized for minor ailments, something they had "volunteered" upon themselves in the hope that they might miss the sailing of the ship about to take them on what they thought might be a "one-way" ride.

When the convoy finally sailed, Dr. Norwood said, only one man aboard the LST, besides himself, had ever been out of sight of land. Since his medical duties were not too exacting he offered to take on the additional duty of ship's chaplain. Every Sunday morning he held a short religious service. Attendance was voluntary but to his amazement, during the entire trip there was one hundred percent attendance by every officer and man not on watch. He could only ascribe this religious fervor to a firm belief in the one-way ride theory. Among other interesting incidents of the voyage, the one I remember was of the Officer of the Deck who thought that by zigzagging he could keep the ship out of the rays of the moon. He did not want his ship to be the target of a Japanese submarine that might be lurking in the shadows.

Another confirmation of the psychological concern of amphibious recruits came from young Wally Wemyss, a powerfully built, newly commissioned ensign, who arrived as a member of a unit with the peculiar code name "Brass Hat." The "Brass Hat" unit was organized at the San Diego Training Station for the purpose of manning the small Higgins boats being shipped out to Australia. It was a good-sized outfit, with about four hundred enlisted men and forty young officers, but because the word "amphibious" had become associated with their Higgins boat activities, there were grave forebodings among them as to their future.

This may have been the reason that when the "Brass Hat" detachment was changing trains at Los Angeles en route to the transport awaiting them at San Francisco, the more fearful took the opportunity to go "over the hill" for keeps.

Wally Wemyss was a good man to handle this unit although he had had no prior naval experience—not even an indoctrination course. He had applied for a commission in the Navy, got it, and was put on duty even before he had a uniform. He told the recruiting officer he would like to go someplace where there would be excitement and action, and thought submarine duty or amphibious duty would be just about right. So he ended up in the Amphibious Force in the Southwest Pacific, where he subsequently found the excitement he was looking for.

Nearly all the young officers in our outfit were college graduates. The few officers who had come up through the enlisted ranks of the regular Navy were almost always a few years older. These old-timers invariably had their ships or craft in better physical and mechanical condition than the Reserve officers and almost without exception had a physical trait of their own that was noticeable—they were, to a man, more serious-minded and unsmiling. The better discipline aboard their ships was easily seen. The young Reserve officers were more eager and venturesome, and as they formed the overwhelming majority of the force, planning was patterned to their capability.

All these instances of untried personnel and untried ships were quite disheartening, for it was these men and these ships that would have to carry out a new and exacting technique of amphibious landings. How to beach their ships through a surf, ward off a bomber attack, navigate at night through poorly charted waters, and load cargo for quick discharge, were but a few of the things the crews of these flat-bottomed ships must be expert in if they were to survive.

The first step was to modify the training program to include the new techniques. Commander Jamison and his instructors at Port Stephens were assigned this job. The transition in the training procedures from that laid down in Navy publications regarding amphibious operations to a new and untried technique caused some shaking of heads. Jamison and the Marine members of his staff were thoroughly familiar with the procedures that had been used so successfuly in the North Africa and Guadalcanal landings. Now they were to teach new procedures and they were not sure they liked it.

Jamison's tact and good judgment overcame the difficult period of transition not only within his staff but also in his dealings with the commanders of the Marines, Australian Diggers, American GIs, and the "make you learn" skippers of naval ships. He even quieted the complaints of the local civilians when beaching ships ruined their oyster beds, a thriving business thereabouts.

Besides the development of a new and questionable technique, and the training of inexperienced troops and crews, there were other matters that were equally important and worrisome. An amphibious operation requires a forward base from which to operate or an assortment of auxiliary ships such as hospital ships, repair ships, tankers, supply ships, and water barges. The construction of an amphibious base at Milne Bay was still in the planning stage. The only auxiliary ship assigned to the Seventh Amphibious Force was the repair ship *Rigel* (AD-13) and we were still waiting for her.

7:

Planning First Combat Operations

NO COMMANDER IS EVER QUITE SATISFIED THAT HE HAS THE needed number of properly manned ships and properly trained troops to do a foolproof combat job. Such was the case when General MacArthur directed the Seventh Amphibious Force to land elements of the Sixth Army on the small islands of Woodlark and Kiriwina.

Our training activities and repair facilities were beginning to function smoothly, but it was only a beginning. The output was not yet ready for combat.

Starting from zero, two months previously, there was now a unit of about 2,500 Australians and Americans as instructors and maintenance personnel at the Amphibious Training Centers (ATC)—facetiously called "allergic to combat"—at Port Stephens and Toorbul, giving an inadequate training course to 20,000 ground troops per month. At other places naval instructional units were making ready the newly arrived LSTs, LCIs, and LCTs. The ship handling by the crews was usually quite good, but they had much to learn in gunnery, communications, ship maintenance, cargo storage, and beaching operations before they were ready for combat. Unfortunately, we could not wait for the finished product in either quality or quantity before moving into the forward area.

The unglamorous, hurriedly organized and vital Maintenance and Repair Section was headed by Commander Loar Mansbach, an ex-warrant officer who knew how to get things done. He was assisted by two Reserve officers, Lieutenant Commanders J. L. Landenberger and J. W. McLaughlin—the former a graduate naval architect and the other an electrical engineer. They had the help of a group of civilians sent out by General Motors and other large industrial concerns, to keep the engines their firms had built in operating condition. Without these usually middle-aged men and their practical operating and supervising experience, our maintenance crew could never have met their schedule.

One of the first big jobs of the newly formed repair unit at Brisbane was the unloading of a group of LCTs from the ships that carried them from the States. The LCTs were too small to undertake an ocean crossing under their own power. Some of them arrived in sections aboard freighters, others were carried fully assembled aboard an LST. This report of the first unloadings is made by the man who did the job:

> Nine LCTs arrived Brisbane aboard LSTs. One of the LSTs was taken upriver across from the Public Library and anchored fore and aft. Thousands of Aussies were packed on the banks of the river and making "book" on whether the Yanks would make a "go" of it. Following Navy Department instructions, the ship was listed to one side by pumping water into some of her tanks. With about a ten-degree list, the cables holding the cradle and the LCT were cut. To most everyone's surprise, the LCT slid off and didn't set off the enormous wave that was expected. The launching of the others was easy after that.
>
> The LCTs that arrived in three sections aboard freighters were unloaded at the wharf and assembled in the water alongside the ship which carried them. The three sections were bolted together, and surprisingly, there was no excessive leakage. The aligning of the sections prior to bolting was sometimes troublesome, particularly if they hadn't been pre-fitted before they were loaded aboard ship. And it was really a problem if there was a strong wind and the surface of the water became disturbed.

As soon as each LCT was made seaworthy, it was turned over to the crew—one ensign and ten men—who had accompanied their craft on its piggyback journey across the Pacific. If there was any one group of Reserve officers for whom I had the greatest admiration and sympathy, it was the young LCT officers. Usually, they were the only officer aboard and as such were responsible for safety of the craft, and also for the harder job of maintaining discipline among the small crew, many of whom were often older than themselves.

Before they learned much about their craft or crew they might be sent in big convoys or on independent forays, for days at a time, with no one to turn to for help and advice. One young LCT officer told me that his only prior experience in leadership had been as chairman of his fraternity dance at the University of Texas. His only prior seagoing experience consisted of three afternoon trips aboard a subchaser on the Hudson River during the ninety-day "wonder-blunder" course at Columbia University.

The maintenance of the various types of beaching ships was a continual headache.

The engines broke down faster than our organization and Australian shipyards could put them together.

Once, nearly a third of our craft were undergoing overhaul simultaneously. Some operating troubles were due to green crews, but most were due to the lack of spare parts. Hardly a ship arrived in the area with its quota of spare parts. That was because ships were pushed out of the building yards with a minimum of equipment aboard.

The reason for this deficiency was understandable, but it did not salve the feelings of those who had to keep the ships running. Each shipyard was attempting to establish a record in the number of ships that could come off the assembly lines. No credit was given for providing adequate spare parts. Any extra equipment and machinery that might become available was reserved for new construction. Just before leaving the States, one know-it-all member of the crew of the *LST-458* expounded his theory on spare parts:

"We ain't gonna get no spare parts. Why should we? We are a one-way ship and they know we ain't coming back. It stands to reason."

Repeated requests to the Navy Department for spare parts brought so little result that we suspected Admiral Halsey's maintenance group at Nouméa—where the ships stopped en route to Australia—were hijacking, from the supply ships, the parts that rightly belonged to us. An investigating officer was sent to Nouméa and found that they were no better off than we were, and suspected we were the hijack culprits.

A spare part incident concerning the Michiana oil filters, used in diesel engines on the LSTs, was described by McLaughlin:

> . . . These white filters began to clog up after a few thousand hours use and none were available in the area. The Bureau assured us that a large shipment was on the way and even noted that they were in the shaft alley of the *LST-469*. This is the craft that was torpedoed—and where did the torpedo strike? Right in that shaft alley. . . . However, this situation was somewhat eased by the ingenuity of Mr. Else, one of the General Motors technicians, at whose suggestion we bought up all the women's white stockings we could find on the East Coast of Australia. . . . These stockings made reasonably good substitutes for the factory-made filter covers.

One bit of engineering ingenuity that did not come to my attention at the time—and never did reach the attention of higher authority—involved cutting a large hole in the bottom of an LST. Getting holes in a ship's bottom from enemy torpedoes, guns, or bombs was a normal expectation of war and no bothersome questions were asked, but for a repair gang to deliberately cut a big hole in a ship's bottom was something else again.

This particular LST was skippered by an overly confident Reserve officer—an ex-liquor salesman—who saw no need to waste government money in getting a pilot

An LCT (6), in 1943 the Navy's newest large tank lighter, drops its ramp on a beach, ready to take aboard a 32-ton Army tank.

to take his ship up the Brisbane River when he was quite competent to do the job. Unfortunately, in rounding a particularly sharp turn a propeller struck a submerged rock. The resulting damage necessitated dry docking, but the dry dock could be made available only during one tide—a few working hours at the most.

On further examination, it was found that the propeller shaft, as well as the propeller, was badly bent. The only spare shaft in the area was in the hold of this same LST, and underneath all the cargo. There was not enough time to unload the cargo in the usual way, that is, working from top to bottom to get at the shaft.

After considerable thought—about three minutes—the repair officer decided to reverse the unloading process, and start at the bottom where the shaft was in storage. So he cut some steel plates from the bottom of the ship, pulled out the spare shaft and other necessary parts, fitted them in place, and replaced the plates, all within the space of three hours. Although the job was eminently successful, it might not have been, and so the matter was kept in a "top-secret" unofficial category.

There was a great difference in the material condition of the ships as they arrived in Australia. In some cases it was due to variation in the upkeep skills of the ship's crews, but more often to the variation in the quality of workmanship at the building yards. McLaughlin claimed he could tell which yard built a ship by looking at the waves in the deck plates. The only shipyard to which he gave a plus mark was Orange, Texas, and he was not a Texan.

So many of the beaching type ships arrived in Australia in poor physical condition that it was impossible to get enough of them ready in time for the comparatively minor but simultaneous landings on Woodlark and Kiriwina. Inasmuch as the benefits from the occupation of these islands accrued in equal measure to the South Pacific Forces of Admiral Halsey as well as to the Southwest Pacific Forces of General MacArthur, it was agreed that Halsey's forces would loan some of his ships and troops to augment those of MacArthur in this operation.

The Woodlark-Kiriwina landings were not expected to be difficult as there were no Japanese on the islands, or so we were informed, and the few hundred natives were presumably friendly. The islands were about two hundred miles northeast of the eastern end of New Guinea. The principal danger lay in an attack by enemy bombers, submarines or surface raiders, particularly while the ships were at the beaches. To reduce the danger of being sighted, ships were scheduled to approach the islands during darkness, unload their troops and cargo, and be away again before daylight. General Krueger was in charge of troop participation and I was in charge of amphibious participation.

The purpose of the occupation was to obtain airfield sites for short-range fighter planes of the Fifth Air Force. These would be used to escort long-range bombers on the last lap of their raids against the Japanese base at Rabaul. The fighters would also be in a good position to intercept Nip bomber raids against Admiral Halsey's South Pacific Forces at Guadalcanal as well as those against General MacArthur's Southwest Pacific Forces in New Guinea.

As more ships and naval personnel dribbled into Australia they were fitted into the operation with little regard to their previous training. Among the new arrivals by air was Commander R. M. Scruggs, with orders to command a group of LSTs which had been given some preliminary training at Panama City, Florida. Quite a go-getter, he wanted to know where the war was and when he could get going. As it was the Easter weekend, Brisbane was reasonably subdued and quiet. It seemed out of keeping with his idea of a nation on the perimeter of the war zone. But he plunged right into the job of getting his LSTs into combat condition, and he was a pretty hard driver. As some of his ships would take part in the Woodlark-Kiriwina operation, I sent him with a small group from my staff to Milne Bay to embark in a native lugger provided by the Australians, and from there to make their way to the islands for an up-to-date reconnaissance under cover of darkness. There was always the possibility that Scruggs' scouting party might alert the Japanese as to our intentions, if there were any in the area, but we had to take that chance as our photographic intelligence unit was not well organized at that time, and information from former planters in the area, particularly Kiriwina, was very meager.

The charts used—the only ones available—were reproductions of a map done by a German missionary in 1909, apparently from memory. We learned later that Kiriwina had been oriented seven miles out of bearing, and as expected, the information from former residents proved unreliable.

The reconnaissance of the beach approaches made by Scruggs' party was helpful, but, since it was made hurriedly and during darkness, it proved far from adequate. They found no evidence of any Nips. Both islands were almost completely surrounded by coral reefs and channels through them were difficult to locate. Even getting to the islands was a navigational hazard for the sixty-foot, inter-island lugger which carried the group. The difficulties were aggravated by the need for traveling at night and hiding during the daylight in overhanging foliage of the many small islands along the route. The lugger had been hired on the assumption the captain knew the area like his own jungle backyard, but even so, his craft was hung up twice on coral heads during his night navigation to Kiriwina. This news caused plenty of worries as to how inexperienced amphibious skippers would fare in nighttime navigation through waters that were dangerous even to lugger experts.

General Krueger coordinated all phases of the planning at his Camp Columbia headquarters, near Brisbane. Commanders M. T. Farrar and Bern Anderson from my staff represented me at these conferences. To meet the Army's shipping requirements called for the use of every beaching ship that was able to move, including those still en route from the States that might arrive in time. There would be no ships in reserve for contingencies.

Then the planners had to make some last-minute eliminations of troops and cargo from the initial convoys, because of the loss of an LST and an LCI.

The *LST-469,* in convoy from Sydney to Brisbane, was torpedoed by a lone Japanese submarine. The attack came while most of her crew were at their evening meal. The torpedo hit and the loss of life was unusually heavy. This taught the LST skippers a costly lesson—never assemble the entire crew in one compartment when there is a possibility of submarine attack.

An odd sidelight of the attack was the loss of Commander Scruggs' personal baggage which had been stored in the torpedoed compartment. Among his effects was a napkin ring engraved with his name. Five years after the war ended an

Australian sent the ring to Scruggs, but did not say how it came into his possession.

Unlike the damage to the LST due to enemy action, the damage to the LCI resulted from bad weather conditions. During a severe storm the *LCI-227,* one of the three on training duty at Port Stephens, broke loose from her moorings, and was blown dangerously near a large rocky ledge. It looked as though she would be a total loss. However, with the Army furnishing small boats, the Australians supplying a salvage tug, and the Navy sending in its two remaining LCIs to heave away on lines attached to the ship, an investment of $750,000 and a much-needed ship was saved.

Although the Woodlark-Kiriwina operation had lost the immediate services of the *LST-469* and *LCI-227,* as well as those of a couple of other craft because of breakdowns or late arrivals, we found that if the Army would be economy-minded in troop and cargo requirements we could just get by with the remaining available shipping.

But carrying the troops and cargo to the vicinity of the islands was only part of the problem. After the ships arrived, they would have to find their way in darkness through coral reefs and onto the beaches, complete their unloading, and be on their way again before daylight. The initial convoy would have the hard job—find a channel through the coral, blast one out if necessary, buoy it, and build up sandbanks on the beaches on which the ships could drop their ramps to off-load. Finding experienced beachmasters, harbor masters, and shore party commanders to carry out these important duties was out of the question. There were none available at that time. The men assigned these jobs would have to figure out how to do them after they got there.

The beachmaster's job at Kiriwina promised to be particularly onerous, and the assignment was given to Ensign Wally Wemyss because he was strong, uninhibited, and had lots of initiative. He had been on duty at Toorbul since his arrival as part of the training staff. But we almost lost him a few days before he got started on his new assignment. Returning one night from Brisbane to Toorbul with a boatload of trainees, he lost his way, ran over an Australian mine field, was fired on by shore batteries, and enjoyed a dangerously exciting time.

All the planning for Woodlark and Kiriwina was based on the assumption that the landings would be unopposed. The LSTs, LCIs, APDs, and LCTs were lightly loaded to permit quick discharge during darkness and withdrawal from the islands before sunup. Shore construction crews were to work at night only and hide in the jungle during daylight. This would also be the procedure for succeeding echelons which would arrive each night with additional personnel and equipment until antiaircraft batteries had been set up and airfields were operating in sufficient strength to protect daylight convoy movements.

Coinciding with Woodlark and Kiriwina landings, Admiral Halsey's South Pacific

Forces would land a division of troops on the beaches of New Georgia in the Solomon Islands, more than three hundred miles to the eastward. His Solomon Island activities were under continuous surveillance by Japanese planes and it was hoped they would concentrate all their attacks in that area and overlook the Southwest Pacific convoys. And such proved to be the case.

The landing force which Halsey moved to New Georgia was well-protected by a continuous air cover of thirty-two planes during daylight hours and, at supporting distance, by five aircraft carriers, four battleships, nine cruisers, and a large number of destroyers.

Our Southwest Pacific convoys would be less well-protected. They would have an antisubmarine screen of a few destroyers although, lurking within supporting distance, would be a division of cruisers under British Rear Admiral V. A. C. Crutchley. He would be able to handle light surface raids but in case of a major Japanese effort we would need to rely on Halsey's fleet, much farther away—provided they got the word in time.

The main concern in the Southwest Pacific was lack of air cover for the convoys. General Kenney's Fifth Air Force could not provide adequate air cover, principally because his fighter planes were "short-legged" and could not stay on station long enough to be effective. However, Kenney believed his planes could bomb the nearby Nip bases so effectively they would not be able to launch an attack against our landings even if they knew about them. As a further precaution, he proposed to keep some of his fighter planes on ground alert available to come to our aid if it became necessary. We were a bit skeptical of this arrangement and particularly doubtful that Air Force ground-alert planes based in New Guinea could ever reach our convoys in time to ward off an enemy bomber attack, but we had no choice in the matter. We looked with envy at the preparations in Admiral Halsey's force where carrier planes would provide continuous daylight cover.

The Woodlark and Kiriwina operations were militarily important to General MacArthur as a beginning in the encirclement of Rabaul. To the Seventh Amphibious Force, they would be a tryout of the organization and of the capabilities of beaching ships and crews under unusually difficult navigational conditions. If no enemy was encountered, it would in effect be an advanced training exercise, and we hoped it would turn out that way.

8: Woodlark-Kiriwina

30 June 1943

PLANS FOR THE FIRST LANDING IN HOSTILE TERRITORY OF THE Seventh Amphibious Force were completed about mid-June 1943. There was a good bit of nervousness among all of us as the time for commencing the operation drew near. We knew our own limitations of partly trained and untried crews and plans had been patterned accordingly, but how about the ships and troops that were being borrowed from Admiral Halsey? How would they fit into the overall picture? We had done no training together.

Ships, troops, and cargo from the South Pacific as well as from the Southwest Pacific were assembled for the jump-off at staging ports in Australia and in Milne Bay. To be closer to the combat area, General Krueger moved with his staff from Brisbane to Milne Bay. I prepared to follow as soon as some urgent matters had been settled concerning the repair ship *Rigel,* troops training, and the 2nd Engineer Special Brigade.

The *Rigel* had reported to the Amphibious Force a few weeks previously and since then she had been working around the clock with the repair unit in Brisbane. She couldn't begin to handle all the jobs that awaited her but even so there was an even greater need for her in the forward area to take care of a lot of small craft that would be operating thereabouts, and Brisbane would be too far in the rear to permit their shuttling back and forth. Shore facilities were being constructed at Milne Bay, on the edge of the operating area, to meet the most urgent needs of our ships. Until they were functioning, the *Rigel* would have to carry that load. The shipyards of Australia, and her supply bases and hospitals, would continue to take care of the big jobs.

My presence in Milne Bay would permit me to keep in close touch with our craft and the conditions under which they operated. And another important reason for my being there was its proximity to General Krueger's headquarters. In the Southwest

Pacific there was no unity of command of the various services below General MacArthur's level, which was contrary to the principle of unified command in all operations in other combat areas. Our landings were planned and carried out on the basis of cooperation. It was a bit unorthodox but it worked—perhaps because General MacArthur was always in the background and ready to handle any recalcitrants.

In most of our upcoming operations General Krueger's force would supply the troops and the Seventh Amphibious Force would supply the ships, so it was quite important that our planning groups be readily available to each other to consult on matters of common interest, such as availability of ships, staging areas for the troops, ammunition, food, and casualty handling for both troops and ship personnel.

Before leaving for Milne Bay I was directed to take over the operational control and training of the 2nd Engineer Special Brigade which was stationed at the widely separated ports of Rockhampton and Cairns. The date of the take-over would be after they had made a small boat landing on 30 June at Nassau Bay on New Guinea's north coast. I was also to undertake the amphibious training of the 9th Australian Division at Cairns, more than eight hundred miles north of Brisbane. The 9th Division was a seasoned combat outfit from the Middle East, scheduled for the landing operation that was next after Woodlark and Kiriwini in the plans for the isolation of Rabaul. As this next operation would be carried out solely by beaching craft on specific beaches of New Guinea, the amphibious training was limited to the job in hand rather than to the all-around training given to the troops at Port Stephens where the big assault transports, the *Manoora, Kanimbla,* and *Westralia* were included in the program.

A training unit from the Port Stephens outfit was sent to Cairns. Port Stephens was beginning to lose its usefulness. It was too far away from practically all of the troop campsites which were now spread from Brisbane to Cairns. Trains were overburdened with wartime freight, military trucks were at a premium, roads inadequate, and harbors congested. To relieve some of the overland transportation difficulties, I gave orders to close the training setup at Port Stephens and move to Toorbul, a far less desirable spot but six hundred miles farther north and that much closer to the main troop encampments.

My operational control of the 2nd Engineer Special Brigade was bound up with certain restrictions. The brigade consisted of 3 engineer boat-and-shore regiments, each composed of 104 officers and 2,067 men, organized into one boat battalion and one shore battalion. A few brigades had been organized in Massachusetts during the previous year for the purpose of manning large numbers of the 36-foot and 50-foot Higgins boats which it was expected would participate in a British cross-channel operation, a sort of Dunkirk in reverse.

The brigade was composed of a few regular Army officers from the Corps of

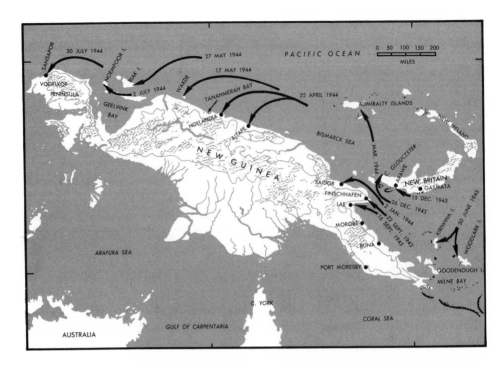

ASSAULTS ON NEW GUINEA AND ADJACENT ISLANDS

Engineers, but in the main the troops were a heterogeneous collection of yachtsmen, small boat engineers, garage mechanics, and volunteers—with lots of enthusiasm but little military know-how. When the cross-channel operation was delayed, these brigades became surplus to European requirements. MacArthur requested that he be sent any that were available with the hope they could help him in his 1942 supply problems along the New Guinea coast, since the Navy was apparently unable to help him at that time. The 2nd Brigade was the initial answer to MacArthur's request. One of the units of the brigade was assigned the job of assembling Higgins boats from sections that were sent out from the States.

As finally worked out, the brigade would come under my operational control during the assault phase of any landing after Woodlark and Kiriwina. When the Army commander was established ashore after the landing operation, the control of the brigade and its boats would pass to the Army commander of the task force. Just how they could best be fitted into amphibious operations would be a matter of trial and error.

On completion of the new arrangements, Seventh Amphibious combat headquarters was moved to Milne Bay. The move was far simpler for me than it had been for General Krueger—all we had to do was sail the USS *Rigel* to Milne Bay. To accommodate his field headquarters a campsite had to be hewn out of the jungle. My staff and I would have the comparative luxury of living aboard ship.

Only a small part of my staff (those concerned primarily with planning and operations) accompanied me to New Guinea; the others remained in Brisbane aboard the administrative flagship the *Henry T. Allen,* with the personnel files, pay accounts, and official records.

The plane trip to Milne Bay with my streamlined staff was a well-remembered experience. The small landing field at the western end of the bay was merely a series of steel mats laid between groves of coconut trees that was visible when it was not raining. Since the rain commenced every day at 2 P.M.—you could almost set your watch by it—it was necessary to arrive before that time. Unfavorable winds and a pilot who was new to the area put us well behind schedule. There were anxious moments as the sky became overcast and a light rain started to fall. There was not enough gas in the twin-engine plane to search for some other friendly airfield. We were preparing for a crash landing in the jungle when the clouds parted and the field appeared underneath. The plane glided in low over the coconut trees and came to a landing in oppressive heat and dampness. Deep, sticky mud was everywhere. A marker nearby indicated the furthest spot the Japanese had reached in their attempt to capture the place a year previously.

Since Milne Bay would play such an important part in the future operations of the Seventh Amphibious Force, it merits some description. Seen from the air, it is a beautiful, narrow body of water, about twenty-six miles long with an average width of five miles. Except that it provided excellent anchorage areas, everything else about it was unpleasant.

Other than the relatively few plantation areas, the grass shoreline marked the beginning of a mangrove swamp. Jungle foliage overhung the water. Crocodiles infested the streams. Scrub typhus, elephantiasis and "jungle rot" were commonplace.

Every night malaria-bearing mosquitoes came out in swarms and their bites laid everyone low, the mighty and the meek alike. In this respect Navy men were far more fortunate than their Army brothers who lived ashore, for the ships could usually anchor outside the flying range—about four hundred yards upwind—of the insects. Even so, all hands afloat, like everyone ashore, were given a daily dose of atabrine. The drug was a malaria suppressant, but had the undesirable side effect of turning the user's skin yellow.

When the *Rigel* arrived, she anchored in a bight of the Bay near the north shore, partly shielded from reconnaissance planes by jungle growth. She was a most welcome relief from the dankish smells ashore.

At the time of my arrival in Milne Bay, Seabees were engaged in the construction of an amphibious base, a base for PT boats, a supply base, small docks, munitions depots, a network of roads, and a small naval hospital. Similar work was being undertaken for the Army, but on an even more extensive scale, by the Army Engineers.

The conditions under which the Seabees worked were only acceptable because of the urgency of war. In addition to the danger from malaria and skin diseases, they had to endure stifling, humid heat. Deep, gooey mud was everywhere; it was not uncommon to see bulldozers mired and slowly sinking out of sight, or men working in sludge up to their waists. In spite of these difficulties, remarkable progress was made, but even so, many months would pass before these shore facilities could meet the needs of the forces afloat.

We desperately needed, at once, repair ships, water barges, supply ships, and the many other special types that are required to support a combat naval force operating a long way from its home base.

But the most crying need was for a hospital ship for immediate use in the forward area. Even before battle casualties started coming in, the medical staffs of the amphibious ships in Milne Bay were unequal to the task of caring for those stricken with tropical diseases. There was doubt that a hospital ship would be assigned to the Seventh Amphibious Force—they were few in number and our priority was not very high—but as a partial substitute we thought we might be able to convert an LST into a "first-aid" ship if we could spare one and if the Navy Department had no objections. A newly promoted and imaginative medical officer, Lieutenant Commander E. F. Norwood, had submitted a sketch for just such a conversion.

We well knew that the Navy Department jealously guarded its right to authorize any modifications of the original design of any ship, and changing the "innards" of even as LST was not to be undertaken lightly. Getting a Navy Department reply to such a request might take anywhere from a few weeks to several months, and even then the request might not be approved. Anyhow, an official request was sent to Washington outlining our reasons and needs. Then, to "save time," we went ahead with the LST conversion plan on the assumption it would be approved.

Valuable as each LST was for assault operations, a "first-aid" ship would be even more valuable. The *LST-464* was chosen because she would arrive at Sydney within a few days where the shipyards could do the work. Two days after her arrival, the conversion job was under way and her character changed from a fighting ship to a ship of mercy. This entailed the installation of a watertight door in the tank deck bulkhead to afford access to the forward troop compartment from either port or starboard. Spaces were converted into a receiving room, sterilizer room, and operating room. The wounded could be brought in over the ramp onto the tank deck, and passed into a receiving room through the hatch. On the tank deck were installed 78 hospital beds, 4 refrigerators, plenty of lockers, 22 toilets, and 19 wash basins.

A column of Seventh Amphibious Force invasion ships heads for Kiriwina and Woodlark.

The repair ship Rigel *(AD-13) joined the Seventh Amphibious Force in time for the Woodlark-Kiriwina landing and was designated Admiral Barbey's flagship.*

Assembling this equipment in the States would not have been a matter of conse-quence, but getting it in war-short Australia required a lot of priorities. The ship's medical staff consisted of six doctors, one dentist, and a number of corpsmen, all of whom were obtained by "thinning out" other ships and shore bases.

Our first-aid ship did a magnificent job throughout the war. Ironically, nine months after her conversion, and after she had handled some thousands of sick and wounded, a letter was received from the Bureau of Ships regretfully turning down our conversion request: "It is desired that all LSTs continue to operate in the manner for which they were designed." The letter further added that "a hospital ship will be sent to your area when one becomes available." The letter was placed in those files most likely to be lost in combat, and the *LST-464* continued to operate, if not in the manner for which designed, at least in the way we most needed her.

But the first-aid ship was only the first in a series of high priority conversions made in the combat area. The matter of a water barge was next on the agenda. Keeping our smaller ships supplied with fresh water was a vital matter. The LCTs and other little craft were originally designed for short distance operations in the English Channel where they could always return to their home base if they wanted a drink of water. But in New Guinea they had to depend on rain water obtained from canvas catchalls that covered their top deck. Water from the streams ashore was generally not usable because of pollution from the native villages. And so an LCT was converted into a water barge, obtaining its water from uninhabited islands or from streams far removed from native villages, and rationed it to the needy.

Another "must" in immediate ship requirements was administrative flagships for the little LCTs. On their longer trips, someone had to act as guide, keep track of the personnel records and pay accounts, and supervise their activities.

Fortunately, we had received a number of wooden-hulled coastal transports about the size of small tugs. They were officially designated APc's, but were usually referred to as "apple carts." Just why we got them was a bit of a mystery for they were designed to carry small groups of troops from dockside to dockside, and docks in New Guinea were a rarity. It was assumed we had them because they were not in much demand elsewhere, probably because of maintenance difficulties due to their hulls being infested by teredos. However, our repair section overcame much of this difficulty by installing copper sheathing at the water line. These small craft soon filled many gaps in our requirements, although none were used for their designed purpose.

A few were converted for use as "tenders" and as flagships for LCT flotilla commanders; one was converted to a floating post office; and one was converted to a "planning" ship. This last "apple cart" was equipped with a mimeograph machine, one typewriter, a chart room, extra bunks, and other equipment needed by our planners as they moved from one isolated Army headquarters to another in the preparation of joint plans.

As more ships joined the Amphibious Force and our operations became larger, the demand for special types of auxiliary ships became more pressing. A few LSTs were converted into "repair ships" and others into "casualty ships." Other conversions were made from other types of ships as the need arose.

The smaller conversion jobs were done at Milne Bay by Commander Mansbach, the repair officer, and his small staff. In addition to the usual work on damaged hulls, bent propellers, and broken-down machinery, they devised ways of blasting damaged LCI screws off their shafts; built a dry dock in the mudflats of the shoreline; and developed other curious devices for ship maintenance that were a marvel of improvisation.

As I look back I am amazed at the great amount of work turned out by Mansbach and his associates in the suffocating heat and drenching rains of Milne Bay. Their work was frequently interrupted by lone Japanese bombers who would usually come over at sundown, drop their load and get away in the gathering darkness. Whenever we received radar warning of their approach, all ships not immobilized would get under way, skirt the shoreline and zigzag until the raid was over. Then they would return to their anchorage, lights would be turned on, and the job of repairing ships and building bases would go on and on.

I was never to see the completed shore facilities at Milne Bay. By the time it was in full operation, U.S. combat forces were well on their way toward the Philippines and other bases had been established along the route. But Milne Bay served a vital need in the early days of our operations as a replacement for the bases much farther away in Australia.

The landings on Woodlark and Kiriwina Islands were scheduled for the night of 30 June 1943. Every usable LST, LCT, and LCI in the Southwest Pacific, plus those borrowed from Admiral Halsey's South Pacific forces, was participating in this operation. That night, at Milne Bay, we anxiously awaited word aboard the *Rigel*. Radio silence was to be strictly observed on every ship in the landing force unless disaster engulfed them, such as an attack by a raiding force. Every hour of silence was an hour of good news. The ships had been in enemy controlled waters for twenty-four hours and it seemed unbelievable that they had not been sighted by Japanese reconnaissance planes, although overcast weather and a series of squalls provided some measure of protection.

The hazards were not only from the Nips. There were also the navigational dangers of inexperienced crews trying to make a landing in pitch darkness on a beach surrounded by coral. And we prayed that none of our few ships would be permanently hung up on a reef.

Not until the first group of ships returned to Milne Bay did we get the details of what had happened. There had been no Japanese air or surface opposition. Within a few hours of the main landing at Woodlark, the antiaircraft batteries were in position. It was expected the fighter strip would be functioning within a week. The Kiriwina job had proven more difficult because of greater beaching hazards from coral. Even so, the air strip there would be completed well in advance of our planning date.

The landing on Woodlark had been made by six LSTs shortly after nightfall on 30 June 1943. There had been no navigational mishaps en route, but navigating the tricky channel through the reefs and keeping clear of the coral heads during the intense blackness was tricky business and no job for amateurs. To safeguard the precious LSTs, Commander Scruggs personally piloted each LST of his division in succession through the reefs to its allotted place on the one comparatively decent beach. This procedure was all right for an unopposed landing, but hereafter these skippers of his LSTs would have to do their own piloting, and furthermore it would have to be done against shore opposition.

The landing at Kiriwina went less smoothly, for the reefs were more difficult and the coral-studded beaches were almost unapproachable. For that reason no ships larger than LCIs could be used. The LCIs carrying a total of 2,250 troops had been accompanied by 12 equipment-laden little LCTs, each towing behind them even smaller craft. They had had a pretty rough time as they tried to follow their guide, an APc. Commander M. T. Farrar, our planning officer who doubled as convoy commander of the Kiriwina group, gave a graphic picture of the initial operation of these new ships with new crews in new waters:

> I was in the Able Peter little Charlie (APc) that led this weird assortment up the non-existent channel. It wasn't too bad, only a couple of LCTs forgot to follow the leader and were stranded for a time, and one got lost, but the LCIs steamed along like the old Pacific Fleet. When they neared the shore and separated to take their own position on the beach "all hell broke loose." The beach approaches were full of niggerheads and at one time or another it seemed that every one of the LCIs and LCTs went hard aground. Our boy Wemyss (Navy beachmaster) is a jewel. He has the courage and strength of a lion. With his three small boats and ragtag boat crews we "unstuck" each LCI and LCT and piloted them within at least wading distance of the shore.

Until a pier could be built it would be necessary to use the small LCTs to supply the bulk of the cargo for the building of the airstrip and for other construction on Kiriwina. It was quite a job for these craft, each with their one young and inexperienced officer and an even less experienced crew of ten young men. For the next two months, they would be engaged in almost continuous round trips of hundreds of miles in waters that even native luggers found hazardous.

The few hundred natives on both islands were poor physical specimens, but were friendly and helpful as laborers. The women, as well as the men, chewed betel nut which stained their teeth a disgusting brown color. But this unpleasant habit had one desirable result. It kept our men away from them.

Young Wally Wemyss, the beachmaster at Kiriwina, had more than his share of trouble. He not only had the job of blasting a channel through the reef and getting ships in their right slots on the beach at night without lights, and their cargo discharged during heavy rain and darkness, but the far more difficult job of taking care of the visitors. It seemed to him that every staff colonel in the Southwest Pacific had arrived to make an inspection of what was going on and that each one expected to be comfortably housed in accordance with his rank. This, at a time when a dry sleeping place under a tree was luxury treatment. He petitioned us to keep the visitors behind their desks in Australia.

The Woodlark and Kiriwina operations emphasized one aspect of amphibious operations in particular which heretofore had not been considered seriously, and that was seasickness. Squalls and gusts of wind rolled and pitched the small ships to such an extent that more than fifty percent of their troops were helplessly seasick—a serious matter if they had to fight their way ashore. Forecasts of sea conditions would need to be given more weight in future planning.

When all reports were in, we found considerable satisfaction in knowing that our inexperienced force had met all commitments on its first try. More than 16,000 men, with equipment and supplies, had been transported 185 miles beyond the advance base at Milne Bay through poorly charted waters, subject to Japanese air, surface, and submarine attack, without the loss of a single man, ship, or craft.

But there were a couple of communication slip-ups that might have caused trouble. Before the start of the operation, the commanding officers of all ships were impressed with the need for radio silence. MacArthur's headquarters in Brisbane was particularly emphatic that all matters pertaining to the operation be kept secret until the airfields had been completed and the garrisons in a position to defend themselves—a matter of a few weeks.

To the surprise of all of us at Milne Bay, we intercepted two messages shortly after the ships started homeward from the initial landing. One was from the socialite commander of a division of LSTs who not only broke radio silence but also used a top secret code to issue invitations to a dinner party on his return to Townsville, Australia! The other was a radio broadcast from MacArthur's headquarters announcing the successful landing. Apparently, some public relations man at his headquarters had gotten the word about the "landing" but not the word about the "silence." As far as we knew, however, these communications slip-ups did no harm.

Although the Seventh Amphibious Force had gained experience in ship and boat handling around sand bars, coral reefs, and through surf, in daylight and in darkness, no experience had been received in defending against bomber attack or in landing troops against shore opposition. Except for some reconnaissance planes and two inconsequential bombing raids against Woodlark, the operations had been completely free from enemy attention. This may have been due to the unobtrusiveness of the effort, but more probably was due to the all-out Japanese reaction to Halsey's landing, three hundred miles to the eastward, which left them nothing for Woodlark and Kiriwina. Halsey's forces in New Georgia and Rendova had been subjected to heavy bombing and surface raids and their troops ashore had met strong opposition.

Seventh Amphibious Force responsibilities to Woodlark and Kiriwina did not end with the landing of assault troops. MacArthur had made our organization responsible for the flow of supplies to the island garrisons until piers were built and it appeared safe for the Army Service of Supply to take over this support job with civilian-manned freighters. This procedure became standard for all future operations.

During the two months the Amphibious Force carried supplies to the forces on these islands, medical officers aboard the ships would often be called upon to treat ailing natives. Among the medical officers called upon was Lieutenant (j.g.) Fay Begor who was attached to a group of LCIs. During his many supply runs he developed a large charity practice among the natives, which was one reason for their strong friendship and helpful cooperation.

As a military feat, the landings on Kiriwina and Woodlark Islands were of no great moment, but it was an essential first step—or so we thought at the time—in the capture of Rabaul.

9:

Assault
on Lae
16 September 1943

THE NEXT OPERATION FOR THE SEVENTH AMPHIBIOUS FORCE
was a combat job where strong resistance might be expected both from the shore and
from the air. The 9th Australian Division was to be landed on beaches adjacent to the
strategic village of Lae, an important Japanese outpost in the defense of western New
Guinea. The village was important to the Allies as an essential step in the isolation of
Rabaul. This small port on the Huon Gulf of New Guinea is about 370 miles
northwest of Milne Bay. After landing the troops on two beaches, about 16 miles to the
east of Lae—well out of range of its coastal batteries—the amphibious force would
then maintain a flow of reinforcements and supplies to the beaches while the troops
fought their way into the town. The two beaches were of firm black sand, about 400
yards long and 20 yards wide. Back of them were mangrove swamps.

The capture of Lae was not a job for the 9th Division alone. It was to be a
three-pronged affair: while Australian troops were transported by sea to the landings
eastward of Lae, American troops would start an overland attack along the coast
northward from their base at Buna, and the 7th Australian Division would be
airlifted to the village of Nadzab for an attack on Lae from the rear.

Expectations that the defense of Lae would be stubborn were heightened by a
captured Japanese document written on the seventeenth of July 1943, and signed by
Lieutenant General Hidemitsu Nakano, commander of the Japanese 51st Division.
Translated, it read:

The whole fate of the Japanese Empire depends upon the decision of the struggle for Lae-Salamaua. These strongholds must be defended to the death. We must crush the enemy both on land and in the air. Whatever plans to land troops he may attempt, we must destroy speedily and decisively at the water's edge. Every officer and man must develop his strength and resolution so that one man is the equal of ten.

Despite the brave words of the Japanese commander, his troops were faced with an impossible situation. He had to defend a wide area with not much over 20,000 troops, and these were reported in a weakened condition from fatigue, short rations, and malaria. His men would be pitted against three divisions of hardened Allied troops striking at them from three directions.

When the step-by-step plans for the reduction of Rabaul had been outlined by General MacArthur at a conference of his senior commanders, it had been estimated that amphibious ships, troops, and planes could be made available for the Lae operations about two months after the landings at Woodlark and Kiriwina. That would be during the early part of September 1943.

Such matters as the exact date and hour for the amphibious part of the operation were to be arranged by agreement between Major General G. F. Wootten, the commander of the 9th Australian Division, and myself. The availability of troops and shipping, state of the tide and moon, and time of sunrise were determining factors in these matters. We both wanted a night approach and an early daylight landing. Wootten did not want his troops landed in darkness in jungle territory, and I wanted the landing in early daylight so we could get our ships unloaded and away before any Japanese planes found them unloading on the beaches and bombed them. The landing date agreed upon was 4 September 1943.

Two weeks before the landing date, our amphibious plans, and the plans of all the ground troops involved, had been coordinated except for those troops to be airlifted to Nadzab by General Kenney's Fifth Air Force. Kenney could not commit himself on airlifting the troops until weather forecasters produced favorable predictions. For a time it looked as if our amphibious landing would have to take place without the simultaneous participation of any airborne troops operating in the rear of Lae.

But this possibility did not bother General Wootten. "Just land me on the beaches," he said, "and I'll get into Lae while the Air Force is still looking at its weather maps." As it so happened, the 7th Australian Division was airlifted to Nadzab the day after our amphibious landing on the outskirts of Lae. Coordinated operations with the Army Air Force were always a bit uncertain because of their dependence on the vagaries of the weather.

There would be no prior strafing of enemy beaches by friendly planes nor any air cover for ships during the landing. This was because our shore-based fighter planes could not reach the beachhead as early as 0630, and both Wootten and myself were unwilling to delay the landing to a later hour. A later hour would have required the convoy to approach the beaches during daylight, exposing it to enemy observation while en route and thus forfeiting the element of surprise. Surprise was more important than an uncertain air cover.

Since the ships in the convoy would not have any air cover during the landing, it would be necessary to load them very lightly for a fast discharge and quick getaway. Three to four hours on the beach should be enough for this purpose as we doubted the Japanese would be able to launch a bomber attack from any of their main air bases within that time. Also, we knew the Fifth Air Force would work over enemy airfields at Lae and other places within their reach during the week preceding the landing, and it seemed improbable the Nips would have much left in the line of planes to bother us while getting our troops ashore. As a precautionary measure, a group of fighter planes would be kept on ground alert at Dobodura—an airfield near Buna and about 140 miles from Lae—and thirty-two fighter planes would be in the air over the convoy routes a few hours after daylight.

As an added precaution, the destroyer *Reid* was stationed about fifty miles to the eastward of the landing area with a fighter-director team aboard. This arrangement extended the radar warning system for enemy planes approaching from the east and north, and would give our fighter planes some additional time to meet any oncoming attack.

It was not a very pleasant assignment for the *Reid*, all alone and in the path of any Japanese bombers. But there was always the possibility she would not be bothered, as one destroyer might not be considered worthy of a concentrated plane attack when there was bigger game ahead.

The threat of a bomber attack on the convoys and the possible loss of some ships was a matter of grave concern to General Wootten as well as to myself. Because of the light loading of the ships, Wootten would have to start his operations ashore with a bare minimum of requirements. The loss of any of the LSTs might well restrict the flow of essential reinforcements and supplies in follow-up echelons, for we were working on a pretty thin margin as far as ships were concerned.

The joint planning for the operation was done at Wootten's headquarters in a former plantation at the western end of Milne Bay. In addition to officers from the two staffs, there were also representatives from destroyers, submarines, and PT boats. The Fifth Air Force was represented by a junior officer who was present as an observer rather than a planner. Every night the planners reported to their respective commanders on all matters that had been under discussion. The senior commanders would get together on major decisions.

Preparations for the Lae operation were helped when the Amphibious Force staff was increased by twelve career officers. These new arrivals were the result of

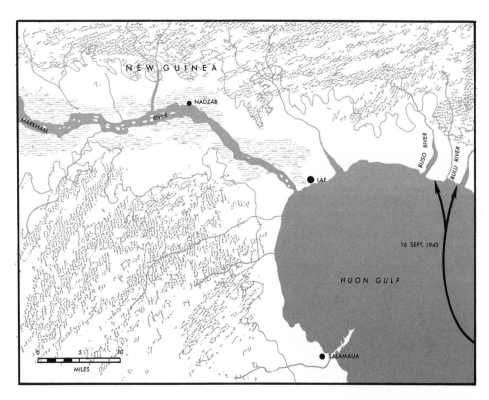

LANDINGS NEAR LAE

MacArthur's personal request to the Navy Department that my staff be augmented by twenty-five experienced officers for the important upcoming series of operations. Although thirteen of the officers were siphoned off in Australia, the twelve that finally reached us at Milne Bay were an excellent group. And they were badly needed. Our skeleton staff was nearing exhaustion from the long hours, the heat, and the lack of recreation.

Among the newcomers, the two most experienced in the type of warfare we were about to undertake were Captain F. W. Benson and Commander Charles Adair.

Adair's first job was a reconnaissance mission along the New Guinea coast to find a suitable bay or inlet which could be used as a small forward base in operations against Salamaua and Lae. His report gives a picture of the primitive and haphazard manner in which we gathered bits of intelligence information in those early days:

> Before making the trip by small boat, I wanted to get a set of photographs of the coast line which would be of assistance in investigating the whole area. The Air Force provided me with a B-17 piloted by Colonel Hutchinson. They also provided an escort of four fighter planes because we would be taking pictures close to Japanese bases.
>
> We photographed the coast line to within a short distance of Salamaua, the nearest

Lieutenant Commander James E. Van Zandt, U.S. Naval Reserve, conferring with Admiral Barbey. Van Zandt was typical of the outstanding Reserve officers who served with the Seventh Amphibious Force. He had resigned his seat in Congress to see action in the Navy.

The destroyer Conyngham *(DD-371) became the flagship for the Seventh Amphibious Force just before the Lae operation. Although unsuitable as a flagship, she was used in this capacity on a "make do" basis for almost a year.*

Japanese air base. We returned to our base at noon and by seven o'clock the next morning I was given three complete sets of photographs made by the K-17 camera. I can't be too complimentary to the U.S. Air Force for their cooperation.

The next day, accompanied by the Marine officer from our staff and two Australian Army officers, I boarded a forty-foot motor boat which the Army loaned us for the survey trip. The boat formerly belonged to the Mayor of Sydney, Australia. It had a crew of three Army enlisted men.

We spent a week investigating every inlet on the New Guinea coast to a point just south of Salamaua. We sounded the water for depth at every prospective base site. As I was a so-called expert, I personally swung the lead for most of these soundings.

The day before we went on our trip and the day after we returned, Japanese planes attacked all boats in the area, but we weren't bothered during the entire survey.

As an indication of the shoestring conditions under which we were operating, all available beaching ships were engaged in running supplies to the garrisons at Woodlark and Kiriwina and could not be released from this work until two weeks before the scheduled date of the Lae landing. During these two weeks, we had to assemble ships at the jump-off ports, distribute operating plans, hold rehearsals, and load troops and supplies for the assault. There just was not enough time to do all the things that needed to be done in the way they ought to be done.

During the final rehearsal we thought we had lost one of our little LCTs. Its cargo was particularly valuable for it carried General Wootten's communication equipment. This valuable LCT was the last one in the column of the rehearsal force of assorted ships and craft which sailed steadily throughout the night. In the morning all ships hit the Normanby Island training beach except our little LCT with the General's equipment. A search of the area brought the little fellow back many hours later. The young, dedicated, and devoted ensign in command had steered the craft all night, by himself, to be sure the job was done right. His orders had been to pick out a dark blob on the ship ahead and never let it out of his sight. During darkness, peering through the wheelhouse slot, he had steered steadily and faithfully toward the dark blob ahead. Unfortunately, the dark blob he had followed all night was his own jack staff.

As landing operations go, the Lae affair was not likely to make much of a dent on history. But in the Southwest Pacific it was a matter of great importance. The hodgepodge of ships that comprised the Seventh Amphibious Force was to be tried out in a beach assault for the first time. Failure or success would determine the pattern for future operations of MacArthur's forces. Furthermore, the landing had to be made without benefit of air cover or prolonged naval bombardment. It would be executed somewhat like a commando raid, except that it would be made in early daylight and the troops would go ashore and stay there.

There was some concern as to how the lightly armed amphibious ships would conduct themselves if subjected to a bomber attack. And there were a number of other uncertainties. The men of the 9th Australian Division were experienced desert fighters, but this would be their first experience in an amphibious landing and jungle warfare. And then there was the matter of the Engineer Special Brigade that would be operating with us. It would be the first time any part of the brigade had been wholly integrated into our amphibious activities, and we wondered as to their capability, particularly because of their earlier difficulty in making a small boat landing through the surf at Nassau Bay.

The first combat job which had been assigned them—and before they came under my operational control—was the transportation of about one thousand American troops from Morobe, an American-held area, to Nassau Bay about forty miles farther along the North New Guinea coast and in a Japanese-controlled area. The brigade had been brought to Milne Bay aboard freighters, and from there had worked their way in their own boats to our PT base at Morobe, about three hundred miles along the coast.

Although Nassau Bay was in Japanese-controlled territory, no opposition was expected as reconnaissance indicated there was nothing more than an enemy outpost on Nassau Bay.

Unfortunately, on the night chosen for the Nassau landing—30 June, to coincide with our Woodlark-Kiriwina operation—the weather was bad, with heavy rains and strong winds. Some of the boats lost their way en route to the landing area and those that arrived capsized in attempting a landing through the heavy surf. Fortunately, there was no enemy opposition and no lives were lost, but the loss of supplies was a serious blow. Our planning officer, Commander Charles Adair, flew over the area the following day. His description of a beach strewn with disabled boats and supplies made us skeptical of their combat use under any but fair weather conditions.

The plans for the Lae landing called for one battalion of the 532nd Engineer Boat and Shore Regiment of the Engineer Special Brigade, 1,060 men, to be transported from their encampment on the shores of Morobe Bay to the landing beaches about 75 miles away.

The Australian assault troops were to be landed in waves at short intervals. The first echelon of 560 troops would land in boats from four APDs. The second echelon would follow with 18 LCIs carrying 3,780 troops, and then the Engineers would be landed. The Engineers were organized as a shore party, and also as an advance construction group. That meant they would unload the landing craft as they arrived, develop roads in the immediate area, and move the supplies and ammunition to convenient locations in the jungle. They were to be carried from Morobe to the landing area in their own boats—10 LCMs (50-foot Higgins boats) and 40 LCVPs (36-foot Higgins boats). The same convoy would include Amphibious Force craft:

four LCTs carrying a cargo of antiaircraft guns, two subchasers to act as antisubmarine patrol, and an APc to guide them on their way. As soon as the Engineers reached the beaches they would become part of the Army command. In addition to their usefulness for shore party activities, General Wootten proposed to use their boats to ferry his troops across some streams between the Army landing area and the village of Lae, 16 miles to the west.

My flagship for this operation would be the destroyer *Conyngham* (DD-371). A destroyer is not a suitable flagship to control an amphibious landing, principally due to lack of communications facilities and the inability to berth and feed the Army and Navy staffs that should be embarked. Communication had to be maintained with all units in the convoy, with planes in the air, with troops ashore, and with distant supporting forces. Our ingenious communications officer, Lieutenant R. J. Schmidt, U. S. Naval Reserve, fitted the *Conyngham* with extra communication facilities on a "make do" basis. These arrangements were unequal to the task, but as there was no other choice, the Seventh Amphibious Force used a destroyer as flagship in all subsequent landings until a communications ship was assigned almost a year later.

The importance of keeping the flagship separate from local operations was brought home to the British during their unsuccessful amphibious expedition to Dakar in 1940. In that operation, the British commanding general at one time was on board a bombarding ship heading north at twenty-five knots while his troops were heading south in transports at twelve knots.

Compared with the much larger later operations, the planning for Lae should have been a simple affair. Only about 17,000 troops and 12,000 tons of supplies and equipment would be carried in 156 miscellaneous ships and craft. But it was not an easy matter, principally because the various planning staffs were new to their own jobs and to each other. Also, Australian and American planning procedures were different. Planners were unsure of the combat capabilities of the various units to be fitted into the plans. The troops, in camp at widely separated points along the New Guinea coast, would have to be picked up by inexperienced crews of a miscellaneous assortment of ships of varying speeds which all had to reach their allotted place off the landing area at dawn on D-day.

There were many beaches in the vicinity of Lae, and the Nips could not be in big numbers on all of them. On that assumption, it was probable that most of the opposition would come after the troops had landed and were heading toward the village. Intelligence information indicated that there were about eight thousand Japanese concentrated in Lae itself within a strong labyrinth of defenses.

A new format was adopted for the Lae operational plans. The one used at Woodlark and Kiriwina proved too bulky and detailed for use by smaller craft. The new format contained a few pages of "General Instructions" explaining the purpose of the operation and a few statements on how it would be carried out. Then, a few more pages to show the job to be done by each group of ships. Only the senior commanders who had adequate administrative offices would get the complete copy containing weather forecasts, information about enemy forces, and other detailed data on the general situation. The small ships and craft would get only the part that pertained to them and the "General Instructions" pages. All they had to know was "where their slot was and how they got into it." We hoped the plan would work. It did. It became our standard format thereafter, albeit a bit unorthodox when compared with Naval War College procedures.

Although there were four large troop transports—the *Henry T. Allen* and the three Australian ships—assigned to the Seventh Amphibious Force, they were not used in this operation for the same reasons they were not used at Woodlark or Kiriwina. The *Henry T. Allen* was not suitable for the forward area because of her poor material condition. The Australian ships, the *Manoora, Kanimbla,* and *Westralia,* were too large and valuable to be employed without adequate naval escort or air cover. For the time being, they were used in the rear areas for troop training and troop transportation.

Not since the ill-fated British assault on Gallipoli in 1915 had any Australian troops participated in an amphibious landing. And this time the technique would be different. The troops would be landed from especially designed beaching ships and on beaches out of the range of coastal defenses. Within minutes after the first assault waves were on the beach, equipment would be landed which would include, among many other things, bulldozers and miles of steel matting to provide a roadway for vehicles. Our defense preparations had two unavoidable deficiencies: there would be no air cover during the assault; and the protective screen of destroyers would be too weak to ward off a Japanese cruiser attack—a very real possibility.

On 2 September 1943 troops of the 9th Australian Division moved aboard the landing ships in Milne Bay. Final rehearsals had been completed and the men were ready. Other ships took aboard equipment and supplies at Buna and the Engineers Special Brigade stood by at Oro Bay.

At nightfall, my temporary flagship, the destroyer *Conyngham,* led the troop-loaded convoy along the New Guinea coast to the assault area, thirty-six hours away. There were no stops en route other than a slowdown at Buna to permit some supply ships and a tug to join the convoy. Aboard the *Conyngham,* in addition to General Wootten and a few of his staff, were two Australian planters who had lived in the vicinity of Lae for the previous twenty years. They were our advisers regarding the beaches, swamps, and jungle trails in the landing area.

The Nips undoubtedly had some expectation of an attack, somewhere, sometime soon. Their snooper planes must have reported the increased activity in all New Guinea ports and attached some meaning to the sudden increase in the bomber attacks on their air bases. They had attempted to blunt U.S. preparations by stepping up their own bombing raids. At noon on 3 September, Japanese planes attacked ships in the harbor of Morobe, but they did little damage. More importantly, they missed sighting the large troop convoy which was even then headed for the assault area and not far from their line of flight. It was one of the more fortunate circumstances of the Lae operation.

One hour before sunrise on 4 September, the *Conyngham* left the convoy and speeded ahead to identify the two landing beaches, designated Red and Yellow, which were a few miles apart.

Identification of the beaches was not easy. The shoreline was low with few distinguishing marks. In places, trees overhung the water. Clusters of coconut palms and a river bed were the main aids to identification. Radar was of little help because of the unfavorable shore contours. The Australian planters joined us on the bridge but were not as helpful as we had hoped for. Apparently they were not familiar with the topographical features as seen from the sea at dawn. But Commander Adair, chief planner and staff navigator, because of his considerable experience with boating in jungle areas, was able to pilot the *Conyngham* to the right spot. In the semidarkness each ship of the convoy jockeyed itself into its allotted position for the landing, using the flagship as a reference.

The weather was clear, almost no wind, and but little surf. Conditions were ideal for the assault. So far, plans had been carried out with clocklike precision.

First, the five destroyers laid down a short bombardment to uncover hidden batteries and to knock out any snipers lurking among the coconut trees near the beach. Small boats, lowered from the APDs and loaded with their assault troops, headed for the shore under cover of the bombardment and behind a pall of smoke resulting from the gunfire. When the boats were twelve hundred yards from the beaches, the bombardment stopped and the boats continued their approach. The first wave of Australians hit the sandy shore just eighteen minutes after sunrise and moved inland to an abandoned coconut plantation by way of narrow roads through the mangrove swamp. There was no organized opposition. A few Japanese lookouts who had strapped themselves to the upper trunks of palm trees were knocked from their perches by the bombardment, and the Aussie troops took care of the rest.

But the landing was not to be as free of action as we were beginning to hope. Eighteen LCIs, carrying almost 4,000 troops, were just nosing into the beach when 3 Japanese bombers and 6 fighters came in low and fast from the direction of Lae. They made one pass, strafing ships and beaches and dropping bombs. Two LCIs were badly damaged; the *LCI-339* received a direct bomb hit through the main deck, and the *LCI-341* suffered a near miss which blew a big hole in her side. The ships had to be abandoned and the crews took temporary cover in the jungle.

Naval casualties during the landing were fewer than might have been expected, but I was particularly sorry to learn they included my young medical friend, Lieutenant Fay Begor, who had been so helpful to the natives of Kiriwina. Another tragic loss was the young commanding officer of one of the LCIs that was damaged by the first plane attack. He had come out of the original bombing unscathed, but during the night he had returned to his ship to examine the damage with the hope that his ship—his first command—could be salvaged. A lone Nip bomber on night reconnaissance dropped its load and he was killed.

Succeeding groups of ships and boats arrived right on schedule. The shore party segment of the Engineer Special Brigade, with more than 1,000 men and the steel matting for road building, was particularly welcome. The LSTs, each carrying 400 troops and about 40 trucks and miscellaneous stores, were unloaded and on their way back to the rear bases within a few hours. Even the little LCTs, with one exception, met their unloading schedules although each one carried 120 tons of stores. In less than 4 hours, more than 8,000 men and 1,500 tons of supplies had been landed in the initial assault. The one lone LCT which could not meet her schedule was left stranded on the beach by the receding tide. She survived a bombing attack, retracted, and finally joined a returning convoy that night.

The rapid unloading of the bigger ships, the LSTs, was made possible because the stores and equipment they carried had been loaded on trucks so all that had to be done was to roll the trucks down their ramps to the firm sand ashore. This was not an economical use of cargo space, but the need for getting the ships away from the beaches within a few hours was the determining factor. Moving the trucks inland over narrow trails through the mangrove swamp was quite a problem, in spite of the use of steel matting. I saw a few trucks slowly sinking in the gooey mud, and perhaps they are still there, but probably out of sight.

Only one LST had any difficulty retracting from the beaches. She appeared to be hard and fast. However, with the aid of the tug *Sonoma* pulling, and three destroyers making waves close aboard to break her loose, she finally came off in time to join the retiring convoy.

Owing to communication difficulty between Wootten's field headquarters and my flagship, we had no information as to his progress ashore. Accompanied by two members of my staff, I finally found him in a coconut grove about one mile inland, surrounded by walkie-talkies and telephone cable. More than twenty-five miles of telephone cable had been landed for this operation. He was bubbling with enthusiasm and confident his troops would be in Lae within two weeks. And they were, but not without much hard fighting before that happened.

General Wootten's troops started the sixteen-mile advance toward Lae along a swampy coastal plain about one mile wide. The going was tough: mangrove swamps, jungle undergrowth, and razor-edged Kunai grass had to be overcome. Torrential streams had to be crossed. Cleverly concealed Japanese pillboxes took their toll and almost ever day enemy bombers came over and dropped their loads. Nearly every night their raiders would hover over Red and Yellow beaches, drop flares and then bombs in the vicinity of the LSTs unloading cargo in the darkness below. Fortunately these attacks caused very little damage. (Except for the initial assault, all the LSTs arrived at the beaches after nightfall and departed before sunrise.)

But if the Allies found the going a bit rough, the Japanese garrison in Lae found it even rougher. Every day American planes bombed them, and every night American destroyers shelled them. The punishment was too great and on the twelfth day, the sick and tired remnants of the Nip garrison abandoned the village and started their trek to join up with their countrymen to the westward.

An interesting sidelight of the Lae operation was a coast watcher radio report to MacArthur's headquarters. This particular coast watcher was one of a number of Australians who remained hidden on the mountaintops of New Guinea, reporting daily by radio the movement of any large groups of Japanese troops or ships. As the sun rose on the morning of 4 September, the day we landed, he excitedly reported great numbers of Japanese ships landing heavy reinforcements for their garrison at Lae—but it was our ships and our troops he was sighting.

From the naval point of view, the assault phase of the operation worked out far better than we dared hope. The only casualties had resulted from the early morning raid of enemy bombers from Lae. We learned later that the Japanese bombers had arrived on the Lae airfield at sundown the previous day with the expectation of making an early morning attack on our ships at anchor at Morobe. Our amphibious landing on nearby beaches gave their bombers an unexpected uncovered helpless target.

The probability that the Japanese air force would react violently to the landing was confirmed a few hours later. Although Allied bombers had been pounding nearby Japanese airfields during the previous week, their air force had plenty of punch remaining. While I was still ashore at Wootten's jungle headquarters, our radar outpost, the destroyer *Reid,* reported that three large groups of enemy planes were approaching from the direction of Rabaul. The Fifth Air Force figher planes covering the convoy routes and those on "standby" at Dobodura were directed to intercept. There was some satisfaction in knowing that all ships, except the two damaged LCIs and one little LCT, had left the beaches and were on their way to their home bases. When under way, they had the great advantage of an escort of destroyers to assist in warding off an air attack, and more importantly, they had freedom of movement.

Commander Charles Adair joined Admiral
Barbey's planning staff just before the Lae
landing. One of his first tasks was a
reconnaissance mission.

Captain F. W. Benson, U.S. Navy, was
indispensable in applying his experience
to maintain the many small craft used
in the assaults.

Men and supplies spew out of landing craft onto the beach at Lae, New Guinea.
Unloading was completed only a few hours after the initial assault.

As soon as I returned to the *Conyngham*, she left at full speed to join up with one of the oncoming LST convoys so she could help in their defense. Fortunately, the warning of the impending bomber attack was received in time to permit Allied fighters to intercept a group of seventy Japanese planes in the vicinity of the picket ship *Reid*. In the air battle that followed, twenty-three enemy aircraft were destroyed and the rest disappeared over the horizon. The *Reid*, in addition to doing a splendid job of air warning and fighter directing, defended herself against three dive bombers; she escaped unhurt and may have brought down one plane.

The Japanese planes which escaped the fighters headed toward our base at Morobe. They ran directly into the *Conyngham* and then sighted the oncoming convoy of loaded LSTs. Four dive bombers attacked the *Conyngham* and the rest headed for the convoy. When the "General Alarm" was sounded, indicating an attack was imminent, I was below decks enjoying a shower bath after my all-night watch on topside. The ship's skipper, Commander James H. Ward, commenced swinging the *Conyngham* from side to side at such high speeds and such sharp turns that it was almost impossible, in my half-clad condition, to get to the upper deck.

Before I could reach my usual seat in the starboard wing of the bridge, the bombs began to fall. Sitting in my seat was a young torpedoman named Brennenen, with his binoculars trained on the incoming planes. As I zigzagged in his direction he started to get up, but he was a fraction of a second too late. A bomb had landed close alongside and some of its fragments ricocheted across the deck. One piece, about the size of a walnut, pierced his body just above the hip bone. I caught him as he fell. He was the only casualty on the ship, and miraculously he lived to fight another day.

The ship received minor hull damage from bomb fragments, but in exchange shot down one of the four attacking planes and crippled another. As soon as the attack was over—it only lasted a few minutes—she straightened up and headed at full speed for the convoy still under heavy attack a few miles ahead. But it was all over before we got there.

Twelve torpedo bombers and ten dive bombers had concentrated on the six loaded LSTs, and five dive bombers had attacked the four escorting destroyers. The torpedo planes had come in just above the surface of the water to release their torpedoes when fifteen hundred yards away. The slow, hard to handle and lightly armed LSTs were no match for the attackers. The LST-473 received two bomb hits on her upper deck, and the LST-471 caught a torpedo near her stern. Flames engulfed a large part of the deck of the "473." It was a great tribute to the discipline and new-found skill of her crew that they extinguished the fire before it ignited the large quantities of gasoline and ammunition she carried.

Both ships were dead in the water on our arrival but the attacking planes were nowhere in sight. The high speed and maneuverability of the escorting destroyers permitted them to escape undamaged; their gunners claimed two planes. The four undamaged LSTs and their escorting destroyers continued on their way to Red and Yellow beaches with supplies and reinforcements for the Australians who were doing the fighting ashore.

There was little satisfaction in knowing that the attack might have been much worse but for the courage of these inexperienced amphibious crews who, regrettably, had suffered a large number of casualties, as had the Australian soldiers they were carrying. Two of our small group of LSTs would be out of commission for a long, long time.

The first Medal of Honor awarded within the Seventh Amphibious Force went to the helmsman of the *LST-473*, Johnnie D. Hutchins, seaman first class, of Lissie, Texas. Johnnie was in the demolished pilothouse, mortally wounded but still alive, after the bombs hit. Then two torpedoes were seen heading for the ship. With his last ounce of strength, Johnnie guided the ship clear of the torpedoes. He died with his hands on the wheel.

The LST skippers maneuvered their clumsy ships to avoid torpedoes and bombs far better than had been expected, and their antiaircraft fire accounted for two enemy planes. One matter of major importance did come out of the battle. There was a great lift in the morale of the crews of the LSTs; a feeling of confidence in their youthful skippers; and a growing belief in their capability to defend themselves. No longer would they style themselves "large, slow targets."

Two LSTs were diverted from a returning convoy to tow the disabled *LST-473* and *LST-471* to the advance base at Morobe, with the ever useful *Conyngham* acting as the sole escort. At Morobe the cargo from the disabled ships was transferred to the two empty LSTs who were soon on their way again to the fighting front.

The slightly wounded men were transferred to first-aid tents at Morobe while the more serious cases were taken aboard the *Conyngham* for transportation to Buna where there were better medical facilities. Identification tags were attached to the dead and then they were wrapped in blankets and turned over to the local Graves Registration Service. Grave lot numbers and location were obtained. Belongings were inventoried and turned over to the ship's supply officer. In the absence of a chaplain, the medical officer of the *LST-471*, Lieutenant Commander E. F. Norwood, conducted burial services at the improvised cemetery. An Australian firing squad and bugler participated in the services.

The formal report of the medical officer contains this rather informal account of his medical activities:

> After arrival in Morobe there were repeated "red alerts" and by late morning of September 5th the loss of sleep, nervous strain, and knowledge of dead comrades to be re-
> trieved from wreckage resulted in the crew appearing as though "the mighty hope that

makes us men" was growing pretty slim. Before proceeding with extraction of bodies a "stout shot" of medical brandy or whiskey was dispensed to each officer and member of the crew. There was no known coronary disease among these men but even the most ardent member of the W.C.T.U. could not have doubted grog's therapeutic advantage had she witnessed the immediate physical and mental change that took place.

The Japanese air force had not given up the fight. Not a night would pass without our convoys being trailed by snoopers who dropped a few bombs. Every night ships at anchor and the shore installations at Red Beach, Morobe, Buna, and Oro Bay would be bombed. Every night these small raids took their small toll of personnel. I particularly remember a big awkward, blond boy—more suited to the farm than to the sea—who was the coxwain of my barge. At sundown each day my prudent coxwain would leave the flagship with a wisecrack about having a grandstand seat watching the upcoming attack of bombers, and then happily secure the barge to a channel buoy, well out of harm's way. One night a poorly aimed bomb missed both the flagship and the entire village of Buna, and unfortunately landed right in the middle of the barge. There were no survivors.

The duties of amphibious representatives at Oro Bay, Buna, and Morobe had become so numerous and so vital to the operations that we had to draw on badly needed personnel from our ships and staff to help out the units at those places. These units not only acted as a go-between with the Army, Air Force, and Australians, but handled the many activities that were usually taken care of by the Service Force— such as grave registration, repair, overhaul and fueling of ships, stevedoring, handling of casualties, and other logistic chores too numerous to mention. But in those early days there was no Service Force in the forward area; we had to build an organization that did the same work under a different name.

Although a steady flow of new personnel had come into the area, activities had become so widespread that the supply could not satisfy the demand. Among the new arrivals were two, not-so-young, Reserve officers whom we greeted with some misgiving because their backgrounds led to some uncertainty as to how they would fit into our organization. As it turned out, each remained with our force until its dissolution in China in December 1945. Each did an outstanding job in his own field, but there the similarity ended.

The first one, Lieutenant Commander William F. Jibb, had been ordered to the staff as a public relations officer, although we did not know we needed one. Jibb had done some newspaper work in Florida and had paid his way through the University of Florida by wrestling alligators. A resourceful individual of great courage, Jibb carried out many difficult assignments far removed from his public relations job and became a very valuable member of our team.

The second one in the group of new arrivals was Lieutenant Commander James E.

Wearing their flat "tin hats," Australian soldiers pour out of the open bow of an LST, ready to participate in the invasion of Lae, New Guinea, September 1943.

Van Zandt. He had enlisted in the Navy in World War I and in between wars had continued his participation in the Naval Reserve. Although a bit older than his Reserve associates we were prepared to welcome his experience, tempered with the thought that he was a recently resigned congressman from Pennsylvania. When Van Zandt asked for duty in the combat area we wondered if what he really wanted was to get close enough to the front lines to say he was there, but not close enough to get hurt. Well, we would soon find out.

So, to get him out of our hair and back to his constituents as soon as possible, if that seemed advisable, we sent him to the roughest and toughest assignment under our roughest and toughest commander of LSTs. But Van Zandt fooled us. By his skill, courage, and common sense he was soon in command of his own squadron of LSTs, and I had the privilege on more than one occasion to commend him for "gallantry in combat."

Some months later, on a quick trip to Washington, I was a luncheon guest of a small group of congressmen. After a short talk about the progress of the war in the Southwest Pacific, I was asked about the well-being of their old colleague, James Van Zandt. I told them of my misgivings on his arrival and how they had proven so unfounded. I thought they would be greatly pleased at hearing about his fine record, but instead there was an awkward silence. I think it was Congressman Walter Judd who expressed the feelings of the others with his remark, "and just why did you think a congressman wouldn't want to do his part?"

In order to build up the personnel of our newly established shore-based units as the Amphibious Force moved along the New Guinea coast we had to draw upon and finally abandon some rear area activities. In this shift of personnel, the restless and newly promoted Lieutenant (j.g.) Wally Wemyss, who had been on duty at Kiriwina, was moved to Buna. Whenever he had a few hours off from his own job, he would fraternize with the 19th Bomber Squadron stationed in the nearby Dobodura area. He enjoyed flying as an unofficial naval observer on many bombing raids. On the return from a raid on Rabaul, the pilot would fly low over the coastline and it was Wemyss' job to identify the Japanese barges being used for transport of personnel and supplies. He also substituted for one of the gunners if either one was wounded or killed—this happened on three occasions. He enjoyed his dual role of half seaman and half flier.

One day Wemyss got real mad at the Japs' "dirty tricks department." He had been wandering around Buna minding the Navy's business when the air raid siren sounded. He dove head first for the nearest foxhole, but his legs were wholly exposed when the bombs dropped. On this particular raid the Nips used an antipersonnel bomb—a very thin casing filled with barbed wire, razor blades, nuts, bolts, and other oddments. Although Wemyss was not badly hurt, he had over a hundred scars on his legs to show for his exposure. In retaliation, he and a bomber pilot friend of his, Captain C. C. McGlasson, worked up a dirty trick scheme of their own.

They learned that if a number of open bottles were tied together with a fifty-pound weight so that the necks of the bottles were facing earthward, the resulting noise when dropped from a plane would be a terrifying screech, and perhaps the ack-ack gunners would seek cover. Only the lead plane was to be equipped with bottles. The planes following the lead plane at a considerable distance would carry their usual load and it was hoped they could drop their bombs without ack-ack interference. About fifty bottles were tied together, in one bundle, with vines from the New Guinea jungle and weighted down with empty shell casings. The lead plane carried about twenty of these bundles.

Wemyss made the first of these bottle raids on Rabaul. Instead of referring to him as "bombadier," he was designated the "bottledier." He made two more such raids before his naval unit commander told him to stick to his purely naval duties at Buna. Shortly after Wemyss' withdrawal, the bottle raids were discontinued. The theory was fine, but unfortunately the Nip gunners concentrated on the leading plane before they heard the screech of the bottles, and the volunteers for the job of "bottledier" became fewer and fewer.

The crews of the PT boats in their nightly forays against Japanese shipping led an exciting life. I remember one incident in particular because of the unusual circumstances. A wounded Japanese medical officer had been captured, but died soon afterwards. A PT boat skipper, in a humanitarian gesture, decided to give the dead Japanese a proper burial at sea. When his boat left harbor that afternoon for its usual nighttime raid, it carried on deck the dead officer covered with a Japanese flag. The burial was to take place at sunset. Unobserved, a group of Japanese planes came out of the setting sun and dove in for the kill. Then the leading plane pulled out of the dive and the others followed suit. No bombs were dropped. A reasonable explanation is that the lead plane observed the Japanese flag and assumed it to be one of their own boats on patrol. A simple humanitarian act had saved a PT boat from destruction.

Our amphibious ships had not been designed for combat but circumstances altered their role. Their gunners had to become good marksmen if they wanted to survive. Those who had shot down a plane in combat were particularly pleased and proud and wanted the world to know it. The custom soon developed of painting a small Japanese flag on the side of their bridge to represent each plane shot down. As the campaign progressed, the flags became so numerous on the LSTs, the LCIs, and even on the small subchasers and little LCTs, that a newcomer might wonder if there was any relationship between the number of flags and the availability of paint.

10: Capturing Finschhafen

22 September 1943

THE AUSTRALIANS CAPTURED LAE ON 16 SEPTEMBER 1943, JUST twelve days after ships of the U.S. Seventh Amphibious Force landed them on nearby Red and Yellow beaches. The remnants of the Japanese garrison, perhaps six thousand, had escaped into the jungle. They were making their way overland to meet their fellow countrymen coming down the New Guinea coast as reinforcements for their troops at Finschhafen, the small port that guarded the western side of narrow Vitiaz Strait between New Guinea and New Britain.

The capture of Finschhafen, one hundred miles up the coast from Lae, was another step in the plan to surround and isolate Rabaul. But it was not expected to be undertaken until one month after the capture of Lae. This time schedule, however, now had to be advanced. Finschhafen had to be captured before its garrison was reinforced by Japanese troops now heading that way.

Except for air cover, everything had gone so smoothly in the Lae landing that we thought we knew more about amphibious operations than we actually did. With better protection from enemy bombers, so we thought, we were ready for anything.

It was in this frame of mind that I was called to a conference at MacArthur's field headquarters at Port Moresby the day after Wootten's troops entered the town of Lae. Lieutenant General George Kenney was present as commander of the Allied Air Force, and Lieutenant General Herring represented the Australians. I represented the Navy. There was a sense of urgency in the air. MacArthur wanted to know how soon the Australians could make troops available to land at Finschhafen and how soon the Seventh Amphibious Force could assemble the ships to carry the troops.

My reply was that the ships could be made ready in seventy-two hours, but I noted that Finschhafen bordered on Vitiaz Strait and I did not like the idea of exposing them to enemy bomber attack in those narrow waters without better air cover than we had been getting. The loss of any more LSTs would hold up the next operation. General Kenney was somewhat subdued from his usual self-assured manner. He was probably having some second thoughts about Air Force ability to protect convoys by having fighter planes on "standby alert" and his ability to overcome the Japanese bomber threat by attacking them at their bases. At all events, after a bit of nudging by MacArthur, he agreed to provide two layers of air cover over the beaches and over the convoys as soon after daylight as his planes could get there.

General Herring doubted that his Australian troops and supplies could be made ready for loading in less than four days at the very earliest. The optimistic landing date finally agreed upon was 22 September 1943, just six days hence. The troops would need to be embarked from the Lae area on the afternoon of the twenty-first, and those from Buna one day earlier. That left just three days to prepare the plans, assemble the ships and load the troops. The hour of landing was left for the Australian Army commander and myself to decide. General Wootten, the Army commander who would supply the troops, was near Lae with his staff. My staff was in Milne Bay, 265 miles away. A PT boat with some of my planners hurried to Buna, a midway point, and met me there on my return by air from Port Moresby. After some preliminary discussions, Commander Adair continued on to meet with General Wootten and his staff, in their jungle headquarters tent outside Lae.

In anticipation of a landing in the Finschhafen area our intelligence unit had been gathering information from natives and former planters about nearby beaches, shoals, rocks, and surf conditions. Apparently the only suitable landing place was a coral-sanded beach located in a small bay about seven miles north of Finschhafen. It was about six hundred yards long, but because of offshore rocks only the northern half was considered suitable for landing craft. A sandbar was believed to be located off the beach and there was some question whether LSTs and LCIs could get across it. It was an easy place for the Japanese to defend, if they chose, because it was flanked on the southern end by a rocky promontory and on the northern end by the Soong River. Back of the beach were steep, heavily forested mountains.

It had been hoped that more precise information could be obtained by an on-the-spot reconnaissance and so a party of six white and four native amphibious scouts had been put ashore from a PT boat near the proposed landing area during the night of 11 September, and withdrawn two days later. They had been unable to get the detailed information desired regarding sandbars, coral reefs, or water depths because of Japanese and native activity in the vicinity. No defenses were noticed on the beach itself, but machine-gun nests were believed to be located on the rocky promontory at the southern end.

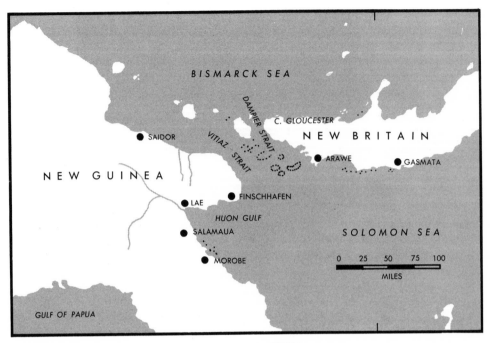

EASTERN NEW GUINEA

Intelligence information was handicapped by a lack of photographs. Although some low verticals had been taken by a photo-reconnaissance plane on 19 September and delivered to our planners that night, they proved of little help. Because of some photographic slip-up they did not cover the beach area, and there was no time for another run.

At that time the Fifth Air Force only had one plane mounted with the type of equipment essential for detailed beach pictures. Commitment in other fields of photographic reconnaissance was so heavy, and dependence upon busy operational units for fighter cover so restricting, that the Air Force could only supply a small fraction of the many pictures desired for our operations.

The narrow waters of Vitiaz Strait and the lack of maneuvering room in case of bomber attack continued to haunt me. I wanted the landing to be made in darkness so that the ships could be unloaded and away from Vitiaz Strait before any daylight bombing attack developed. Landing ships and boats on the right beach during darkness would not give us any trouble, I thought, particularly as there would be a three-quarters moon that night. But I was overly optimistic for I had not given due weight to the poor visibility that would be created by the smoke and dust from naval gunfire in a dew-laden atmosphere.

The Australians wanted a dawn landing as they did not relish the idea of going into a strange jungle during darkness. We compromised by scheduling the landing one hour before daylight. This would permit the troops to be landed on the beach during darkness but daylight would be with them before they had to fan out into the jungle.

The plan as finally agreed upon by Wootten and myself called for all the troops and fifteen days' supplies to be landed on the first day. To expedite the unloading time of the ships, Wootten agreed to assign one hundred soldiers to act as stevedores. They were not part of the assault force. They would return to their garrison duty at Lae and Buna on completion of their unloading job. It was a most successful innovation.

The fifteen days of supplies to be landed on the first day was deemed necessary to reduce the number of ships engaged in re-supply runs until Finschhafen itself was taken and an airfield established from which planes could provide cover for our convoys. We had come to have great respect for Nip bomber capabilities, and we were getting closer to their operating bases. We hoped the new Allied airfield could be built in fifteen days, but if not, we felt the LCTs and LCMs could temporarily meet urgent re-supply requirements by hugging the coast on night runs from Lae.

The plan was written up during one day and one night. One hundred and forty copies were mimeographed aboard the faithful little *APc-15* while shuttling between various command headquarters, and finally turned over to a speedy PT boat to expedite delivery to the scattered units. In some cases, the plans were received but a few hours before the sailing time. In others, plans were delivered to ships under way. Again the destroyer *Reid* was posted as a radar picket ship. Again the shore party was organized from elements of the Engineer Special Brigade. They were confident they could navigate the one hundred miles in their own small boats, but it proved a bit too tough for them. The Australian Navy took over the responsibility of providing a small beach party. Before we had time to worry about the pitfalls of hurried planning and questionable beach information, we were on our way.

As operations go, Finschhafen did not amount to much. But even so, 3 days were hardly adequate for careful, precise planning for putting ashore in less than 3 hours on unfamiliar beaches, 5,300 troops and some thousands of tons of supplies from 70 ships and small craft. The problem was not made easier by the fact that the ships, the troops, the aircraft, and the supplies were located in different bases along some hundreds of miles of the New Guinea coast. This left little time for consultations and no time for rehearsals.

Among the unpleasant possibilities about which little could be done in our preparations for Finschhafen was that of a raid on the convoy by a Japanese surface fleet. We knew that our heavier-than-usual shipping activity at Buna, Lae, and Red Beach had been observed by enemy reconnaissance planes and recognized that the

Nips might interpret it as another thrust up the coast. If so, they might decide to send some cruisers from Rabaul to raid the convoy as it entered Vitiaz Strait. We optimistically hoped, however, that they would interpret this increased activity as merely part of the build-up of our forces at Lae. Later intelligence information indicated that such was the case.

The only Japanese response to this activity was an increase in the frequency of their bomber attacks on Lae and Red Beach, but they were not in sufficient strength to bother our preparations. The last attack was made at sundown on the eve of our departure from Red Beach for Finschhafen. The LSTs were completing their loading and the escorting destroyers, including my flagship the *Conyngham,* were patrolling offshore when six Nip bombers made a high level attack. Fortunately, they concentrated on the destroyers. Antiaircraft fire kept them at a safe distance and their bombs landed harmlessly. One plane was seen to crash in the nearby hills.

The movement of the various groups of ships to Finschhafen took place according to plan, a creditable performance since the charts we used were eleven miles in error. The night was partially overcast and navigation difficult for the smaller craft. They had sailed from different places at different hours and were required to arrive in darkness within a few minutes of each other at an open sea meeting place. The different small convoys reported sighting two enemy snoopers, but there was some question whether the snoopers had in turn sighted any of the convoys. An advance group of our destroyers was patrolling the northern end of Vitiaz Strait when, at 4 A.M., they picked up on their radar screen a number of pips in the direction from which Japanese surface raiders might come. Too quickly, the destroyers illuminated the area with star shells, only to find in the brilliant light the small boats carrying our Army shore party who had lost their way. But the damage had been done. The star shells had alerted Japanese on the nearby beaches and complete surprise was no longer possible.

All ships and craft were in their allotted places on schedule, except the boats carrying the shore party which were an hour late because of their navigational troubles. Right to the minute the boats from the APDs were loaded with troops and headed toward the beach. At the same time, four destroyers began their short pre-landing bombardment. A slight mist over the area trapped the smoke and dust from the bombardment and the assault boats disappeared into the smog. Seven minutes before the troops were scheduled to put foot on the beach, the destroyer bombardment ceased and the troops were on their own, but under cover of the machine guns in their own boats which sprayed the beach ahead.

In the darkness and haze the boats had difficulty keeping in touch with each other and finding their own particular slots on the beach. Compasses were of little use as the steel in the helmets and rifles of the troops acted as magnets on the compass needles. In spite of these difficulties, all but four of the boats hit the north beach

LSTs with their noses to the beach at Finschhafen, New Guinea, just after a dawn landing.

(Scarlet Beach) within a few minutes of the scheduled time. Two of the four boats had veered off to the left, landed on the rocky southern promontory, and ran head-on into a Japanese pillbox. One of the boats carried the beach party. Its leader, Lieutenant Commander Band, Royal Australian Navy, a very popular officer with all the services, was caught by a hail of bullets and died before he could be brought to a hospital.

There was no opposition to the landing on Scarlet Beach itself, but as the troops started inland, Japanese resistance became increasingly worrisome. The LCIs, each carrying two hundred troops, followed the small boats and with but one exception all arrived in their proper slots. Two of the LCIs were grounded on a sandbar for a few minutes about fifty feet off shore, but by using full power ahead, they finally bounced their way over the bar and got their troops within wading distance of dry land. All the LCIs were under fire from machine gun nests on the promontory at the south end of the beach, but the fire was not very effective against the plastic splinter shields around the 20 mm guns, the conning tower, and the pilothouse. The LSTs had an easier time; daylight was just breaking when they put their noses on the beach; and besides, the sandbars had been properly buoyed by the beach party by that time.

Some vicious shore fighting lay ahead for the Aussies. As they moved inland they met stubborn resistance from Japanese ground troops, and were pounded unmercifully from the air. Those who had been in the North African campaign said Finschhafen was far worse than anything they had received from the Germans and Italians. On one particular day they counted 115 specific air attacks. Not until 3 October, 11 days after the landing, were Finschhafen and the surrounding area in Australian hands.

Everyone realized that the landing part of the operation had been blessed with a lot of luck that might not come our way a second time. Although the naval personnel losses were light, casualties to the small craft that strayed from the beach approaches were serious for they had run into a solid shelf of coral that damaged their propellers. Hereafter, I would approach very cautiously the idea of landing any assault troops on an unknown beach during darkness.

Following the pattern established at the Lae landing, enemy bombers started attacking as soon as they could get there—which meant a few hours after daylight. But during these few hours our own fighter cover had arrived. Shortly after 9 A.M., while ships were finishing their unloading, a vanguard of four Japanese planes appeared and were promptly engaged by a group of our own fighters which had arrived a few minutes earlier. One enemy plane was shot down and the others dropped their bombs in the vicinity but without damage. Within the hour, all ships were unloaded and we breathed a sigh of relief as the last group of ships was formed into a convoy and we started on our return.

A Japanese snooper plane was following us and we felt he was passing the word to a bomber squadron which was even then winging its way in our direction—but we had the satisfaction of air cover overhead and plenty of maneuvering room for the ships. Just before noon, one of our own unseen fighter planes came up on voice radio with: "The plane you now see falling ahead of you is sent with the compliments of the Fifth Air Force." Sure enough, about one mile ahead of the flagship was a falling plane, and the Japanese snooper was no more. But he had done his bit in guiding his countrymen toward the convoy.

In less than an hour, the picket destroyer *Reid* signalled that a large number of enemy planes were approaching and that she had notified our fighters where to intercept them. The planes hurried to make contact and our ships moved into an antiaircraft formation. Within minutes we received word that seventy Jap planes had been engaged, thirty had been shot down, and that our fighters were chasing others headed in the direction of the convoy.

Eight enemy torpedo planes accompanied by seven of their fighters broke loose from the melee and began a low level attack on the convoy. Three destroyers were strafed by the fighters at masthead height. The wakes of seven torpedoes passed between the zigzagging ships, but all missed due to the skillful maneuvering of the ships, their heavy antiaircraft fire, and our own fighter planes, which followed some of the enemy planes almost to the surface of the water.

War had suddenly become a very personal thing. One enemy plane, very close, was headed directly toward the wing of the bridge on which I was standing. The pilot wanted to hit us and kill us before we hit him and killed him. He missed and crashed in the water alongside. War had made us enemies and brought us together from points half a world apart in a strange tropical setting.

The *Reid* picked up two Japanese survivors from a plane that was still afloat. One was badly hurt and offered no resistance, but the other had to be knocked out by an oar before he could be taken aboard.

Fourteen of the fifteen Japanese planes which had taken part in the attack on the convoy were destroyed—in most cases they came down in flames, sometimes missing our ships by only a few yards. Our only plane casualty in this part of the battle was a fighter who boldly followed his target right into the midst of our ships' antiaircraft fire. His plane was hit. As his plane fell, he parachuted into the water and was picked up by one of our destroyers. His target crashed. The remainder of the trip was without incident. An enemy snooper plane continued to shadow us into Buna, but no attack was made.

So ended the assault phase of another amphibious landing. Each of the three landings to date had been made with the same ships, but each had been made under far different circumstances. We were learning the hard way. We now knew we would never like nighttime landings, and we also knew there is nothing like an air cover of friendly planes to save a convoy from possible disaster.

The supply phase of the Finschhafen operation would now get under way. Captain R. M. Scruggs, the LST group commander, had this to say about the first of these supply runs:

My job was to bring in the first reinforcement echelon to Scarlet Beach on the night of D-day. The landing site was a small bay, approximately 1,000 yards across, and the only coral-free beach in the vicinity. The beaching site was to be indicated by the troops winking flashlights out to sea at a prearranged time. However, the Japs had been conducting an air attack on the beach just prior to our arrival, and the troops would not turn on the lights for fear of drawing down additional attacks. This resulted in our thinking that we were wrong in our navigation. However, after about an hour's delay, they turned on the marker lights, and we went on in.

Jap snipers were on the points of the little bay and their whining bullets kept us (as far as possible) behind something that would stop a rifle bullet. However, nobody was hit. One or two Jap prisoners were brought aboard by the Aussies with ropes around their necks. The big Aussies were leading the little Japs around like dogs. These were the first prisoners I had seen. They would look down at the deck as though they were deeply ashamed of themselves. I suppose this was the result of their philosophy that it was better to be killed than captured. Sometimes the Japs would have no means of committing suicide before capture and such circumstances resulted in their being taken alive.

11:

Landing at Arawe

15 December 1943

AFTER THE FINSCHHAFEN LANDING CAME THE ONE AT ARAWE, finally scheduled for 15 December 1943. But it was not planned that way. It was not the small harbor of Arawe, but the village of Gasmata on the south coast of New Britain that MacArthur had scheduled as the next landing spot in the overall plan for the isolation of Rabaul.

Gasmata was not much of a village, but even so it was the most important one on New Britain's south coast. It had a small port with an airfield and good beaches nearby. The airfield was a small one, but it had been useful to the Japanese as an emergency fighter strip, and presumably would be useful to us. The harbor had been in use as a staging area for barge traffic from Rabaul to many small garrisons along New Britain's south coast, and this traffic was an important element in Nip defenses of the area.

Lae and Finschhafen had already been taken, and somewhat ahead of schedule. They were but stepping stones on the road to the capture of Cape Gloucester on the northwestern coast of New Britain. Cape Gloucester was highly important to the Japanese as it was their major western outpost in the defense of Rabaul. For that same reason it was equally important to the Allies. But General MacArthur was reluctant to undertake the capture of Cape Gloucester as long as all the south coast of New Britain remained in Japanese hands, and since Gasmata was the pivotal point in their southern coastal defense system, it was slated for capture.

A regimental combat team of the 32nd Division had been assigned to take Gasmata and the 1st Marine Division had been assigned to the capture of Cape Gloucester shortly thereafter. As usual, different troops, but the same ships.

Preliminary planning by the various staffs had been started and aerial and ground reconnaissance of prospective beaches in the vicinity of Gasmata had been made. A scouting unit from the amphibious camp at Fergusson Island had been landed from a PT boat and stayed ashore for ten days. Most of their time had been spent in the jungle dodging hostile natives and Japanese until they were finally brought out, half starved and miserable, by the boat which had landed them. The leader of the group had been saved one time when he and his native guide were crawling through the brush toward an enemy outpost and a Nip sentry carelessly lit a cigarette within a few feet of them. But they had little to show for the risks they had taken. The information they brought back merely confirmed what we already had learned from friendly natives and aerial reconnaissance.

The near capture of the scanty unit increased reluctance to undertake further scouting forays if the needed information could be obtained through other means. However, in spite of experience in these matters, each new Army commander of each new operation usually wanted a scouting party landed prior to the assault in the hope of obtaining useful on-the-spot information not available otherwise.

As the planning for the Gasmata operation progressed there developed a growing concern as to its feasibility. To get the matter into the open, MacArthur called a conference in his office in Brisbane. The conference started off with pessimistic statistics. Gasmata was but 193 miles from the big Japanese air base at Rabaul, the nearest Allied airbase was more than three hundred miles away, and our more important bases were even further.

Because of these relative distances, and because of a scarcity of fighter planes, General Kenney said he could not guarantee an air cover in sufficient strength to break up a Japanese bomber attack on the landing force. As a consequence most of us felt that an attack in the Gasmata area might well result in heavy losses in ships, and perhaps in men. I pointed out that if such proved to be the case the Cape Gloucester operation might have to be postponed as we could not count on the arrival of new ships to fill in the gaps.

The question then arose as to whether the Gasmata project should be abandoned, and if so, what was the alternative. There were no other satisfactory landing beaches on the south coast of New Britain. The whole coastline was coral-bound and all known beaches were too small to handle a landing party of any size. The few small harbors being used by Japanese barges and fishing craft were but tiny inlets that could be reached only by shallow, winding channels through the coral reefs.

Amid the gloom resulting from lack of ships and planes to do what we felt needed to be done, General MacArthur adjourned the meeting until the following morning.

The USS Carter Hall *(LSD-3) was a new type of amphibious craft that looked like an ordinary cargo ship but became a "floating drydock" in an assault operation.*

Amphibious trucks (DUKW), at home on either land or water, prove their usefulness in the landing at Arawe.

In spite of the passage of time, some words are so burned into one's memory as never to be forgotten. Among them are MacArthur's bitter words as we filed out of the room, "There are some people in Washington who would rather see MacArthur lose a battle than America win a war."

That night and the following morning at breakfast, Vice Admiral A. S. Carpender, the Seventh Fleet commander, and I examined again all the charts and all the available data regarding New Britain's south coast in the hope of finding some landing site that might meet our purposes and yet not be so hazardous an undertaking as Gasmata.

We finally agreed that the least objectional spot was the little harbor of Arawe. It had the advantage of being eighty-six miles to the west of Gasmata and hence that much closer to our newly established air base at Finschhafen, and that much farther from the enemy air bases at Rabaul. But the only beach in the vicinity of Arawe was too small to handle more than a few boats at one time and so the main attack would have to take place on the village itself. Its shallow harbor was a fairly large coral-infested body of water between an island and the mainland, with an inner harbor where most of the Nips were encamped. This inner harbor could only be reached by small shallow-draft craft—not drawing over a few feet—winding their way through a tortuous reef-bound channel. For this reason the old standbys, LSTs and LCIs, could not be used there. An attacking force would need amphibious tractors that could climb over the reefs for a direct approach to the town. But there were very few amphibious tractors in the Southwest Pacific and they all belonged to the Marines who had been reserving them for use at Cape Gloucester.

From Carpender's and my point of view, one of the good features about Arawe was that the Nipponese garrison was not believed to be very large and, because of their apparent inaccessibility, were likely to be careless in their defense preparations. Like Gasmata, but on a smaller scale, the Nips had been using Arawe as a staging area for their barge traffic along the coast, but it had very little strategic value.

When the conferees met the following morning Admiral Carpender proposed the cancellation of the Gasmata operation and the substitution of a landing at Arawe instead. He outlined the various advantages and disadvantages as we saw them with heavy emphasis on the matter of air cover. He admitted it was a risky job and that it could only be undertaken with amphibious tractors. General Kenney, apparently somewhat relieved, said he could supply the necessary air cover at Arawe which he could not do at Gasmata, and supported the idea. Krueger commented that less troops would be required at Arawe and that the troops previously scheduled for Gasmata could be used to advantage elsewhere, and that he was all for it. After some further discussion as to its feasibility and desirability, MacArthur gave his approval and directed the planners to get busy immediately. The Gasmata operation was cancelled and planning for Arawe started that same day.

The troops of the 112th Cavalry Regiment (dismounted) were designated for the landing because they were available and in the forward area. They had never been in combat nor had they had any amphibious training. Even troops with more experience would have had difficulty getting ready in the three weeks time allowed for this complex, though small operation. Under the circumstances, they did a fine job.

As soon as the necessary arrangements could be made the regiment was relieved of its garrison duty at Woodlark and moved to a staging area on Goodenough Island. Five days before the date scheduled for the assault, the regimental commander, Brigadier General J. W. Cunningham, requested a small reconnaissance party be landed on the very small beach, designated Blue Beach, a few miles to the eastward of Arawe. They stayed a few hours, reported a few Nips in the vicinity, but apparently saw no defenses, and doubted that they had been observed.

The landing plan as finally agreed upon was the result of a number of compromises. Navy planners were much concerned over the troop commander's desire for two subsidiary surprise landings to be made one hour before daylight and before the main landing. One was to be made with 150 men on small Blue Beach, and the other on small Pilelo Island, at the entrance to the harbor, to seize a suspected radio station. The main landing would not get under way until daylight.

Experience with a night landing at Finschhafen made us shy away from a repetition of this type of operation. However, the troop commander was encouraged by the report of the reconnaissance party and felt that landing a small force via rubber boats on Blue Beach under cover of partial darkness—last quarter moonlight —with no prior bombardment, might result in complete surprise, and perhaps go off without any resistance. If the small Blue Beach landing was successful, it would provide another entrance point into the village. The main assault on the inner harbor would, of necessity, be carried out by troops transported in slow and cumbersome amphibious tractors and amphibious tanks that could climb over the many coral reefs lying in the path of a direct approach. Even when the channel was buoyed, it would be too shallow for use by other than light-draft craft such as Higgins boats, or possibly LCTs.

All the available amphibious tractors and tanks, better known as alligators and buffaloes, with their crews, were borrowed from the 1st Marine Division, training at Goodenough Island for their own operation a few weeks later. It would be our first experience with such vehicles. We obtained enough of them to carry the initial assault force of almost one thousand men. They would be landed under cover of destroyer bombardment and rocket fire. On the basis of available information, we believed this force could easily cope with the Arawe garrison of an estimated five hundred Japanese. High-angle rocket fire would be provided by one subchaser and two amphibious trucks (DUKW). Behind the initial assault force seven hundred men would trail in Higgins boats, to make their way through the circuitous small-boat channel as soon as it was buoyed by the naval beach party.

In addition to the hazards to the assault troops from the defenders ashore, there would always be the danger of an attack by Japanese aircraft, surface vessels, and submarines on our troop-carrying convoy, either while en route or in the landing area. And the Japanese had the planes and ships to do it if they thought it worth the effort. To protect against a sea attack from the eastward, Admiral Crutchley of the Australian Navy, with a division of Allied cruisers, would patrol the area about twenty miles to our rear. Our western and most vulnerable flank would be covered by a group of PT boats patrolling Vitiaz and Dampier Straits. While they could hardly stop a raiding force of ships, they might do some damage with their torpe-does and at least give warning of an enemy approach so that the convoy could fall on Admiral Crutchley's cruisers. It was too risky to station Crutchley's few cruisers in the confined waters of Vitiaz and Dampier Straits where they would be exposed to submarine, air, and surface attack.

The Arawe operation, though small, provided a number of firsts. In addition to the alligators and buffaloes, it would be the first time we had used rockets and the first time we had used a "floating dry dock" in an assault operation. The USS *Carter Hall* (Landing Ship, Dock), a new type of amphibious craft, had joined the Seventh Amphibious Force a few weeks previously. She looked like an ordinary cargo ship when under way, but she could carry all our amphibious tractors and tanks in her hold. In the assault area the ship's hold would be flooded, gates in the stern would open, and the tractors and tanks would crawl out under their own power.

Another first would be the use of an Australian transport, the *Westralia,* in a landing operation. Instead of carrying her own boats, she would carry the landing boats of the naval beach party and the shore party. There were two reasons for this: first, the beach party and shore party needed their own boats to use after the departure of the ships, and second, we wanted the *Westralia* to leave the assault area as soon as possible. We did not want her to wait to pick up her own boats when there was a good probability an air attack would develop. We had all too few of her type and she was too valuable to take a chance on losing.

Like the *Westralia,* the *Carter Hall* was scheduled to leave the landing area as soon as she had unloaded her alligators, buffaloes, and boats, and the troops they carried, which we hoped would be shortly after dawn.

Since there would not be any large ships at Arawe to handle casualties (usually cared for by the Navy until the Army could establish their facilities ashore) my staff medical officer organized several surgical teams, each composed of two medical officers and ten hospital corpsmen. For Arawe, two teams were placed in the small LCTs, since no LSTs would be used in the landing. It was a makeshift and highly successful arrangement. Fortunately, there was no need for this crude improvisation for future landings.

Another innovation that would be employed at Arawe for the first time was a new type of beach party. In previous landings improvised beach parties had not been wholly successful. At Woodlark and Kiriwina the beach party was a makeshift group, we thought, adequate to meet the needs of a no-opposition landing. But it was not. At the Lae landing, the responsibility was given to the Army Engineers who also were the shore party. It was hoped that this group could do both jobs and thereby save on the requirements for naval personnel, of which there was an acute shortage at the time. We soon learned that a good shore party did not necessarily become a good beach party.

At the next landing, near Finschhafen, the work was assigned to Australian naval personnel, inasmuch as we were landing Australian troops. But lack of rehearsal time and differences in technique created communication delays between the Aussie troops ashore and the American ships off the beaches. Also, the need for a medical officer and hospital corpsmen to form part of the beach party contingent became apparent.

Operations up to that time had been on a small scale, but we could see future requirements would demand a number of trained and competent beach parties, available on call, and flexible enough to meet the requirements of any size operation.

Lieutenant Commander Royce N. Flippin was placed in charge of the program and told to obtain volunteers and start training in the Milne Bay area. The size and organization of the parties was left to his discretion, but their duties at the beach were carefully spelled out.

Flippin proved an excellent choice. He was a good organizer, an athlete, and fearless. He gathered a group of men of similar characteristics. By 1 October, Beach Party Number 1 was in training and a second commenced a month later. There was no such thing as a time period for the training. The training would be continuous, broken only by the assault operations to which beach parties would be assigned for short periods. Their duties would be hazardous. They were to go ashore with the first assault boats and commence their job of buoying channels, erecting markers on the beaches for incoming craft, handling assault casualties, taking offshore soundings, blowing up beach obstacles, and maintaining voice communications between the troops ashore and incoming boats and nearby ships. They must work closely with the Army shore party which would unload the ships at the shoreline, but it was up to the beach party to see that the ships arrived in the right slots for quick unloading. The beach party would remain ashore until the troops were in full control of the situation. They would then return to their home base and prepare for the next beach assault.

When the Arawe landing was scheduled, Flippin was ready and assigned to command the first beach party unit. The medical section of his unit was prepared to give first aid treatment to the wounded and evacuate them to an LCT carrying a surgical team.

Although the beach party problem was solved, we were not so fortunate in finding an experienced shore party. The Engineer Special Brigade had provided the shore parties for the Lae and Finschhafen landings, but their men were still engaged on those jobs and they had no others who were trained and available. The best they could do for us at Arawe was to provide a number of small boats and crews to man them. As a substitute, a shore party was organized from available groups of men wherever found. The result was an untrained body of men unfamiliar with each other and their job. It was one of the prices paid for these hurried landings and makeshift arrangements.

After some last-minute conferences, the troops were loaded aboard their ships at Goodenough Island and sailed for Buna where the naval escort joined them. The troop commander, with some of his staff, was aboard my flagship, the destroyer *Conyngham,* which first led the convoy of thirty-six ships in a deceptive movement toward Finschhafen. Shortly after midnight we headed toward the landing area. The night was clear and a last-quarter moon partially illuminated the formation of ships.

Men were tense and watchful at their battle stations. At 3 A.M., only one hour away from the assault area, a lone Japanese reconnaissance plane suddenly appeared overhead. We could hear the drone of the engines as he approached. He flew over the convoy twice, the last time at four hundred feet. With remarkable restraint, no one opened fire. Experience had taught that if we held our fire there was a good chance the snooper would not illuminate the convoy with flares—perhaps of uncertainty as to what was below him. Fortunately, some lightning and thunder appeared to the eastward which apparently unnerved the snooper for he dropped his bombs without damage and "high-tailed" it for home. We could only guess as to what he had seen and what he would report.

At 4 A.M., on 15 December 1943, all ships maneuvered into their places in the landing area. The two APDs moved into position with the men they carried for the hoped-for surprise raids on Blue Beach and Pilelo Island, and each lowered its fifteen rubber boats. The rubber boats, carrying ten men each, quietly paddled toward their objectives in the darkness. At the same time, the *Carter Hall* discharged alligators and buffaloes through its stern, and the *Westralia* lowered its assault boats.

No signals were exchanged, no guns were fired, and fifteen rubber boats continued toward Blue Beach and fifteen toward Pilelo Island. The partial moonlight silhouet-

Aerial view of the Arawe area, showing Cape Merkus and Pilelo Island.

Troops of the U.S. 112th Cavalry Regiment advance over the coral reef at Arawe,
15 December 1943.

ted the ships. Every sound of an anchor chain or voice reverberated in the stillness of the night. It seemed unbelievable that any Japanese in the vicinity could be unaware of our presence. Perhaps we would get away with our surprise landings after all. As the rubber boats neared Blue Beach, they merged into the jungle background and were out of sight of the watchers on the ships.

And then the silence was broken! We could see the flashes and hear the sound of machine guns. Not knowing whether our men had reached the shore, the APD and her supporting destroyer withheld their fire for a few dangerous minutes, and then began firing in the darkness toward the gun flashes ashore. After a few salvos, the guns on Blue Beach were silenced, but it was too late to save the raiding party. Only one man, a sergeant, reached the beach and later told of his experiences. The boats were only about one hundred yards off shore, paddling very quietly, when all at once they were caught in an enfilading fire of machine guns. Most of the men jumped overboard to reduce their exposure to fire, but twelve of the fifteen boats that were headed for Blue Beach were riddled with bullets and sank. In view of the unexpected opposition, it was suspected that the reconnaissance party which had been landed a few days previously had been observed and the Nips had built up their defenses accordingly.

The rest of the pre-dawn plan was more successful. The group of fifteen rubber boats that landed on Pilelo Island reported they had met with little resistance and had captured the radio station without much trouble.

With the coming of daylight, the buffaloes and alligators headed for the inner port. The alligators, in particular, were slow and awkward and had difficulty keeping in formation. A few were hung up on the coral reefs but most made the inner harbor under cover of the bombardment of the destroyers and rocket craft. There was little resistance from the Japanese garrison. The bombardment, particularly by the rockets, had been very effective. Then a squadron of Fifth Air Force B-25s bombed and strafed the area so that the defenders had little desire to remain and die for the Emperor, and quickly faded into the rain forest. The beach party which had landed with the buffaloes set to work immediately to mark a channel through the reefs for the small boats waiting to enter the harbor.

Within two hours, all 1,700 assault troops and the troop commander were ashore; the harbor of Arawe was in our hands; the *Carter Hall*, *Westralia*, APDs and all destroyers except my flagship, the destroyer *Conyngham*, were homeward bound. We stayed behind to search the waters for any men who might be hanging to any wreckage off Blue Beach. The Subchaser *699* and boats from Flippin's beach party joined in the search. Overhead, a group of P-38s, which had arrived shortly after daylight, acted as air cover.

The search for Blue Beach survivors—all but sixteen were rescued—was about completed when the radar picket ship warned of enemy aircraft approaching. The P-38s failed to intercept them, and the Japanese—thirty-three bombers and torpedo planes—came in. The *Conyngham,* the biggest ship in the area, received most of their attention, although five of them picked on the Subchaser *699.* Bombs began to drop ahead, astern, and on each side, but there were no direct hits. Torpedoes came at the *Conyngham* from every direction as she maneuvered between their wakes with guns blazing. It did not seem possible that she could survive; but she did, due to the skillful handling of her skipper, Commander James H. Ward, and a lot of luck. And the same might be said for the handling of the *SC-699* by her skipper, Lieutenant (j.g.) James W. Foristel, a former lawyer. That morning, the "Shootin' *699*" claimed credit for picking up seventy-one survivors off Blue Beach and shooting down one plane. Not bad for a subchaser!

During the several plane attacks on my flagship, I was probably more aware of what was going on than anyone else because I had nothing to do. Everyone else was concentrating on doing his own particular job. The skipper and the bridge personnel were swinging the ship at high speed to avoid the torpedoes and bombs; the lookouts were reporting incoming planes; guncrews were doing what guncrews are supposed to do; ammunition crews were feeding the guns; the firemen and engineers were driving the ship at more than her rated speed; everyone had a job and was busy doing it, but me. I was just a spectator in my seat on the starboard wing of the bridge. It would have been far easier on the nerves if I could have shot a gun or handled a wheel.

Like most air attacks, this one lasted only a few minutes. The planes swarmed over us and were gone. There was some minor damage to the supply dumps ashore and a few casualties, but the ships and boats were not hit. The *Conyngham* headed for its home base at Milne Bay and upon arrival I again transferred my flag to the *Rigel.*

For the next few weeks our little LCTs, towing even smaller craft, and guided by APc's, maintained a flow of reinforcements and supplies from the newly established base at Finschhafen to the newly acquired base at Arawe. Hardly a day would pass but these little craft had to fight off plane attacks either en route or while unloading. During these attacks the *APc-21* was sunk and the *SC-743, YMS-50, APc-15,* and four LCTs were damaged. But these little fellows were getting better and better in defending themselves, and soon had Japanese flags painted on their pilothouses as credit for planes shot down.

Among the reports of the Arawe operation, the one that arrested my attention came from the beach party commander. Written matter-of-factly, it described two men manning a machine gun in an open boat and engaging an enemy plane in combat. Apparently the incident was too commonplace to call for identification of the participants. The report said:

. . . after the sinking of the *APc-21,* one small boat crew fought off an enemy plane attempting to strafe the survivors. The bravery of this crew undoubtedly saved the lives of several men. The identity of the crew is unknown.

With the assault phase of the Arawe operation over, attention turned to other matters. Important command changes had taken place in the rear area. During the preceding two weeks, Vice Admiral T. C. Kinkaid had relieved Vice Admiral A. S. Carpender as Commander of the Seventh Fleet. Apparently the rift between Carpender and MacArthur had reached the breaking point. The change of command also brought a number of staff changes at the Seventh Fleet Headquarters, which would not affect forward area planning and preparations for Cape Gloucester, but might have a bearing on future operations.

Just eight days after my return to Milne Bay from Arawe, I would leave again to head the convoy carrying troops for an assault on Cape Gloucester—one likely to be bitterly defended.

12:

Cape Gloucester

26 December 1943

ON 26 DECEMBER 1943, JUST ELEVEN DAYS AFTER THE SEVENTH
Amphibious Force had landed troops at Arawe, the 1st Division of the U.S. Marines
were scheduled to be put ashore at Cape Gloucester, on the northwest coast of New
Britain. At least a week of joint training of all troops and ships was an essential
requirement for a smooth-functioning operation. But the best we could do was to
supply the ships for a few practice landings at each of the embarkation points.
Almost all of our amphibious ships were engaged in running urgently needed
reinforcements and supplies to the isolated garrisons at Finschhafen and Arawe. We
did not like these shoestring arrangements and the Marines liked them even less.

The 1st Marines were veterans of Guadalcanal. Their landing from APAs at
Guadalcanal in August 1942 had been unopposed, but they had won glory and gained
experience in jungle fighting in the following six months of that bloody campaign.
Now they were to be landed again from another type of ship and with another type
of technique—and they were not sure they liked it.

They disliked the idea that their troops would be assault-landed directly on the
beaches from LCIs and LSTs instead of from boats carried to the landing area by big
fast transports (APAs) as had been done at Guadalcanal; they disliked the idea of
relying on land-based Army air support instead of on Navy planes from aircraft
carriers offshore as they did at Guadalcanal; they disliked the idea of the naval
bombardment force departing from the area immediately after the landing and
leaving them stranded with an uncertain supply line as had happened, to their grief,

at Guadalcanal; nor did they like the idea of preparing for the operation without extensive training in the ships that would carry them to the beaches.

In spite of these dislikes and misgivings, the Cape Gloucester landing was a grand success. Marine historian Frank Hough in *The Island War* called it "the most nearly perfect amphibious assault in World War II." George McMillan, historian of the 1st Marine Division, in his book, *The Old Breed,* had this to say:

> Whatever its approach to perfection, the assault phase of the Cape Gloucester campaign was the only one of the four major landings made by the 1st Marine Division during which things happened—as nearly as can be expected in war—when they were supposed to happen. The landing went according to plan.*

When the Marines first learned they were designated for the Cape Gloucester operation, they were recuperating in Melbourne, Australia. The first step was to move them from Melbourne to encampments in the New Guinea area in Liberty ships. The Libertys were cargo ships and not suited to carrying large numbers of troops. With makeshift plumbing facilities on the open deck, sleeping accommodations in cargo holds, and stand-in-line messing arrangements, they were a poor substitute for the specially designed Navy transports to which the Marines were accustomed before they came under MacArthur's command.

Even the camp sites in the New Guinea area were not to their liking. There was no available site that could take the entire Division at one time so one regiment was sent to Milne Bay, one regiment to Goodenough Island and one regiment to Oro Bay—all about eighty miles from each other. Amphibious Headquarters was at Milne Bay and Air Force Headquarters at Port Moresby. Coordinated planning was difficult. The Marines were highly concerned about the operation that lay ahead and longed for the day they would get away from the Southwest Pacific command.

There was good reason for them to expect that Cape Gloucester would be vigorously defended for the Japanese well knew that if Cape Gloucester fell, the fate of Rabaul was sealed. There were no villages or harbors in the vicinity of Cape Gloucester. Most of the coast was coral-bound but with a few fairly good beaches on the north coast. The approaches to the beaches were a bit difficult due to a series of scattered coral reefs about six miles to seaward. Numerous coral islets and pinnacles lay between these reefs and the shoreline. The hulk of a Japanese destroyer aground on one of the outer reefs gave silent evidence of the hazards of navigation in this area. The wreck became a useful reference point in aerial photography and in chart making during our preparations.

To MacArthur, the capture of the Cape Gloucester area meant far more than another step in the encirclement of Rabaul. It would open the straits between the

* The other three major landings of the 1st Marine Division were not made in the Southwest Pacific.

western Solomon Sea, where his forces were operating, and the Pacific Ocean, where he wanted to go, to extend operations along the New Guinea coast and into the Philippines. Those were his plans, but not those of the Joint Chiefs of Staff—at that time.

Between the western end of New Britain and a jutting peninsula on New Guinea are two narrow straits, Dampier and Vitiaz, separated by small Rooke Island and some neighboring islets. MacArthur's forces had captured Finschhafen which dominated one side of the straits, but as long as the Japanese held Cape Gloucester and its airfields on the other side, passage through the straits would always be a risky undertaking.

The Marines were perfectly confident they could handle any Japanese in western New Britain—estimated to be about eight thousand—once they got ashore, if they could land without being chewed up in the process. The amphibious force was equally confident the Marines could be landed without being chewed up.

While our planning ship, the *APc-15,* with one or more staff planners, and a yeoman, typewriter, mimeograph machine and much paper, shuttled between the various staff headquarters developing a workable landing plan, the other members of the staff gathered information regarding the beaches; converted LCIs into rocket boats; converted more LSTs into casualty ships; moved salvage tugs and repair ships closer to the landing area; and stockpiled supplies at Lae, Finschhafen and Arawe so that the troops at those places could keep going for the next few weeks without outside help. Ammunition, food, and equipment requirements for the Marines were transported by our amphibious ships to forward bases not only for their jump-off requirements, but also for their follow-up requirements. Every available ship was in use. There would be no reserves to fall back upon.

The beach party of eighteen men under Lieutenant Commander Flippin, which had landed with the first assault wave at Arawe on 15 December, had done a magnificent job in that operation in laying buoys and marking channels under hazardous conditions. But they would now be needed at Gloucester, so after three days at Arawe they were withdrawn and reorganized to meet the requirements of the new operation.

Aerial reconnaissance provided some excellent pictures of the various beaches, surf conditions, reefs, probable defenses, and swamp area. The wrecked Japanese destroyer was a good marker for determining the rise and fall of tide and also the depth of water over the reef.

A series of three scouting teams were landed at various times in the vicinity of Tuali village, about eight miles southwest of Cape Gloucester. These teams were in the main composed of Marines who had been temporarily attached to our amphibious scout camp on Fergusson Island for training.

It had become customary for the various Division commanders to send a few of their men to Fergusson Island for scout training before engaging in the reconnaissance of any area in which they were interested. Although most of the information the Navy needed for its purposes could be obtained from aerial reconnaissance, troop commanders usually felt they could get more and better information on matters of particular interest to them, such as trails, defenses, and back country terrain, by reliance on ground reconnaissance. One of the requests we always made to a scouting team was to bring back a Japanese prisoner if at all possible, but none ever did.

The three Marine reconnaissance teams which had landed near Tuali village and the PT boats which carried them had plenty of excitement and a few close calls, but they obtained little new information. One PT boat was almost lost when caught between two lines of Japanese barges. We doubted the information obtained was worth the risk. The Japanese became aware of the reconnaissance near Tuali and to that extent it may have been of some value in diverting their attention to the wrong landing beaches.

The need for an effective naval bombardment of the Cape Gloucester beach area, just prior to the landing, was considered of vital importance. The staff gunnery officer, Major J. M. Blais, U.S. Marine Corps, a former member of the 1st Marine Division, was particularly valuable in this phase of planning. The landing would be supported by the gunfire of four cruisers and a number of destroyers. Naval bombardment is very effective against fixed targets, but of little use when firing into a matted rain forest that extends almost to the shoreline. Furthermore, the flat trajectory of naval gunfire was not effective in driving the Japanese out of their pillboxes; aerial bombing of specific targets was better but, unfortunately, we could not count on pinpoint accuracy nor precise timing. Nor was strafing of the beaches with aircraft of much help.

We had found that strafing the beaches with a bullet every six feet was not very effective and furthermore all naval gunfire had to be withheld while the planes were over the beaches. What was needed was a plunging, high-explosive type of fire laid in a barrage just ahead of the troops as they hit the shore. Commander Dwight Day, our assistant repair officer, was the man who supplied the answer.

On the decks of the *LCI-31* and *LCI-34* he installed racks to hold twelve rocket launchers. Each launcher could fire twelve 4.5-inch rockets. Each rocket had a fixed range of about 1,200 yards. Since the launchers were in a fixed position, the rockets could only be aimed by heading the ship and hence the launcher in the direction of the target.

The launchers when installed were angled out from zero degrees for the launchers farthest forward, up to three degrees for those farther aft on each side, which gave them a front coverage of about three hundred feet. To provide coverage in depth, the LCI with her rockets would proceed toward the beach, slightly ahead of the first wave of troops. A salvo of twelve rockets would be fired to land just inland from the

Marines and materiel cram this Coast Guard-manned LST, bound for the invasion of Cape Gloucester, New Britain. At the landing it was unloaded in less than three hours.

A Japanese bomb nearly scores a hit, but luckily falls between two combat ships at Cape Gloucester.

Coast Guardsmen fight off attacking Japanese planes at Gloucester. Bomb splashes show how close the LST came to getting hit.

Christmas Day, 1943. U.S. Marines aboard a loaded LST en route to Cape Gloucester. On the twenty-sixth, they successfully drove the Japanese back into the jungle.

A Japanese destroyer grounded off
Gloucester helped determine the tide
changes when planning the assault
operation.

LCI(R)s (R for rockets) were a Seventh
Amphibious Force innovation for
bombarding the beaches ahead of the
waves of landing troops.

Part of the second wave of Marines to hit the beach at Cape Gloucester land from the LCIs.

Bow doors of beached LSTs open to disgorge men and materiel on the Gloucester beach. Decks are yet to be unloaded.

Marines push a jeep ashore at Cape Gloucester. Others carry litters for the casualties to come.

Another jeep is pushed through the surf. Coast Guard and Navy-manned LSTs participated in the invasion.

Trucks roll down the ramp of an LST to mire in the mud caused by a sudden tropical rainstorm on New Britain Island.

LSTs, their huge jaws open, line up on the beach, disgorging Marines and materiel for the New Britain campaign.

Constantly on the alert for Japanese snipers, Marines move across a Cape Gloucester stream.

shoreline, and a new salvo would be fired for each hundred yards the ship moved forward until the ship itself ran up on the beach. If it worked out as planned, the troops would move onto the shore with a flaming barrage of bursting rockets always ahead of them. Skillful timing and navigation were an essential part of the bombardment. The effect of the rocket tryout on a small island near Milne Bay was devastating. The rain forest was cut as with a giant scythe. We hoped their use at Cape Gloucester a few weeks later would be equally devastating.

The air support for the Cape Gloucester operation was the most extensive of any planned to date. To weaken Japanese air capability all their nearby airfields would be targets for intensified bombing during the week prior to the landing. Although this bombing would reduce the Japanese ability to make air attacks against our assault force, experience had shown they could quickly rebuild their air strength with planes flown in from supporting bases.

In spite of the separation of the headquarters of the Sixth Army, 1st Marine Division, Fifth Air Force, and Seventh Amphibious Force, all of whom were concerned with the planning, the final plans were well coordinated, although the complete air plan was not available until two days before the sailing date.

A series of excellent air photographs had been obtained for the planners. Skillful photographic interpretation furnished the needed information regarding beach characteristics and accurately located reefs and shoals from which navigational charts were prepared and distributed to all ships. To assist the coxswains of the small boats in identifying the proper beaches, each one was given a silhouette of the shoreline and surrounding hills.

The 2 main beaches chosen for the assault on the basis of the information supplied by the photographs, designated "Yellow One" and "Yellow Two," were approximately 6 miles east of Cape Gloucester. A subsidiary landing was to be made on "Green Beach" near the village of Tuali about 7 miles on the other side of the Cape. The Japanese airfield consisted of 2 runways built on the western-most tip of the Cape. One runway was within 50 yards of the shoreline. The firm sand behind the beaches, according to the photographs, only extended a few yards inland and then gave way to a rain-forested swamp which extended about one thousand yards to the base of the jungle-covered "Target Hill," 450 feet high. Most of the fixed shore defenses and troops were believed to be concentrated at the airfield, and at "Target Hill," and perhaps at Borgen Bay, a few miles to the westward, but only roving patrols were likely to be encountered on the beaches selected for the landings. As guns on "Target Hill" dominated all the surrounding beaches, that was one of the first points that must be captured by the landing force. But the speed with which the troops could get to it would be determined by the depth of water in the swamp they must cross. The depth of water would be determined by the recent rainfall, and the rainy season was about to commence. Few Japanese were likely to be encountered in the swamp, but strong opposition might be expected as our troops moved westward along the shoreline to the airfield.

To eliminate the danger from the guns on "Target Hill" while the troops were being disembarked on the beaches, the Air Force was asked to give it a thorough going over with high-explosive bombs and then follow it up with a few tons of phosphorus bombs to clear out any remaining Nips. Hopefully, smoke from the phosphorus bombs would be trapped by the humid atmosphere, and drift slowly downward and blanket the activities in the beach area.

The Marines were a bit skeptical of this proposal because of the danger the beaches might become so smoke-bound that the boat coxswains would lose their way. The use of phosphorus smoke was a "first" for us in this kind of operation, but possible gains appeared to outweigh possible losses and phosphorus bombs became part of the plan.

One part of the plan that conformed to previous landing force procedure was a shore party formed from the men in the combat division, rather than from men of the Engineer Special Brigade as we had been doing. However, a detachment of the Engineer Special Brigade would supply the boats for use of the shore party. The lessons learned at Guadalcanal had made the Marines especially conscious of a shore party's importance and so they designated and trained 1,300 of their own men for this particular chore. They preferred it that way.

Guadalcanal had also impressed upon the Marines the possibility of an interrupted flow of supplies and so they insisted that their assault force be accompanied by enough ammunition, equipment, and food to last them twenty days. This was somewhat more than had accompanied the troops in our previous landings, but if the Marines felt their shore party could offload ships promptly and keep the beaches clear, we were willing to try it. It meant, however, some landing craft would be immobilized on the beach unloading supplies almost continuously on D-day, during the most probable times for an air attack, a situation we did not like. Although there would be friendly planes overhead during most of the day, it was doubtful if they could stop an enemy air attack in its entirety. The final plans provided for 12,540 men and 8,150 tons to be landed on D-day, 26 December.

Just before the Marines at Goodenough Island embarked aboard their troopships, General MacArthur visited them. His parting words to Major General W. H. Rupertus, the commanding general of the 1st Marine Division, were a bit unusual: "I know what the Marines think of me, but I also know that when they go into a fight they can be counted upon to do an outstanding job. Good luck."

The assault troops from Goodenough Island and Milne Bay were assembled at Oro Bay and Finschhafen, the jump-off points. Repair ships, salvage tugs, supply ships, and water barges had been stationed in bays and inlets close enough to the landing area to be useful and yet not close enough to get hurt. The *LST-464*—the 175-bed hospital facility—was stationed at Buna. Surgical teams were embarked in specially equipped casualty LSTs. These ships would be used for the emergency handling of the wounded and evacuate them to the *LST-464* at Buna or to the 300-bed naval hospital at Milne Bay.

At last, the detailed preparations were complete and a rehearsal held at Cape Sudest, nine miles south of Buna. By Christmas Eve, all ships were loaded. At 6 A.M., Christmas Day of 1943, the main convoy left Cape Sudest for the assault on Cape Gloucester just twenty hours later. It was a dispiriting Christmas Day for the thousands of men embarked in strange ships heading into hostile waters; one that few of them would care to remember.

Four hours after departure, a Japanese coast watcher reported the movement of the ships and three hours later a Japanese reconnaissance plane was shot down by our air cover. We learned later that their reports led the Japanese at Rabaul to assume that the convoy was headed for Arawe with reinforcements—a most fortunate error from our point of view.

Apparently the convoy was not sighted as it passed through Vitiaz Strait and rounded the western end of New Britain. Christmas night was dark and moonless with overcast skies. Four cruisers led the Force and I followed them in the destroyer *Conyngham,* with a miscellaneous assortment of more than one hundred combat ships and amphibious ships stringing along behind for many miles in protective formation. No signals were exchanged, either by radio or visually. Each ship kept its position by "hanging on to the heels" of the ship ahead. I fidgeted all night on the bridge, but Major General Rupertus, who was on my flagship, slept unconcernedly below. At the first light of day every ship moved into its assigned position and the cruisers and destroyers opened fire on the air strip, the beaches, and on "Target Hill." Under cover of this fire small craft buoyed a channel through the reefs and marked the shoal spots. Mine sweepers searched the area for mines.

Some of the Marines were a bit nervous about this landing. Only five weeks before, at Tarawa in the Central Pacific, the 2nd Division of Marines had suffered heavy losses from Japanese machine guns as their boats stranded on the reefs during the assault. There were many reefs around Cape Gloucester and the Marines wondered if this show was likely to be a repetition of Tarawa.

Yates McDaniel, a war correspondent for the Associated Press, was aboard one of the APDs which carried the boats for the first wave of the assault to Yellow Beach One. He was a veteran of our landing technique and therefore qualified to speak with authority to the "first-timers" among the troops. A long time afterward, he told me that to allay their apprehension, he announced he would go ashore in the first wave—which he did—because of his confidence in the precise planning and careful preparations of the Seventh Amphibious Force and the strong probability that the Marines would reach the beach without casualties, which they did. McDaniel felt his words and action may have lessened the tension in the group around him.

Exactly to the minute, the small boats loaded with troops from the APDs started shoreward under cover of the naval bombardment, followed by more troops in a group of LCIs. When the naval gunfire ceased, thirty heavy Air Force bombers headed for "Target Hill" and dropped their load of high explosives and white phosphorus smoke bombs. A heavy pall of smoke drifted slowly down the hill, as we had hoped. The heavy bombers had hardly left when forty medium bombers dropped their load. As soon as the medium bombers left the LCI(R)s opened a thunderous fire with their rockets and laid a flaming curtain ahead of the boats from the APDs as they were putting their troops ashore. The smoke from "Target Hill" had now descended to the water, cutting off the view of the assault troops both from "Target Hill" and the supporting ships outside the reef. A great sigh of relief went up when the first of the assault boats came out of the smoke belt and signalled, "No shore opposition."

The landing was a complete surprise. Yellow Beach had fewer Japanese defenses than any place in the vicinity. From captured Japanese documents we learned later that they expected the landing, if made, would take place at Borgen Bay, a few miles to the westward where the beaches were much better, so they had concentrated their defenses at that point and at "Target Hill" and the airfield. "Target Hill," an obvious defense position, was so battered by gunfire and bombs that the defenders were unable to offer effective resistance to the Marines who struggled through a waist-deep swamp to capture the hill within a few hours of the landing.

Shortly before 0900, with ships on the beach, enemy aircraft were reported approaching from the direction of Rabaul. Our protective cover of aircraft tried to intercept but missed. That was because the Jap planes had turned south toward Arawe owing to wrong information from their "snooper" plane. They dropped their bombs at Arawe but did little damage as there were no ships in the harbor.

All day long the movement of LSTs to and from the Yellow beaches continued. At 1430, while two groups of LSTs were on the beach, there was another warning of a strong force of enemy planes approaching. Four squadrons of Air Force fighter planes were directed to intercept and did, but ten enemy dive bombers broke through and made a series of well-coordinated attacks against the ships caught inside the reef. They sank the destroyer *Brownson,* damaged the destroyers *Lamson, Shaw,* and *Mugford,* and the *LSTs 66* and *202.* Ships outside the reef, including my flagship, although attacked, had plenty of maneuvering room and were able to avoid any damage. For the next ten minutes the air was full of flaming planes. From the air battle overhead, American pilots floated down in parachutes and Japanese came down in burning planes. Black columns of smoke rolled skyward from crashed bombers and fighters that dotted the ocean.

In this atmosphere of high tension, one of war's tragedies took place. Captain R. M. Scruggs, U.S. Navy, who was in command of six LSTs unloading on the beach, gave this account of the incident in his pictorial diary:

> I happened to be on the LST on the right flank, standing on the bridge talking to her skipper and admiring the smoking volcano in the background. The ships were still at General Quarters from a Jap air attack a short time before, and the gunners were trigger-happy. Suddenly the lookouts yelled, "Planes approaching low on the starboard beam." On looking up we saw approximately a dozen twin-engined bombers coming low over the point at an altitude of about 500 feet and heading straight for us. It looked as though we were really sitting ducks as the LSTs were only separated by 150 feet and sticks of bombs laid across them would almost certainly result in one hundred percent hits. Within a few seconds the planes were in range, and I told the skipper, "Let them have it." But before the Captain could give the orders to commence firing we were able to recognize the planes as our own B-26 light bombers. Instead of giving the order "Commence firing," the Captain tried to pass the word "Friendly planes. Don't fire." However some of the gunners had already started shooting, and since our ship had opened up, all the other five joined in. The planes swept across our stern and the big white stars of the Army Air Force became so obvious that many of the gunners ceased firing, but not before two planes were mortally hit. One of them crashed immediately into the water. The second caught fire and went into a long glide, burning more and more, until by the time it crashed about a mile away it was a solid mass of flames.
>
> The bombers were making a low-level attack upon Japs occupying a point about a mile and one-half to the left of where we were beached. There was a prohibition against friendly planes flying low over friendly ships, and it was the disregard of this rule by the Air Force that resulted in the unnecessary destruction of two of their bombers.

A saddened group of LSTs completed unloading and started on their return to their base when just before sundown, another plane attack was reported as imminent. This time there were no mistakes in identification. Eighteen Japanese torpedo bombers, escorted by a squadron of fighters, were intercepted by Air Force fighter cover and every one was shot down. The Japanese Air Force had had a bad day, with a total of sixty-four planes lost. After these heavy losses, we doubted they could continue air attacks of any strength on our convoys or on the beaches, and such proved to be the case.

From a military point of view, the first day at Cape Gloucester had been most successful. The Marines landed on the beaches without loss and moved toward their objectives much faster than had been expected. However, shore opposition was mounting and the wounded were coming in from the front lines in increasing numbers.

Among the innovations initiated in this landing, the one that gave us the most satisfaction was the expeditious handling of the casualties. Men wounded ashore were immediately taken to the nearest LST on the beach. Each LST carried a doctor and small medical staff. Additionally, one ship in each group of LSTs carried a surgical team of four doctors and a staff capable of handling three hundred casualties. All seriously wounded were handled by these field-equipped "casualty" ships. The same ships transported all the wounded to base hospitals within a few days, and probably saved many lives.

Another innovation that far exceeded expectations was the outstanding perform-ance of our LCI(R)s—the "R" designating rockets. After the operation we com-menced a program for converting 16 LCIs for this purpose. Some of the new ones carried 288 and the later ones 312 rockets. Some months later the Navy Department developed an LCI(R) which we found had too deep a draft, was hard to handle, and was overmanned.

Our own LCI(R)s became a valuable part of the amphibious effort, not only as rocket ships but for many other purposes. Each one was equipped with smoke pots so that within minutes they could circle a convoy or a harbor and lay a smoke screen that would blot it out from attacking planes. Each one was also equipped with fire hose, chemicals, explosives, and pumps; and their crews were especially trained in fire fighting. They could blast passages through reefs or slots in the shoreline in which LSTs could be berthed.

These versatile LCIs with the wicked punch successfully fought large fires aboard more than twenty ships and assisted the Army in fighting fires in ammunition and supply dumps ashore. All the officers and crews of the rocket ships were a credit to the Seventh Amphibious Force and to the Navy. The youthful skippers of the *LCI(R)-73* and *LCI(R)-338*, Lieutenants (j.g.) Maynard Taylor and C. R. Good-man, were especially outstanding in courage, ability, and resourcefulness.

There were few defenders on the beaches at Cape Gloucester and those that were there never fired a shot. The LCI(R)s may be given much of the credit for that. The devastating effect of their fire is illustrated in an incident reported by Lieutenant E. F. Norwood, the medical officer on an LST. A hospital corpsman followed, at a discreet distance, the first assault wave of Marines ashore. Looking about for some possible souvenirs, he saw a rifle barrel with a bayonet attached sticking upright from a brush-covered hole. He casually gave a tug to the bayonet which did not move, and then as he watched, it gradually disappeared. Frightened, he got help from a nearby patrol of Marines. They surrounded the hole and out of it emerged three shell-shocked Japanese.

For the next four months the Cape Gloucester campaign would drag on in the bloody and weary routine of tired, mud-sloshing Marines pushing the Japs out of western New Britain under conditions unpleasantly like Guadalcanal. The Seventh

Amphibious Force would continue its chore of maintaining a steady flow of reinforcements and supplies to their comrades ashore, and in addition would be making other landings, with other troops, on other beaches.

One of the amusing sidelights of the Gloucester follow-up campaign concerned James Van Zandt, former congressman from Pennsylvania. He had now become the commanding officer of the *LST-457*, one of the shuttle ships running supplies from Buna to Cape Gloucester. Once, just before the *LST-457* left Buna, three neatly garbed and dedicated Red Cross ladies reported aboard with authorization—from GHQ in Australia—to take passage on an LST to Cape Gloucester. There they proposed to establish a Red Cross camp to bring a little comfort and cheer to the worn-out troops fighting ashore.

Van Zandt tried to warn them off by describing the conditions under which the men were fighting. He told of the torrential rain with mud everywhere and said the average Marine's idea of heaven was a stream in which he could take a bath without stepping on a crocodile or being shot, although he might be willing to settle for a dry foxhole.

The girls were quite determined in their desire to do their bit to relieve the homesickness of the lonely boys ashore, and besides they had the backing of high authority in the rear areas. And so Van Zandt, somewhat reluctantly, turned over his cabin to them and sailed for the fighting front. When a few miles off the landing area he sent a dispatch to the troop commander, Major General Rupertus, reporting his arrival with 400 troops, 100 vehicles, 300 tons of bulk cargo, and 3 Red Cross girls and requesting instructions. The instructions came quickly: "Land troops, vehicles, and cargo on Yellow Beach. Keep girls locked up and return to Buna."

Four months later, when the Marines were relieved of their job in western New Britain by soldiers of the 40th Army Division, the ships of the Seventh Amphibious Force had moved many hundreds of miles to the westward, and, at that time, were busily engaged in landing more than 70,000 troops at the villages of Aitape and Hollandia on the New Guinea coast.

13:

Capture of Saidor

2 January 1944

PLANNING AND PREPARATIONS FOR THE CAPE GLOUCESTER OP-
eration were buoyed by the thought that, with the operation over, there might be a
few weeks surcease from "hurry up" planning and partial rehearsals. There was the
hopeful expectation that resupply runs to Lae, Finschhafen, Arawe, and perhaps
Cape Gloucester might then be reasonably free from bomber and strafing attacks, for
men and ships were beginning to show the strain. We even dared hope that some
amphibious ships—some were barely able to keep going—might then be given a few
weeks for much needed repairs, and some of the men could perhaps even make a visit
to Australia.

But this was not to be. On 20 December, just as the staff breathed a sigh of relief
that plans and preparations for the Cape Gloucester show were on schedule, but still
6 days before the landing, General MacArthur's headquarters ordered another one.
This one was scheduled for the 126th Regimental Combat Team of the 32nd
Division. We were to land them on 2 January, or within 48 hours thereafter, at
Saidor, a small Japanese base on the coast of New Guinea, 115 miles west of
Finschhafen, another step on the way to the Philippines.

By that time I was physically and mentally exhausted from many last-minute
arrangements for Cape Gloucester and hardly in a mood to give concentrated
attention to the preparations for another operation, and my staff was in the same
condition. However, we examined all the available intelligence data on the Saidor
area and then roughed out a tentative landing plan. The details would have to be

worked out by those staff members who would be left behind, while I was en route to
Cape Gloucester. They would work in concert with Army planners at Goodenough
Island. Final plan approval would have to wait upon my return a few days later.
There would be no time for basic changes. On 24 December GHQ stated that the
Saidor landing must take place on 2 January, 1944, and no later.

This meant that the troops designated for Saidor, with all their supplies and
equipment would have to be loaded aboard the ships on 31 December, only five days
after the Gloucester landing, and under way on New Year's Day. There was neither
time nor ships available for practice landings or full-scale rehearsals. As it was, we
would be hard-pressed to get enough undamaged ships back from Cape Gloucester in
time to complete the loading on the thirty-first. Fortunately, the troops designated for
Saidor had previously completed the six weeks' amphibious training course at Milne
Bay in preparation for the landing at Gasmata, for which they had been originally
scheduled but which was later cancelled.

Even though no rehearsals would be required, the many details that had to be
worked out would have overwhelmed a less experienced staff. They had to determine
how many ships would be required and what type of ships. Among these types
would be rocket ships, gunnery ships, escorting ships, troop-carrying ships and supply
ships, just to name a few. Since all available ships were being used at Cape
Gloucester, assignment to the Saidor operation would have to await their return. They
would still have to transfer casualties to a base hospital, have towing gear checked,
and take on fuel, ammunition, fresh water, and provisions before they could proceed
to Goodenough Island to load the troops and equipment for Saidor.

About 7,500 men and 3,000 tons of supplies would have to be landed in the first 3
hours after dawn on D-day, 2 January. At least 50 ships would have to sail in the
assault convoy. An equal number of ships and an equal amount of supplies must
follow in a few days. Shore bases must be informed as to what was expected of them.
There was no big central base in the New Guinea area where all supporting activities
could be carried out simultaneously. Our small, slow ships would have to load
ammunition, fuel, and supplies at a number of improvised bases extending from
Milne Bay to Finschhafen, a distance of over 375 miles.

While one section of the staff arranged for the readiness of the ships, another
section—in conjunction with the staff of the troop commander—worked out such
details as loading the ships so that their trim would conform to the slope of the
beaches. Other details for the planners included each ship's position in the convoy; its
position on arrival in the landing area; the amount and length of time for gunfire
and rocket fire; the landing beaches; target designation; the number of boats and
troops for each assault wave; spacing between waves; assignment of beach parties;
and the preparation of charts showing the location of shoals and reefs. Finally, all the

data and instructions had to be assembled in a single, concise, accurate, complete plan that must be mimeographed and distributed to a large number of widely separated ships and stations—all in a matter of five days' time, including Christmas. There was little time for sleep. I returned from Cape Gloucester on 27 December. By 29 December the plan was signed and distributed by PT boat, and on 31 December the troops and supplies were being loaded at Goodenough Island. All ships were loaded and under way to the landing beaches on New Year's Day.

General MacArthur had decided a speed-up in landing operations was necessary in order that American troops might join up with the Aussies, who were pressing along the coast from Finschhafen in their pursuit of the Japanese who had escaped from Lae and Finschhafen. Saidor was chosen as the landing spot because it had good beaches, a good airstrip, and was weakly defended. The Japanese had been using it as a staging area for coastal barge traffic. Its principal value to the Allies lay in the potentialities of its airstrip. There were no fixed defenses and its garrison did not exceed 500 men. About 50 miles on either side of Saidor, however, were two Japanese strong points: Sio to the eastward with 12,000 men, and Madang to the westward with 18,000 men.

The Saidor landing was an excellent example of MacArthur's concept of "hit them where they ain't" and "bypass the strongpoints." Both terms might be translated into "big gains with little losses."

Seventh Amphibious Force planners had time for only three short conferences with those of the Sixth Army and the 32nd Division at Goodenough Island, and one conference at Air Force headquarters. The Navy plans were written between Friday noon and the following Monday morning. We began to feel the holidays were the favored jump-off dates; first there was the Christmas Day movement to Cape Gloucester and now the movement on New Year's Day to Saidor. Holidays, apparently, were merely the incidental trappings of a peaceful civilization and had no place in war.

The coastline in the Saidor area is coral-fringed over most of its length. A few breaks in this coral barrier led to three small, hard sand beaches, chosen because their steep slope would permit the landing craft to get their bows well up on the shore and thus provide a dry landing for the troops. Aerial photographs also showed that the area immediately behind the beaches was free of swamps—something unusual in most parts of New Guinea and New Britain.

Since there was no choice in the date of the landing, plans had to conform to the tidal and lunar conditions that could be expected on January second. The first-quarter moon would set shortly after midnight. This was a bit of luck; ships could probably approach the area in complete darkness and perhaps escape observance by coast watchers or snooper planes. We were also lucky in the matter of tides. They occurred

Admiral Barbey, in company with Brig. General Clarence A. Martin, U.S. Army, Commander 32nd Division, and Brig. General R. N. L. Hopkins (right), Australian Imperial Forces, watches the 2 January 1944 landing on Saidor, New Guinea.

Troops of Company C, 126th Infantry Regiment, cross the Seng River near Saidor.

at just the right time and were not over three or four feet, and that could be handled quite readily.

The landing was scheduled for fifteen minutes before sunrise. There would be no air bombardment preceding the assault as Air Force bombers could not get to the area in time—they could not arrive until an hour after sunrise. The advantage of a surprise landing at dawn more than offset any advantages of a pre-attack bombing.

One of the newly trained naval beach parties was brought to the forward area to accompany the landing force. A boat detachment from the 2nd Engineer Special Brigade was attached to the shore party.

The troops embarked at Goodenough Island on 31 December were in excellent spirits. They were fresh, and with new equipment. But the crews of the ships which carried them were a tired lot worn out from the grueling runs to Gloucester and the frequent air attacks. The ships were loaded and under way for the assault area on schedule. I led the convoy of 55 ships in the *Conyngham*. With me was the regimental commander, Brigadier General C. A. Martin, and a few of his staff.

Until midnight of 1 January, the weather was clear with a quarter moon partially lighting the convoy. The convoy had the usual assortment of destroyers, APDs, LSTs, LCIs, PCs, SCs, rocket ships, and salvage tugs spread over a good many square miles of ocean. The ships were darkened. A Japanese reconnaissance plane droned overhead but we doubted that he had seen us, and held fire.

Shortly after midnight the moon set, the weather became overcast with scattered showers, and the convoy became enveloped in almost total blackness. We worried that our smaller craft might lose their way or collide in the darkness. Their magnetic compasses were not reliable due to the masses of steel in the armored tanks and equipment they carried, and they had no gyrocompasses.

When dawn came, every ship, to our great relief and admiration, was in its allotted place at the scheduled moment. I was often amazed how these youthful skippers could become such proficient seamen in so short a time. But when the stakes are high, men learn fast.

As the first light touched the sky, the destroyers opened fire on the beaches and the nearby jungle. The troops were embarked in small boats from the APDs and headed through the reefs toward the shore under cover of the naval bombardment. As the first wave of boats neared the beach the destroyers stopped their firing and the rocket-ships started their barrage, which formed a moving curtain of fire just ahead of the advancing troops. Following the small boats came the personnel-carrying LCIs which beached and landed troops dry-shod over their ramps. Then the LSTs landed more troops, tanks, and bulldozers directly on the beach through their big bow doors. The nearby jungle was a shambles, but the troops got ashore without an opposing shot. As the Japanese defenders fled into the jungle at the opening of the bombardment, they left cooking stoves with the food still on them.

In less than 3 hours, 7,500 troops and 3,000 tons of supplies and equipment were landed without a single casualty. The shore party functioned smoothly. Exits from the beach through a narrow strip of jungle were cleared within 15 minutes after bulldozers were unloaded from LSTs. The speed of the planning and the expertness of its execution could only have been possible with troops like those of the 126th Regimental Team who had become thoroughly indoctrinated with every detail of Seventh Amphibious Force technique.

As soon as the last man was ashore and all the tons of cargo unloaded, the convoy was re-formed and with their destroyer escorts headed for their home bases. So far, so good.

Surprisingly, there had been no immediate reaction by the Japanese Air Force. We happily assumed such good fortune was probably because no Japanese coast watcher or snooper plane had picked up the convoy during the previous night. But we were wrong. The convoy had been reported by a Japanese coast watcher as it passed Sio, and also by a snooper plane. The Japanese had lost the convoy when the moon set and the rains began, guessed at its destination, and guessed wrong.

It was not until 1600 that afternoon that 30 Japanese planes arrived in the Saidor area and attacked the landing beaches. The attack was partially broken up by friendly aircraft.

Some slight damage to shore installations and a few casualties resulted from the attack, but by the time the planes arrived the targets were few. The ships were long gone, and most of the equipment and supplies had been dispersed into the jungle. The Japanese planes never did sight the homeward bound convoy.

The landing was a resounding success from every angle. The next day the troops ashore reported the capture of the Saidor air strip and the clearing out of all Japanese in the immediate area.

For the Seventh Amphibious Force, the first assault phase of the Saidor operation was now over. The second phase was about to begin—the job of transporting reinforcements and supplies to the troops ashore. With our dwindling number of ships and increasing number of commitments, that was not easy. But within a few weeks the rest of the 32nd Division was landed at Saidor and shortly thereafter they joined up with the Australians who had reached a point on the coast a few miles to the eastward.

The Saidor landing compared favorably in size with that at Cape Gloucester, but received little attention in the world press, although war correspondents were present. Perhaps because there were no dramatic moments. The planning and execution was a hurried one—too hurried to build up suspense—and everything worked the way it was intended to work. The weather produced the right amount of overcast at the right time, the tides were right, and even the moon gave us the right amount of light, when we wanted light, and hid itself when we wanted to hide. Each ship slid into the right slot at the right moment. The beaches were just the type the skippers always prayed for and seldom got. There were no enemy air attacks of any consequence. The whole operation was just too perfect to be newsworthy.

14: Morale Difficulties

WITH THE SAIDOR LANDING OUT OF THE WAY, AND THE NEXT one—the Admiralty Islands—not scheduled until 1 April 1944, there was the prospect that the tempo of operations for the next two months would ease sufficiently to permit sending some ships to Australia for badly needed overhaul and recreation for their crews. Makeshift repair facilities in the forward area were having trouble keeping the ships running and of course suitable recreation facilities were non-existent.

The continual tension and strain of amphibious operations was getting everybody down. No longer did the men quip about the soft life of the sailors stationed in Australia who had fresh milk, fresh vegetables, movies, girls, and extra pay, whereas all they got in New Guinea was atabrine, medals, and a chance to die. When they spoke of those things now it was in deadly earnest. Most of the men had been in the forward area for more than six months. Crowded spaces, heat, rain, and air raids were with them always. Shore recreation was necessarily limited to walks or swimming at nearby beaches where warm soft drinks and warm beer might be had. And even this bit of recreation was likely to be interrupted by a "red alert," or a warning about sharks.

Professional athletes occasionally visited the ships to lay out a recreational program. Among them was Gene Tunney and George Halas, coach of the Chicago Bears. But there was little they could do. Most of the ships were small and their anchorages were usually fronted by jungle or swamp or sharp-edged Kunai grass, with an occasional narrow beach along the shoreline. The native villages were filthy. It was hardly a situation that lent itself to organized sports. And then there was the rain. Four inches a day was not uncommon during the wet season.

To satisfy even the simplest needs was not easy. Ice was hard to come by. Ice cream and cold beer were rarities. Australian beer was treasured, not only because of its strong alcoholic content but because the quality of much of the "state-side" beer had deteriorated to such an extent that even novices could tell the difference.

Movies aboard ship, regardless of their vintage, were always well attended. Crews of small ships without projectors would visit their bigger and more fortunate sisters whenever they were together. Because of the danger from night bombing attack, all ships were kept darkened—movies had to be shown below decks in spite of the stifling heat. Usually the films were badly mutilated from many showings and frequent splicings by amateur operators. Even so, the audiences stayed to the end to watch and suffer.

Life was particularly rugged on the small craft—the LCTs, SCs, and APc's—but they enjoyed a freedom from regulations and etiquette of the naval service not enjoyed by the larger ships. Commander B. C. Allen, Jr., who commanded large numbers of them during the New Guinea campaign, had this to say:

> All these craft were designed for short-range operations from established bases, but instead were employed (at least in the initial part of our advance) well ahead of any shore base. They had limited storage space for dry provisions, and even less for chilled and frozen—usually a household refrigerator. Provisioning was a constant headache with the little fellows who had to depend on tenders or the generosity of larger ships. When fresh provisions were received, they disappeared with a gulp.
>
> It was an outdoor life, and the men were surprisingly healthy. With only primitive medical facilities it was necessary to depend on shore bases for care of the truly ill.
>
> Church parties were sent to larger ships when possible. Very occasional services on board were conducted by visiting chaplains.
>
> There were no racial problems.
>
> One thing seemed to stand out. These were all tiny ships, so personal contact was close from top to bottom. Under these circumstances the well recognized personal influence of the captain was greatly magnified. The result was that the ship and its entire crew tended to be as the captain—good, bad, or indifferent. This had an interesting sidelight. With responsibility on his shoulders, the average captain tended to increase in stature.
>
> Most of the combat was with enemy planes, and the men stood up well. This was particularly true if they could shoot back, even ineffectually. Mounting extra machine guns on the craft paid big dividends, both in morale and in enemy planes shot down.
>
> There appeared to be a definite limit to the amount of fatigue and danger the average individual could take without respite. We had a few cases where the limit was shaved closely, and if encountered at all, came after the event. Such cases were few in number.
>
> It is well to emphasize again that there was practically no resemblance between the designed purposes and the actual employment of each of these types of craft. They were

built for short-range operations from established bases, and ended up on extended duty well forward of all normal support. It was a case of "make do" from start to finish, and they did very well.

To provide some of the essential services for many of the small ships of the growing amphibious force, a few LSTs had been converted into repair ships. The *LST-453* was one of the first of these conversions—a sort of improvised repair and "mother" ship. In September 1943, she had been stationed at Buna. At that time most of the amphibious ships were busily engaged in carrying supplies to the recently captured ports of Lae and Finschhafen. Because Buna was a convenient port of call for the little craft in their goings and comings, the *"453"* was stationed there to take care of those that could not take care of themselves. The other converted LSTs were stationed at equally unpleasant places and performed equally important duties.

Lieutenant O. L. Norman, the commanding officer of the *LST-453,* described the frustrations of a skipper of one of these station ships and the conditions under which they operated, in a letter dated 31 October 1943:

> This ship is operating as a tender for small craft; disbursing provisions, medical supplies, spare parts, fuel and fresh water, and in addition overhauling LCTs and performing maintenance work on other ships, including destroyers and thirteen LCIs. Last month the ship serviced fifty-four vessels; this month it will be approximately sixty.
>
> There is no storage space. Ammunition that has not been issued is stacked on the main deck and fully exposed to enemy action.
>
> There are not enough seamen aboard to carry out the duties of a supply ship, operate the boom, and carry on the normal ship's work.
>
> The doctor's understanding is that the ship is to act as a semi-hospital and offer medical services for small craft in the area—but he has neither the personnel nor equipment for these duties, and could not even perform a major operation.

And then Lieutenant Norman inserted an optimistic note of determination:

> Regardless of conditions stated above, the overhaul of LCTs is on schedule, doing repair jobs at the rate of twenty-five per week.
>
> Your attention is called to the constant air attacks this ship is subject to. The ship's company has had no more than five full nights' sleep in the past sixteen days. The alerts usually last from one to two hours and have lasted from midnight until 0500. Weather conditions and the ship's construction do not permit rest or sleep in the daytime, and even if they did, the work schedule would not permit it.
>
> The fresh water situation is critical. Until nightly air attacks cease, the evaporators are going to be shut down after dark in order to black out the ship. A water barge is requested.
>
> The ship's armament offers no protection against medium bombing and is inadequate against low altitude attacks. Enemy night attacks are now without opposition. We have been lucky so far, but there is no assurance that luck alone will continue to protect us. Additional armament and night fighter protection is requested.

Most of the personnel of this ship and the smaller craft have been in out-of-the-way stations and advanced areas for months with no form of recreation or diversity. It has been all work and no play. Older men can do without recreation, but it is difficult to maintain the morale of younger men.

A moving picture projector and supply of films should be furnished. There are projectors in the rear areas. This equipment should be made available to advanced areas.

Libraries aboard ship should be restocked. The present meager supply has been read and reread by practically every man aboard.

The present deplorable mail situation should be corrected immediately. The men would rather have mail than anything else.

The concluding paragraph contains the very satisfying statement that "this ship is ready and willing to serve in any area, advanced or otherwise, that the Navy may designate."

Life on the *LST-453* was but little different from life on the hundreds of other ships and craft operating along the New Guinea coast, and in some respects it may have been better. The *"453"* did not have to navigate through hazardous waters nor face machine-gun fire from enemy-held beaches. The difficulties under which the ships were operating was well known, but there was little that could be done except in minor details. What was needed was more ships and replacement personnel. This would have permitted occasional visits to rear areas by the ships and crews. Up to this point the urgency and size of the operations in the Southwest Pacific had increased faster than the number of new ships and new men to handle them. The workload, instead of diminishing, continued to increase. In January 1944, a 400-ton pontoon drydock was assigned to the *LST-453*. Whenever she moved from one forward base to another she towed the drydock with her in order to better service the smaller craft. Until conditions changed, every man would have to carry more than his share of the overall load.

The mail service was never entirely satisfactory. The secret and sudden movement of ships and their frequent absences from their usual bases made it almost impossible to pick up and deliver mail with any degree of regularity. But the service was greatly improved when an APc was converted into a mobile post office which was placed on a rural delivery route to all the jungle hide-outs where any of our ships might be holed up.

The *LST-464*—the floating hospital—was our main reliance for medical services. She was staffed with a surgeon, internist, dermatologist, urologist, EENT specialist, hospital corps officer, and initially about forty hospital corpsmen. Later, an anesthetist and psychiatrist were added. Additional surgeons were placed aboard for temporary duty if needed. The total bed capacity was 175, but the limited messing and laundering facilities made a rapid turnover of patients desirable.

In the early operations she was stationed at advance bases, usually Cape Sudest,

In a setting reminiscent of the Ozarks, a Coast Guardsman dangles a fishing line in the water. In this Navy rest camp high up in the New Guinea hills, war-exhausted enlisted men relax before returning to active duty.

Morobe, or Buna, in order to receive casualties from amphibious craft and then transport them to hospitals in Milne Bay.

Handling of the dead was always a touchy subject. Identification, place and type of burial, and the disposal of the personal effects of the deceased were matters on which relatives nearly always wanted precise information. Most burials took place in military cemeteries in the forward area. Occasionally it was necessary to conduct a burial at sea, and in such cases a careful note was made in the ship's log of the exact latitude and longitude of the burial site. I remember writing to a boy's mother about the circumstances of his death, and the necessity for a burial at sea, and the type of services conducted by the chaplain. She wrote a pathetic letter of acknowledgement. What seemingly caused her the greatest grief was the sense of loneliness at her boy's being left behind in the vast Pacific Ocean.

Because of the nature of their duties, doctors were more familiar with the thoughts and feelings of the men about them than the other officers aboard ship, and a review of some of their reports gives a balance to the morale picture.

Most doctors agreed that the percentage of psychiatric patients was remarkably low considering the conditions under which we operated—far less than the percentage of patients usually found in the larger cities. This was probably due to potential cases being screened out before they were sent overseas.

Dr. Wayne P. Chesbro, in charge of a psychiatric ward housed in a tent at Milne Bay, reported that almost without exception his patients were enlisted men—probably because most officers had broken their home ties, were college trained, had learned to think and live by themselves, and with officer status the conditions were a bit more tolerable. But for the young men who had never travelled far from home and had close family ties, the strain was terrific. There was no one to lean on. Assigned to a ship in the combat zone with limited water supply, stifling heat, lack of recreational facilities, crowded living space, little privacy, and intermittent bombings, the period of adjustment was a bit too much for some of them to bear. Terror, apprehension, homesickness—all rode individually with these boys. Those with a poor home background suffered most. Those with a good background and self-reliance stood it best.

Among the psychiatric cases was a tall young Negro who was rendered speechless the first time in combat. He could not recall his name. He would not answer to questions. Another boy came out of the same encounter talking of God all the time. He refused food. One of the mental patients wrote to President Roosevelt:

> Dear Frank: Us boys out here haven't heard a fireside chat for a long time. Tell you what we will do. If you will come out here and give us one we will burn down the whole damn tent to give you enough fire. How about it?

A chaplain leads prayers on board an LST en route to Cape Gloucester, New Britain.

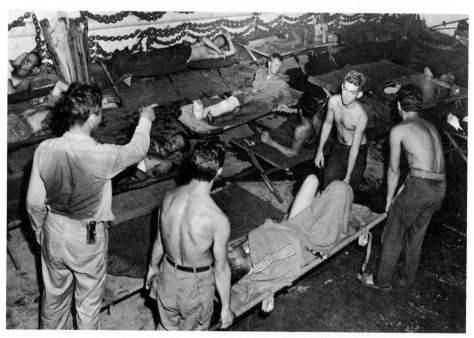

An LST serves as a "floating hospital" to bring battle casualties out of the fighting zone. Limited facilities made rapid turnover of patients imperative, and many were transported to hospitals at Milne Bay.

Other variations included men with a persecution complex who were dangerous to attendants and to doctors.

I remember a young ensign who was aboard an LST when the ship was attacked by bombers in the harbor of Morobe. His General Quarters station, about as far down in the ship as one could get, had to do with supplying ammunition from the storage bins to the guns on topside. But the terror and strain of waiting for the bombs to fall was just too much. When the battle was over he was found in a dark cubby hole on his hands and knees, sobbing and praying. It seemed best to transfer him to the rear area, but one young LST skipper with a better understanding of human nature than most requested the young man for his ship. Later I learned that the terror-stricken ensign had been assigned to a topside job with a gun crew. There, with no fearful waiting, and busy firing at attacking planes, he did a creditable job in his new battle assignment.

But not all men recovered from their initial fright. A young sailor on the *LST-470* was assigned as "captain of the head" because of his ineptness for more difficult jobs. But he was a good man, cheerful and hardworking. His first assignment at General Quarters was to a fifty-caliber gun; he was good at target practice, but in actual combat he was just too scared to handle a gun. Because he was so well-liked by officers and crew, he remained with the ship doing menial jobs, but he never got over his fear and was never again given a battle station.

The overwhelming number of men did their jobs well and uncomplainingly and often gave more thought to the welfare of their shipmates than to themselves. It was not uncommon to hear a wounded man ask "Doc" to take care of his buddy first who needed attention worse than he did.

As might be expected, there were a few weaklings in every outfit who gave first thought to their own safety. Because of these few it was necessary to guard all assault boats the night before an amphibious landing. On one or two of our landings, saboteurs had temporarily disabled a few boats by draining out the fuel or tampering with the engine to prevent their departure in the first assault wave. But these were exceptional cases.

Liquor had its uses and its problems. Beer aboard ship was stored under lock and key; a few cases would be issued to recreation parties for use ashore. A small amount of hard liquor was available for the judicious use of each medical officer.

Liquor was not always confined to medical purposes. It occasionally became a useful commodity of exchange. The *LST-470* was once badly in need of some very scarce repair equipment. Her needs could not be supplied by official requisitions; however, when the ship sailed she had the needed equipment including a welding rod, strap iron, and other carpenter and shipfitter supplies, all because of the medical officer's judicious use of a little alcohol in the right places.

Keeping the liquor under lock and key was not easy. A raid on the liquor locker was considered quite justifiable by otherwise law-abiding men. Ingenious "stills" were uncovered, operating on fermented peaches and canned blackberries.

Once, after hearing that ships arriving from Australia were loaded with liquor which was being bootlegged to combat ships, and desiring to set an example to other ships of the force, I ordered an inspection of my flagship. I headed the inspection party, accompanied by the ship's commanding officer, my aide, and a few other officers. I expected to hear bottles of liquor plop over the side as we approached the more secluded places. But we heard and found nothing.

Apparently whatever small amount of liquor we had aboard was properly secured in the medical officer's locker. I was righteously pleased. Years later, in Washington, D.C., Congressman W. S. Mailliard, who had been my aide on the inspection tour, told me why we never found any liquor. As I left my cabin by one door, some reckless souls entered by another door with all the contraband liquor on the ship and stowed it there until the ship had been inspected, when it was returned to its former hiding places.

In general, living conditions aboard ship were much better than ashore. The ships were clean, there was decent plumbing, the food was better and, except when in port, there was freedom from insects and mosquitoes. But there was no protection from the sun's rays, which could penetrate the coarsest awnings. Ship life also had the disadvantage of being almost always in a state of combat readiness as the ships moved through enemy waters enroute to and from one assault operation after another. This meant the crews slept at their battle stations with their clothes on. Lack of sleep and frequent bombings wore down the stoutest hearts.

For the soldier or Marine who had been landed in an assault operation on an enemy-held beach, life was pretty rugged for the first month or two. Not only did he have to contend with the Japanese, he had to contend with deadly tropical diseases as well. Heat, mud, rain, jungle, and danger were all about him. There were far more casualties from disease than from Japanese bullets. But these conditions did not last unbearably long before the situation ashore would stabilize. The Japanese would withdraw from the area and our troops would develop a reasonably comfortable community life. Air raids would become a rarity, outdoor movies would be possible, civilian entertainment groups would arrive, and regular mail service would be established. A good many months might pass before they were again called upon to take part in a new assault operation.

Occasionally naval stations would be established ashore in some of the forward areas. They often had more trouble in providing comfortable campsites than did their Army compatriots. At the Naval Station at Finschhafen a newly arrived sanitary officer reported a most unsatisfactory condition of the "heads." He finally had one built with mahogany seats, beautiful surroundings, and good screening. "It was duly commissioned. It was so cozy it became sort of a clubhouse and flew its own pennant."

All things considered, there was probably little to choose between the soldier's life ashore and the sailor's life afloat. But there was one distinct advantage of those who lived aboard ship—they did not have to worry about the problems created when nurses, WACs and Red Cross workers began to arrive in the quieter sections of the combat zone ashore. Women were not fitted for the crude conditions of outdoor living. A few among thousands of men often led to trouble. They would have served their country better by remaining in the rear areas.

Native women were no problem. The majority were unattractive and some were repulsive, particularly those suffering from yaws. They wore grass skirts, with nothing above their waists. Women from the missions wore grass skirts down to the ankles; those employed on plantations had their names tatooed on their shoulders, and wore skirts at knee length.

Native villages were small—not over ten or twelve thatched huts—usually built near a stream or on the coast. Whenever fighting took place in their vicinity, the natives would disappear into the hills. When the situation had quieted, a few would drift back and attach themselves to the military as handymen.

A floor show at Buna was once staged by four "Fuzzy-Wuzzies" who did a war dance. After the dance they sang "Silent Night" in Pidgin English. Then they gave an encore of "Old Folks at Home," which they had learned from the missionaries in prewar days.

There were very few chaplains attached to the Amphibious Force. Some were excellent; some were too inexperienced and youthful to provide the counselling and spiritual guidance needed by young combat-hardened veterans. Not infrequently a sympathetic medical officer would satisfactorily take over the duties of an absentee chaplain.

One young chaplain who had been advised to work with the sick and wounded and illiterate in their correspondence with their families entered upon his duties conscientiously and perhaps too enthusiastically. One day he came in to see me, and then somewhat to my surprise, asked for my wife's address. He proposed to write her about what I was doing and how I was getting along.

On another occasion a different but youthful and fervent chaplain appeared on the bridge shortly before dawn as we led a convoy through a narrow channel into an enemy-held harbor, which we believed to be heavily mined. The men were all at their battle stations, tense and nervous in almost complete darkness. There was a strong probability that our first knowledge of the presence of Japanese would be shells crashing into the ship or mines detonating under the keel. It was under these circumstances of tension and strain that the chaplain asked for the use of the loud speaker to lead the crew in a short prayer.

The use of the loud-speaker system during the approach to battle is always reserved for messages of the utmost importance; but a short prayer might fill a needed void, and so the chaplain was told to go ahead. Unfortunately, his opening words were hardly comforting to a nervous and imaginative group of young men who were even then wondering if the next second would be their last. He asked whether each member of the crew in these fateful moments was prepared to meet his Maker. He was cut off the air.

War is a savage business. To every decent individual must come the difficult task of accommodating one's principles of human conduct with the brutalizing one of killing and destruction. To a chaplain the task of accommodation must be particularly difficult, perhaps impossible.

15: Admiralty Islands Operations

THE ADMIRALTY OPERATION STARTED OFF SIMPLY ENOUGH. TO complete the isolation of Rabaul, the Joint Chiefs of Staff had directed General MacArthur to undertake the capture of the Admiralty Islands and Hansa Bay on the New Guinea coast with the forces of the Southwest Pacific, and for Admiral Halsey to continue his movement up the Solomon Islands with South Pacific forces to capture the Japanese port of Kavieng.

In addition to its role in the isolation of Rabaul, there was an additional reason, and a very important one, for the occupation of the Admiralty Islands. They contained the fine big harbor of Seeadler which could be developed into a major naval and supply base, ideally located to support the Allied advance to the westward. As far as operations go, the Admiralty Islands affair did not amount to much, and yet the place in history of a great military man may have rested on its outcome.

The Admiralties group includes the main islands of Manus and Los Negros, and a number of smaller ones, about two degrees south of the Equator. The weather there is uncomfortably hot and sticky. The islands are situated about 220 miles north of Cape Gloucester and 345 miles northwest of Rabaul.

Kavieng, the other important link in the encirclement chain, was a heavily defended port on the western end of the island of New Ireland, but much closer to Rabaul—barely 160 miles to the northwestward.

With these two defense outposts in Allied hands, the northern and western gap in the encirclement of Rabaul would be effectively closed.

Hansa Bay, on the New Guinea coast and 140 miles to the westward of Saidor, was included in this series of operations because of its protective position with relation to the Admiralties, and also because it was a good stepping stone in MacArthur's advance to the westward.

In view of the exposed position of these three places, the Admiralties, Hansa Bay, and Kavieng, it was not advisable to undertake any amphibious operations against them without strong naval support from carriers, battleships, and cruisers to provide protection from the Japanese fleet which was then believed concentrated at Truk Island, 626 miles to the north. Admiral Nimitz had the necessary combat ships to provide this protection, but because of operations in the Central Pacific, he could not make them available until 1 April. And so the date of 1 April 1944, was tentatively set by the Joint Chiefs for the assault on the Admiralties and Kavieng. The Hansa Bay operation would take place about three weeks later. (There were not enough amphibious ships in the Southwest Pacific to carry out the Admiralty Islands and Hansa Bay operation on the same date, although that would have been desirable in view of the availability of the Pacific Fleet at that time.)

In January 1944, we had little positive information on Japanese strength in the Admiralties and the estimates by different intelligence officers varied widely from an optimistic one thousand to a pessimistic five thousand troops. (MacArthur's intelligence officer had submitted an estimate of slightly over four thousand). Whatever the number, it was not likely to change materially within the next few months in view of Japan's recent loss of Cape Gloucester and the uncertainty of their local air and sea control. Allied intelligence led us to believe that most enemy troops would be concentrated in the vicinity of the two airfields, one of which was on the small island of Los Negros immediately east of the larger Manus Island where the big airstrip was located. Although Manus and Los Negros were two islands, they were almost contiguous for a considerable part of their length, being separated only by a small, shallow strait. The separation between these islands widened at their upper end to form the magnificent Seeadler Harbor, which was entered from the north through a number of small coral islets. Between these islets there was only one good navigable entrance which was presumably well-protected by coastal guns hidden in the underbrush.

The First Cavalry Division had been designated by General MacArthur to make the assault. Other units would be added to the Division, including engineers and construction battalions, so that the total occupying force would approximate forty-five thousand men.

Early in January 1944, the 1st Cavalry Division under the command of Major General I. P. Swift moved from Australia to the jump-off base at Oro Bay on the north coast of New Guinea. The Division had no combat tradition more recent than

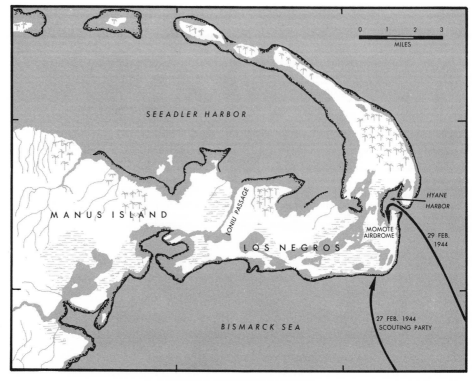

ADMIRALTY ISLANDS LANDINGS

the Indian Wars. During World War I, it had maintained the Mexican border patrol. The Cavalrymen were a spit and polish outfit, far ahead of any troops we had worked with heretofore. Their horses had been left in the States and as dismounted troops they had been undergoing amphibious and jungle training for the last few months at a site near Brisbane. They would have almost three months more to put the finishing touches on their training before going into combat. My flagship anchored in Oro Bay so that the amphibious planning staff could work closely with their planners.

It was quite satisfying to have almost ten weeks to prepare for the Admiralty landing. The last landing, at Saidor, had taken place during the preceding week. Six days before that we had landed the 1st Division of Marines at Cape Gloucester, and eleven days before that we had landed the 112th Cavalry at Arawe. Most of our ships were still fully engaged in the business of getting supplies to the combat areas, and would be for some time, but the hurry-up pressure on our force had eased enough to permit sending a number of ships to Australia for major overhaul, and allow others to undergo minor overhaul in the forward area. Some men—as many as could be spared from the operating ships—were being flown to Australia for short recreation periods. It was a happy interlude.

More good news came in the arrival of additional officers and men to help overcome the personnel shortage. The new arrivals included some officers for my staff, one of whom was Rear Admiral W. M. Fechteler, reporting for duty as my deputy. He had recently been promoted to flag rank and, although he had had no amphibious experience, that could soon be remedied.

After some preliminary arrangements, joint training and planning with the 1st Cavalry Division got under way. Plans called for the landing to be made on four beaches inside Seeadler Harbor. There seemed to be no other choice. Only inside Seeadler Harbor were there adequate beaches to support a major operation. The ocean side of both Manus and Los Negros islands was nearly inaccessible due to rocks, coral, and high surf. The only other possible landing site examined was small Hyane Harbor on the eastern side of Los Negros. But it was not much larger than a lagoon, with a small, sandy beach at the southern end. It was far too small for any operation of the magnitude we had in mind. Besides, its channel entrance was less than fifty yards wide—between unmarked coral reefs—and its maximum depth was only three fathoms. The approaches and beach were considered suitable only for small boats in a minor assault.

Before ships could safely enter the large Seeadler Harbor—fifteen miles wide by four miles long—the coastal batteries at the entrance would have to be destroyed, an uncertain business at best. And then there was the question of coral pinnacles and mines within the harbor. We knew the general location of the pinnacles but they were not buoyed, and we knew about the mines because they were U.S. mines—our own planes had dropped them there long before the date of the planned invasion. That called for extreme care in navigation and for minesweepers to precede the invasion force.

Joint plans for the 1 April landing were completed on 23 February 1944. This allowed ample time for all the different elements comprising the landing force to be assembled and for the Navy to get its ships fueled, loaded with ammunition and supplies, and dispersed to the various ports to pick up their particular quota of troops.

On 24 February, while the plans were still being distributed, an urgent dispatch was received from General MacArthur's headquarters which changed everything. In his dispatch, MacArthur directed that one squadron of the 1st Cavalry Division and some special detachments, about 882 men in all, be landed on Los Negros Island not later than 29 February, just five days hence. The dispatch referred to the landing as a "reconnaissance in force" and directed that the assault troops be carried in APDs, but if much shore opposition developed after the landing, the troops were to be withdrawn. General Krueger, who was then at Finschhafen, 140 miles away, was directed to coordinate the planning.

Also included in the dispatch was the information that, on the previous day, three

B-25 planes had flown to Los Negros and remained in the vicinity for over an hour, flying at times at treetop height. The pilots sighted no Japanese. The airfield was overgrown with grass. The island had probably been evacuated, although a small caretaker garrison might have been left behind.

The old "hurry up" was with us again. Within the next 3 days we would have to prepare another set of landing plans in conjunction with the Army, find some APDs not too far away and get them to Oro Bay, load them with troops, provide them with destroyer escorts and have them under way for an amphibious assault in the Admiralties, 500 miles to the north. It was quite a job. Only 3 APDs were available and they could carry a total of 510 troops, and that was not enough by nearly half. The 9 available destroyers would have to do double duty as troop transports, although they were totally unsuited for this role. (It is probably the only time in World War II that U.S. destroyers were used to carry troops in an amphibious assault.) After these preliminary arrangements had been agreed upon, General Swift and I, with a few of our staff, left by plane for General Krueger's headquarters.

MacArthur's decision to make a "reconnaissance in force" during the last week in February—five weeks ahead of the time scheduled for the full scale assault—was based on more far-reaching considerations than the immediate one of a local victory. He knew that the Joint Chiefs of Staff were even then considering the direction the Pacific war should take after the fall of the Admiralties, Kavieng, and Hansa Bay. Under examination were the opposing views of General MacArthur and the naval high command.

At every opportunity, MacArthur had advanced his theory that the quickest and least costly route to the defeat of Japan lay along the north coast of New Guinea and thence northwestward into the Philippines. He felt that this route was not only desirable from a military point of view, but that it fulfilled a moral obligation to liberate the Philippine people, at the earliest possible moment.

The naval point of view, as advocated by Admirals King and Nimitz, was that strategic considerations favored an island-hopping advance of the Fleet through the Central Pacific, capturing and establishing naval and air bases en route and containing or destroying the Japanese Fleet. The naval plan would bypass the Philippines and instead would make a landing on Formosa or on the north coast of China as the last step in the isolation of Japan. Both plans envisioned cutting Japan's supply lines to Southeast Asia, bombing her cities, and a final all-out assault on her beaches.

Supporters of each viewpoint had little sympathy for those of the others. MacArthur was quite outspoken and frequently voiced the opinion that "island-hopping with its great loss of lives is not my idea of the way to win the war," and would then cite as an example the heavy losses incurred by the Central Pacific forces in their assault on Tarawa.

Admiral Barbey welcomes a new arrival to his staff—Rear Admiral W. M. Fechteler reported for duty as his deputy early in 1944. Left to right: Rear Admiral Barbey, Rear Admiral Fechteler, the Officer of the Deck, Vice Admiral Kinkaid, and Captain Noble.

Coast Guardsmen unload trucks and other supplies onto landing barges destined for the beaches of Los Negros in the Admiralty Islands.

The decision of the Joint Chiefs of Staff as to future routes in the Pacific would carry with it the allocation of troops and ships and planes between the two areas. MacArthur well knew that if the decision favored the Central Pacific, the New Guinea operations might be his last and he would be left in solitude in the backwash of the war.

For Admiral Nimitz, the determination of the future direction of the war had less personal meaning, because the Pacific Fleet would always remain under his command. If the decision went against him, his island-hopping campaign would probably be cancelled and the Fleet would act in a supporting role of MacArthur's troops as they advanced along the New Guinea coast.

The political factor favored the New Guinea route if we were to keep faith with the guerrilla fighters in the Philippines and Indonesia. The military factors were less clear in determining the cost in lives and time of the two routes.

Along the New Guinea coast were a series of Japanese strong points, at Hansa Bay, Madang, and Wewak, with a total estimated enemy troop strength of more than fifty thousand. Beyond them was the Aitape-Hollandia area with probably another twelve thousand men from there on; every few hundred miles there were equally strong points lying across the route to the Philippines.

On the other hand, the route through the Central Pacific was marked by a series of presumably well-defended atolls, some of which would have to be taken by frontal assault to provide air and naval bases for the Fleet, and these assaults might prove costly and time consuming. There was considerable optimism within the forces commanded by Admiral Nimitz that future losses, in any attack on island bases, could be kept within acceptable limits. This optimism resulted from the successful carrier strike on Truk on 16 and 17 February which uncovered unsuspected Japanese weakness and probably indicated that other supposedly well-defended atolls might be similarly weak.

The carrier strike on Truk turned up the additional information—which was of immediate interest to MacArthur—that the main body of the Japanese fleet had withdrawn from the Truk-Rabaul area and apparently was concentrated far to the westward. This meant that MacArthur's troops could now be landed in the Admiralties without awaiting naval protection from the Pacific Fleet and gave MacArthur an independence of action he had not heretofore enjoyed.

While the future course of the Pacific war was under study by the Joint Chiefs, MacArthur had decided to submit for their consideration a bold new maneuver. It was based on a memorandum which had been prepared by his imaginative senior planning officer, Colonel Bonner Fellers. The Fellers' memorandum contained the daring type of operation that appealed to MacArthur's sense of the dramatic. The submission of this proposal was delayed pending the capture of the Admiralties when his military position would be more secure and consequently its acceptance more probable.

The proposal provided for the cancellation of the Hansa Bay operation, substituting instead a landing in the Hollandia area on the north coast of New Guinea—hundreds of miles to the westward of any previously considered operation. It would mean landing at a point that might be heavily defended and in between a number of Japanese strong points. It was a risky job and could only be undertaken under the protection of the Pacific Fleet, which would have to be interposed between the Hollandia landing force and the Japanese Navy. But the whole project would have to await the capture of the Admiralties and the establishment on them of allied bases.

With these thoughts in mind, MacArthur sent off his urgent 24 February 1944 order for a "reconnaissance in force" on the Admiralty Islands, just five days later. If "reconnaissance in force" developed into an immediate seizure of the islands, he would be in a good position to submit the Hollandia proposal to the Joint Chiefs while future Pacific strategy was still under consideration.

None of the commanders in the forward area liked any part of this "quickie" assault on the Admiralties. General Swift wanted a minimum of 2,200 troops in the initial assault. I did not like the idea of even a small amphibious landing—regardless of what it was called—relying solely on a few destroyers and APDs. We could not use the slower LSTs, LCIs, and LCTs, because they simply could not get there on time. They would have to come later. Because of the surf, no landing could be made on Los Negros from the open sea nor could our small force be sure of driving its way through the entrance into Seeadler Harbor. There was no alternative but to use small shallow, coral-infested Hyane Harbor, with its fifty-yard entrance and narrow beach.

General Krueger, always the cautious pessimist, liked the idea of a "reconnaissance in force" in Hyane Harbor even less than the rest of us but he was not the type to voice his objections. Whatever GHQ wanted he would attempt to carry out to the minutest detail without argument. Because of his disbelief in the air reports of Japanese troop strength on Los Negros, he requested a Navy seaplane to carry a small scouting group of one officer and five men to the island to obtain on-site information. They landed outside the surf on 27 February and made their way ashore in a rubber boat. Their disturbingly brief radio report received later that day led to some jittery moments.

While the scouting party was having a bad time reconnoitering on Los Negros, 3 APDs and 9 destroyers were being loaded to carry the assault troops from Oro Bay. A maximum of 1,026 troops was all that they could carry. It was a pretty meager force to go out on such an important mission. Only the lightest equipment—no vehicles or even kitchen gear—was carried and the men were restricted to bare essentials. Although the APDs had been converted to carry troops and light equipment, the destroyers had neither the boats nor space to carry troops. All of the 1,026 men and equipment would have to be landed ashore in the 12 boats carried by the APDs. This meant that the assault boats would not only have to carry ashore the men from their own APDS, but they would have to make a series of round trips under fire, through a narrow channel, to pick up the men from the destroyers lying outside the harbor. It was a long haul for the boats and an arrangement that nobody liked, but there was no alternative.

If all went well on the first day, a follow-up force of 1,500 combat troops and a naval construction battalion of 1,200, including some special detachments, would be sent forward, bringing the total to 3,726 men at the landing beach. The reinforcements were to be loaded aboard six LSTs and ready to sail, if ordered to do so, from Finschhafen on D-Day, 29 February. In addition to the troops, these LSTs would carry nine LCVPs and 2,500 tons of stores and equipment. Each LST would tow one LCM. Two minesweepers would accompany the convoy for possible use in big Seeadler Harbor if the entrance channel to that harbor was found to be undefended. The reinforcement convoy would go forward only after the results of the landing were known. It would take them close to 30 hours to make the 295-mile trip from Finschhafen.

Based on the information provided by GHQ, the planning instructions carried these paragraphs:

> The enemy is believed to have greatly reduced his strength in the Admiralty Islands and to be evacuating that area.
>
> In the event that little or no enemy opposition is encountered and the landing force is firmly established ashore (on Los Negros), the occupation and development of the Seeadler Harbor area and Momote airdrome (Los Negros) area will proceed. If resistance to the landing is too great, the landing force will withdraw.

During the final loading hours at Oro Bay on 27 February, the cruisers *Phoenix* and *Nashville* and four destroyers arrived from Brisbane. These could be used to augment our bombarding force at Hyane Harbor. General MacArthur and Admiral Kinkaid were aboard the *Phoenix,* and I went aboard to report the status of preparations. I told them I proposed to remain behind and complete the arrangements for the reinforcement echelon, and had designated my deputy, Rear Admiral Fechteler, to command the attack force. To my surprise, MacArthur turned to his aide and said in a somewhat irritated manner, "Substitute the name of Fechteler for that of Barbey wherever appearing in the communiqué." Apparently, the communiqué had been prepared although the landing had not yet taken place.

I gave General MacArthur and Admiral Kinkaid copies of the plans which had only been completed the day before. There was some concern among those present as to the correctness of the Air Force intelligence information.[1]

We could only guess at the reason MacArthur wanted to accompany this small "reconnaissance in force" operation. He had not taken part in any previous operations where the stakes were much larger. We guessed that he wanted to be present when the decision had to be made whether to continue the assault or to withdraw.

Late on the afternoon of the twenty-seventh, the little force of 3 APDs and 9 destroyers carrying 1,026 troops left Oro Bay for Hyane Harbor, 500 miles away. The next day they were joined by the *Phoenix* and *Nashville* with their 4 accompanying destroyers *Daly, Hutchins, Beale,* and *Bache,* which took position about 11 miles ahead.

After the convoy had sailed, a message was received from Krueger's scouting party which was still ashore at Los Negros: "Could not get to river—lousy with Japs." The alarming phrase, "lousy with Japs," could mean that our small assault force would run into serious trouble, but then again it might only mean that the scouts had sighted some pockets of Japanese whose total number might be in the low hundreds. We preferred to think that they could not have sighted any great numbers while dodging about in the jungle. At all events, there was no suggestion on anybody's part to change anything because of a cryptic message.

As far as we knew, the convoy had neither been followed or even sighted by snooper planes. All ships arrived in their assigned places outside Hyane Harbor shortly after dawn on 24 February. Boats from the APDs were loaded with their troops and headed for the narrow harbor entrance under cover of ships' gunfire and bombardment from shore-based aircraft. As the boats neared the entrance between the capes, they ran into some heavy machine-gun fire, but the destroyers soon silenced these enemy batteries and the boats were able to make their way into the harbor and then turn left toward a narrow, sandy beach two hundred yards away. Four men were killed and six wounded en route to the beach, but at the beach itself there was no opposition. The Japanese, caught by surprise and, wishing to get out of the area of bombardment, had backed into the jungle to reorganize. The first wave of boats hit the beach two minutes after the scheduled time and the other waves of boats followed a few minutes later. It was a precision operation that could only have been carried out by highly trained and experienced boat crews. And then came another bit of good luck. A heavy rain set in which shielded our small boats from gunfire as they

---

[1] From captured documents, it was later learned that the Japanese commander, Colonel Yoshio Ezaki, had issued orders for his troops to keep out of sight during daylight hours and that they were not to fire at any reconnaissance planes. The air strips were partly overgrown with grass as they had not been used recently, and the jungle was merely reclaiming its own.

returned to the destroyers for more troops to ferry through the narrow entrance channel. Good luck had almost become a trade mark of the operation.

The completeness of the surprise was shown by the hastily abandoned kitchens which were found within twenty-five yards of the water's edge. Within an hour and a half troops had captured the nearby Momote air strip and overrun a command post which contained many valuable documents. It began to look as if the operation would be a pushover. General MacArthur came ashore at 4 P.M., and with Brigadier General W. C. Chase, the troop commander, looked over the situation and then returned to the cruiser *Phoenix*. He immediately sent a dispatch ordering forward the reinforcements which were then waiting at Finschhafen. Shortly afterwards the two cruisers and their four accompanying destroyers left the area. At sundown Rear Admiral Fechteler departed with his ships except for two destroyers which were left behind to furnish gunfire if needed by the forces ashore.

But matters ashore were not turning out as smoothly as had been expected. Returning patrols brought General Chase the disquieting news that the enemy was in far greater strength than had been estimated earlier in the day. In the face of the new situation, General Chase withdrew his troops to a smaller perimeter, for his tiny landing force was now on its own and faced with a probable night attack from a much larger force. The attack came shortly before dawn. Fortunately, it was not well-coordinated and Chase's troops were able to hold their own, but in doing so they suffered far more casualties than they were prepared to handle. Captured Japanese mess tables were used as operating tables. Other wounded were ferried to the two destroyers lying offshore. The ranks of the American troops were getting thinner.

Intermittent fighting continued throughout the next day. At dusk on the second night, the Japanese again attacked, in greater numbers and with more determination than before. It was a bloody hand-to-hand affair in the murky jungle. General Chase narrowly escaped capture. Great issues depended on small group fighting and individual courage. There were moments when it appeared the Japs would overwhelm our troops, who could not retreat; their backs were to the sea and they had few boats. Throughout the night destroyers illuminated the Japanese areas and pounded them with five-inch gunfire.

When daylight came, the exhausted troops were exhilarated as they saw the reinforcement echelon of six LSTs approaching, commanded by Captain R. M. Scruggs. Near the channel entrance Scruggs embarked in a small boat which headed for the beach, but the coxswain was hit by sniper fire. Scruggs returned to the flagship and called to the skipper, "Give me another coxswain and give this one the purple heart." Scruggs then led his ships into the harbor where they beached, firing as they moved into position. The convoy had been escorted by three destroyers and two minesweepers, a most welcome addition to the naval gunfire support force.

Men of the 50th Coast Artillery fire on Japanese positions on Los Negros Island in the Admiralties.

To guard against possible ambush by Japanese snipers, each man on the alert position in this patrol boat carries a carbine. Natives pole the dugout through the jungle on Manus Island.

Seabees had landed, expecting to put the airfield in usable condition. But this was not to be. For the first few days they functioned as combat troops, using the blades of their bulldozers to dig trenches, bury the enemy dead, and provide a shield against Japanese bullets. The first night ashore they formed a part of the defensive perimeter. It was the third straight night of fighting for General Chase's weary men. Again the Japanese attacked and again in greater numbers and with greater ferocity. In defending their sector, the Seabees had ten men killed and fifty-nine wounded. The defensive perimeter was broken many times and often the decision was in doubt. During one bad point in the attack, the destroyers stationed off the harbor entrance were able to set up a barrage across a narrow strip of land that prevented the Japanese from the north from joining in the attack on our troops at the airfield. It may have been a decisive barrage.

Even after the arrival of Scruggs' reinforcement echelon, the situation remained so critical that General Chase sent urgent messages for help. General Krueger came aboard my flagship at Oro Bay on 3 March to see what could be done. He was worried, as were all of us. He wanted some additional combat troops to arrive at Hyane Harbor by the following morning. The only transports that could make the run overnight were the three APDs which had just returned from Hyane Harbor. Twelve hundred and fifty troops were loaded on them, and on some accompanying destroyers, and in a few hours they were on their way at high speed. The next day these troops had taken their places in the defense perimeter and some of General Chase's men could fall into an exhausted sleep after almost four days of continuous hand-to-hand fighting.

But the worst was now over for the troops ashore. The Japanese attack on the night of 3 March had been repulsed with such heavy losses that they could not again mount a sustained attack.

Reinforcements of men and ships were sent forward almost daily, and a few days later enough cruisers and destroyers were available to take under fire the coastal batteries guarding big Seeadler Harbor at the northern end of the islands. Within a week two minesweepers entered Seeadler Harbor and swept up eleven magnetic mines. Other ships entered to buoy the coral pinnacles and soon more ships arrived with additional reinforcements. From then on, it was a mopping up operation. The remnants of the Japanese garrison retreated to the hills, but it was not until 3 April that U.S. forces could properly say they were in complete occupation of Manus and Los Negros, and that naval support could be withdrawn.

That the operation succeeded was due to boldness and a lot of luck, and to the poor preparations and lack of organization on the part of the Japanese. For a time, however, it looked as if the operation had been headed for disaster.

Naval gunfire played a vital part in this perilous operation. When asked about naval support, General Chase replied: "They didn't support us; they saved our necks."

For the Seventh Amphibious Force the operation was over. There was no longer any danger from a Japanese naval or air attack, Liberty ships could safely enter Seeadler Harbor and the development of a big naval and air base was soon under way.

And so another assault landing was behind us. In all the others, plans were made on the assumption that the troops were going ashore to stay and reinforcements and schedules were laid out on that basis. But this one was different; maybe we would stay and maybe we would not. The Japs were to decide that.

The landing as originally scheduled for 1 April, with overwhelming force, would have overrun the islands in a few days with a minimum of casualties. Heavy air and naval bombardments would have preceded the landing and probably silenced any shore batteries. Minesweepers, survey ships, tugs, small boats, heavy equipment, artillery, supplies, reinforcements, and construction battalions would have been available when required. As it was, all these elements of a landing force went forward piecemeal, unscheduled, as ships were commandeered and urgent pleas were met.

Because of faulty intelligence and the need for haste, a small number of ships and troops was given an almost impossible assignment. In the first few days, the outcome was often in doubt. The fine leadership of General Chase and the courage of his men saved the day. The troops could not have been withdrawn. A disaster at Los Negros would have set back the Pacific campaign several months at least. The psychological effect of an American defeat on the Japanese would have been tremendous. MacArthur's ability as a military leader would have been questioned and his proposed campaign along the New Guinea coast might have been cancelled.

We learned later that the Japanese had about four thousand men in scattered defensive units throughout the two islands, all within easy supporting distance of each other. Fortunately, the Japanese commanding officer had felt sure that the weak landing in Hyane Harbor was but a diversionary attack and that the main effort would follow shortly at the entrance to Seeadler Harbor, and so he refused to concentrate his forces against General Chase during those first two critical nights when the outcome hung in the balance. Had he done so, there is little question that General Chase's force would have been overrun. After the second night it was too late, for reinforcements had arrived and Chase was saved.

Looking backward, I have often wondered if MacArthur ever questioned his own judgment in this matter.

16: Planning the Hollandia Operation

ON 5 MARCH 1944, GENERAL MACARTHUR RECEIVED THE WORD that he had been hopefully waiting for—U.S. troops were in firm control of both Los Negros and Manus islands. The uncertainty was now over and the Admiralty operation was destined to take its place among the spectacular amphibious successes of the war.

That same day MacArthur dispatched to the Joint Chiefs of Staff the proposal to cancel the Hansa Bay directive and substitute instead an attack on Humboldt Bay, Aitape, and Tanahmerah Bay. Also that day his Chief of Staff, Major General Sutherland, left by air for Washington to press for its adoption.

The proposal could not have been presented at a more opportune time. The newspapers were carrying glowing accounts of MacArthur's Admiralty campaign which the United Press called "one of the most brilliant maneuvers of the war." The Associated Press described it as a "masterful strategic stroke" and the London Sunday *Times* was equally enthusiastic.

If the Hollandia operation—the overall name for the attack on Humboldt Bay, Aitape, and Tanahmerah Bay—should be approved, the naval forces in the Southwest Pacific would need to be augmented by many types of ships from among those assigned to the Central Pacific. Most urgently required would be some big aircraft carriers to raid enemy airfields within striking distance of Hollandia, and small aircraft carriers to provide cover over the landing area. MacArthur's land-based planes were too far away and too short-legged to do the job. Large numbers of troop carriers, cargo ships, and escort ships would have to be borrowed to carry the nearly 80,000 men that would be involved. And a vital requirement was that a major part of the battleship and carrier strength of Nimitz's Fleet interpose itself between the Hollandia area and a strong Japanese task force reported to be concentrated at Palau, about two steaming days to the northwest.

To gain some preparatory time, MacArthur directed his senior commanders to undertake preliminary planning and submit estimates of troop, plane, and ship requirements with General Krueger as coordinater. As soon as we could get together, General Eichelberger and I with a few of our staff assembled at General Krueger's headquarters in Finschhafen and started work on an outline of a plan of attack and an estimate of our needs. A good bit of guesswork was involved as there was little reliable intelligence to go on. Within a few days, however, estimates were sent to MacArthur's headquarters, and a few days later Krueger, Eichelberger, and I were called to Brisbane to meet with Admiral Nimitz and his Chief of Staff, Rear Admiral Forest Sherman, who had flown in from Pearl Harbor upon approval of MacArthur's proposal by the Joint Chiefs of Staff. Tentative plans were reviewed and agreement reached as to the number of ships that Nimitz could loan MacArthur, the dates they would arrive, and the dates they would be returned to the Central Pacific. The date of return was an important consideration in view of some pending operations in the Central Pacific.

In addition to approving MacArthur's move into Hollandia, the Joint Chiefs of Staff in their directive of 12 March 1944, laid out the future course of the war in the Pacific. This provided for Nimitz's forces to occupy the Marianas beginning 15 June, and the Palau Islands beginning 15 September. The occupation of Mindanao by MacArthur's forces, supported by the Pacific Fleet, was scheduled to begin 15 November. These moves were "preparatory to a further advance to Formosa, either directly or via Luzon."

The Hollandia landing date was set for 22 April 1944. That meant all detailed plans must be completed within the next two weeks to permit their distribution to the 217 ships involved—which were scattered all over the Pacific—and give them time to assemble at their respective jump-off points to take on fuel, troops, ammunition, and cargo and move into assigned positions in the invasion convoys. Difficult adjustments had to be made in ship schedules as the Seventh Amphibious Force was still heavily engaged in supply operations to Gloucester, Saidor, and the Admiralty Islands. Liberty ships would have to take over these jobs much sooner than they normally would have done.

Joint planning posed more than the usual problems because of the great distances that separated the headquarters of General MacArthur and Admiral Nimitz and their various commanders. General MacArthur was in Brisbane, Australia. Admiral

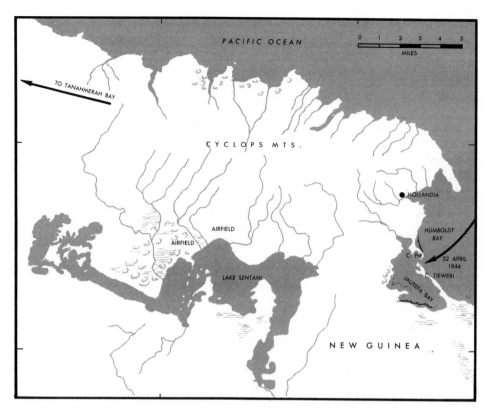

THE HOLLANDIA OPERATION

Nimitz was in Pearl Harbor. General Krueger, the commander of the Sixth Army who had been designated to coordinate all Allied planning in the Southwest Pacific, was at Finschhafen. General Eichelberger, who would command the ground forces, was at Goodenough Island, three hundred miles to the eastward. My flagship was anchored at Buna, about midway between the two places. Air Force headquarters was at Brisbane, and the headquarters of those bits of the Australian Navy that would operate under my command was at Melbourne. The various units of the Central Pacific Force that were involved were scattered from the Hawaiian Islands to the Solomons.

Considering the conditions under which our own small staff worked—stifling heat, loss of time and frustrations due to the separation of the various planning staffs, utilization of borrowed ships unfamiliar with our operating procedures, and the complexity of the problem—I consider it a remarkable achievement that the naval plans were completed and ready to be distributed in a period of eighteen days. On 6 April, eight hundred copies of the plans—which included detailed instructions to every unit involved—were mimeographed and on their way to everyone who needed to know.

Each ship had its own particular job. Some were sent to Finschhafen and Goodenough to conduct refresher amphibious training of combat troops. Others loaded stores and ammunition. Tankers moved from port to port to provide the needed fuel. Cargo ships were loaded with everything from paving material to bulldozers. Hospital ships, salvage tugs, minesweepers, floating dry docks, and other miscellaneous types were assembled and readied for action.

This increased activity was duly noted and reported by Japanese reconnaissance planes. We learned later that the Japanese correctly guessed that a new invasion was imminent, but incorrectly guessed its destination. Rabaul was considered a likely point, but they also considered Hansa Bay or perhaps Wewak—somewhat further to the west—as probable attack areas. Defenses at those places were built up, their garrisons alerted, and search planes guarded the approach zones. Hollandia was not in the area of probabilities as it was believed to be too far to the westward, and so its defenses were neglected. It was a backstop and supply base for Hansa Bay, Wewak, and other Japanese strong points to the eastward, and so its planes, airfields, and supply dumps were expanded with that purpose in mind.

To fill in some of the intelligence gaps regarding the Hollandia area, Lieutenant Jim Gratiot of my staff embarked in the submarine *Dace* on 18 March for a photographic reconnaissance of the beaches. The ship remained in the area for two days while the shoreline was photographed, soundings made, reefs plotted, and tidal data gathered. The *Dace* also carried a small scouting party of "coast watchers" made up of seven Australians and four natives under the leadership of the picturesque "Bluey" Harris. They were to remain ashore until picked up by a submarine two weeks later. It was hoped that any important information they would gather would be sent back by means of portable radios which they carried. Unfortunately, they were betrayed by some local natives and ambushed by Japanese. "Bluey" Harris and four others of his party were killed outright. The other six members escaped to the jungle and led a hunted and near starvation existence until Allied troops landed one month later. One of the survivors, with a harrowing tale, arrived alongside my flagship in a native canoe shortly after we had anchored in Tanahmerah Bay. He thought he was the only survivor of the Harris party.

For the first time in the Seventh Amphibious Force's series of joint operations with the Army Air Force, planning liaison was on a satisfactory basis. Not infrequently in the past there was uncertainty as to just what air support could be expected and the liaison officers who were assigned to us were too junior in rank to commit their seniors. But this time it was different. Some senior amphibious force planning officers were assigned to the Army Air Force staff and some senior planning officers of their staff were assigned to the amphibious staff. This welcome exchange helped each force to understand better the capabilities and limitations of the other. It may have been furthered by the fact that naval air officers from the Pacific Fleet were temporarily assigned to the Seventh Amphibious Force staff to assist in the planning, use, and control of carrier-based planes.

During the planning phase we were heartened by a series of heavy air raids by the Army Air Force which virtually neutralized the Japanese air fields at Hansa Bay, Wewak, and Aitape. These were followed by long-range bomber attacks on the Hollandia air base which caught a large number of enemy planes on the ground. And then Vice Admiral Mitscher's carrier planes from the Pacific Fleet swooped in and finished up where the Army Air Force had left off. There would be no squadrons of Japanese planes to hamper operations as they had done at Lae, Finschhafen, Arawe, and Gloucester.

Two hundred and seventeen ships of miscellaneous types would be available to the Seventh Amphibious Force to transport, protect, and put ashore 79,800 Army and Air Force personnel. These would be landed in jungle territory where there were few roads and little food, and in the face of an enemy of uncertain strength. The plans called for all the men plus 50,000 tons of supplies, 232 boats belonging to the Army Engineers, and 3,000 vehicles to be landed in the first 3 days. The ships would then return to the rear area for more men and supplies.

Some troops would have to be transported more than a thousand miles from embarkation point to the landing beach. Some would have to be transported in LCIs which were hardly suitable for anything longer than an overnight trip. But we had no substitutes. All Seventh Amphibious Force ships and all those borrowed from the Central Pacific Force were pressed to do just a bit more than they were designed to do. Some of the ships would not see each other until they met at a rendezvous point on the convoy's route.

The plans provided for three simultaneous landings to be made shortly after daylight on 22 April 1944 by three separate task forces at three different places—one at Hollandia (Humboldt Bay), one at Tanahmerah Bay, and one at Aitape.

Hollandia was a little town facing Humboldt Bay—a potentially fine harbor providing anchorage for a large number of ships. The bay contained a few small beaches and a jetty. Japanese headquarters were located in Hollandia and it was probable that any defenses they had would be concentrated in that area. Thirty miles to the westward and across a mountainous ridge was Tanahmerah Bay, the second landing point, with two short, narrow beaches backed by a swampy terrain. No Japanese defenses had been sighted in this area.

On a plateau about ten miles inland, and equidistant from Humboldt Bay and Tanahmerah Bay, were three good airfields. MacArthur wanted those airfields and the good harbor in Humboldt Bay to support his further operations to the westward.

Four U.S. commanders meet aboard a U.S. destroyer during the Hollandia operation. Left to right: Rear Admiral Daniel E. Barbey, U.S. Navy, in charge of Seventh Amphibious Force operations; Major General Horace Fuller, U.S. Army, commanding 41st Division; Rear Admiral William M. Fechteler, U.S. Navy, deputy commander of amphibious forces; Lieutenant General Robert L. Eichelberger, U.S. Army, commander I Corps.

Men about to participate in the Hollandia landing are briefed aboard an LST en route to the invasion areas. As many as 600 to 800 troops were frequently carried on one LST, together with their equipment.

High-altitude aerial photograph of the Humboldt Bay-Hollandia area under bombing attack.

Humboldt Bay-Hollandia area, low-altitude aerial reconnaissance photograph. Smoke in the distance is from a bombing attack.

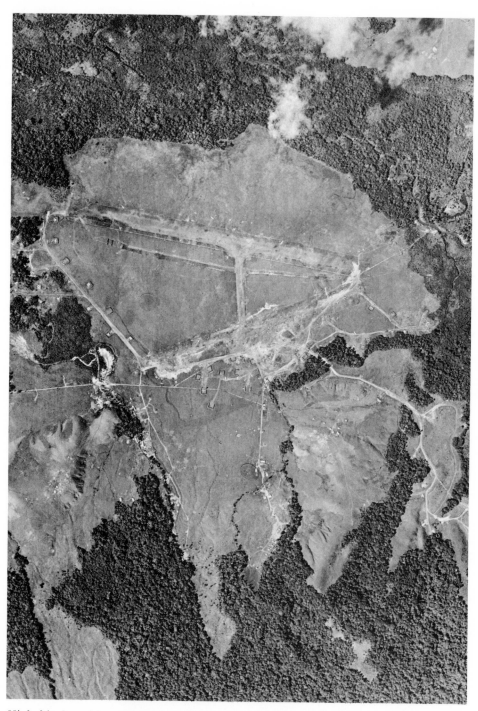

High-altitude aerial reconnaissance photograph (31,500 feet) of the Hollandia airfield, taken shortly before the invasion. General MacArthur needed the airstrips to support his further operations to the westward.

The third landing would take place at Aitape, 120 miles to the eastward. A small air-field nearby could be useful and there was the need to establish a military force in that area to protect MacArthur's eastern flank from possible attack by the strong Japanese forces at Wewak.

Usually, with the planning completed by the amphibious commander's staff, the next step in the procedure cycle would be the assignment of those plans to the various task force commanders whose staffs would prepare more detailed plans for their particular part of the overall operation. But this was not so for the Hollandia operation.

On completion of the planning, my staff was divided into three sections—each assigned to a task force organized to carry out one of the three landing jobs. To help fill out the requirements for these improvised task force staffs, officers and men were drawn from training and rear area activities. The Deputy, Rear Admiral W. M. Fechteler, was given command of the Humboldt Bay task force; the Chief of Staff, Captain A. G. Noble, was given command of the Aitape task force; I assumed local command of the Tanahmerah Bay task force with supervisory command of all three task forces.

Unfortunately for the smoothness of transferring some staff members from a headquarters job to a task force job, instructions were received from General MacArthur on 10 April—four days after the completion of our plans—that it might be necessary to extend operations to the Wakde area immediately after the landing at Hollandia. General Krueger was directed to submit, prior to 22 April, a summary of naval, air force, and army requirements for this new operation. In effect this meant preparing tentative plans and requirements for an entirely new operation before we sailed for Hollandia, and by a staff that was even then being dispersed to new duties.

Wakde is a small island a few miles off the New Guinea coast and about 115 miles to the westward of Hollandia. The Japanese had built a small airfield on Wakde and also some airfields on the mainland, a bit further to the westward. It was feared that planes from these fields might harass our efforts to develop the Hollandia area into a naval and air base.

Tentative plans and estimated requirements for a Wakde landing were submitted to MacArthur's headquarters a few days later, but they were not very satisfactory to any of us for they were based on very meager information regarding tides, shoals, navigational hazards, and enemy defenses. The one encouraging feature of the proposed operation was the intelligence information that the enemy garrison was not believed to exceed five hundred men. But experience in the Admiralties landing had made us a bit wary of some intelligence information.

Those staff members not engaged in the Wakde planning took part in the rehearsals for the Humboldt Bay-Tanahmerah Bay-Aitape landing, which were held in the vicinity of Goodenough and Finschhafen from 8 to 10 April. So many ships had to be brought together from great distances that there was little time left for a thorough job, and rehearsals were quite incomplete in many details. However, assault troops practiced getting from a landing craft to the beach while wading through the surf with heavy packs on their backs and rifles held aloft. The shore organization was tested, and in two cases the coordination of rocket fire and air attack to cover the final approach to the beaches was given a good workout. As usual, none of the commanders was quite satisfied with the shortness of the training period.

To disguise U.S. intentions as to the real landing area, the first convoy to Hollandia was to sail north from Finschhafen to the Admiralty Islands, then west until opposite the landing beaches. While this was two hundred miles longer than the direct route, there was less chance of detection by Japanese reconnaissance planes that would be searching off the New Guinea coast. Also, this route provided a rendezvous point in the Admiralty Islands where the LCIs could assemble a day ahead of the main body. This layover time permitted troops to be disembarked from their cramped quarters and exercised on the beaches before continuing on the long trip to Humboldt Bay, Aitape, and Tanahmerah Bay.

Just before the ships of the Seventh Amphibious Force dispersed to their various rendezvous points, a disquieting dispatch was received from the Navy Department that demanded immediate disciplinary action against a young ensign in my command. While on duty on the New Guinea coast, he had committed the unpardonable act of sending the skull of a Japanese soldier to a young lady, who had foolishly allowed herself to be photographed with it. The International Red Cross and the State Department were deeply concerned. The implications were serious. The Navy Department demanded that the culprit be found and stern disciplinary action be taken.

The officer was quickly found, but prompt disciplinary action was something else again. Such action called for a General Court Martial to be convened, senior officers to be designated as members, attorneys appointed, briefs prepared, and all the other time-consuming features of a trial arranged, for even in time of war the rights of the accused must be carefully protected.

But there was no time for all these niceties of legal procedure. Ships were taking off in every direction for a major amphibious landing. Something less formal, less drastic, and much speedier would have to be substituted. The officer was brought before the commander of the Seventh Amphibious Force, reprimanded and transferred out of the area. A radio dispatch was then sent to the Navy Department advising that disciplinary action had been taken, but omitting all details. The flagship then sailed for Hollandia and observed strict radio silence which had the advantage of not having to answer awkward questions.

17:

Hollandia
22 April 1944

ON 17 APRIL 1944, FIVE DAYS BEFORE D-DAY, THE SLOW SHIPS AND those furthest from the rendezvous point sailed from their various staging areas. Shortly after daylight on 20 April (D minus 2 day) the assault convoy of 164 ships joined up at a point northwest of the Admiralties. The second and third convoys were following at 24-hour intervals.

The assault convoy formed a special circular cruising disposition with a diameter of thirty miles. Radar picket ships were stationed ten miles ahead and on each flank of the destroyer screen to provide early warning of approaching enemy aircraft. To facilitate the separation of each task force when the time came for them to head for their respective beaches, the Western (Tanahmerah Bay) Task Force was placed in the center, the Central (Humboldt Bay) Task Force on the right flank, and the Eastern (Aitape) Task Force on the left flank. The convoy speed was maintained at nine knots because of the slow LSTs. Fortunately the weather was overcast, which made it difficult for enemy aircraft to pick up our movement.

A Japanese plane had sighted one section of the convoy while it was en route to the Admiralties. Apparently that convinced the Japanese the convoy was headed northward for Truk, or perhaps eastward to Rabaul or Kavieng. At all events, the next day (D minus 2), enemy planes from Truk searched the area behind the convoy but never made contact, that day or subsequently. Again we were blessed with luck.

Carrying out the procedure of previous landings, I used a destroyer—this time, the destroyer *Swanson* (DD-443)—as operational flagship. Embarked with me was

Lieutenant General R. L. Eichelberger who was in direct command of the ground forces of the Western and Central attack forces. Lieutenant General Walter Krueger, the overall commander of the ground forces, was embarked in the destroyer *Wilkes,* and General MacArthur was embarked in the cruiser *Nashville.*

There were anxious moments, the second night out, when radar contact was made with a large number of unidentified ships directly ahead of the convoy. All ships went to General Quarters. It could be the Japanese fleet which had eluded Admiral Mitscher's carrier task force operating somewhere to the westward. Because of radio silence, we did not dare inquire. After a suspenseful half hour the pips disappeared from the radar screen; we learned later the contact was with Mitscher's carrier task force.

Shortly before nightfall on D minus 1, the Eastern Task Force—sixty-seven ships under Captain Noble—left the main convoy and headed for Aitape. The Central Task Force with Rear Admiral Fechteler left a short time later and headed toward Humboldt Bay. The Western Task Force continued on its way toward Tanahmerah Bay. As far as we knew, the convoy had not been sighted by any snooper plane or submarine, nor had the two reinforcement convoys behind us been sighted.

The approach was favored by a continuation of overcast sky and gentle breeze. The only ripples on the water were caused by the movement of the ships as each one sought to arrive in its assigned position at the exact moment before dawn. It would be unwise to become silhouetted against the dawn sky before we were ready to open fire. General Eichelberger joined me on the upper bridge of the *Swanson.* Both of us wore life jackets, as did everyone else. We reviewed our plans and wondered if we had provided for all foreseeable contingencies. We speculated on the possibility that the convoy had been sighted and might even then be sailing into a trap.

The conversation shifted to less important matters, such as the cost and nuisance of replacing the life jackets which would disappear before the day was over. The Navy had taken upon itself the job of providing a life jacket for every soldier it carried, and the soldier in his turn was obligated to wear the jacket until he was safely on the beach. He would then leave it in a convenient place for the naval beach party to pick up and return to the ship for use by another soldier in another landing.

Unfortunately, the GIs had found out, as had their Aussie counterparts, that the life jacket was a very useful article ashore. It could be used as a pillow or as a lining to a fox hole, and undoubtedly for many other purposes of which the Navy had no knowledge. At all events, the Navy never recovered more than a small proportion of the life jackets that left the ships, and we assumed that today would be no exception.

I had not seen much of Eichelberger since the wind-up of the Buna campaign more than a year previously. In spite of his fine job in that operation, he had been assigned to unimportant training duty in Australia where he had fretted his time away.

Because of his outspoken, critical, and sometimes belligerent manner, he had not endeared himself to the top command in the Southwest Pacific. But now he was back on combat duty again and I enjoyed our close association.

As dawn broke on D-day, every pair of eyes on every ship was strained toward the shore. With binoculars, I compared the contour of the hills and the shoreline with the photographs taken by the submarine *Dace* just a month before. Yes, we were right "on the beam" and I was ready to give twenty years of my life if the convoy could get in close enough to open fire before being discovered, fired upon, and perhaps blown out of the water.

Cruisers, destroyers, and rocket ships were in their assigned firing positions, and transports prepared to lower their boats. It seemed unbelievable that all those ships had arrived off the beaches and that the Japanese had not sighted them and opened fire with their coastal batteries. The wait for each ship to reach its assigned position seemed painfully long. And then the signal was given—a flare went up and every combat ship let go with its guns simultaneously, each gun on its own pin-pointed target. In the half-light it was a gorgeous spectacle.

Small landing boats, alligators, and buffaloes loaded with troops headed for the beach. It was the first combat experience for many of the troops; they were frightened and shivering, and each probably quite convinced that some Japanese bullet had his name on it. To the old-timers—anyone who had been on a former landing—there was less concern for each had become convinced that no Japanese bullet was meant for him.

When the boats and amphibious tractors were half way to the beach, the guns stopped firing and the carrier planes, in a perfectly timed attack, completely covered the beach area with bombs and machine guns.

Through binoculars we could follow the small ships of the special service group as they fanned out into their assault positions. These were the mine sweepers, the tugs, and salvage craft that would provide the equipment to blow up reefs, buoy channels, mark beaches, and help out any landing boat that got into trouble.

The shore-bound boats were flanked by LCIs, each equipped with 288 rockets, fire equipment, and smoke bombs. So successful had these craft been at Cape Gloucester that Commander Dwight Day was now in command of an improved version of an entire group of these craft which he had developed.

Just before the troops hit the beach, the planes stopped their attack and the rocket ships opened fire. The rockets were far more devastating than the planes and guns because of the concentration of their plunging fire in the landing area. When the rocket fire stopped, the troops could be seen stepping from the boats onto the beach.

The Japanese offered no organized shore opposition, which was quite understandable considering the lack of fixed defenses and the surprise nature of the landing.

*An LST, crammed with heavy fighting equipment, supplies, and troops, approaches the
assault beach at Tanahmerah Bay, 21 April 1944.*

*Japanese shipping takes the brunt of the "softening up" bombing of the Humboldt Bay
area prior to the landing.*

Occasionally, we would hear some scattered rifle firing, and there were a few machine-gun bursts from an islet in the bay, but this was quickly silenced by a few rounds from the *Swanson*. Our troops found a few uncompleted pillboxes on the beach but that was all. It seemed more like a rehearsal than the real thing. But we had learned from experience that lack of opposition at the shoreline did not mean we would be free from opposition further inland.

At Tanahmerah Bay, General Eichelberger and I anxiously awaited word from Aitape and Humboldt Bay as to the progress of those landings. We soon learned that there, too, they had met with little opposition at the shoreline. However, they reported evidence of large garrisons, mostly service troops. These apparently had panicked and left behind their personal possessions, half-eaten meals, weapons, and supplies. In a few cases, U.S. troops found the remains of the Japanese gun crews in their pits, burned from the searing fire of the rockets. It was believed that the Japanese garrison, estimated at 12,000, had escaped into the jungle, but would reorganize and establish a new line of defense.

Prisoners—and there were an unusually large number of them—told of their complete surprise at the landings. They were so certain we would not land in their area that when the naval gunfire burst upon them the commanding officer was paralyzed into inaction and his troops panicked in fear.

This certainty on the part of the Japanese that there would be no assault operation in the Humboldt Bay area undoubtedly accounted for the lack of beach obstacles or underwater mines. Their defenses had been constructed to ward off an attack from the air. The ground defenses in the Aitape area were no better. Those at Tanahmerah Bay were merely the outposts of coastal patrols.

Shortly after noon of D-day, General MacArthur came into Tanahmerah Bay aboard the cruiser *Nashville*. Immediately after the ship anchored, he assembled his senior commanders for a visit to the beach. Besides the General and myself, there were Generals Krueger, Eichelberger, and a few members of our staffs. When about halfway to the beach, a signalman in the boat received a message from the *Nashville* that a Japanese plane was headed in our direction.

I ordered the coxswain to head for the nearest destroyer to get the protection of her guns. An open boat without protection seemed hardly the place to concentrate most of the brass of the Southwest Pacific when there was a Japanese plane on the loose. MacArthur, however, thought otherwise. He asked that I direct the boat to continue to the beach, which I did. A few minutes later a lone plane came in, swooped over us, then continued on in the direction of Hollandia. In thinking about this incident and similar ones at other times, there was never the feeling that it was an act of bravado on MacArthur's part, but rather that he was a man of destiny and there was no need to take precautions.

The pre-landing intelligence information regarding the two Tanahmerah beaches was very poor. Contrary to expectations, one of the beaches, the main beach, was not only narrow but backed up by an impassable swamp. Our understanding that a path connected the two beaches was erroneous. There was none. Supplies kept piling up on the narrow strip of sand and the troops were unable to move ahead or very far on either side.

The other beach was fronted by patches of coral that made it unusable except by amphibious tractors and small boats at high tide. The path that was supposed to lead from the second beach to Japanese airfields at Lake Sentani proved to be an almost impassable jungle trail. Because the beach conditions at Humboldt Bay were reported to be in much better condition, General Eichelberger requested that further troop landings and cargo unloadings be made in that area.

Lack of detailed aerial reconnaissance was directly responsible for the faulty troop and cargo dispositions. Fortunately, there were no serious consequences, but that was only because of the weakness of the Japanese defenses.

On completion of the inspection of the Tanahmerah beaches, MacArthur's party returned to the *Nashville* for a brief review of the day's happenings. Reports were being received from Humboldt Bay and Aitape that troops in those areas were rapidly moving inland against practically no opposition. At this time MacArthur made another of his startling proposals. In view of the apparently overwhelming success of the day's operations, why not continue on to the Wakde area—140 miles further along—and strike the Japanese there while they were still off balance? The troops to be used in the assault would be some of those 45,000 reinforcements then en route to the area and due within the next 48 hours.

He asked me if the Navy could carry out its part of such an operation. I was all for it and told him that our preliminary planning had already been done and that such changes as would be necessary could be done by radio. General Krueger was noncommittal, but General Eichelberger was vehemently opposed to the idea. He pointed out that our initial success did not mean we would not run into heavy fighting later and that it would be dangerous to take on another operation before this one was further along. Eichelberger still had bloody memories of the Japanese combat capabilities in the Buna campaign some fifteen months before. As he was to learn later, however, their capabilities had greatly deteriorated since those hard-fought days.

After listening to the various arguments, MacArthur decided to defer the attack on Wakde for the time being and continue to carry out the present operation as previously planned. His decision may have been influenced by the near disaster that had almost overtaken the Admiralty campaign owing to hasty planning and faulty intelligence.

A U.S. Navy plane cruises high to provide air cover for the amphibious craft far below, headed toward the landing beach at Tanahmerah Bay, 21 April 1944.

American troops, helmeted and carrying their fighting packs, ready to land as soon as the ramp drops on the enemy beach at Aitape.

Bird's-eye view of the opening stages of the assault on Hollandia, 23 April.

Not long after the assault troops had landed at Humboldt Bay, strange groups of people came out of the jungle. Among them were 120 emaciated, turbaned Sikhs who had been captured by the Japanese at Singapore and brought to Hollandia as slave laborers. There also emerged an almost equal number of half-starved and sick missionaries of many nationalities and faiths, including a few nuns. The Sikhs were bitter at their harsh treatment and wanted to join our armed forces to get their revenge. All the refugees were taken aboard ships, fed, clothed, and sent to Australia. The Sikhs were later returned to India.

One problem that always plagued every operation and one that neither the ground forces nor the Navy seemed able to overcome was the dispersal of supplies from the beach area. The Army naturally wanted as many tons of supplies as the Navy could deposit on the beach, in the shortest possible time after the assault personnel landed. Unfortunately, the beaches were usually small and narrow, and exits were few and difficult to construct. Humboldt Bay, although far better than Tanahmerah Bay, was no exception. Soon the beaches were piled high with thousands of tons of our own supplies, plus those abandoned by the departing Japanese—an inviting target for any marauding plane.

And then happened what we hoped would not happen. On the second night of the landing a lone Japanese plane dropped a stick of bombs right in the middle of the congested beach area. The resulting explosions and fires among the gasoline storage and ammunition dumps continued for four days. No ships were lost but twenty-four men were killed outright and one hundred were seriously burned—which was more casualties than was suffered in the landings on all beaches on D-day. Twelve precious LST loads of cargo went up in smoke. The fires were finally extinguished by the fire-fighting LCIs which had been especially equipped for use in just such an emergency.

Another victim of plane attack, the cargo ship *Etamin,* resulted from the beach congestion that occurred in the Aitape area. She had arrived with the first convoy on D-day, and anchored off shore awaiting discharge. Priority in unloading was given to the LSTs because they could discharge their cargo directly to the beaches over bow ramps. Soon the small beaches were overcrowded and the cargoes on the big freighters, which had to be lightered to the beach, remained aboard until the situation ashore cleared up.

Five days after arrival, the *Etamin* was still only half unloaded. Shortly before midnight on 27 April, three Japanese planes came in undetected and one made a torpedo hit on the *Etamin.* Quick action by her crew saved the ship. She was later made sufficiently seaworthy to be towed to Finschhafen. That was the only damage of any consequence to the 217 ships involved in the Hollandia-Aitape operation.

Some of the differences between Seventh Amphibious Force landing technique and the text book procedure were the short time allotted to ship bombardment, the lack of reliance on shore-based air support, and the simplicity of beach party organization. Because of the small size of the beach party group, their importance may be overlooked. Our beach parties were organized, trained, and standardized as the outgrowth of a series of trial-and-error procedures.

Lieutenant Commander E. R. Halloran headed the beach party in the assault at Tanahmerah Bay. What he reported was but little different from that taking place in the other landing areas. The extracts quoted indicate the role played by one of the many small units operating within a command, each doing its part. They were little known outside their own sphere of activities:

Three officers and seventeen men assigned Beach Party #3 for duty Tanahmerah Bay. Spent two weeks with combat teams. Indoctrinated in all phases of plans. Personnel and equipment (including such unrelated items as tree climbers, explosives, and walkie-talkies) divided among five boats to avoid possibility of losing all during assault if concentrated in one boat. D-day reveille at 0300. Mess at 0330. Filled canteens and boarded boats at 0400. Final inspection of men, boats, and equipment by beachmaster.

0400 party descended ship's ladders in utter darkness to enter assigned boats. Army troops still milling all around, each heavily loaded with personal gear and combat equipment, and stumbling into their particular seats. Sea choppy. Visibility zero. Difficult to get all boats into proper position. Ship bombardment commenced at 0600. Boats headed for starting line, 9,000 yards from Beach #2. On signal boats under way for beach. Ship bombardment stopped and plane bombardment commenced. When plane bombardment stopped, rocket bombardment started. Rocket bombardment stopped at 0700 and troops stepped on beach. No opposition to landing. Beachmaster set up his command post in center of Beach #2 at 0710, and established communications with his flanks, ships afloat, and with boats of the hydrographic section who were taking soundings offshore. Beach staked out with markers, indicating where boats and ships should land. Hydrographic section reported beach gradients satisfactory for dry ramp landings of LSTs. All LSTs notified to start de-waterproofing all vehicles for fine sandy beach landing. Navy medical unit set up. Slots for LSTs staked out. Sandy shoal 5 feet deep, 10 yards from shoreline. Flagship advised. [We got this information aboard the *Swanson* at 0719, just 19 minutes after the first troops stepped ashore.]

Beachmaster notified flagship that Beach #1 was only 35 to 40 yards wide which was backed by a small stream 9 to 15 yards wide and running parallel to it, and beyond it was a swamp 300 yards wide. Due to coral obstacles fronting Beach #1, necessary for troops to make assault in buffaloes (amphibian tractors). Met by weak gunfire. Area defended by small number of troops. All fled but one. He was shot. Enemy abandoned one mortar, 7 officer's swords, a number of rifles and considerable ammunition. Troops moving slowly up rugged trail toward air strip. Army engineers attempting to bridge stream and swamp. Progress slow. Road that was supposed to connect Beaches #2 and #1 nonexistent. Troops being moved from Beach #2 to Beach #1 by boat over coral at high tide. Beach party demolition section started blasting channel through 600 feet of coral reef to permit boat access to beach at all tides. Heavy rains commenced at 1400 hampering all cargo handling and bogging down land transport. Transports *Henry T. Allen, Kanimbla,* and *Manoora* completely unloaded at 1442, ahead of schedule, and they sailed for rear area. Air alert at 1500 [this was the alert that was sounded while General MacArthur was en route to beach in the landing boat]. LSTs manned their guns. Shore party continued unloading without interruption. At 1552 all clear signal given. Last of LSTs unloaded at 2035. At 2100 beach party dug fox holes and watch set for night. Conference with Shore Party Commander regarding next day's schedule. Secured at 2330. Next morning at 0600 started moving supplies from Beach #2 to Beach #1 to take advantage of high tide. LSTs continued arriving. Beach congested with supplies.

Sergeant on reconnaissance south of beach took Japanese prisoner, an aviation officer, and with help of a Fuzzy-Wuzzy (native) and an outrigger canoe brought him to the beachmaster at 0900. Two infantrymen, just landed, rushed at the prisoner with their bayonets, forcing the beachmaster to draw his .45 to protect the prisoner. Prisoner sent under guard for treatment of his wounds to Beach Medical Officer, Lieutenant Commander E. C. Klein.

For eleven days, Lieutenant Commander Halloran and his beach party worked with naval ships and army troops. The party was small in numbers, but mighty in accomplishment. At noon on 3 May, they closed camp and returned to the rear area to resume training and preparations for a new landing.

While Beach Party No. 3 was struggling with the congestion at Tanahmerah Bay, Eichelberger and I, with our staffs, moved to Humboldt Bay aboard my flagship. In accordance with prior understanding, I would retain command of the task force until the troops were firmly established ashore. This took place on the third day after the landing and I prepared to leave the area.

In Hollandia, General Eichelberger and I visited the small one-story building which had served as the headquarters of the Japanese commanding general. The tiny office was cluttered with overturned furniture and scattered papers. A large chest was filled with paper money. On one side of each bill were Japanese characters; on the reverse side English lettering designated its value in pounds, shillings, or pence. Since the natives of New Guinea did not use money, we assumed the bills had been printed for use in Australia when and if it was captured.

While we were both still aboard my flagship, Captain Arleigh Burke came aboard with a message from Admiral Mitscher. Burke was then Chief of Staff to Admiral Mitscher, whose fast carrier task force had protected our western flank and made some highly successful raids on nearby Japanese air bases.

Mitscher advised that his force was leaving the area to resume scheduled operations in the Central Pacific. Eichelberger wanted me to request Mitscher to remain and conduct more air strikes to the westward. It was a precautionary move, but I did not think it was justified by the existing situation.

MacArthur and Nimitz had agreed that Mitscher's task force would be released as soon as the landing phase of the operation had been completed, barring some unusual complications. So far there had been none and so I would not request any extension. It was the only time that Eichelberger and I disagreed on any matter of importance during many days of association in the campaigns in the Pacific.

From then on, the Navy's job in the Hollandia-Aitape area consisted only of bringing in more troops and supplies and building a naval base at Humboldt Bay, but the Army had much hard fighting ahead, particularly in the Aitape area. The Japanese troops in Wewak, which had been bypassed, made a difficult overland march of ninety miles and reached the outskirts of the Aitape area during the early days of July. Nearly ten weeks was taken for this hazardous jungle trek, a journey they could have made along the coast in one night in small boats if they had not lost control of the sea to roving PT boats. Twenty thousand Japanese continued their attack on Aitape for almost a month before they withdrew, a beaten and disorganized mob. They tried to make their way through the jungle to points of safety, but disease, lack of food, and harassment by Allied troops and nature took their toll. Few of them survived to the end of the war.

While the Army was fighting ashore and developing airfields, the Navy continued the job of carrying reinforcements and supplies and building a naval base. The period of probable quiet ahead provided me time for a quick trip to Washington to present our case for more ships and more personnel. The borrowed ships had been returned to the Central Pacific and the Seventh Amphibious Force, again on its own, not only needed replacements of men and ships if the present pace were to continue but an overall increase would be required if MacArthur's plans to move into the Philippines were approved.

The need for dividing the Seventh Amphibious Force and its staff into smaller tasks when simultaneous operations were undertaken, such as those at Hollandia, Aitape, and Tanahmerah, made it almost impossible for the staff to keep abreast of operational and planning requirements. The small, unusually competent staff had many of the advantages that go with close-working relationships between themselves and similar groups of Army staffs, but such advantages were often counterbalanced by the need to use them in some operation hundreds of miles away at a time when urgent instructions from General MacArthur would start a new set of plans for another landing.

General MacArthur had no such difficulty within his own staff. He had a very effective arrangement which permitted planning to go ahead simultaneously in a leapfrog manner on various objectives. He had three planning teams—a blue team, a white team, and a red team. Brigadier White, an Australian, headed the blue team; Colonel Peyton, an army officer, headed the white team; and Captain R. D. Tarbuck,

Two big LSTs with their noses into the sand at Tanahmerah Bay. In the background, more LSTs unload supplies for the occupation forces.

Landing craft come in through the surf with troops and supplies from the assault transports seen on the horizon.

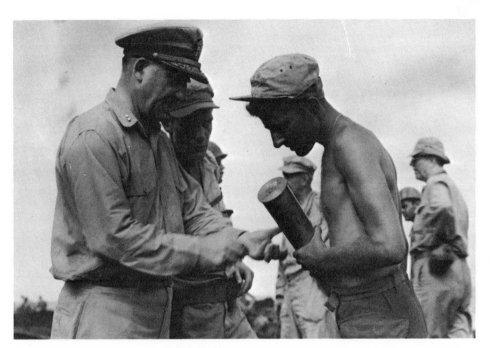

Admiral Barbey examines a Japanese dual purpose antiaircraft and coast defense missile, found at an enemy installation on Hollandia.

Troops of the 185th Infantry Regiment advance inland through knee-deep water along the edge of Lake Sentani, Hollandia.

a naval officer, headed the red team. After the invasion of the Philippines, Tarbuck became my Chief of Staff.

My arrival in Washington was not particularly a timely one for drawing attention to needs in the Southwest Pacific, because all interest centered on the Normandy invasion, which would commence in a few days. General Marshall and Admiral King had left for England to be on hand for the great event. I wanted to go as an observer to learn what I could on all matters that might be helpful in preparation for the scheduled U.S. invasion of Mindanao a few months hence. But the lack of time and the difficulties of obtaining transportation kept me in Washington.

The conditions at Normandy, however, were so different from those in the Southwest Pacific that it was doubtful if any on-the-spot observations would have been particularly useful. An example of these differences was the weather. In the cross-channel operation there was always the chance of fog grounding all planes, or strong winds and a rough sea making landing through the surf an impossible undertaking. In the western Pacific, we could nearly always count on gentle breezes and smooth seas.

In the matter of landing beaches, there were not many suitable places along the coast of France and all of them were well-defended by fixed installations, beach obstacles, and by troops able to quickly shift from one area to another over good roads. In the Southwest Pacific, the many excellent beaches scattered throughout the area were vulnerable to assault and difficult to defend. The Japanese could not be strong everywhere, nor could they readily shift troops from one point to another. They had spread themselves too thin throughout the islands of the Pacific, China, the Philippines, and Southeast Asia.

But the Allied forces attacking the coast of France had several advantages not enjoyed by the Allied forces in the Pacific. They had accurate charts and accurate information regarding tides and beaches. Also, the distance from their home base, England, to the point of attack, was but the width of the English Channel. They had shore-based planes and superiority of air power to cover all phases of the operation. Transports could land their troops, return to their home base and be back with more troops, fuel, ammunition and supplies within a matter of hours. Whereas in the Pacific, planning for an assault on Hollandia, the Marianas, or on the Philippines involved different considerations. Nor was there any likelihood of friendly shore-based airplanes to provide air cover. Carriers would have to provide this service. And the stay in any area would be of short duration because of the need for fuel, ammunition, and supplies.

The Washington end of preparations for the Normandy landing had been completed and all that anybody in the Pentagon could do was stand by and wait.

Uncertain weather had caused a postponement, and then in the early morning hours of 6 June 1944, word came that Allied troops had landed and that all phases of the operation were moving along as scheduled. A few days later, Admiral King returned to Washington and the war, as fought in the Pentagon, went on as before.

The Joint Chiefs of Staff had approved the next steps for U.S. forces in the Pacific commanded by Admiral Nimitz and General MacArthur. The Palaus had been scheduled for capture by Admiral Nimitz's Central Pacific Force about 15 September. In the same Joint Chiefs of Staff memorandum, MacArthur's Southwest Pacific Force had been assigned the job of capturing the island of Morotai, the northernmost isle of the Moluccas.

Morotai, Palau, and the Marianas guarded the eastern approaches to the Philippines. When these islands had been captured and Allied airfields built on them, they would provide some measure of protection to U.S. fleet operations in adjacent waters and a hazard to Japanese operations. Although MacArthur had been authorized to move into the southern Philippines after the capture of Morotai, his further moves had not been approved.

In his talk with me, Admiral King was quite outspoken in his determination that Mindanao would be the western terminus of MacArthur's campaign, and that thereafter the Central Pacific forces under Admiral Nimitz would spearhead the Pacific campaign. He felt that Luzon and the northern Philippines should be bypassed by Admiral Nimitz's forces in favor of an assault on Formosa. With Formosa and the Marianas in Allied hands, he said, Japan would be isolated from her oversea supplies, and her home territory could be pounded into submission from new U.S. bomber bases. He stated that MacArthur's greatest contribution to this overall effort would be the establishment of some air bases on Mindanao that could be used to neutralize Japanese airfields on Luzon until Nimitz could be established on Formosa. He ended our talk with the sarcastic remark that MacArthur seemed more interested in making good his promise to return to the Philippines than in winning the war.

On my return to Brisbane a few weeks later I reported to MacArthur the results of my trip and gave him an expurgated account of my talk with Admiral King. As far as getting more ships was concerned, there was very little good news to report. I had been told that we could expect the assignment of two amphibious headquarters ships to the Southwest Pacific and some increase in ships and personnel when the pressure of operations in the Atlantic eased up. But Admiral King had made it quite plain that any such increase would be limited to what was considered necessary for an invasion of Mindanao. If his wishes were carried out, there would be no invasion of the islands of Leyte or Luzon.

But my report had no effect whatsoever on General MacArthur's plans. He directed his staff to go ahead with preparations for the invasion of the island of Morotai, then southern Mindanao, then Leyte, then Luzon, and finally, with a mopping up campaign of the rest of the islands in the Philippine group. I remained in Brisbane for the next few weeks to work on the naval end of these plans.

18:

Operations at Wakde-Biak

17, 27 May 1944

PRELIMINARY PLANS HAD BEEN DRAWN FOR THE WAKDE OPERA-
tion prior to my departure for the States and a tentative landing date had been set for
21 May 1944. It was believed that the situation in the Hollandia area would have
stabilized sufficiently by then to release enough troops and ships for that comparatively minor job.

Wakde is a small island—about one and a half miles long—lying two miles off the
mainland of New Guinea and 140 miles to the northwestward of Hollandia. The
small airfield there was not in itself much of a threat to Hollandia, but when tied in
with other enemy fighter and light bomber fields on New Guinea's mainland, it was
a serious nuisance, if not a threat. Wakde, being the closest, would be captured first
and the others would be taken in succession as ships and troops became available. It
was expected that in a short time these small enemy airfields would in turn become
Allied fields on the perimeter of a potentially great U.S. naval and bomber base at
Hollandia.

But a snag developed in these plans. The soil in the Hollandia area was incapable
of holding up under heavy bomber operations. Since the closest American bomber
base was over four hundred miles to the rear, there was urgent need to find a new site
to the westward—one that could support land-based planes of all types. Such a base
was necessary before making any major move with land forces in the direction of the
Philippines.

Intelligence information indicated that the Japanese in their search for good airfield

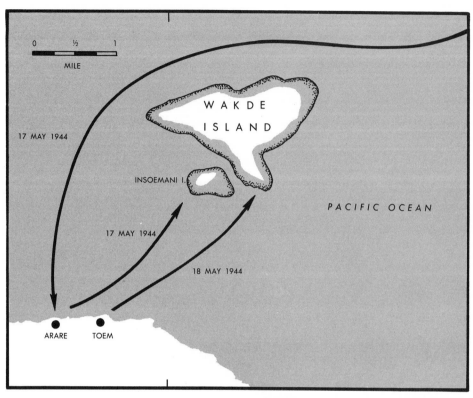

0 ½ 1
MILE

17 MAY 1944

WAKDE ISLAND

INSOEMANI I.

PACIFIC OCEAN

17 MAY 1944

18 MAY 1944

ARARE   TOEM

WAKDE ISLAND ASSAULTS

sites had found most of western New Guinea suitable only for fighter and light bomber strips. The coastal area was too spongy to support heavy bomber operations, and the inland area was too mountainous. As a result the Japanese had built heavy bomber bases on offshore rocky islands like Biak—the nearest one to Hollandia and three hundred miles to the northwest, on the route to Mindanao. Until Biak was captured, MacArthur's advance to the Philippines would be halted. As much as he disliked a frontal assault on an island basis with its heavy losses, there was no alternative. On small islands, where there was no escape, the Japanese would fight to the bitter end.

But before moving on Biak, MacArthur had to get control of Wakde, about midway to Biak, as that little island could not be allowed to threaten the supply line.

The capture and use of the airfields on Wakde and Biak could not be delayed. But there was another and equally important reason why MacArthur wanted to get these attacks under way as soon as possible. It was part of his military philosophy, voiced at every opportunity, to move fast and keep the enemy off balance. If these bases were important to the Japanese, they would assume the same bases would be important to us. Not until the fall of Hollandia were the Japanese likely to have considered an amphibious attack on these islands as imminent, and not until then would they start putting their defenses in order. If such was the case, the sooner the attack, the weaker the defense. Subsequent events proved that MacArthur was right again.

To expedite matters, the Wakde operation was advanced from 21 May to 17 May, and the Biak operation was scheduled for 27 May—ten days later. It was hoped that within these ten days Wakde and the adjacent mainland could be captured, its airstrip put into operation, and that the amphibious shipping used in its capture could be released and readied for the Biak assault.

For the Wakde operation, almost 20,000 troops, including engineers, service troops, and air force personnel, with the ships to carry them, were assembled in the Hollandia area. Captain A. G. Noble, my chief of staff, was designated as the attack force commander.

The mobilizing of 20,000 troops to capture a small island with an enemy garrison of perhaps 500 may have seemed a disproportionate effort. But Wakde was only part of the problem. A landing would first have to be made on the mainland, almost opposite Wakde and two miles away, to avoid any interference from enemy troops in that area. Not far from the proposed landing site on the mainland were a number of Japanese posts, including a few small airfields, with a garrison strength of about 10,000. Most of these troops could be brought to bear against any landing force within a few days.

There was not time enough for a careful reconnaissance nor for any full dress rehearsal. But as most of the troops and ships committed were veterans in this type of warfare, no great concern was felt in these particulars, although there was some concern in the matter of air support.

Another matter that gave us some concern was the need to rely on merchant ships to maintain the flow of supplies. As operations became bigger and more involved, it had become increasingly difficult to provide navy-manned ships for this purpose.

Among the great assemblage of ships at Hollandia were a number manned by merchant crews. These ships had been chartered by the War Shipping Administration to augment the Navy-manned fleet of tankers, cargo ships and, sometimes, ammunition ships. The rules and regulations under which they operated did not fit into emergency situations in the war zone. Captains of the merchant ships had little control over their crews, who often seemed more interested in overtime pay and bonuses than in the war effort. A newly arrived merchant crew always seemed to anticipate bomber raids—not close enough to hurt anybody but close enough to give them a bonus.

During the Wakde preparations, Commander Earl P. Finney visited about twenty merchant-manned Liberty ships in Hollandia harbor in an effort to obtain fuel oil for

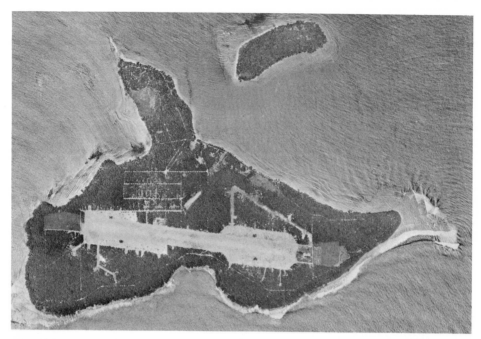

High-altitude aerial reconnaissance photograph showing Wakde Island Airdrome, the prize General MacArthur was after.

The landing on the island of Wakde, only a few miles from the New Guinea mainland, was bitterly opposed by the Japanese. Here, bombs fall on the Wakde airstrip, destroying many planes and immobilizing the airfield for counterattack.

First and second waves of the invasion troops crowd together on the beach at Wakde, pinned down by Japanese machine gun and sniper fire.

American dead being removed from Wakde, 18 May 1944.

destroyers assigned to the operation. The Navy tanker which was to furnish the oil
had not arrived, and the situation had become serious.

Nearly all the merchant captains were willing to help, but they were hampered by
union regulations. The urgency of the situation made no difference. The destroyers
would have to arrive alongside on weekdays—no weekends—between 0800 and 1200
or 1300 to 1630, otherwise the merchant crews would refuse to handle lines or to
make fuel hose connections. But they might be induced to do so on an overtime basis.
Fortunately the Navy tanker arrived in time and the destroyers were fueled around
the clock.

Wakde, like most islands of the Western Pacific, is surrounded by coral reefs. An
attack on it would come as no surprise to the Japanese as it was in the direct line of
the U.S. path to the Philippines. The only question in their minds would be the date
of the attack, and whether they should defend Wakde to the last man or abandon it
and move to a position on the mainland.

The first step in the operation was a sea-launched attack which took place as
scheduled on 17 May 1944, near the small mainland village of Toem, two and a half
miles from Wakde. After an hour's bombardment by cruisers, destroyers, and rocket
ships, the troops landed without any opposition. If any enemy troops had been in the
vicinity they were probably only coastal patrols who undoubtedly fled toward their
headquarters at Sarmi, eighteen miles to the westward.

As soon as the landing force had secured the Toem area, artillery was brought into
position and commenced bombarding Wakde. All that day and most of the night, the
artillery, naval ships, and shore-based planes hammered away at the island. The next
morning the assault took place.

Intelligence had reported no more than 500 Japanese in the defense force and it was
believed they were in the process of evacuation. Considering the pounding that the
garrison had received, only token opposition was expected. This expectation was
wrong. Captured documents showed that ever since the U.S. landing at Hollandia
the Japanese had been expecting us and had used the intervening time to build up
their defenses. For two days, against overwhelming odds, the Japanese literally
fought to the last man, losing 759 dead and one prisoner. Our Army had 110
casualties, the Navy, 10—a high rate compared with former operations. The real
heroes of the landing were the rocket-firing LCIs. They steamed in close to the beach,
remained on the flanks of succeeding waves of assault boats, and poured in a deadly
cover of rocket fire. But for their extremely effective barrage and the excellent control
of Captain Noble, the casualties would have been far heavier.

With the advantage of "hind-sight" I feel that the proposal made by MacArthur at
his Tanahmerah Bay conference, almost a month earlier, for an immediate assault on
Wakde would have resulted in a quick low-cost victory. At that time, there were no

fixed defenses on Wakde. They came later. In addition, we would have had the support of carrier planes to help pound the defenders into submission.

The average soldier, sailor, or airman riding a ship headed for an amphibious landing has little knowledge of where he is going or what to expect when he gets there. Once ashore, his thoughts and feelings are limited to a few square yards around him. He has little information and not much interest in the overall operation. What one man saw and felt and thought when first engaged in combat is vividly told by the public relations officer of the Seventh Amphibious Force (Lieutenant William F. Jibb) in a letter to his wife. Written immediately after the landings on Toem and Wakde, it is quoted in full because it may express the reactions of other young men among the more than 200,000 that the Seventh Amphibious Force had previously landed on the beaches of New Guinea, New Britain, and adjacent islands. Some of these landings had been made against light opposition and some had been heavily opposed. The landing at Toem on the mainland on the first day was unopposed, but the landing on the island of Wakde on the second day met bitter opposition. Here is the letter:

> I left the embarkation point [Hollandia] loaded with stuff which at the time seemed important but later became classified with the nondescript.
>
> In the jungle pack were five pairs of heavy woolen socks, two undershirts and two shorts, one pair of jungle green suits, one first-aid kit (extra), ammunition for the .45 and gun, toothbrush, shaving equipment, helmet and one pair of leggings.
>
> Over one shoulder the rifle, over the other a kit of writing equipment for notes on pictures or human interest stories. On the belt around the waist a .45, a canteen filled with water (should have taken two), first-aid kit, sulfanilamide dressing packs, ammunition slips, and I believe that was all—except for a jungle knife. Then a camera with film and I was off to the war—for my first landing.
>
> A few days aboard a transport in order to get to my destination. In other words—Destination Unknown. The first night I slept in the bunk and after that on the deck because it was cooler. Hard steel but quite comfortable. Up at dawn or before every day. And just could not wait for the landing—keep in mind it was my first and I was really looking forward to it. I was heading to shoot the Japs, with a camera.
>
> D-day had arrived and here they came like the proverbial bill collector. No sun—just moon and stars. Up at 3:00 A.M. (which we write 0300) and down for chow and it tasted good—about the best I ever ate. Excitement ran high among all because, with the exception of a few of the old regulars, it was new to most of us.
>
> It was dark when I clambered into the landing boat with all my gear. I sat on the bottom of the boat while it was lowered and thought. No use looking around for nothing was showing—not even a cigarette could be lit. No undue noise for we were only so many thousand yards off the landing beach [Toem]—which was Japanese.
>
> We scampered around the water and finally the Navy opened up. A most beautiful

presentation—a bombardment by the U.S. Navy. Much like a technicolor movie. Beautiful colors—blues, greens, yellows, reds—all streaking shoreward, and some over our heads. When the shells came over you could hear them whistling through the air—some called them whistling willies. I only hoped each time one passed over that it had enough steam to keep going.

My standing up is much different from what it will be when I make the second landing tomorrow. That comes a little later in the story, so be patient.

The boat beached and out we poured—third wave—onto the beach. My long legs flying for cover with a camera in one hand, a gun in the other, and a pack on my back which must have weighed 150 pounds by now, plus a belt which probably tipped the scales at 40 pounds. (They did not weigh that much but they surely felt like it.) And of course we landed in chest-deep water which got me wet from chest down but luckily I had put my cigarettes in my helmet and they were safe on top of my short hair.

Shot pictures all that morning—the landing was with the rising sun against the Rising Sun. Found some chow and then wandered up the beach.

All that afternoon three other photographers and I tried to find something to take pictures of but no luck. A few native huts blown to the ground—but no Japs. Wandered back to the beachmaster's place and decided to spend the night with him. He was a newspaper man in civilian life so we talked over things and about dark ate a K-ration can and drank water from the canteen. Discussed the landing to be made tomorrow and decided that I would go with him in the third wave again with one of my photographers who is taking moving pictures. The other one I sent in another boat.

Slept in a foxhole that night and the next morning could hardly get out of it. My legs were tied in knots. My back ached and I felt like the devil. Had a half-pint of gin and took a stiff drink myself and gave the rest to the other fellows around for their morale or something. Anyway it was about the most enjoyable drink I ever had and the most necessary, I guess.

I climbed into a landing boat which was headed for the island Wakde on which we are to land in the third wave. The Navy has been blasting it for some hours. We are off shore waiting for the signal. The first wave starts in and of course we are interested in their reception. Nothing much happens to them and the second lands and then we start in—this time for keeps. The second gets ashore without much effort. But a few hundred yards off shore we see return fire from the Japs and some of the bullets hit the barge in which I am riding.

Up to this point the movie photographer and I have been having a swell time taking pictures of what is happening. When bingo a bullet hits our boat. Someone yells: "Duck for cover—Jap fire." But he might have saved his breath. Nugent (photographer) and I are down in the boat—and I almost alongside the keel. I hear the tattoo of the fire hitting the side of the boat. And I have heard some of the bullets come right through the sides of the boat which does not make me a bit happy.

Excitement is high of course and there is much whispered conversation as though anyone is much interested in what we are saying. And it is needless to tell you that I did not get curious at this point and try to see what was happening. I am not the least bit interested in who is shooting or who is shooting back. By now I am wishing I am back where things are quiet.

We are told to get ready for the landing. I shift my pack to my back, my writing case over my shoulder. My gun—carbine—is in my left hand and the camera case in my right. The boat lurches on the sandy beach and we take off.

Let me describe it this way. I was about the last off the boat and we were landing in waist-deep water. I got nothing wet higher than my knees. And I was about the first to get behind a log.

I am shooting pictures, I am told, and the pictures I got bear out the statement, but honestly I do not remember it at all. Up and down the beach, and up and down behind logs. Of course some damn Jap sniper is trying to catch me but he is having one hell of a job I am moving so fast. He never catches up with me with his bullets. I wonder why I am picked out for a target, when it is called to my attention that I am wearing a .45. I immediately take it off and put it inside the camera case. Then I am left alone except for an occasional pot shot.

During the landing a soldier to my left was killed—the bullet went right through his helmet and into his skull and into his neck. Of course at the time I did not know it. Someone to my right noticed the soldier slump over his rifle and called it to the attention of the first-aid corpsman who landed with us. He froze—scared to death. I rose from behind the log and an enlisted man ran with me across the 75 feet where he lay. Our path lay across an open stretch and of course some sniper peppered the ground around us but he was too slow. We made it and turned the soldier over to find him already dead. So back we scampered behind the log. Intentions can be one thing but having the strength or legs to go places is another. I had the intentions but do not know where the strength came from.

From there on it was a matter of shifting from one log to another. We were pinned on the beachhead for 30 minutes. After that I decided to leave and wander inland to get pictures for by that time the action on the beachhead had subsided.

We finally got to a deserted hut about a half-mile from where we had started and found that I had run out of film. I went back for more film. When I got back we went into the hut to look around at the trinkets and stuff. Out we came and met up with a platoon of soldiers. I asked the lieutenant in charge if they were reinforcements and he said, "Hell no, we are the first combat troops in this area." I froze for we had been wandering in Jap territory without knowing it. They took off and we joined up with them.

I do not suppose we got more than a hundred yards when a machine gun from our rear opened on us. Everyone dove for cover. I dove for a tree but no matter where I went someone continued to pop at me. And to make matters worse I dove into a red ant nest. So between the ants and the sniper I was in hot water for many seconds—I do not suppose it was longer than that when I took cover behind a concrete wall. There I took my first deep breath in what had seemed hours.

Nugent and I got separated. He went with the half of the platoon that went ahead to the airstrip and I joined the squad to clean out the machine-gun nest. Back we went and cleaned them out and then killed a sniper in the hut into which we had wandered. He was sitting up near the roof shooting through the roof. Why he did not shoot one of us I do not know. But he did not.

From there we (I used "we" but I did not shoot a Jap with a rifle—only a camera) began cleaning out snipers in slit trenches. One unit killed three and I jumped over the slit trench to get a good picture. Just after I shot the picture one of the live Japs still in the trench opened up and they shot him—but he was just below me as he shot and of course there is no use telling you that I was not scared. Thank God, I do not freeze when I am scared—I move and fast too. Right down behind a tree.

Up again to shoot pictures. But in a minute they shoot another below me. Seven in one slit trench no more than 7 feet long and well hidden with dead leaves and trunks of palm trees fallen across it.

Well, the story goes about the same from here on. Up and down all day—remember many hours have passed and I am getting hungry and when I do get back to the beachhead it is 1630 (4:30 P.M. your way of telling time) and I am tired and disinterested in the war, the landing and everything else. And when I flop on the ground I am only interested in one thing—sleep.

The most eerie experience was coming back from the front lines on the island. Everyone is moving up in those circumstances and few come back. When I got ready to come back I was alone in the idea. I found it hard to come back the trail by myself. Jap snipers were still around somewhere—I never saw one alive for more than 10 seconds and always I saw them just as some army boy had drawn a bead on the particular one. I thought I had good eyesight but it is not that good.

Anyway, I started back. Standing erect because the Americans were still advancing and I did not want them to mistake me for the enemy. And being up straight I imagine I presented a beautiful target to a sniper. I suppose if one had shown up in my path I would have run—I do not know. But I do know I would not have taken a picture of him. Not alive.

It's rather funny how things happen. On landing one boy to my left was killed and one to my right was wounded. One behind me was wounded—I have a picture of him but I do not remember him or his being wounded in the landing.

And the boy who froze up—the first-aid man—was up for citation at a previous landing when he faced two Japs head on to save the life of a doctor. So you can never tell just what might happen.

I guess you are interested in my reaction on landing. Well, I was not scared because I was too busy thinking of where to seek cover. I got my fright after it was all over when I thought of where I had been and how lucky I had been.

Being shot at is not so tough. You just figure the Jap would not get you and if he shows himself you will kill him. And when you land and are behind a log, the reaction is one of loneliness. Although you rub shoulders with other men you feel quite alone, because you know everything depends on you and you alone.

That is about all—it is not much. The Army boys have a tough job staying there after the landing and cleaning things up. Some Navy stays too. But we take our pictures and get off. It is a tough racket—let me tell you that.

Food is hard to get—mostly rations. Water is hard to get and thirst becomes a phobia. The rain, the mud, the mosquitoes, the wet clothes, the raw feet from the sand that gets into your shoes cutting the skin off, and all the rest is just plain HELL.

The Biak landing, which followed ten days later, was bigger and more difficult; MacArthur's headquarters had labelled it as one of "strategic urgency." For one reason or another, Seventh Amphibious Force operations seemed to have fallen into the urgent category, but as time went on it became easier and easier to meet urgent deadlines because more and more of the ground forces involved had some combat experience. As for naval ships, nearly all of their crew were veterans of many landings.

The plans for Biak, with Rear Admiral Fechteler as the attack force commander, called for 30,000 men, including combat troops, engineers, service and Air Force personnel, to be assembled for loading Seventh Amphibious Force ships as soon as they were released from the Wakde operation. This number was adequate to handle an enemy garrison of 2,000. Unfortunately, the Japanese on Biak numbered nearer 11,000, and they were well-armed, courageous, and skillfully led.

Biak is the largest of a small group of islands lying about one hundred miles to the eastward of the Vogelkop (the western-most peninsula in New Guinea). The island is about forty-five miles long and twenty miles wide. Like all the other islands in the area, it was surrounded by coral reef and had no natural harbor. As a substitute for harbor facilities, the Japanese had built two small jetties from the shore to deep water outside the reef.

The landing plan conformed to the pattern developed for and successfully used in previous beach assaults. The convoy approached the landing area under cover of darkness. At first daylight, assault craft were launched and headed for the beach under cover of a short but heavy bombardment. Previous experience had shown that the Japanese would withdraw from a heavily bombed beach and retreat to caves or prepared positions in the vicinity of their airfields. The Biak operation was no exception in that respect.

On the first day of the attack, American casualties were almost negligible. The real losses came later in the fight for the airfield, some miles distant from the beaches and beyond the range of shipboard guns.

Troops and supplies in a steady stream continued to reach the beach throughout D-day. Late that afternoon four Japanese twin-engined bombers accompanied by several fighters appeared out of the west in two waves flying very low, about five hundred feet, and aimed their bombs at LSTs still unloading on the beach. None of the bombs exploded—apparently they were dropped from too low a height to arm.

The bombers never had a chance to escape from the concentrated gunfire of the ships, and they must have known it. After dropping their bombs, they tried to crash dive the nearest destroyers, but failed to reach their targets. Their sole success was to badly damage Subchaser 699. In its report the 699 claimed credit and a hash mark for shooting down a bomber which crashed a few yards off its starboard bow. A few seconds later another plane, on fire, headed for the destroyer flagship, missed it and continued in a direct line for the 699. One wing of the plane was torn off as it hit the

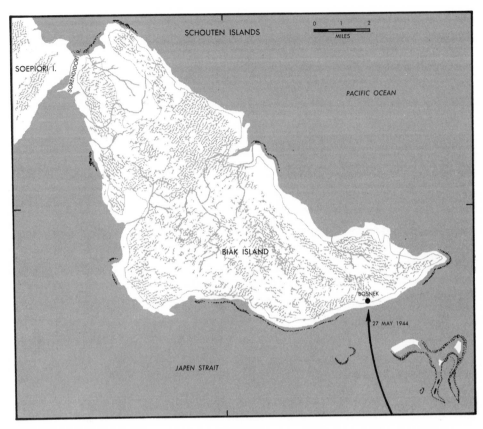

BIAK

water thirty yards away. The rest of the fuselage ricocheted, crashed on the deck of the subchaser, and exploded. The pilot hit the mast with such force that he cracked it. Most of the ship's rigging was swept overboard. Fire swept the *699* from the pilothouse to the depth charges at the stern. Parts of a human body were scattered over the conning bridge. Bits of wreckage were everywhere.

The ship carried her full complement of three officers and twenty-five enlisted men, of whom two were killed outright and one badly burned. Also aboard was Lieutenant Commander P. C. Holt, in his capacity as landing craft control officer. The force of the plane's explosion blew the ship's officers and twelve of the crew overboard. Lieutenant Commander Holt assumed command and fought the fire with seven slightly injured men who remained aboard. Within minutes the good old standby, the salvage tug *Sonoma,* was alongside and helped fight the flames.

The men in the water were picked up by another subchaser and then Commander "Rainy" Day came alongside with one of his fire-fighting LCIs and within twenty minutes the fire was out. That night the *SC-699* started her long tow to Australia for a major overhaul. This was the same little subchaser that did such a fine job at Arawa, called by her crew the "Shootin' *699*." Like a magnet, she seemed to attract danger. That the ship was saved and so few lives lost was due to the resourcefulness and courage of Holt and the seven men who fought the flames with him. Included in Lieutenant Commander Holt's official report was the laconic statement that he had assumed command as "the captain had gone overboard without leaving any orders."

Because of lack of office space and clerical help on the smaller ships, the preparation of official reports was always a problem. Sometimes reports were submitted in longhand, and sometimes not at all. One from the rocket gunboat *LCI-73,* which took part in the Biak landing, is more complete than most and gives a good account of a landing as one rocket LCI experienced it.

In the Biak operation, the *LCI-73* was assigned to a station in the center of the leading wave of assault craft where she was to bombard the beach and the area directly behind it with 4.5-inch rockets and automatic weapons, then strafe the two jetties that extended out from the beach and over the coral reefs. That done, she was to search for channels through the reefs and locate suitable beaching points for LCIs, LCTs, and LSTs. The following are chronological excerpts from her D-day reports:

    0645   Proceeded into beach just ahead and in center of first wave of LVTs [Amphibious tractors].

    0707   Mortar and machine-gun fire coming from beach.

    0711   Obtained correct range for rockets and started firing, working barrage inland for 300 to 400 yards. Fired 180 rockets.

0714 to
    0717   Strafed landing area with 40mm. and 20mm. until guns could no longer bear without endangering our first wave.

               At this time it was seen that the landing was not being made at the designated beach. Smoke from the cruiser and destroyer bombardment had limited the visibility making it necessary to come within 400 yards of the beach before seeing the shore line.

0720 to
    0735   Searched for jetties and other possible landing points.

0740 to
    0830   Received word jetties had been found. Proceeded to their vicinities. LCIs were landing troops on them but suitable landing points needed for LCTs. Found two channels in coral reefs and had two LCTs land their cargo there.

0850 to
    0856   At request of Army, fired rockets and strafed Jap machine gun emplacements at east end of Green Beach.

    0908   Fired rockets ahead of infantry as they advanced east of Green Beach.

0911 Shelled enemy hut.
1216 Strafed enemy barges.
1307 Passed close by "T" head of jetty east of Mokmer village. Inspected for Japs and strafed. Jetty in excellent shape.
1550 Fired rockets and strafed enemy positions in support of infantry advancing along west coast toward Mokmer.

For the next eight days the *LCI-73* and her two sister LCIs kept searching for enemy coastal positions, meeting all army requests for assistance and fighting off enemy plane attacks. They were particularly proud of their defense against planes.

D-day plus 2

0815 All guns fired on Jap zero plane and several hits observed. Plane did not go down immediately but disappeared over island. Later on, destruction of this plane was confirmed and accredited to this ship by army artillery post who reported plane had fallen in water out of our sight.

D plus 3

1829 Fired on enemy planes. Some hits probably made but plane did not fall.

D plus 4

2048 Enemy plane dropped flares in vicinity of ship. Saw plane and opened fire. Hits probably made. Plane reported to have fallen, but we cannot claim it as shore batteries and other ships were firing on it at same time.

D plus 6

1642 Attack by eight planes on ships in vicinity of Mokmer jetty. At least two were shot down by ships under attack. Another plane which escaped that fire came within range of our guns and was definitely shot down. The plane was seen to burst into flames.

Same day

1656 Enemy planes again attacked. As they flew west they came within our range. All our guns fired. One plane immediately crashed.

D plus 7

1109 Fired on planes attacking destroyers. No planes observed to fall.

On the ninth day, *LCI-73* returned to Hollandia with an exhausted crew, not much fuel, and no ammunition. During all that time of almost continuous contact with the enemy, with shells and bombs landing on all sides of her, she never suffered a hit or a single casualty.

The Japanese failure to make any large-scale plane attack on the day of landing led to the feeling that they had written off Biak and were not going to waste any more troops or planes in its defense. But we were wrong. The Japanese had not done more because they were not ready to do more. Captured documents showed that immediately after the fall of Hollandia they undertook to strengthen their position in the Vogelkop and the islands lying in the path of MacArthur's advance to the Philippines, and that included Biak.

A division of Japanese troops had been embarked in Shanghai during the last week in April as the first step in this strengthening process, but the convoy never got beyond the Philippines. Successive torpedo attacks on the convoy by the U.S. submarines *Jack* and *Gurnard* forced the Japanese to abandon these particular troop reinforcement plans.

The Japanese were finding as much difficulty, perhaps more so, in providing the necessary planes to block MacArthur's advance as in providing the troops. The Allied shore-based air force and the Navy's carrier planes had all but wiped out Japanese air power in that corner of the Pacific. But with the landing of American troops on Biak on 27 May, the Japanese reacted as swiftly and fully as their resources permitted.

By drawing on their reserves, they were able to assemble 166 planes with partially trained crews and flew them into Vogelkop on 1 June to augment the 18 already there. On 31 May, 2,500 Japanese troops were embarked at Mindanao in 2 cruisers, 3 destroyers, and 1 transport under escort of the battleship *Fuso,* 2 heavy cruisers, and 5 destroyers. Their plan was to land the troops at Biak on 3 June under the air cover of their planes from the Vogelkop fields. This strong Japanese naval force might have overwhelmed the 4 Allied cruisers and 14 destroyers—all the Southwest Pacific Force could muster to oppose them—if they had been aggressively led. But instead of carrying out his mission, the Japanese commander landed the troops in the Vogelkop and the escorting force returned to Davao in Mindanao.

After the war, we learned that this timid action resulted from the Japanese commander's belief that the Allies had assembled a powerful naval force, including a carrier, in the vicinity of Biak, and his fear of a trap. That mistaken belief was due to erroneous reports received from inexperienced reconnaissance planes.

On 2 June, five days after the Biak landing, the hastily assembled, partially trained, and malaria-ridden pilots of the newly arrived Japanese planes in the Vogelkop took off on their part of the plan to attack Biak and Wakde. In the heaviest air raid on U.S. forces since the landing at Gloucester, six months previous, fifty-four Japanese planes arrived off Biak at 4:40 P.M. Eight beached LSTs had just completed their unloading and received the brunt of the attack. There were no Allied planes present as all had been grounded at Wakde and Hollandia due to a weather front. The Japanese air attack was pressed home vigorously for over an hour but the new pilots did not have the skill of those of former days; the only damage was a near miss on an LST. The attackers lost twelve of their dwindling supply of planes to the concentrated gunfire of naval ships and shore batteries.

The pilots, not discouraged, returned to their home bases with exaggerated reports

Biak Island in the Schoutens is the destination of this string of LSTs, heavily laden with the equipment for invasion.

LVTs discharge from an LST and head for the beach at Biak. It was important to have the LVTs pointed towards their goal when they emerged, as they were not quickly maneuverable when waterborne.

*Coast Guardsmen stand on the alert beside their 20mm. antiaircraft gun at Biak. They are
ready to give Japanese raiders "the works" should planes venture within range.*

*The barrels roll as troops unload gasoline and oil, lifeblood for the American planes and
mechanized equipment used in the invasion of Biak.*

of the damage they had inflicted on Allied shipping and so the next day, 3 June, a new attack of forty-one planes came in at 11 A.M. Again no Allied air cover was present, having been delayed again by a weather front. As before, the attackers concentrated on the three destroyers in the area and on the amphibious ships discharging cargo at the beach. The attack lasted for half an hour and then Allied planes arrived and drove off the enemy. Again our shipping suffered little damage due to skillful maneuvering and the inexpertness of the attacking pilots. None of our ships were hit by bombs and there were but few casualties from bomb fragments and strafing. The Japanese lost eleven out of forty-one planes.

Intercepted messages, reconnaissance planes, and submarine sightings kept the Seventh Amphibious Force headquarters well informed about Japanese activities in this part of the Pacific. Although we knew what they were doing, we could only guess at their intentions. Not for a long time did we learn of the various Japanese plans to aid their beleagured garrison on Biak with troops, planes, and a segment of their fleet.

The Allied landing at Hollandia had taken place with such suddenness that the Japanese were wholly unprepared to meet it with a major fleet engagement. But the Biak affair was something else again. When they finally learned that the major U.S. fleet strength had returned to Central Pacific bases, they hoped to regain Biak by feeding in some ground troop reinforcements from the Vogelkop with the support of the ships and planes in that area, but their Vogelkop forces were unequal to the task.

Although MacArthur's Southwest Pacific Force had but four cruisers and accompanying destroyers, they were able to maintain nearly continuous patrol of the western and northern approaches to Biak. Almost daily, Japanese planes from the Vogelkop made attacks on this task force, the troops and ships at Biak, and on the airfields at Wakde. Each attack weakened the Japanese strength without commensurate gain. Their major success was a sneak attack by two bombers on Wakde, the evening of 5 June. A hundred air force planes were parked there, wing to wing, and the Japanese destroyed about two-thirds of them. Other enemy successes were the underwater damage done by a torpedo plane to the cruiser *Nashville,* and a direct bomb hit on the destroyer *Kalk* engaged in escorting some LSTs.

With the hope of eluding Allied cruisers, six Japanese destroyers, three of them towing troop-loaded barges, departed from the Vogelkop on the morning of 8 June, intending to land reinforcements that night in a small bay in the western end of Biak. Shortly after noon, Allied light bombers from Hollandia sighted and attacked them, sinking one destroyer and damaging three others. After the attack the enemy destroyer force reorganized itself and continued on its mission. Some hours later the three destroyers cast off their troop-laden barges and fled in the darkness. Some of the barges may have reached Biak but not enough to have had any effect on the outcome of the fighting ashore.

In spite of these reverses, and because of Biak's importance to their planning, the Japanese high command, on 10 June, assigned two 18-inch gun battleships, the *Yamato* and the *Musashi,* and some cruisers and destroyers, with orders to eliminate all Allied naval forces in the Biak area and land sufficient troops to retake that island. The battleship task force, made up of units based in the Netherlands East Indies, assembled at the island of Batjan, about five hundred miles to the westward of Biak. The landing of reinforcements was to be made on 15 June. If the Japanese had carried out their plan it would have been the most powerful enemy naval offensive faced by the weak naval forces of the Southwest Pacific during its two years of operations. But new factors forced the Japanese to call the landing off.

Word of the attack by Nimitz's carrier planes on Guam and Saipan on 11 and 12 June added to our reconnaissance information, and convinced the Japanese that a major amphibious operation was about to be undertaken in the Marianas. It was the type of situation the Japanese fleet commander had been waiting for. He cancelled the operations against Biak, ordered all major units of his fleet concentrated in the Philippine Sea and naval planes redistributed from the Vogelkop to bases further north. At their new bases, they would be able to assist in the forthcoming battle of the Philippine Sea. This redistribution of forces left the Japanese garrison on Biak to their fate and MacArthur's luck had held again.

We can only speculate as to what might have happened if Nimitz's invasion of the Marianas had been delayed a week. If so, two powerful Japanese battleships accompanied by cruisers and destroyers, covered by an air flotilla from the Vogelkop would have been thrown at an Allied cruiser force weakened by the loss of the *Nashville*—and an Allied air force weakened by the loss of planes at Wakde. If the Japanese had destroyed the Southwest Pacific cruiser force at Biak and gained local control of the sea, it is quite possible that MacArthurs' further advance would have been so delayed as to reorient the direction of the war in the Pacific. Undoubtedly, more consideration would then have been given to the Navy's proposal to bypass Luzon and move directly into Formosa after capturing the Marinas.

As it turned out, the Japanese combined fleet was badly mauled by Nimitz's Pacific Fleet in the battle of the Philippine Sea on 19–20 June 1944. That defeat, for the time being, left MacArthur's Southwest Pacific Force free to continue its steady move toward the Philippines, but the Japanese still had powerful naval and air forces that might be thrown across its path.

While the Army continued its job of mopping-up ashore, the amphibious Navy would continue its part of the job of carrying reinforcements and supplies. When the

Biak airfields were firmly in U.S. control and able to provide air cover to incoming merchant shipping, the Navy would turn over this work to Liberty ships operating under the Army Service of Supply.

Until 1 July 1944, the Seventh Amphibious Force had been its own service force in the New Guinea campaign. On that date the Seventh Fleet Service Force, which had been functioning in Australia, extended its activities to the forward area. Most of our converted LSTs and small-craft conversions were transferred to the service force at that time, renamed, and continued on the same type of work as heretofore. Our old friend, the *LST–453,* became the *ARL–40* and was renamed the *Remus.*

19:

Operations at Noemfoor-Sansapor

2, 30 July 1944

AS SOON AS THE PRESSURE WAS OFF BIAK, GENERAL MACARTHUR was in a position to resume the Allied offensive toward the Philippines. One of the obstacles in his path was the small island of Noemfoor, about seventy miles west of Biak and that much closer to the western end of New Guinea (the Vogelkop peninsula). Noemfoor's three airfields had provided bases for some of the Japanese raids during the early stages of the Biak fighting. Under Allied control they would be useful when the projected attack on the Vogelkop took place.

Noemfoor is circular in shape with a twelve-mile diameter, and like Biak almost completely surrounded by reefs with a narrow coastal plain backed up by heavily forested hills. Unlike Biak, however, aerial photographs indicated the possibility of a number of usable channels through the reefs.

On 15 June, MacArthur directed his senior commanders in the forward area to prepare plans for an assault on Noemfoor on 2 July 1944. Finding the troops and the ships for this job was not easy. Fighting was still going on at Aitape where Allied troops faced a Japanese force of almost 20,000 men. Obviously no troops could be obtained from that area—in fact, they needed help. Nor could any troops be released from Biak as there were die-hard pockets of Japanese still holding out in caves in the hills and all U.S. troops on that island would be fully engaged for the next few weeks in rooting them out. The cruisers and destroyers needed for bombardment and escort purposes in an attack on Noemfoor were not immediately available as they had left

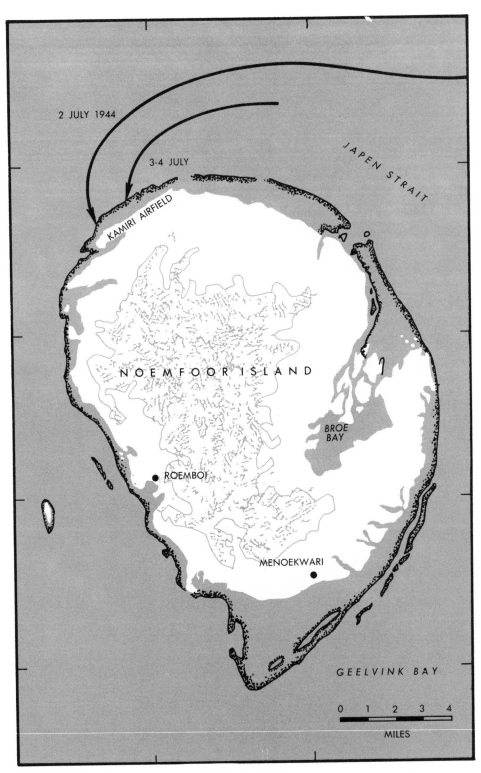

2 JULY 1944

3-4 JULY

KAMIRI AIRFIELD

JAPEN STRAIT

NOEMFOOR ISLAND

BROE BAY

ROEMBOI

MENOEKWARI

GEELVINK BAY

0 1 2 3 4
MILES

NOEMFOOR ISLAND

for the Admiralty Islands for fuel and ammunition. And there was the usual acute shortage of amphibious shipping.

Since there would be no amphibious ships to lift reserve troops standing by at Hollandia, it was arranged that the reserves would consist only of a parachute regiment which could be flown in and dropped on the island, if required.

Shortly after dawn on 2 July, a brief, but heavy, air and naval bombardment cleared the beach of defenders, most of whom withdrew into the hills.

It was an easy landing. The LCIs found the channels through the reefs and the amphibious tractors lumbered their way over the coral. The Japanese had planted a few hundred land mines near the beach, but they were easily identifiable and did no damage.

The sandy beaches provided good footing for the troops as they headed along the shoreline for the nearest airfield. Within a few hours, the Kamiri Airfield was in our possession. With memories of the Biak operation in mind, the troop commander, Brigadier General E. D. Patrick, felt that the ease of operation at the beachhead was no indication that stiff opposition would not be awaiting him as he moved inland. Also, prisoner interrogation indicated twice as many Japanese defenders as had been estimated. To prevent being left short-handed, Patrick asked that the paratroopers held in reserve at Hollandia be dropped on Kamiri Airfield the following morning.

That there was so little opposition at the beaches, or even at the airfield, was surprising as the Japanese had enough men in the garrison to have given a lot of trouble. However, their troops were poorly led, morale was low, food was scarce, and they had no stomach for fighting.

Although there were a number of enemy airfields within striking range of Noemfoor, none of them had enough planes to make an air raid on the day of assault. That was because nearly all planes had been moved to the defense of the Marianas Islands, and what few planes remained behind were grounded due to a weather front which persisted for most of the day and sealed off Noemfoor from the south and west. In all our various operations, the vagaries of weather seemed to favor us more often than the Japanese.

More than 7,000 troops were landed at Noemfoor on that first day. It was more like a training exercise than an attack on a supposedly well-defended island.

Next day the paratroopers were flown in from Hollandia and dropped on the Kamiri Airfield. The drop was not a success. Some of the planes flew in too low and many men suffered broken legs. The next day another battalion was flown in, again with unsatisfactory results. Nine percent casualties was just too much. Not until the Corregidor operation, eight months later, were there any further attempts to land paratroopers in the Southwest Pacific.

While the overall technique of our succession of landings remained the same, some variations crept in to conform to changing conditions. For example, in the three

Calm despite the prospect of a hard battle ahead, these American soldiers relax amidst the supplies and equipment on the LST that is taking them to Jap-held Noemfoor Island.

American paratroopers float in over the Kamiri Airfield on 4 July 1944 to reinforce the infantry units that made the initial landings on 2 July.

An American salvage detail sorts out the supplies left behind by the retreating Japanese during the invasion of Noemfoor. In the center is the tail assembly of a Jap bomber.

The paratroopers who landed via parachute on Noemfoor the morning of Independence Day return to camp after their attack, tired but still smiling.

Hollandia landings, unlike the earlier operations, there was no need for the light loading of LSTs to permit them to off-load and be away from the beach within a few hours, to evade enemy air attack. During the Hollandia landings, we had complete mastery of the air because of the temporary presence of aircraft carriers from the Pacific Fleet. And, from that time onward, the strength of the Japanese Air Force and the quality of its pilots steadily declined so we no longer feared their air attacks as had been the case at Lae, Gloucester, and other places. A round-the-clock unloading schedule could be maintained as soon as a beachhead was established.

At Noemfoor another variation from the standard procedure was the tryout of paratroops to provide reinforcements on the day following the landing. The rest of the landing followed a more familiar pattern. The LCI rocket ships did their usual spectacular job of taking out the beach defenses, and the demolition team carried out its blasting job of widening a channel through the coral reef. In all this welter of activity of hundreds of boats and small ships attempting to negotiate an uncertain passage between coral pinnacles, the defenders made but one shell hit on the many targets. And that was on an amphibious tractor, clambering over a reef while en route to the shore. One man was killed and five injured—the only casualties from enemy action for this phase of the operation.

Noemfoor emphasized again the less than satisfactory results obtained from the prior landing of scouting teams in the vicinity of enemy-held beaches. An army scouting team was put ashore on 21 June from a PT boat near the Kamiri Airfield, remained two days, and was then taken off. Their purpose was to obtain information regarding enemy defenses and beach conditions. All they learned after a dangerous game of hide and seek was that the enemy was on the island in considerable strength. No usable information was obtained on beach conditions, such as tidal movement, depth of water over reefs, boat channels, and other data needed for an assault landing.

As usual, our staff found this information could best be obtained by a careful study of photographs taken from planes or through submarine periscopes. The thrill of scouting adventures always seemed to attract plenty of volunteers who liked to live dangerously. On the negative side of these forays was the probability that the scouting team would either be observed or captured and thus alert the enemy as to our intentions. This time, the scouting team was sighted and the Japanese correctly assumed that a landing in that area could be expected. Even so, they were so poorly led and so dispirited that their defense preparations were limited to laying some ineffective mines at the landing beach. A more determined enemy could have caused a lot of trouble with this advance knowledge.

With the landing phase over, the Noemfoor operation would be routine: bringing in reinforcements, putting the airfields in serviceable condition, and digging the Japanese out from the caves where they had taken refuge.

As soon as the 5,000 Noemfoor natives were sure that the Americans would win, they came out of their hiding places in the hills and joined in the hunt for the Japanese. In the final count, 1,900 Japanese had been killed and 186 taken prisoners—an unusually high prisoner percentage. The operation had cost the Americans 61 killed and 343 wounded.

One of the pathetic stories of this campaign was the Japanese treatment of 3,000 Indonesians shipped to the island a year earlier as slave laborers. Only 403 of them survived the ordeal of back-breaking work, semi-starvation rations, and sickness.

On 3 July, the day after the landing at Noemfoor, with the intensity of fighting at Aitape building up, and with mopping-up operations still under way at Biak and on the New Guinea mainland opposite Wakde, orders were received to prepare for a landing near Cape Sansapor on the Vogelkop peninsula on 30 July. Seventy miles to the southwest of Cape Sansapor was the Japanese air base at Sorong and 140 miles due east was their base at Manokwari. Cape Sansapor was chosen for the landing because no enemy troops were believed to be in the immediate vicinity and photographic reconnaissance indicated it was suitable for airfield construction.

The Vogelkop is a large peninsula at the northwestern end of New Guinea. When that bit of enemy land was captured we could truly say that, except for mopping-up operations, the New Guinea part of MacArthur's campaign would be over. With the Vogelkop in Allied hands, MacArthur would then be able to project his campaign directly into the Philippines, via a couple of island stepping stones en route.

The Vogelkop is a rugged country with steep mountains, heavy rain forest, and deep valleys. For all practical purposes there were no roads. Communication between the Japanese bases was maintained by barge traffic along the coast. There were a number of good beaches, but they were often separated from each other by almost impassable mountain ranges. Most of the beaches were free of reefs. It was an ideal set-up for the landing of an amphibious force that had control of the sea and air. There was no possibility the enemy could concentrate a land force for defense of the beaches.

Aerial reconnaissance had shown no Japanese activity in the vicinity of Cape Sansapor, which was near the northernmost point of the peninsula. Good beaches, nearby, seemed to be free of reefs. Patches of flat ground in the immediate vicinity appeared suitable for the development of a number of fighter and light bomber air strips. Although the enemy air bases at Sorong and Manokwari together had about 18,000 troops, they did not pose much of a threat. They had few planes and these would have little opportunity to function because of Allied air raids. Their combat troops would be unable to concentrate as the Japanese did not have control of the coastal routes.

Columns of LCIs, closely followed by an LST, lead the way to the invasion of Cape Sansapor. The antiaircraft guns, which go ashore with the troops, are manned and ready for enemy attacks from the sky.

Sansapor, 30 July 1944—a landing with only one casualty. Landing craft unload on the beach, while the warships wait on the horizon for the word to open fire—but the word was not needed.

American soldiers file down the ramps of an LCI, prepared for the worst, but happily surprised by the best—no opposition at Sansapor.

A patrol of infantrymen, on lookout at a river entrance, move cautiously inland on Cape Sansapor.

In nearly all our previous operations, the primary purpose of the landing was to capture the nearby enemy airfields and then convert them to Allied use. But now General MacArthur intended to avoid landing on the beaches near the air bases of Sorong and Manokwari, both of which were believed to be heavily defended, in favor of a landing near an undefended midway point where U.S. forces could construct their own fields. With a heavy bomber base at Biak, and fighter fields at Noemfoor and Sansapor, MacArthur would be in an excellent position to provide air support for troops in the tentatively scheduled assault on the island of Morotai, the last stopping place before U.S. forces landed in the Philippines.

As most of the senior commanders, other than MacArthur, had moved their headquarters to the Hollandia area, coordinated planning was simplified. (MacArthur did not move Southwest Pacific Force Headquarters from Brisbane to Hollandia until 30 August 1944.)

The Navy's part in the Sansapor operation was very simple. The beaches were narrow but good, with very little surf or coral; and there were no large groups of enemy troops in the immediate vicinity. No preliminary bombardment would be necessary. It would be primarily a ferrying job with little risk. Three cruisers and nine destroyers under the command of Rear Admiral Russell S. Berkey, U.S. Navy, would form a protective screen to the north and west of the landing area as insurance against any raids by Japanese naval units. But such raids were unlikely. After losing two carriers and suffering disastrous plane losses in the Battle of the Philippine Sea a couple of weeks previously, the Japanese fleet was in no condition to undertake major operations for the time being.

The Army's job at Sansapor would not be as simple as that of the Navy, and might involve a lot of hard fighting later on. Although no opposition to the landing itself was expected, an estimated 18,000 Japanese troops stationed in the vicinity of Sorong and Manokwari would eventually have to be reckoned with.

Reconnaissance had shown no signs of enemy activity in any parts of the Vogelkop other than at main Japanese bases and barge control points.

The proposed landing site was one of the few places that lent itself to reconnaissance by an on-the-spot scouting party. Because of the isolation of the area, there appeared little danger of observation by the enemy, and there was the probability that good information could be obtained regarding soil conditions for airfield construction and a suitable area for use as a PT base.

Accordingly, a series of reconnaissance parties were landed from submarine and PT boats, and remained ashore, unobserved, for three and four days at a time. These parties included members of the Army, Navy, and Air Corps qualified to gather data on matters of particular interest to each service. It was the most thoroughly reconnoitered landing ever undertaken in the Southwest Pacific and made under conditions that seemed more like peace than war. On the basis of these observations, a landing beach was chosen that was about twelve miles to the northeastward of Sansapor.

If there was a serious threat to the landing, it would have to come from some of the thirty-one Japanese airfields within striking range. But this threat did not seem a likely one as most of the airfields had been pretty well stripped of their planes and apparently no new planes had been flown in. We were confident the Allied Air Force could handle those that remained.

The naval attack force consisted of the usual balanced group of APDs, destroyers, rocket LCIs and smaller craft—48 ships in all—plus Admiral Berkey's covering force of 3 cruisers and 9 destroyers. The amphibious ships carried a landing force of 13,500 combat troops, 7,000 service personnel, and 7,000 Air Force personnel. This may have seemed an unusually large combat force considering the probability of little or no shore opposition, but they might be needed later if it became necessary to move against the Japanese bases at Sorong and Manokwari.

The landing was carried out as planned, commencing at seven o'clock in the morning of 30 July 1944. No enemy was sighted and no shots were fired. A few hours later, two small islands adjacent to the landing area were captured against token opposition. One man in the landing force was shot during this secondary operation. The next day a battalion of U.S. troops moved in small boats along the twelve miles of coast to the village of Sansapor. On sighting them, the small garrison of Japanese troops fled to the hills.

Although this important operation resulted in only one combat casualty, the casualties from the dreaded scrub-typhus were unpleasantly large. Before the end of August, more than eight hundred troops had become infected with a fatality rate of 3.6 percent. The disease was finally brought under control by the same methods which had proven so successful at Biak—impregnating troop clothing with a solution of Dimethyl Pthalate (DMP) and clearing the grass and brush from occupied areas and spraying with DDT.

There was no serious fighting ashore in the Vogelkop peninsula. Small groups of Japanese patrols were encountered as U.S. troops expanded the beachhead. By the end of August, the Japanese had lost 385 killed and 215 captured, but most of the captured were Formosan and Korean laborers. Except for the construction of the airfields and the problem of resupply, the Sansapor job was over.

For the Seventh Amphibious Force, the Sansapor operation marked the end of a trek of 1,500 miles in just one year—from one end of New Guinea to the other.

During that time the Seventh Amphibious Force had to transport and land, every few weeks, groups of approximately 30,000 Allied troops in little-known jungle areas where they had to search and destroy a stubborn enemy, and build a new community while doing it. And the requirements of this new community covered almost every phase of modern living.

To name a few: each community had to have roads, airfields, housing, lighting, sewage, gas stations, churches, fire stations, jails, hospitals, movie theaters, clerical space, post office, and cemetery—plus the construction equipment to create all these things, and the manpower to operate them.

Although some of these activities could be performed in the open air, most were carried on in quickly assembled Quonset huts. All equipment for these new communities had to be brought by freighters from areas half a world away, to embarkation points where amphibious ships would carry it to the combat area. In the combat area someone would be waiting to receive it, and someone would be waiting to use it.

The basic features of the new community would be feverishly built and functioning within a few days of an assault landing. Within a few months a stable, well-run base would be operating.

It was a marvel of organization. I gave up trying to learn the details of how it was put together. It was saddening to know that within a few months each of these bustling communities which we had seen hewn out of the jungle would be abandoned and the remnants left to the natives and the jungle.

And this moving of whole communities of 30,000 men and their equipment—in the case of the Hollandia operation, more than 100,000—was made possible because of the slow, awkward, wonderful LSTs; the ships whose construction was turned down by the Navy Department just three years previously, in the belief they would fulfill no need in a modern war. When war did come a few weeks later, a more realistic appraisal was made and construction was started on more than 1,000 of these LSTs Without them it is difficult to imagine how the war could have been successfully fought.

20: Morotai
15 September 1944

WHILE THE VETERAN SEVENTH AMPHIBIOUS FORCE WAS CON-
tinuing the job of carrying reinforcements and supplies to newly acquired bases at
Wakde, Biak, Noemfoor, and Sansapor, I retired to Brisbane to work with MacArthur's headquarters on plans for the invasion of the Philippines.

As a preliminary to this invasion, plans were outlined for the capture of intermediate points on the route between the western end of Dutch New Guinea and the
island of Mindanao. These intermediate points were needed to provide bases from
which shore-based aircraft could cover the westward movement of the amphibious
force.

The first landing in the Philippines was scheduled for Sarangani Bay, a large bay
on the southeastern end of Mindanao. The tentative date had been set for 15
November 1944. The Joint Chiefs of Staff had given its approval of moves up to
Mindanao, but not beyond.

The first of the intermediate operations would be a landing on Morotai, a small
island about halfway between the Vogelkop Peninsula and Sarangani Bay. The
scheduled date was 15 September. The next intermediate landing under consideration
was on Talaud Island, about midway between Morotai and Sarangani Bay.

On the same dates these operations were being carried out by General MacArthur's
forces, the Central Pacific forces would start another series of operations against the
islands of Peleliu, Ulithi, and Yap. The Pacific Fleet would provide cover for both
series of operations.

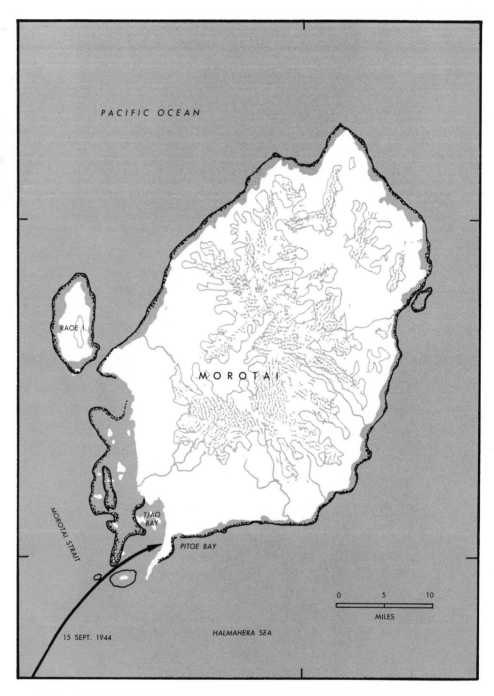

PACIFIC OCEAN

RAOE I.

M O R O T A I

MOROTAI STRAIT

TJAO BAY

PITOE BAY

15 SEPT. 1944

HALMAHERA SEA

0   5   10
MILES

THE LANDING AT MOROTAI

If the future course of the war in the Pacific followed the direction which had been outlined to me on my visit to Washington, then the landing at Sarangani Bay might well be the last major landing by the Southwest Pacific forces and General MacArthur's future role would be limited to the construction of air bases in southern Mindanao. These bases would be used to beat down Japanese air power in Luzon while the Pacific Fleet escorted Admiral Nimitz's Central Pacific forces on an invasion of Formosa.

But MacArthur had other ideas. He directed his staff to outline plans for the seizure of the Misamis Oriental area in northern Mindanao on 7 December, and ordered his Red Team of planners to prepare for an invasion of Leyte, in the Central Philippines.

Beginning with Morotai, there would be a change of emphasis in Southwest Pacific planning. So far, major attention had been directed to the threat of Japanese air attack and little attention to the possibility of a surface attack. As the zone of operations neared the Philippines the situation was reversed. Although Japanese air power had deteriorated, the remnants of their fleet were still a powerful force driven by "backs to the wall" desperation.

Because of this new situation, all further operations toward the Philippines by MacArthur's forces, as well as those of the Central Pacific, could only be undertaken under the protection of the Pacific Fleet. These operations would now be in waters where the entire remaining strength of the Japanese fleet might be concentrated. To simplify the protective job of the Pacific Fleet, the landing at Morotai by MacArthur's forces was scheduled for the same date, 15 September, on which Nimitz's forces were to land on Peleliu Island, in the Palau group. Peleliu and Morotai were only 470 miles apart and the Pacific Fleet could provide simultaneous protection to both landings.

While our staff in Brisbane went ahead with preliminary plans for Morotai and the Philippines, the War Department directed General MacArthur to proceed to Honolulu to meet with a "very important person"—presumably the President—on 26 July. We all assumed, correctly as it turned out, that the future course of the war in the Pacific would be determined at this meeting. MacArthur was accompanied by his chief planning officer, Colonel Bonner Fellers.

We learned later that President Roosevelt, accompanied by Admiral W. D. Leahy, had arrived in Honolulu on 26 July aboard the cruiser *Baltimore*. For the next two days the President conferred with Admirals Leahy and Nimitz and General MacArthur. Although Admiral King and Generals Marshall and Arnold were not present, their views on Pacific strategy were well known to the conferees. The opposing views of Admiral Nimitz and General MacArthur were presented and discussed.

Admiral Nimitz proposed that the area in southern Mindanao, slated for capture by MacArthur's forces, be developed as a strong air base for use in neutralizing Japanese air power throughout the Philippines; that the Central Pacific forces should make an amphibious landing on the island of Formosa, bypassing en route the island of Luzon; and a later landing by Central Pacific forces, if necessary, should be made on the north coast of China. With these places in U.S. possession, Nimitz stated, Japan could be cut off from her vitally needed supplies in southeast Asia and, furthermore, would be vulnerable to air attack from the newly established bases on her perimeter. Faced with this situation, it was believed that Japan would capitulate and that the Philippines would then be liberated without the need for a costly ground war in Luzon and other islands.

General MacArthur approached the matter from a different point of view. He felt it was as much as moral issue as a military one. He did not think the military conquest of the Philippines would be as costly, lengthy, or difficult as the conquest of Formosa and yet the same military purposes would be accomplished. He stressed the fact that the United States government, as well as himself individually, had promised 17,000,000 Filipinos that Americans would come to their rescue, and that this promise must be kept.

No definite commitments were made at the time but before MacArthur left Honolulu he confided to Colonel Fellers that he believed his views had been accepted by the President, and if so, it was undoubtedly due to the recommendation of Admiral Leahy. A short time later the Joint Chiefs of Staff issued directives for a landing on Leyte on 20 December by the forces of the Southwest Pacific Area, but advised that a "decision as to whether Luzon will be occupied before Formosa will be made later."

Now that there was some certainty as to just what was expected of the Southwest Pacific forces, the planning could go ahead with more confidence. Outline plans for Morotai, Sarangani, and Leyte were looked over and then the representatives of the various services left Brisbane on 8 August for their respective headquarters. I boarded my flagship—the *Blue Ridge*—at Hollandia and immediately commenced preparations for the amphibious phase of the invasion of Morotai on 15 September 1944.

Morotai, a small island lying about fifty miles to the northeast of the much larger island of Halmahera, is one of the Molucca group. These islands lie across the direct route from the Vogelkop to Mindanao. With their airfields, they were a threat to all sea traffic en route to the southern Philippines from the southeast.

There were two divisions of Japanese troops and a number of partially manned airfields on Halmahera, but on Morotai our intelligence staff reported not more than 250 troops, and an abandoned airfield.

Most of Morotai is heavily forested and mountainous, but a small level peninsula at the southern end was believed to be suitable for airfield development. In view of the

The first wave speeds towards the beach at Morotai, another step in MacArthur's steady advance to the Philippines.

The beachmaster at Morotai, Lieutenant Manning Williams, giving instructions to the next boat waves approaching the beach.

Troops lose no time in hitting the beach as they go over the side of an Army DUKW at Morotai.

LCI(L)s unload at 'Red' beach, Morotai Island, 15 September 1944. These ships were powered with eight 6-cylinder landing craft engines arranged in a "quad" unit on each shaft, with reversible pitch propellers.

While the Japanese put up very little resistance at Morotai, the landing was difficult because of a dead coral reef covered with slimy mud. Equipment dropped into potholes and became hopelessly stuck and literally had to be lifted out by hoisting gear.

Troops move with care across the battered beach at Morotai after landing from the LCIs in the background.

General MacArthur viewed the bombardment of Morotai from the cruiser Nashville. *Then, only a few hours after the initial landing, he waded ashore through mud and water for a quick inspection.*

small Japanese garrison, our troops could expect to capture the island with very little loss, although the reef-bound shoreline presented some problems in landing there.

Although Japanese strength on Morotai was inconsequential as far as any effective defense was concerned, the number of combat troops on nearby Halmahera, and the possibility that airfields there might get a new supply of planes, posed a potential threat.

To eliminate the potential air threat from all directions, the Fifth Air Force and the fast aircraft carriers from the Pacific Fleet, during the week preceding the landing, staged a series of heavy bombing raids on all enemy airfields on Halmahera, the Celebes, Mindanao, the Palaus, Yap, and Ulithi. These raids proved so effective that when the landings finally took place, the Japanese had almost no serviceable planes within striking range. Most of their undamaged planes, it was learned later, had been withdrawn to Luzon.

But the threat from the combat troops on Halmahera could not be disposed of so easily. If they had landing barges and other small craft capable of transporting the troops across the fifty miles of open water to Morotai, there was always the possibility they might attempt a counter attack, particularly after the landing force was established ashore and combat ships had withdrawn. To guard against this possibility, a squadron of PT boats was included with the initial naval force to maintain a continuous search-and-destroy operation against all Japanese barges and small boats venturing into the open water area.

Forty thousand combat troops and service personnel, not counting Air Force units, were assembled at the ports of Aitape, Hollandia, Wakde, Biak, Noemfoor, and Sansapor. Most of them had been engaged in campaigns drawing to a close in those areas and now they were readied for the new leap forward.

Preparing for an attack on Morotai was considerably different from the preparations for the attack on Lae, just one year before. At that time Japanese aircraft roamed at will throughout the skies, ships were few, and LSTs substituted for hospital ships and repair ships. Our crews were inexperienced, our intelligence was scanty, our confidence was uncertain, and our skill yet to be learned.

Now all that had changed. Japanese air power had withdrawn to the Philippines. There was no longer any need for the partial loading of LSTs so they could be discharged within a few hours and away from the beach before the expected enemy air attack took place. Our ships could now take as much unloading time as necessary, for U.S. planes controlled the sky. And my flagship was no longer a destroyer with limited staff space and inadequate, makeshift communication facilities.

The Seventh Amphibious Force flagship was now the *Blue Ridge,* a large ship especially designed for amphibious operations. With its ample communication facilities, I could keep in touch with troops ashore, beach parties, salvage operations, every ship of my own force, the planes overhead, the submarines operating nearby, convoys bringing supplies and reinforcements, and the various headquarters in the rear areas. This radio contact eliminated much of the guesswork as to what was going on around me. Only an officer who has been in the position of an operational commander, faced with the need for making quick decisions affecting the lives and safety of great numbers of men and ships, can fully appreciate the importance of instant communication with all his units.

Although photographic reconnaissance of the Morotai beach approaches was incomplete, there was enough information to show that a real job awaited us. Coral heads and pinnacles apparently extended about one hundred yards to seaward from the shoreline. There was no observable channel. Two small jetties apparently bridged the reef area. Only about five yards of sandy beach lay between the water line and vegetation. We did not like what we saw, but counted on amphibious tractors and demolition crews to do what was necessary to get the assault forces ashore.

The first section of the convoy sailed from Aitape on D-5, 10 September 1944. As it passed the various assembly ports, the other sections of the convoy joined up; finally, more than a hundred ships comprised the attacking force. Escort carriers, borrowed from the Central Pacific, provided air cover and an antisubmarine patrol. Five cruisers and their accompanying destroyers provided close naval protection against any light enemy raiding force. More naval protection, but farther away, was provided by Pacific Fleet carriers and battleships off the coast of Luzon or Mindanao, where they could knock out enemy air bases and keep a lookout for any threatened movement by major units of the Japanese Navy.

The convoy included the usual assortment of transports, LSTs carrying troops and cargo, LCIs carrying troops and others fitted as rocket ships, as well as the salvage tugs and miscellaneous small craft with their beach parties and demolition teams.

The make-up of the Morotai convoy differed little from those that had gone before, although this time the LCTs were towed by LSTs which joined at Wakde. They would be towed all the way to the assault area, a distance of seven hundred miles. It was the longest tow we had yet attempted and there was some concern as to what might happen in case of an air attack or heavy weather, for the hurricane season was approaching. But such fears were unfounded. There were no air attacks for our own planes had prevented that, and the weather was ideal.

As usual the convoy was formed in a circular disposition which spread over a great many miles. Destroyers were stationed on each flank and ahead as protection against submarine attack. General MacArthur was aboard a cruiser. The speed was only eight knots as that was the best the worn-out LSTs could do.

The third day out, the convoy had a "rash" of men falling overboard. The ships were hot, the sea was calm, and the water looked cool. There was little danger when a man fell overboard—the usual procedure was for the ship losing the man to circle about until he was picked up and then rejoin the formation. Sometimes it was not necessary even to go to that trouble, as the ship next astern would pick up the man as he drifted by. It was all a lot of fun, even though a few sharks were sighted occasionally. But the sharks only gave zest to the overboard game. There was some hint that bored men had formed pools and were betting on recovery times. There would be no sense in trying to break up this sport by threatening to leave behind anyone who was careless enough to fall overboard. A more effective means was found. A simple signal was sent to the convoy: "No more men will fall overboard." It caused a ripple of amusement throughout the convoy and some wondered if the admiral thought he was God. But it worked. Presumably the skipper of each ship took the necessary preventive measures.

The Morotai convoy arrived off the landing area on schedule, at dawn, 15 September. Cruisers, destroyers, and aircraft bombarded all known or suspected Japanese positions on Halmahera and Morotai with very little return fire. Troops headed for the Morotai shore in amphibious tractors and small boats. The going was difficult. Some of the boats grounded on coral heads; tractors were snagged by sharp pinnacles; LSTs and LCTs spewed their vehicles into the swamplike bottom where many foundered before reaching the firm sand. Most men reached shore by wading across the reef in waist-high mud and water. Fortunately there was no opposition. Most of the small Japanese garrison had fled to the hills when the bombardment began, and later attempted to join their fellow troops on Halmahera by small boat.

The medical arrangements followed the general policy developed in recent months in which specially equipped LSTs provided emergency surgical care at the beachhead for all Army casualties until Army facilitites became available ashore. Surgical and nursing care were provided for casualties being evacuated in all LST echelons returning from the landing area. Although all the available medical services in this particular operation were not needed, it was good insurance and a great morale builder.

To provide these medical facilities, our hard-working repair force in the forward area—still without Navy Department knowledge—had altered an increasing number of LSTs until we now had a total of 27 functioning as casualty ships, in addition to their normal duties, for this operation. Thirteen of these casualty LSTs carried surgical teams equipped to undertake immediate major surgery and to evacuate a total of 85 beds and 200 ambulatory cases on each LST. The other LSTs were less well-equipped and carried a smaller medical staff but they were capable of handling the less serious cases.

There was no reduction in vehicle and cargo capacity for forward journeys in these converted LSTs and only an unimportant reduction in the number of bunks available for crew or troop use.

Another medical activity of great usefulness, first tried out at Morotai, was to send planes in on D-day to spray DDT on all areas likely to be occupied. This was done because of the prevalence of tick and typhus infection anticipated in the landing area. In addition to spraying, the same precautionary measure so successfully employed at Sansapor was again carried out—that of impregnating the clothing of all hands going ashore with Dimethyl Pthalate.

With complete control of the air, the difficult job of getting troops and supplies ashore went ahead without enemy interference. Pontoons and ships' boats were used to build causeways from the LSTs to the shore. Bulldozers were diverted from their main job of road building to hauling out submerged vehicles. Bigger ships outside the reef offloaded to LCTs, LCMs and even smaller boats. It was a slow job, but finally there was enough equipment ashore for the engineers to build a pier over the reef which could even handle the unloading of a Liberty ship. But it all took time, and meanwhile other landing areas on the other side of the island were found which offered fewer obstacles.

A few hours after the initial landing I accompanied General MacArthur as we waded to the beach through fifty yards of treacherous mud for a quick inspection of shore activities. While ashore, MacArthur gave me some startling news. He had just received a copy of a dispatch sent by Halsey to Nimitz recommending that the next major landing be made, at an early date, at Leyte Gulf and that all intermediate landings be cancelled. Halsey made his recommendation on the basis of the feeble Japanese reaction to his sweep with a strong naval force along the Philippine east coast. He believed the Japanese far weaker than previously supposed. MacArthur said Nimitz had supported the recommendation and he intended to do likewise. He felt quite certain that the Joint Chiefs of Staff would approve it. He was jubilant. He was returning immediately to Hollandia and asked me to join him there as soon as possible. I agreed to leave Morotai the following night unless some unusual situation developed.

The next day saw a continuation of the unloading difficulties of the first day, while Allied aircraft continued bombing enemy air bases on Halmahera. On the afternoon of the second day a plane from the escort carrier *Santee* was shot down; the pilot, Ensign Harold A. Thompson, parachuted into the strait leading to the Japanese base on Kau Bay, Halmahera. A raft was dropped to him and he drifted to the partial protection of a pier; later he managed to paddle to a fishing hulk lying three hundred yards offshore but within easy range of coastal guns. Our planes kept Japanese batteries under constant attack to protect the stranded aviator, but two had been downed and one pilot lost. If Thompson was not picked up by nightfall, the Japs would be sure to get him. A seaplane tried to pick him up but was driven off by Japanese shore fire.

A hurried conference was held aboard my flagship, the *Wasatch,* to work out a sea-rescue operation that had to be put in effect and completed within a few hours. There was no time for detailed discussion. The rescue had to be undertaken by PT boats under cover of planes which would try to keep the coastal batteries occupied by strafing and by the use of smoke bombs. It was a dangerous job that could only be assigned to volunteers.

Commander S. S. Bowling had arrived in Morotai that morning with a flotilla of PT boats. Although unfamiliar with the waters, he said the *PT-489* and the *PT-363* would like to take on the job, with Lieutenant A. M. Preston in command. The boats not only had to avoid the Japanese shore batteries, but the mines dropped in the strait by our planes to bottle up any Japanese naval ships in the Bay—and presumably the Japanese had done a bit of mining on their own. Rear Admiral T. L. Sprague, who commanded the escort carriers, arranged to provide the necessary planes. Only a few hours of daylight remained and the rescue area was more than fifty miles away.

The two PT boats reached the entrance to the strait somewhat ahead of the planes. They attempted the rescue on their own, but the shore fire was so hot, they were driven back. As soon as the planes arrived a new attempt was made. It was now or never.

The planes did their part almost too well. For almost two hours they smothered the Japanese batteries with strafing runs and bombings and set up a smoke curtain that blanked off the actions of the PT boats from any view from the shore. Unfortunately, the smoke became so heavy at times that a plane had to guide the two PT boats to the downed aviator. But they finally got their man, just as the planes were running out of fuel and dusk was beginning to fall. It was a magnificent spectacle. Fifty planes took part in this operation. Many were hit, but there were no casualties.

The PT boats, also, had their share of good luck. Both boats were riddled with holes, but again there were no casualties. The Japanese, we learned later, were determined to get the downed aviator. They had become convinced that anyone worth such a tremendous rescue effort must be a very important person.

When the air-sea rescue mission was reported successfully completed, I went ashore, conferred with the army commanders, turned over local control of naval operations to Admiral Fechteler, and sailed in the *Wasatch* for Hollandia.

The last step had been taken on the return to the Philippines. For the next couple of months, effort would be concentrated on preparations for the invasion of the island of Leyte. The final chapters of the war with Japan were about to be written and one could sense a victorious ending.

21:

Next Move- The Philippines

BY LATE 1944 GENERAL MACARTHUR'S DREAM OF A TRIUMPHANT return to the Philippines was about to be realized. The date, the place, and the leadership had been decided upon. Only the details needed to be worked out. The date would be 20 October 1944, the place would be Leyte Gulf, and General Douglas MacArthur would be the commander of the greatest invading force ever assembled in the Pacific. Only the Pacific Fleet would be excluded from his direct control, but it would be available to provide the necessary naval protection.

Hollandia became a hub of activity. Every major commander in the Southwest Pacific had moved his headquarters to this area. Good roads were built, wooden barracks and Quonset huts sprang up overnight. Little tent cities dotted the landscape and the harbor filled with ships. Army and navy commanders flew in from the Central Pacific to participate in the planning.

Although the assault phase of MacArthur's Morotai operation had been completed quickly and with little loss, the campaign by the Central Pacific forces against the islands of Peleliu and Angaur had run into serious trouble and the end was not in sight. The attack on Pelelieu had taken place on 15 September, the same date as the one on Morotai. But there the similarity ended.

Peleliu was well defended by more than five thousand Japanese combat troops and an equal number of service troops. Even so, after three days of almost continuous naval and aircraft bombing it was believed a landing could be made without much opposition no matter how skillful the defenders. But such was not the case. When the bombardment of the beaches started, the Japanese retreated to well-prepared positions in the steep rugged hills. No real fighting took place until troops were ashore, when they were caught in a murderous cross fire. From that time onward, for many weeks, the 1st Marine Division was heavily engaged in the costly process of digging the Nips out of their caves.

Angaur, a small island five miles to the south, was captured much quicker and at less cost. Its almost flat terrain offered no hiding place for the sixteen hundred defenders and they were almost wiped out by the five-day preliminary bombardment. When the landing finally took place, there was little opposition.

Forty thousand troops and a major portion of the Pacific Fleet were tied up in the Pelelieu-Angaur operation. Unfortunately, it dragged on during the weeks when every ship and every combat soldier could have been used in the vital Leyte job which was then coming up. More than ten thousand Americans were killed or wounded in the Pelelieu-Angaur campaign, a campaign that some historians consider as unnecessary as the Tarawa affair.

As Hollandia developed into a big rear area base safe from night bomber attacks, we began to see a steady influx of WACS, female nurses, and Red Cross workers. All tried to be helpful, but on the whole they were a nuisance. They required separate living facilities, and they interefered with the privacy of the men who liked to do their sunbathing and swimming in the raw. If we had been given a choice, we would have shipped them home. A favored few, on MacArthur's staff, thought otherwise.

It seemed like a return to civilization to see the thousands of lights in the harbor and watch movies on the open deck. The films were usually old and often in bad condition, but they were always well attended. Sometimes the same movie would be shown twice in the same evening, but no matter, the audience would sit happily through both shows. It was cooler and pleasanter to sit on topside and watch a stale movie than go below to stifling bunks.

For the first time, various USO groups started coming into the area. A large but primitive outdoor theater was built on the outskirts of Hollandia. Bob Hope, Jerry Colonna, John Wayne, and Patty Page were among the entertainers. Usually their shows would be given ashore for the GIs and then repeated afloat to the sailors on the larger ships.

I remember in particular the performance of Judith Anderson who is so well known for her Shakespearean roles. It was steaming hot the afternoon she came aboard my flagship. The men were seated on benches or sprawled about the deck waiting to be entertained.

The conditions were hardly of the type one would choose for readings from Shakespeare. An open deck, bright sunlight, no stage, no scenery, and no costume. I thought it would be an embarrassing flop and that the men were more in the mood

Ships begin to assemble by 4 October 1944 at Seeadler Harbor, Manus Island, Admiralties, for the Leyte operation scheduled for late October. Manus was one of the principal jump-off points for the Leyte invasion.

Bob Hope, always a favorite with the troops, entertains sailors aboard ship at Hollandia.

for the Bob Hope type of stuff which had been enthusiastically received some time before. But I could not have been more wrong. Judith Anderson gave a wonderful performance to the group of men who strained to hear every word. No sophisticated New York audience could have been half as appreciative.

Among the many distinguished visitors who visited our ship during this period was the dynamic Reverend Dan Poling. Perhaps I particularly remember him because we were both from the same part of the United States, attended the same schools, and both had kept in touch with one of our history teachers, who proved to be the favorite of each.

Having MacArthur and his large staff in the Hollandia area and many of his major commanders nearby had many obvious advantages. Previously much time had been lost in commuting between the various command headquarters, but that was now eliminated; also, there was the great advantage of day-to-day personal contact at all staff levels, which made coordinated planning simpler and easier. MacArthur had his headquarters, and a difficult road leading to it, built on top of a high hill about a thousand feet above sea level where the temperature was reasonably pleasant—at least at night. Sweating GI workers had some bitter words for this project.

MacArthur was never able to develop a feeling of warmth and comradeship with those about him. He had their respect but not their sympathetic understanding or their affection. He could not inspire the electrifying leadership Halsey had. He was too aloof and too correct in manner, speech, and dress. He had no small talk, but when discussing military matters he was superb.

Preparations for the Leyte operation, aside from size, were no different than the preparations for previous landings. There was the same sense of urgency, the same great distances separating the various embarkation points, and the same need to borrow amphibious ships from the Central Pacific—a need that had existed ever since the Woodlark-Kiriwina landings. The Seventh Amphibious was never asked to loan any ships, for it was known throughout the Pacific that we were always desperately short of everything.

The island of Leyte is a rectangular piece of land—one hundred miles long and twenty miles wide—running generally in a north to south direction. It is separated from the island of Samar on the northeast by the narrow San Juanico Strait and on the south from the island of Mindanao by the much wider Surigao Strait. To the east is Leyte Gulf, separated from the Pacific Ocean by a number of small islands extending from Samar on the north to Mindanao on the south.

When General MacArthur notified me at Morotai on 15 September that the Mindanao operation was being cancelled and the date of the Leyte operation was being advanced to 20 October, I had a heavy feeling regarding this new deadline. A good part of our amphibious shipping was committed to the resupply of Morotai for the next few weeks, and much of the preliminary planning done in Brisbane would have to be discarded. Often there would be concern on the part of MacArthur's senior commanders as to whether planes, ships, and troops could be readied on the required date for the next operation. But there was never any uncertainty on MacArthur's part. He gave the orders, confident that what he directed to be done would be done.

The new directive provided for the landing of four divisions of assault troops on the east coast of Leyte on 20 October with four reinforcement divisions to be landed a few days later. Two of the assault divisions would be furnished by the Central Pacific and landed by their amphibious forces under the command of Vice Admiral T. S. Wilkinson. The other two assault divisions would be provided by the Southwest Pacific and landed by the Seventh Amphibious Force under my command. My command, the Northern Attack Force, would land troops at the northern end of the Gulf. It would be subdivided into two parts, each part landing one division of troops.

Rear Admiral Fechteler would have local command of the northern half and I would retain local control of the other half. Admiral Wilkinson's Southern Attack Force would land troops twelve miles south of my area. I was also given the additional job of landing detachments of troops on two islands guarding the eastern entrance to Leyte Gulf, and on a small island at the southern end of Leyte Gulf bordering on Surigao Strait.

Some long distances would have to be covered in this operation. From Hollandia to the Leyte beaches is thirteen hundred miles. A few Army units to be transported by the Seventh Amphibious Force would have to be picked up in the Admiralty Islands, another six hundred miles to the rear of Hollandia. With the nine-knot LSTs and the time involved in loading, this meant that some ships would have to sail on the operation no later than 4 October. This allowed about two weeks to prepare and distribute detailed bulky plans of several hundred pages that involved the movement, supply, and safety of many hundreds of ships and the many thousands of troops they carried.

The amphibious force from the Central Pacific had a different problem, perhaps an easier one. Their ships were already loaded with troops and supplies for a landing which had originally been scheduled for the island of Yap. What was needed in their case was a change in the destination and a change in the landing plans, but that was not a simple matter.

My official report of the Leyte operation noted these worrisome thoughts regarding the time element in the preparations:

> All Seventh Amphibious Force shipping was in the meantime carrying out the Morotai operation and its resupply. The last of the ships [from Morotai] arrived back in Hollandia on 6 October or two days after shipping had to begin moving for the Leyte operation. By careful arrangement of the shipping schedule, enough time was obtained

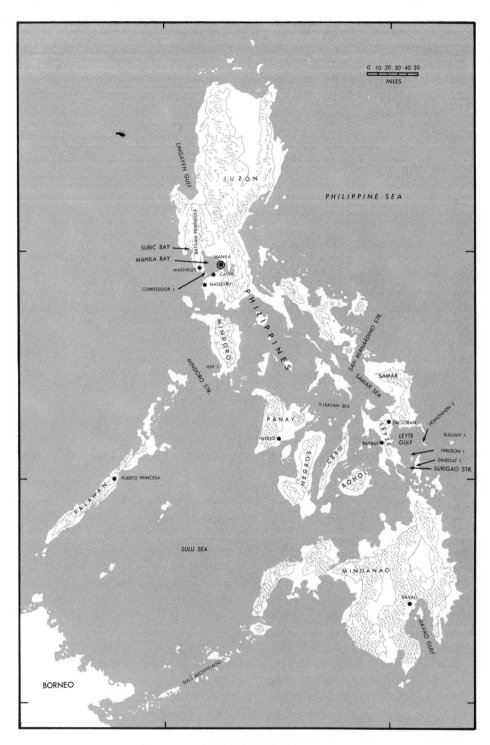

THE PHILIPPINES

between operations to fuel and take on stores, but little else. This has been the customary experience of the Seventh Amphibious Force which has carried out fourteen assault landings and their resupply in the previous twelve months.

The landing at Leyte would be the first one the Seventh Amphibious Force had made in a civilized area and the first time with access to reasonably reliable charts. The ones we were now going to use had been prepared by the Coast and Geodetic Survey in 1902! They showed depth of water, tidal changes, and beach gradients, although not in the detail we wanted. We received excellent information about Japanese troop strength and beach defenses from Filipino guerrillas with whom Allied intelligence kept in touch by submarine and radio.

It was a very satisfying feeling and one of great relief to be able to plan with some certainty as to what might be expected at the landing beaches, something we had not experienced heretofore.

The transports carrying troops were limited to six hundred tons of cargo, the amount they could discharge before dark on the day of the landing. For the same reason, the LSTs were limited to two hundred tons of bulk loading, and to four hundred tons of mobile loaded equipment which could be moved ashore in vehicles.

Charts showed that the beach gradients in the vicinity of White Beach—Fechteler's area—would permit direct offloading from the LSTs to the beach. At Red Beach—my area—there was some uncertainty as to whether this could be done. There were not enough pontoons in the Southwest Pacific to bridge any gap between the LST ramps and the beach and the Central Pacific had no surplus ramps that could be made available.

Lacking pontoons for the LSTs it was felt that, if necessary, they could discharge cargo into smaller craft such as LCTs or LCMs for further transfer to the beach, as had been done in previous operations. It would slow up matters but there appeared no alternative.

During the preparation period we were heartened by the arrival of some experienced senior naval officers who had participated in the Normandy landing. One of these, recently promoted Rear Admiral A. D. Struble, was immediately assigned to command the group of ships slated to capture the northern part of the island of Dinagat and the southern part of the island of Homonhon. The islands lay astride the eastern entrance to Leyte Gulf. The Sixth Ranger Battalion embarked in APDs would make the assault on these islands three days before the main landing, with cruisers and destroyers providing gunfire support.

While Struble's ships were landing the Rangers, other ships would clear the entrance of mines and mark a swept channel. When the channel was reported cleared, two divisions of battleships, some cruisers, destroyers, and miscellaneous craft under Rear Admiral J. B. Oldendorf would pass through and bombard the Leyte beaches on which the troops would be landed two days later. Under cover of this bombardment, demolition teams were scheduled to obtain hydrographic information regarding beach gradients and remove any underwater obstacles.

Other features of the plan provided for a subsidiary A-day landing by a regiment of troops on Panaon, an island in the southern entrance to Leyte Gulf. Struble would also command this subsidiary landing.

Filipino guerrillas had advised that the Japanese had only one division of troops on Leyte—probably 25,000 men—very few planes, and only small detachments on the islands guarding the Gulf entrances. Most planes had withdrawn to Luzon.

It looked as if the Japanese troops on Leyte could be overwhelmed by superior fire power and large numbers, unless they decided to make a last-ditch stand and bring in troops and planes from neighboring islands. The possibility that Japanese battleships or major elements of their fleet would make a surface attack was discounted at Seventh Fleet Headquarters, where Operation Plan 13–44 of 26 September 1944, concerning Japanese intentions, stated:

> 1. (d) It is not believed that major elements of the Japanese fleet will be involved in the present operations.
> 2. It is possible that he will endeavor to strike our attack and reinforcement units with a fast task force of cruisers and destroyers. In addition he will endeavor to concentrate his PT and inshore patrol craft and use them against our landing craft and transports. Attacks by enemy submarines on targets of opportunity may be expected. Participation of Orange [Japanese] BBs [Battleships] in defense of Eastern Philippines area is not considered probable.

Vice Admiral J. B. Oldendorf's task force of six prewar battleships, eight cruisers, and twenty-eight destroyers was fully capable of protecting Leyte Gulf from any raid by Japanese cruisers and destroyers. And it was not believed they would need their full quota of armor-piercing projectiles. On this assumption, the battleships and cruisers had replaced a large amount of armor-piercing projectiles—the type used in surface engagements—with bombardment ammunition. An unduly large proportion, as it turned out.

Captain Ray Tarbuck, the senior naval officer on MacArthur's staff and the head of his Red Team that prepared the basic Leyte plans, had somewhat different and more specific ideas of Japanese intentions. In a memorandum prepared for MacArthur's General Headquarters on 4 October 1944, he noted that the Japanese southern fleet had been divided into two groups, which he referred to as the 1st and 2nd Diversion Groups. The 1st Diversion Group of eight cruisers and twelve destroyers, he predicted, would make a night attack through Surigao Strait on our amphibious forces in Leyte Gulf.

The other part of Tarbuck's analysis that appeared in the same memorandum and should be preserved among history's accurate forecasts was his prediction that the 2nd

Diversion Force of four modern and two old battleships, six cruisers and fifteen destroyers "will attempt to create diversions which are calculated to draw off our slow battleships (Oldendorf's group) and our cruisers and destroyers from screening positions in the Surigao Strait." A chart that accompanied his memorandum showed the possible routes of the 2nd Diversion Attack Force as being either through San Bernardino Strait or around the north coast of Luzon. Whatever route the 2nd Diversion Attack Force took, we were confident Admiral Halsey's Third Fleet would be on guard and fully able to handle the situation.

By 4 October ships and troops were beginning to assemble at the two principal jump-off points, Hollandia and Manus. Vice Admiral T. S. Wilkinson's Southern Attack Force from Central Pacific was among those assembled at Manus as was Fechteler's force from the Southwest Pacific. Wilkinson's troops had embarked on 17 August in the Hawaiian Islands, supposedly for the assault on Yap, but had been diverted while en route and were now at Manus awaiting the 14 October departure for Leyte Gulf.

The expedition of 738 ships, 471 from Hollandia area and 267 from Manus, included battleships, cruisers, small carriers, destroyers, transports, tankers, amphibious ships and an assortment of miscellaneous craft—minesweepers, salvage tugs, and floating drydocks. Approximately 165,000 troops and perhaps another 50,000 sailors were aboard these ships. It was an impressive sight.

The various task groups left at different times, but all with the object of arriving at their own particular time outside the entrance to Leyte Gulf to permit coordinated action on A-day. The Northern Attack Force, my command, included about one-half of the overall number of troops and ships in the operation, which about equalled the number that had taken part in the Hollandia-Aitape landing.

Admiral Halsey's Third Fleet, although part of the operation, would not be under MacArthur's control, but would remain under Nimitz's shore-based command at Honolulu. This divided command created difficulties later.

After some last-minute preparations, including welcoming aboard a number of passengers, the *Blue Ridge* steamed out of Hollandia on Friday, 13 October 1944. Among our passengers were the Army 10th Corps commander, the 24th Division commander, some of their staff, and a few observers from General MacArthur's staff, including the newly promoted Brigadier General Bonner Fellers, chief of MacArthur's planning section, and Captain Ray Tarbuck, his naval planner. The press was well represented by six war correspondents.

After leaving Hollandia harbor, the convoy of 119 ships assumed a modified circular formation with radar picket ships ahead and on the flanks, but well below the horizon. In a few hours every ship was where it ought to be, and we were on our way. Because of the little ships and slow ships, convoy speed was only six knots, but that was enough to take us to a great moment in history.

22:

Leyte Gulf Assault

20 October 1944

MANY YEARS MAY PASS BEFORE ALL THE PIECES OF THE COMPLEX Leyte Gulf (Code named King-Two) operation can be placed in proper perspective and an accurate appraisal made of the many controversial features of the land and air and sea battles in the Philippine area during the last two weeks of October 1944. I won't attempt it.

No one individual was fully aware of what was going on beyond his immediate horizon, and that applied equally to the commander in chief and the lowliest GI. Radio information was often delayed, frequently garbled, and sometimes unreliable.

This account will be limited to the part played by the Seventh Amphibious Force in the overall picture and, as its commander, what I saw and what I thought was taking place on the basis of many dispatches from widely ranging units of the Army, Navy, and Air Force.

We all knew in general whether we were winning or losing but not the accurate details. Every now and then Japanese broadcasts would report the same battle but with different results. Not until days afterwards would we be able to piece together the various bits of information and arrive at a reasonably true understanding of what went on.

I did not keep a journal, but Captain Ray Tarbuck did and used it as the basis of his report to General MacArthur's headquarters. What he saw and what he heard is what I saw and what I heard. He was aboard my flagship, the *Blue Ridge,* as an observer. I am quoting at length from his report.

APO 500
3 November 1944

SUBJECT: PHILIPPINE INVASION, "King-Two" Operation,
             General Headquarters Observer's Log,
             Captain Ray Tarbuck, U.S. Navy

1. The Central Philippine Attack Force was composed of two amphibious forces and I requested orders to the Seventh, since it is an organic unit of this theater. Consequently more of this narrative concerns the Northern Attack Force, [Rear Admiral Barbey] than it does the Southern [Vice Admiral Wilkinson]. War diary form of report is used in order that individuals might form conclusions of their own.

A-6 day, 14 October 1944

A destroyer transfers mail at sea by breeches buoy, coming close aboard the starboard quarter.

Rear Admiral Barbey informs the ship's company over the public announcing system they are en route to invade the Philippines. [Only those who needed to know had been aware of our destination.]

This convoy is to contain 42,000 assault troops of the Northern Attack Force being joined by Rear Admiral Fechteler's convoy tomorrow noon.
Word is received that Admiral Halsey and Vice Admiral Mitscher attacked Okinawa, Formosa and Luzon, shooting down 528 planes and sinking over one hundred ships. Admiral Barbey expects a strong reaction from the Japanese, especially in the air, by night sporadic attacks if they have any air left.

Here in the doldrums there is calm and high humidity resulting in extremely uncomfortable living conditions, especially when it is necessary to wear life jackets.

The Third Amphibious Force [Wilkinson's] is sighted in this area making a double convoy of 555 ships. This does not include the Third Fleet Task Force of 84 combatant ships, the tanker train, nor the 16 CVEs [small carriers] and their escorts. This convoy was mounted in Manus, Finschhafen, and Hollandia.

A-5 day, 15 October 1944

Ten APAs [large transports] and three LSDs [landing ship dock] of Admiral Fechteler's command, carrying the First Cavalry Division, fell into formation. We have our own battleships, cruisers, and destroyers which are not included in the Third Fleet.

Received word that the cruisers *Houston* and *Canberra* have been torpedoed and are under tow. [These cruisers were part of Admiral Halsey's Third Fleet which was operating north of Luzon.] Apparently an enemy striking force is at sea, for Admiral Halsey informs us that he was deploying the Third Fleet for action and that no further support for the "King-Two" Operation can be expected until the situation clears. [The *Houston* and *Canberra* were torpedoed by planes, not ships.] This theater, therefore, is being requested to supply maximum air reconnaissance of Surigao and San Bernardino Straits.

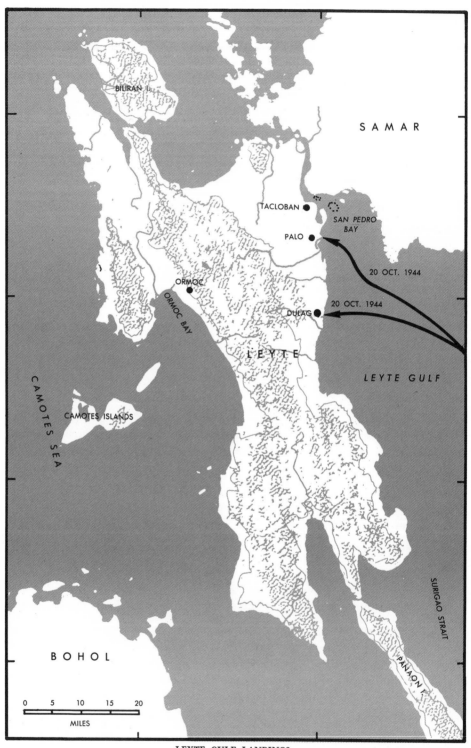

LEYTE GULF LANDINGS

The Third Fleet was scouted today by enemy planes so we anticipate a shore-based air attack upon the Third Fleet after sundown, possibly assisted by surface ships.

The President of the United States sends best wishes for the success of our operation to Sergio Osmena, President of the Philippine Commonwealth, who is now at sea on this expedition.

General Headquarters SWPA [MacArthur's Headquarters] suggests to Admiral Nimitz that consideration be given to the thought that the [Japanese] Second Diversion Attack Force may be the bulk of enemy surface strength in the South China Sea-Singapore area consisting of six battleships, twelve heavy cruisers, four light cruisers and twenty destroyers representing practically all of the enemy's available surface strength. General Headquarters further suggested that this force will sortie through San Bernardino Strait or Surigao Strait.

Enemy reconnaissance aircraft have been over Humboldt Bay which they must have seen to be greatly reduced in shipping. The Japanese, therefore, are cognizant of our convoy's departure.

GHQ also has warned Pacific Fleet that our left flank is unguarded and that if the enemy battle line should appear in that position with our Third Fleet beyond intercepting distance the result will be disastrous. This is the day that the Commander in Chief, Southwest Pacific Area [MacArthur] and his advance echelon party embarks on the cruiser *Nashville*.

A-4 day, 16 October 1944

We have a feeling on board that a Japanese *ruse-de-guerre* is in progress. He may be using his carrier fleet as bait to entice away our fleet aircraft from their mission of preparatory bombing of the rear Philippine airdromes. If this is true, we will have more enemy land-based air to contend with than previously expected and thereby may even lose the air initiative.

Officers and men on board attend aircraft recognition school in the wardroom. Good news is received from Admiral Halsey that he has bagged over seven hundred planes on this cruise and plans to strike the Central Philippines dromes [the ones on Leyte and neighboring islands] on A-2 and A-1.

A B-29 reports two enemy battleships to be at Takao, Formosa. Admiral Halsey says he sent a streamlined detachment toward Ulithi as bait to draw out enemy carriers [which were operating near Japan]. He later sighted three carriers, two cruisers and four destroyers two hundred miles to the northward. The cruiser *Houston* requests removal of all personnel, being in a serious condition.

Admiral Kinkaid says that enemy movements further strengthen his opinion that the Second Diversion Attack Force [Japanese] is a surface group.

The Seventh Fleet Air Wing is warning the Black Cats [U.S. sea planes] that they must discover the approach of enemy ships which might attack the left flank of this expedition.

A-3 day, 17 October 1944

Admiral Struble's forces [Sixth Ranger Battalion] landed on Homonhon, Suluan, and Hibuson Islands without resistance, but in a gale and rough seas. He lost all but two landing boats.

Admiral Halsey has sighted units of the Japanese Fleet which have come out to "mop up." They retired and he pursued. Admiral Halsey considers his forces now secure enough to send more of his carriers to assist in our landing. Admiral Struble reports that his force has captured Japanese prisoners and is sweeping the entrance channel to Leyte Gulf for mines.

A-2 day, 18 October 1944

Admiral Halsey hit Luzon with planes from twelve carriers and sank five large transports, oilers and freighters. One bogie [Jap plane] appears on the radar screen fifty miles to the west. The advance attack group reports sweeping up sixty mines.

Bombardment ships have passed through the mine fields and attacked Dulag village. Beach obstructions have been inspected and considerable opposition is being received from the shore defenses. No underwater obstructions have been found. Machine gun, rifle and mortar fire killed and wounded men of the naval underwater combat demolition team. Sweepers received two air attacks. Guerrilla forces reported that all Japanese aviation on Leyte has been destroyed and that Jap motor torpedo boats have retired. We have apparently obtained air superiority. There are reported to be no Japanese on Panaon Island near southern end of Leyte Gulf.

Red and White beaches, the northern attack force area, are defended with barbed wire, trenches and tank traps with land mines between ditches and trenches. There are many real and dummy pill-boxes with the real ones excellently camouflaged. There are artillery emplacements behind the trenches and mountain guns in the hills according to reconnaissance.

Admiral Halsey is supporting the "King-Two" Operation by covering the San Bernardino and Surigao Straits and is moving his tanker train south to avoid stormy weather. Escort carriers are planning to enter Leyte Gulf and land planes on Tacloban field when proper time arrives.

Information was received that the Far East Air Force, operating from China, has bombed Davao, Mindanao. The Fourteenth Air Force, operating from China, sank a Jap carrier and probably a destroyer in the South China Sea. The Fifth Air Force is due over Cebu. Central Pacific Air, based largely in the Marianas, is hitting Truk and Iwo Jima.

Fleet radio silence is in effect, but from some source a radiophone transmission has been intercepted which described the landing of amphibious equipment on the eastern beaches of Leyte between Dulag and Tacloban. This should have removed completely from the mind of the Japanese Command all doubt as to our intentions. Consequently, Commander Task Force 78 [Commander Seventh Amphibious Force] sent word to his ships that the enemy expected a landing between Tacloban and Dulag and that all hands be prepared for air attacks at daylight.

Preceded by Navy rocket-firing craft, wave after wave of landing craft streak for the beaches at Leyte, Philippine Islands, on 20 October 1944. Offshore, ships of the invasion armada keep their allotted positions, ready for the historic battle.

Three enemy cruisers were reported making high speed on a northerly course out of Makassar Strait. Thirteen large ships have been sighted at Pare-Pare, Celebes.

A-1 day, 19 October 1944

1230: Submarine contact on starboard bow, distance five miles. All ships turned left thirty degrees while screening destroyers attacked with depth charges.

The convoy later resumed its base course. More LSTs joined up from the north. Halsey's Third Fleet, having been prevented from attacking Luzon on A-2, by bad weather, is striking today.

To date the Third Fleet has shot down 954 aircraft and the shore-based aircraft claim 25.

Admiral Halsey's total of Jananese planes destroyed has now reached 1,087 after attacking Clark Field and Legaspi Field on Luzon.
Escort carrier planes have just knocked out eighty-four trucks on the Leyte highway with rockets.

The Japanese Fleet is retiring behind the Ryukyus [chain of islands extending south from Japan].

Our submarines report an enemy troop ship off Manila Bay. Other reports indicate the enemy is landing reinforcements.

A destroyer far ahead has been attacked by air. Everything is going well.

DEs [light destroyers] of Admiral Struble's Ranger Force joined up and then left for Palau.

1800: Sighted Mindanao broad on the port bow.

Destroyer *Ross* struck a mine and while maneuvering to recover exploded another mine. She is apparently under control and will not have to beach. Our crew was ordered to maintain the best possible material condition against underwater explosions.

A-day, 20 October 1944

0400: Entering channel leading into Leyte Gulf.

0420: Reveille. The Rangers have put navigation lights on Dinagat and Homonhon Islands for us [islands at entrance to Leyte Gulf.]

0629: Weather forecast: Scattered intermittant and low clouds, becoming broken over land in afternoon and accompanied by showers. Visibility, fifteen to twenty miles radius; in showers, one or two. Wind northwest, eight to twelve knots. Surf, one to two feet on beaches. Thunderstorms over land in evening, spreading to seaward during early evening, rate possibly twelve to sixteen miles. Wind west, eight to twelve knots.

Destroyers ahead and on both flanks opened fire. Southwest horizon is a ring of flashes.

Air attack from astern; rear of the convoy establishes a curtain of tracers ten miles wide.

We are now in Leyte Gulf. The Southern Attack Force LSTs have crossed ahead to get to the southern beaches. *Phoenix* [cruiser] opened fire, target unknown. [Island of] Samar is visible to the north.

The radar screen is full of bogies. Eight friendly Hellcats appear overhead. The flagship slows down; the transports pass ahead toward the beaches. Destroyers criss-cross the bow and six battleships blaze away with turret fire toward the land. There are so many ships that it is impossible to see the southern shoreline. An LSD passes with a huge pile driver and miscellaneous construction gear. Rockets boats head for the beach at full speed in line abreast.

0750: Battleship *West Virginia* is firing main battery at Red Beach with spotting planes [Kingfishers] circling overhead, as our ship's captain skilfully maneuvers the flagship into the control anchorage. We pass a mine sweeper badly listed and pumping water overboard.

Crazy smoke plumes are rising from the shore and shell splashes rise between the ships and shore. Battleship *Mississippi* is now firing on the northern beaches. She is joined by the *Maryland* whose fire has apparently caused a large shore explosion. Jap ack-ack is fired at spotting planes, but the performance is weak.

9010: Radar indicates two large groups of planes to the northward, distance ninety miles, headed this way.

Light cruisers open fire. Bombardment is getting heavier and monotonous. Hundreds of small boats are now headed toward the beaches, flanked by rocket boats and destroyers. The first wave is going in.

0958: Thousands of rockets hit the beach with the rumble of an earthquake. It is impossible to distinguish one explosion from another; it is just a roar.

Ships and boats maneuver and take stations like a game board. After a week's voyage they are about to land exactly on time. No trained officer witnessing the perfect functioning of such a complex form of warfare could fail to admire the skill and professional judgement of Admiral Barbey and his staff.

1000: The 24th Division and the 1st Cavalry landed on Red and White beaches respectively, other beaches are out of view. Within ten minutes White Beach is penetrated to 100 yards. Enemy returns fire with mortars. The landing was made in about two feet of water. Two landing craft were shot up on White Beach and one sunk. Three LSTs were enfiladed on Red Beach by enemy 75mm. guns, resulting in the death of one ship's skipper and a colonel.

Cavalry meets resistance 500 yards inshore. Ships are delivering call fire. A Jap Sally [plane] is shot down.

A Filipino guerrilla delegation is received aboard the flagship, *Blue Ridge*. They are giving General Irving information on Japanese positions. This delayed General Irving's departure three hours and he left the ship at 1430.

Shells from Japanese shore batteries hit an LST approaching Leyte Island. Minutes later the enemy gun positions were wiped out by infantry. The LST at the right narrowly missed being hit by the fire.

A barrage of rocket projectiles pounds enemy positions on Leyte, ahead of the assault troops, in the opening battle for the Philippines, 20 October 1944.

Watching the progress of the battle at Leyte are Lieutenant General Walter Krueger, U.S. Army, and (right) Vice Admiral Thomas Kinkaid, U.S. Navy, Commander Seventh Fleet.

Captain Ray Tarbuck, U.S. Navy, was an observer aboard the Blue Ridge *during the Leyte Gulf assault.*

Army troops wade ashore as the first wave lands on Leyte.

Word is received that assault troops from Southern Attack Force went into Yellow Beach standing up. Unconfirmed reports indicate that enemy tanks are being taken under fire by our warships and that the air is strafing gun positions.

In the afternoon the *Nashville,* with General MacArthur on board, stood into the Northern Attack area. The General lands at Red Beach on his triumphant return to the Philippines and makes a radio announcement to the Filipino people.

The *Australia* retired from the firing line to anchor near *Blue Ridge* followed by the Australian cruiser *Shropshire.* The cruiser *Boise* sailed by with a deck load of empty powder cans indicative of the large amount of ammunition expended. Bogies are disappearing from the screen as our combat air patrol shoots them down.

President Osmena and Brigadier General Romulo of the Philippines come on board.

1850: Air attack. Starboard guns open fire with the ships south of us backing up the fire. It is getting dark but red tracers light up the sky.

The cruiser *Honolulu* is hit by a bomb which explodes in the magazine handling room, but does not blow her up. Two tugs are standing by to assist her.

By the end of A-day no division has reached its objective, but the First Cavalry had made the most progress.

Advance has been about one mile. Tacloban air strip is captured; Dulag air field is in our hands, but the town of San Palo has not been taken.

Shore batteries have called for the interdiction of two near hills and for star shell illumination to prevent night counter-attack in the dangerous sectors. All night long two destroyers pour shells into the hills and the star shells silhouette our own ships at anchor making us beautiful torpedo targets for enemy planes. The shore line is illuminated by red tracers, lightning, dump fires, gun flashes and beach lights.

The crew is secured from battle stations at dark and a partial gun watch set.

All Jap air attacks today were weak. That is one of the reasons the landing was so successful. It is obvious the enemy would have been more successful had he withdrawn all aircraft into hiding from the carriers during the preparation period in order to husband them for A-Day beach strikes. They have violated the principle of conservation of force and frittered away their air power.

The Seventh Phib Force has been built up and trained under the bombs of enemy shore-based air, so they had their transports stowed and loaded to enable them to discharge everything on A-Day. Now they are standing out, much to the envy of the transports from the Central Pacific, who may have to "take it" while unloading for the next two days.

A plus 1 Day, 21 October 1944

0530: General quarters, enemy air raid.

0600: Heavy star shell concentrations are called for.

0605: Enemy planes attack vessels in this area.

0755: Battleship *West Virginia* again opens fire on the beaches and more rocket boats head towards shore.

Three enemy planes strafe HMAS *Australia*, within a few hundred yards of this ship. Two are shot down but the third one dives into her foremast. Her bridge structure is ablaze and the shear-legs of her mast are broken. Our doctor returns on board with the information that Commodore Collins [Australian] has been wounded and the ship's captain killed.

1050: Avengers covered by Hellcats are engaged in glide bombing enemy high ground positions. Two sailors of a returning landing craft say there is no national ensign on Red Beach so three of them lashed the boat's colors to the top of a decapitated palm tree.

1635: · Air raid at Red Beach. The ships and boats are hours behind unloading schedule, but General Sibert says he is satisfied. Dulag is in our hands. San Palo has been occupied and Tacloban is about to fall. The air strips were mined and are dangerous to bulldozers. It is estimated they will be ready for operation A plus 4 Day.

1900: Enemy planes nine miles on the starboard quarter, firing with 5″ and 40mm. is resumed as they approach. LCIs have been sent up to windward to make smoke. Smoke seems to be very successful at twilight or dawn. During daylight it appears to obscure the gunners' vision without effectively hiding the ship's top hamper.

We receive an air attack from the port side and thousands of red tracers converge over port bow. A large fire is visible on White Beach. Smoke pots are not effective because the smoke is too low and the flame is visible at intervals.

1600: Tacloban has fallen and General Sibert relieved Admiral Barbey of command of the northern operations. [The Navy commander retains command of troops until Army commander is established ashore.]

A plus 2 day, 22 October 1944

Ships carrying reinforcements stood into San Pedro Bay, near Tacloban, with 28,000 men, 45,150 tons of cargo. Fires are seen on Red Beach, and Violet Beach is apparently firing artillery star shells in the early morning.

0650: Lt. Commander Weaver and I land at Red Beach and head for the nearest command post. The area is congested with vehicles, mud, coconuts and clipped trees. The military police are not fully informed as to the location of units and are having considerable trouble routing traffic.

There are so many troops ashore that fox holes are practically touching each other. General Irving has sent two battalions forward through San Palo and one company on reconnaissance patrol to the southward to contact the XXIV Corps. Another battalion is moving up to take the first hill this afternoon. Four enemy 75s which enfiladed the LSTs have just been taken out, three are in good condition, but one has no breach block.

Men have carried many life jackets out of the landing boats for pillows in the fox holes. Fox holes are being covered with palm fronds, shelter halves and landing mat to keep out the rain. There are tank traps in this area.

After an hour's search and wading through swamp, located X Corps Headquarters under a tent fly. General Sibert estimated 350 Japanese killed and said there were no more because they had retired inland avoiding rocket fire and close naval bombardment.

105s were firing alongside this headquarters [Battery B, 63rd Field Artillery]. Few reports are in from the First Cavalry. Total American casualties at this time appear to be 83 killed, 145 wounded. Corps Headquarters is making preparations to move forward, but the General is greatly concerned about the engineer construction progress on his local road through the swamp.

We returned to an LST on the beach by sundown where we obtained a boat to the ship just in time for another air attack. The warships, including battleships, are still anchored near. The convoy ships are firing and one Val and one Hap are shot down; the average is about one out of three destroyed.

Six planes are over the Southern Attack Force and their beaches are covered with tracers. Bombs are dropping near what appears to be Yellow Beach and fires are started. After dark the ships resume their star shell gun fire.

Information is received that the First Cavalry is at Tacloban and the 24th Division is one mile inland. One cavalry brigade is on the ridge ready to advance on Leyte Valley.

A plus 3 day, 23 October 1944

Dawn air attack; did not open fire but made smoke instead. Ack-ack from shore was noticed.

0830:   Warships opened interdiction fire on hill.

0940:   Lt. Commander Weaver and I landed on White Beach. The military police control seems to be well organized here, traffic is running smoothly and dispersal of beach store is systematic. This area has an advantage over Red Beach in that it has a hard-packed sand road.

Took a jeep and headed for Tacloban.

Proceeded to the municipal building. It is a shambles of papers and furniture inside, but has not been destroyed. I saw Colonels Elliott G-4, Wheeler G-3,

Ballintyne G-4, Finley Headquarters Commandant, and Lt. Colonel Cheston, Philippine Army.

A guard of honor consisting of two troops of the First Cavalry was drawn up in front of the government building. They were dirty and tired, but efficient-looking soldiers. Major General Mudge, Commanding First Cavalry Division, personally took charge of arrangements. Broadcasting equipment was set up in the center of the front steps.

General MacArthur and the President of the Philippine Commonwealth arrived in jeeps from the city waterfront. General MacArthur broadcast an address, setting up the Free Philippine Civil Government with Sergio Osmena as its legal president under the supreme authority of the United States.

Lieutenant General Sutherland, MacArthur's Chief of Staff, read the official proclamation which made it effective. President Osmena spoke in appreciation of American support and the Philippine determination to drive out the common enemy.

Colors sounded on the bugle. On the left side of the building the national flag of the Philippine Commonwealth was hoisted. It was made by the sailmaker's mate of the USS *Nashville* and presented on this historic occasion. Colors of the United States were hoisted on the right side at the same time. General MacArthur then decorated Colonel Kangleon of the guerrilla forces with the Distinguished Service Cross of the United States Army for gallantry in action.

There were practically no Filipinos present except representatives of the local government. Apparently the inhabitants of Tacloban had not been informed of the ceremony, or perhaps did not know they were permitted to attend. However, the word quickly spread that the military authorities had turned over civil government to the Filipino people. Although political freedom in this little town is a very small beginning, the act impressed the people as a forecast of policy throughout the Islands. On the way out of town this was clearly indicated by the cheering of the populace.

En route back to White Beach, a distance of about four miles, we pass many trucks and machinery headed for the Tacloban area. Bulldozers are filling in shell craters. Engineers and aviation battalions are clearing base areas. Ambulances are rolling in and tanks moving up.

1815: An enemy plane was discovered overhead, without radar warning. Batteries opened fire. Other enemy planes appeared but none were shot down. I saw no ships damaged but several large explosions occurred on shore on the Tacloban Peninsula. Warships shelled Hill 522.

A plus 4 day, 24 October 1944

0800: Went to general quarters.

0820: Fighters are engaged in dog fights on the starboard beam. We have 18 Navy fighters in the air. Two Jap planes are splashed between Red Beach and our ship. Eight to ten enemy bombers fly over dropping two bombs between the *Blue Ridge* and an LCI and three bombs between the *Blue Ridge* and *Shropshire,* no hits.

Enemy dive bombers launch an attack on the starboard bow. All guns open up with a hell of a roar. The *Shropshire* and a destroyer commence firing also and the aircraft are turning away. Fighter pilots can be heard over the radio "tally-hoing" the enemy. Three planes fall burning, one crashes on shore. One LCI bursts into flames from a hit or a suicide plane crash. One Liberty ship is hit by a bomb. There is too much smoke to identify ships now and the burning oil smoke of the LCI rises 5000 feet, flames about 200 feet. Our combat air patrol is being relieved by a new group arriving on station from the CVEs. The support aircraft circuit announces splashes of over 20 enemy planes.

Our Northern Attack Force has now landed 93,300 men, 160,890 tons on shore. Smoke generators completely cover us with fog, we cannot see through it, but can hear other vessels firing at planes.

1500:   Another Red Alert. A quick count showed 141 ships in the Gulf, LCIs or larger. The sky is full of flak to the south and small boats have begun screening the convoy again with smoke. A Betty, which a destroyer has under fire, flies by our starboard side; a Zero is on the port quarter, but no one seems to be able to hit either one. A Hellcat shoots down a Val and heads to seaward. The Japs are getting bolder and the attacks more frequent. Splash another Val. Total men now on shore, 144,800 with 244,440 dead weight tons.

Commander Third Fleet issued us a warning of increasing enemy submarine activity. Our submarines reported Japanese battleships, cruisers and possibly carriers approaching from the South China Sea and claim sinking one battleship and one cruiser, and damaging another battleship and cruiser. A large group of enemy ships have been sighted approaching this way through Mindoro Strait and other groups are forming up in the Sulu Sea. Apparently there is a naval battle brewing. Third Fleet planes sight Japanese battleships and cruisers in formation headed this way through Visayan waters. They bomb two battleships and a cruiser.

1845:   Two explosions occur to the starboard which sound like bombs, but we cannot see through our smoke screen. The moon is in the first quarter. Nine planes attack from the west and are shot down by fighters in the twilight. Today's count is 41 shot down of which 31 were twin-engine. Received word that Admiral Halsey's battleships have been ordered to guard San Bernardino Straits while we have Oldendorf's bombardment battleships, cruisers, destroyers and PT boats for Surigao Strait.

1855:   Lieutenant General Krueger, Sixth Army, assumed command of landing force operations, relieving Vice Admiral Kinkaid, Central Philippine Attack Force Commander.

Task Force 38 [Admiral Mitscher's carriers] reports shooting down 150 planes, but suffering a bad explosion in the light combat carrier *Princeton* with many casualties. The enemy air fleet, although inferior, is threatening our Third Fleet 180 miles east of Aparri (northern Luzon) with four carriers, two flight deck battleships, cruisers and destroyers. This will force Admiral Halsey to sink the *Princeton*. Word is received that the *Princeton*'s magazines blew up while the cruiser *Birmingham* and two destroyers [*Morrison* and *Irwin*] were alongside rescuing personnel. All three rescue ships were crashed in and badly damaged. The *Birmingham* reported 150 dead and 400 wounded, hospitalization badly needed.

Admiral Halsey is withdrawing air and surface support from this operation, including the fast battleships, cruisers and destroyers, which had previously been ordered to close San Bernardino Strait, for a sweep to the north in search of the enemy's fleet air arm.

A plus 5 day, 25 October 1944

0304:   Five enemy ships in column are reported in Surigao Strait followed by a second group of enemy ships.

About four o'clock in the morning Admiral Barbey's orderly called me to the flag bridge from where could be seen 14″ and 16″ gun flashes to the southward.

0410:   Radio in clear from our battle line (Oldendorf), "We have opened fire."

0415:   "Engaging enemy surface forces in Surigao Strait and South Leyte Gulf. Two battleships, three cruisers and destroyers." Admiral Kinkaid sent a radio to Admiral Halsey, "Are fast battleships guarding San Bernardino Strait?" The answer was "negative."

Apparently Admiral Halsey's order withdrawing these guard ships was sent to force and group commanders of the Third Fleet but was not received by either Commander in Chief Pacific or Commander Seventh Fleet. The reason for enemy concentrated air attacks on the previous afternoon is now apparent, for the enemy's First Diversion Attack Force has sortied through Surigao Strait toward Leyte Gulf to give night battle as predicted in G-3's GHQ Staff Study "Japanese Fleet Possibilities 'King-Two' Operation" of 4 October 1944.

0500:   Radio from Oldendorf's battle line says that enemy surface vessels are retiring, pursued by our light forces. It is later confirmed that the enemy force has been sunk or repelled by available combatant vessels of the Seventh Fleet made up approximately as follows: 6 OBB, 4 CA, 6 CL, 25 DD, 30 PT.

Our pursuing light forces at dawn overtook seven or eight burning enemy ships, which they promptly sank.

Two large magazine explosions were witnessed during the night, so the Surigao Strait losses can be conservatively assumed as follows:

Enemy	*Own*
Sunk—7 unidentified	Sunk—1 PT
Probably Sunk—2 BB	Damaged—1 DD, 1 PT[1]
Damaged—4 unidentified	

Commander Seventh Fleet had placed his combatant ships in the right place at the right time.

0720:   It now becomes apparent that an extremely critical situation exists. The enemy's Second Diversion Attack Force has sortied into the Pacific Ocean through San Bernardino Strait under cover of darkness to attack our escort carriers, convoys, or Leyte Gulf shipping.

It appears that San Bernardino Strait has been left unguarded by a change in orders to the fast battleships, formerly of Task Force 38.2 and 38.4, to form Task Force 34 for a northerly sweep. Escort carrier planes are occupied with long-range reconnaissance, attacking inland fields, covering anchored convoys, providing close support for ground troops, and defending their own ships. Now they must assume the task of fighting off a powerful enemy battle line which is on the loose. Our escort carriers should close our Seventh Fleet battleships if at all possible. Emergency dispatches are being sent to Admiral Halsey calling for fast battleships, some of which could have been made available to checkmate their opposite types in the Jap fleet long before this critical situation developed. The enemy battle line, only two or three hours steaming distance from this anchorage, can outrun and outshoot anything in the area, their minimum ship speed is 25 knots and their two newest battleships are suspected of carrying 18″ guns.

The successful completion of the remaining phase of our transocean amphibious operation is very seriously threatened. Armor-piercing ammunition storage in our slow battleships and cruisers has been partially sacrificed for shore bombardment shell, our ammunition is practically exhausted, torpedoes have been expended, fuel is low and the situation is desperate.

0722:   Escort carriers on duty to the east of Leyte Gulf report that they are under attack by battleships, eight heavy cruisers and many destroyers split in two forces. The amphibious shipping in Leyte Gulf is the bait.

0739:   From Commander Task Force 77 [Kinkaid] to Commander Third Fleet [Halsey]: "Fast battleships are urgently needed immediately at Leyte Gulf." Admiral Kinkaid ordered our slow battleships to assist the escort carriers about 80 miles to the east. We are now suffering the effects of divided command and

---

[1] Actual losses, Battle of Surigao Strait

Enemy:	Sunk—Battleships *Fuso* and *Yamashiro*	*Own:*	Sunk—*PT-493*
	Cruiser *Mogami*, Destroyers *Asagumo, Michishio,* and *Yamagumo*		Damaged—Destroyer *Albert W. Grant (DD-649)*
	Damaged—Destroyer *Shiguire*		PTs *130, 152,* and *490*

dual responsibility. The Third Fleet has been kept intact and taken north as a unit regardless of the existence of modern battleship targets in the south.

Its fleet air is superior to that of the enemy without the use of all our fast battleships off Luzon. In the south our escort carriers have gained ascendency over land-based air. The enemy has placed his modern fast battleships in the theater of operations of our old and slow battleships.

So far as surface ships are concerned, we are strong where he is weak [off Luzon where he does not have to fight battleships], while he is strong where we are weak [off Leyte where we are forced to fight a surface action].

An aircraft reports a Japanese ship sunk in the vicinity of Homonhon Island, which is visible from here, with survivors in the water. Friendly fighters and torpedo bombers are flying around looking for a landing spot at Tacloban Field, which indicates that some of our escort carriers are damaged.

0900:   Sending our battleships [Oldendorf's] to help bring in the escort carriers leaves Surigao Strait an exposed flank, but it is now justified since the enemy Surigao force was decimated this morning.

People here feel that Halsey's Third Fleet battleships are chasing a secondary force, leaving us at the mercy—of which there is none—of the enemy's main body.

If our analysis is faulty it is because we are the ones who are trapped in Leyte Gulf. As soon as the Jap finishes off our defenseless CVEs we're next, and I mean today.

The enemy's strong Second Diversion Attack Force has thus brought our escort carriers and their escorts under fire east of Samar Island. One has received twenty 8″ hits from six heavy cruisers as close as 2,000 yards. Another is helpless and being shelled at close range by a destroyer. Four battleships are closing other CVEs for the kill. Radio dispatches from our beleagured force are pathetic and unbelievable.

1500:   The feeling of being bait in the Leyte Gulf is now relieved as our CVEs and OBBs are returning this way to arrive by dark. In the midst of this battle a lucky four-knot convoy arrived in the Gulf. It consisted of tugs, barges and rafts, containing cylindrical huts and pyramidal tents and other gadgets. How the enemy missed it we will never know.

1800:   Catalinas have arrived and a hospital ship, the USS *Mercy*, is standing in. Admiral Barbey has sent his LCIs and PCs out to rescue survivors of the carriers. One PC reports picking up 200 with others still in the water [26 October].

Before sundown Admiral Barbey sent me to visit Admiral Kinkaid in the *Wasatch* in order to obtain information which would clarify the enemy situation. After conferring with Staff Commander Seventh Fleet, the situation looks brighter. Battleship armor-piercing ammunition has arrived; two ammunition

Admiral William F. Halsey, Jr., Commander Third Fleet, as his barge takes him from his flagship to a conference on Leyte operations.

General MacArthur sees his famous "I will return" pledge fulfilled, as he surveys the Leyte beachhead.

Troops advance inland on Leyte Island, Philippines.

Soldiers build sandbag piers out to the ramps of two LSTs to speed up unloading operations.

Twenty LSTs pour Army equipment ashore near Tacloban airstrip. The equipment moves over causeways hurriedly built by bulldozers scraping the sand and earth from the beach.

ships are in the harbor; most Seventh Fleet battleships and cruisers will be back in Leyte Gulf tonight by eight o'clock; escort carriers will be in the Gulf, except those who choose to remain outside. A previous report of the approach of twenty-six enemy troop transports toward Leyte proved to be in error.

After leaving the *Wasatch* I attempted to find the *Fremont* [Fechteler's flagship] in the dark. This was successful, but our boat got lost in returning to the *Blue Ridge*. The boat compass was broken; there was no chart on board; ships themselves did not know where they were anchored.

After awhile various train vessels became visible. A huge fire flared up on Red Beach. Near Yellow Beach an ammunition dump blew up which sky-rocketed for a long time and supplied sufficient bearings for my boat to return to the *Blue Ridge*. This night our own BBs are guarding Surigao Strait and the eastern entrance to Leyte Gulf, with emphasis on the latter.

Poring over the stack of communications, it is estimated that the following losses occurred today in the battle off Samar Island:

Enemy	*Own*
Sunk—2 CA	Sunk—2 CVE, 2 DD, 1 DE
Probably Sunk—1 DD	Damaged—7 CVE
Damaged—3 BB, 3 CA, 1 DD	

An innovation of this battle is the suicide dive. If the enemy knows its effectiveness we can expect plenty more in future operations. If he has 100 planes which will be shot down tomorrow he might as well "suidive" them today and burn out 100 ships. A countermeasure must be found soon. It looks fatal for APAs and AKAs in future landings unless we replace them with more APDs and LSMs, with LSTs bringing up the supply.

Reports from [Halsey's] Third Fleet credit it with sinking four carriers, a cruiser and a destroyer off Luzon. [This was a separate naval battle from the one outside Leyte Gulf.]

A plus 6 day, 26 October 1944

0100: Battle Division Seven [from Halsey's force] accompanied by three light cruisers is due at San Bernardino Strait, but it is too late to stop the entry of the remainder of the Jap battle line since fourteen of their ships were seen about to enter the Strait an hour ago. Other additional sea reinforcements are due at 0800.

0900: It is now possible to recapitulate the total losses incurred in the naval actions in the Central Philippines in tactical defense of the "King-Two" Operation. No aircraft estimate is practicable at this date.

Enemy	*BB*	*CA*	*CL*	*DD*	*Unidentified*	*Total*
Sunk	0	3	0	0	7	10
Probably Sunk	2	1	0	1	0	4
Damaged	3	6	2	8	3	22

Own	BB	CA	CL	DD	DE	CVE	Total
Sunk	0	0	0	2	1	2	5
Damaged	0	1	1	3	0	7	12

1430: Under way in USS *Blue Ridge* standing out past six battleships, many cruisers and destroyers anchored inside the mine fields. We picked up one destroyer escort, USS *Russell,* and passed through the swept channel about dark after an air attack on the way out.

1800: One Jap plane is trailing us astern as our paravanes leave a phosphorescent wake. Paravanes hoisted on board.

A plus 7 day, 27 October 1944

This is a dangerous area; a naval battle was fought here yesterday, so our own and perhaps enemy ships prowl the vicinity. A black ship is visible to port going in the opposite direction, but neither of us challenge. The Jap snooper has closed to within two miles on the radar screen, but we cannot open fire no matter how close he gets because our best security is our invisibility. One gun flash would bring down his radio key, magnesium flares, and a delegation of night bombers or torpedo planes. Four silhouettes appear to starboard and challenge; they turn out to be friendly destroyers [which is a relief].

A plus 8 day, 28 October 1944

All tension has relaxed and the crew is granted a well-earned holiday routine after ten days on alert, twenty-four calls to battle stations, seven days continual fighting, and forty-six air attacks.

A plus 10 day, 30 October 1944

1800: Entered Humboldt Bay [Hollandia]. It is a mass of ships, lights and blinker signals, a strong contrast to darken-ship for so long.

The battle of the Central Philippines is over. All ships receive the following dispatch, "The Commander in Chief of the Pacific Fleet desires to express to the officers and men of the Fleet his pride and gratitude for the courageous and aggressive manner in which they have done their utmost to destroy the enemy in the recent fighting in the Pacific. To those who have fought in the air, on the surface, and in our submarines, 'well done.' To those brave men who have gallantly given their lives to achieve victory for our country, our reverent and lasting respect. Their high example will inspire us all in the completion of our task of destroying the enemies of the United States."

2. It is regretted that some very pertinent and colorful information has had to be stricken from the journal because of its ultra-secret classification.[2] Its inclusion would have restricted the field of circulation of this report.

[2] The ultra-secret colorful information was written in Captain Tarbuck's personal code. After the war he found the notes but could not decipher them.

3. Being the senior naval adviser permanently attached to General Headquarters, and Chairman of the Committee which drafted the original and first revision of the "King-Two" Plan, I consider it a great privilege to have been granted permission to participate in the Philippine Invasion, and witness that plan in operation.

RAY TARBUCK
Captain, U.S. Navy

23: Comments on Leyte

CAPTAIN TARBUCK'S OFFICIAL JOURNAL PRECISELY RECORDS THE march of events in Leyte Gulf as he saw them. Others saw them differently.

As my flagship entered the narrow waters leading into Leyte Gulf, my thoughts were concerned with mines, the position of ships in formation, readiness to beat off plane attacks, and such other matters as were directly related to the business at hand.

Sailors waited tensely at their battle stations in the sticky pre-dawn darkness, wearing uncomfortable life jackets and helmets. One can only wonder at their wide range of thoughts.

General MacArthur, waiting on the deck of the cruiser *Nashville,* must have experienced one of the great thrills of his lifetime. He could finally say to himself, "I have returned."

One young soldier entering Leyte Gulf aboard a transport must have a memory only of his miraculous escape from a watery grave. The darkened ships were steaming in three long columns, the crews at battle stations, the moonless sky overcast. And then the luckless GI fell overboard. A ship near the head of one column made the chilling report: "Man overboard. Ships astern keep lookout." It seemed a forlorn hope any man could be sighted, let alone picked up, in those swift-running phosphorescent waters. And yet it happened. Twenty minutes later a voice came over the circuit from one of the small craft near the end of the formation, "Man overboard recovered." A marvelous performance by an alert crew!

To the Filipinos, one of the great moments in their history occurred when their

President Osmena and General MacArthur stood on the steps of the Tacloban City Hall on 23 October 1944. The reestablishment of civil government in the Philippines was announced and the flags of the United States and the Philippine Commonwealth were raised simultaneously.

Tears of joy and gratitude welled up in the eyes of the small group of Filipinos who had assembled to hear the reading of the proclamation. On the part of myself and some of the American military about me, there may have been a lack of appreciation of the importance of the occasion and an impatience to have the formalities over with to get back to our jobs. As I left my flagship a few hours earlier, we had just finished fighting off a plane attack; a ship had been bombed and was calling for medical help; a couple of LSTs were caught on a sandbar and having difficulty getting their cargo ashore; Japanese warships were reported heading for Surigao Strait; and a large group of our little craft were nearing Leyte Gulf, an easy prey for enemy surface ships or planes. There was much to do and all of it was urgent. The ceremonies at Tacloban seemed a bit unreal.

In the Japanese headquarters at Tacloban I found a number of propaganda booklets —cleverly written in English and addressed to the Filipinos. The following is a sample paragraph:

> The smashing Japanese victory in Hawaii, Singapore, the Philippines, the Dutch East Indies, and elsewhere does not signify the mere destruction of the Anglo-American fleets or the occupation of vital areas in the southwest Pacific bases. It means more for it starts the beginning of a New Order in East Asia which will give the heretofore oppressed races of Asia the opportunity to rise and assert for their just rights.

At Leyte we learned the real value of smoke-laying LCIs. Japanese suicide planes were a dangerous threat to our shipping. They would head for the biggest ship and all too often break through the ack-ack fire and explode on the deck of their target. Since they could not be stopped by flak or our own planes, the only alternative was to hide. This was done by concentrating anchored ships in the same vicinity and then laying a heavy pall of smoke around and over them. The smoke was particularly effective in a calm or slight breeze, the conditions that usually prevailed during the early morning hours and at sunset—when the attacks usually took place. The enveloping smoke saved many a ship. A Kamikaze pilot was unlikely to enter a smoke screen and sacrifice his life when there was no target in sight.

Hospital ships were forbidden to enter the Gulf for the first few days for fear of Kamikaze attack, and thereafter their stay was limited to three hours, just long enough to pick up the casualties and get out. Since Army hospitals ashore could not be set up as rapidly as anticipated because of heavy rains, the converted *LST-464* remained in the harbor and became the most important medical facility afloat or ashore for several days.

One can get used to anything, I suppose, and bombing raids are no exception. The first time an individual is subjected to a raid he is tense and nervous. But when they take place several times a day, particularly at dawn and dusk, he soon accepts it in the same routine way one accepts the hazards of driving on a crowded freeway. And the admiral in his cabin is no more immune than is the newest recruit in his bunk between decks.

In most landings certain amphibious force capabilities were often called upon by shore activities to help out until their own facilities were well-established and functioning. Surprisingly, the most valuable work of "Rainy" Day's LCI fire fighters, which he designed and commanded, took place ashore. At Leyte, his fire parties saved about one-third of a huge gasoline dump after a six-hour, all-out battle. A number of fire alarms were handled at Tacloban air strip and the LCI fire fighters literally wore themselves out. At this stage of the operation, except for a few CO_2 bottles, the entire fire-fighting capability ashore depended on a few small LCIs.

As reports from planes and submarines filtered in, it became almost certain that the main body of the Japanese fleet was headed for a two-pronged attack on the shipping in Leyte Gulf. One prong, the Southern Force, was headed for Surigao Strait, the southern entrance to Leyte Gulf. The other prong, the Center Force, was headed for San Bernardino Strait, presumably with the intention of passing through it and then swinging to the southeast and entering Leyte Gulf through the same channel that our amphibious ships had used a few days previously. Our planes and submarines had been taking a heavy toll of both of these forces but they kept on coming. At their present speed, they should both be able to enter the Gulf the night of 24–25 October.

On the afternoon of the twenty-fourth, Admiral Oldendorf moved his six prewar battleships, eight cruisers, and twenty-eight destroyers to the upper exit of Surigao Strait and took up a steady patrol, back and forth across the channel. In addition to this patrol, thirty-nine PT boats were stationed along the approaches to the Strait. Their job was to watch for enemy ships with torpedoes.[1] Oldendorf's ships not only had more fire power, but were in an ideal tactical position to meet the threat of the Japanese Southern Force in Surigao Strait. The general feeling was that if the Japanese were foolish enough to attempt it, they would be destroyed. There was even more confidence that the Japanese Center Force could not get out of San Bernardino Strait, for Halsey was guarding that exit with the most powerful fleet that had ever been assembled in the Pacific.

[1] PT boats waited in the blackness to attack with torpedoes when the Japanese ships came through. That part of it was carried out as planned. The Japanese came through and the PT boats dashed to the attack in the glare of enemy searchlights and fired their torpedoes. Only one hit was made. Torpedoes require skilled handlers and few PT crews were equal to the task. Since their arrival in the Pacific they had been used principally in night operations to break up coastal barge traffic with their small deck guns.

Shortly after midnight, the *Blue Ridge* received word that Japanese ships had entered Surigao Strait and were heading north. For the next few hours we watched as occasional flashes of gunfire broke through the darkness. The air was full of dispatches and all the news was good news. When dawn came we learned more about what had happened. The first section of Japanese had entered the Strait with two battleships, one heavy cruiser, and four destroyers. They had come under heavy torpedo attack from our destroyers and gunfire from our battle line. Except for the heavily damaged destroyer, *Shigure,* all Japanese ships had been sunk.[2]

The second section of Japanese approached the Strait with three cruisers and four destroyers, thirty miles behind the first section, but never got into battle. It turned around and discreetly left the scene when it saw what was happening. Planes had been sent out to track them down. U.S. losses were limited to one PT boat sunk, one destroyer and three PT boats damaged.[3]

While all this good news was being passed around we received word of a different type from a different quarter. The San Bernardino exit was no longer being guarded. Halsey had withdrawn all his ships and was chasing six Japanese carriers, three cruisers, and some destroyers that had come down from the north. He had mistakenly believed, on the basis of aviators' reports, that the Japanese Center Force had been so battered in the previous day's air battle that they would not attempt passage through the Strait. We learned later that this Northern Force had been sent down to decoy Halsey away from San Bernardino. Halsey caught the decoy and mauled them badly. Four Japanese carriers, one light cruiser, and three destroyers were sunk, but the Center Force, a far more dangerous unit of the Japanese Fleet, exited unharmed from San Bernardino Strait.

It was not until about 0700 that we got the really bad news that the Northern Section of Admiral Thomas Sprague's 16 baby "flattops" was being fired upon. He had been happily patrolling along the coast from Samar to Mindanao quite secure in the belief that San Bernardino Strait, 150 miles to the northwest, was bottled up. Then surprisingly, his scouting planes reported 4 Japanese battleships, 8 cruisers, a number of destroyers and some shore-based Kamikazes headed in his direction. All his available planes—and there were not many—and his escorting destroyers joined in an attack. But they did not have a chance. Within 2 hours, 2 CVEs, 2 DDs and 1 DE

[2] The real damage to the luckless Japanese force in Surigao Strait was the destroyer torpedo attack which came at them from each side and was so successful that there was little left for Oldendorf's battleships and cruisers to do.

[3] U.S. Losses:
Sunk—*PT-493*
Damaged—*Albert W. Grant* (DD-649),
       PT-194, PT-152, PT-130

Japanese suicide plane sinks the escort carrier St. Lo (CVE–63) *off Leyte Gulf, 25 October 1944.*

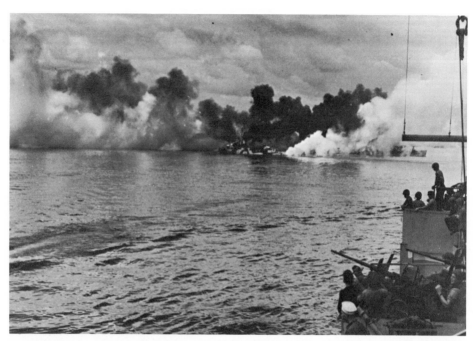

A smoke screen is laid around U.S. warships in Leyte Gulf as Japanese planes approach.

Gaping holes in the bulkhead of the USS Suwannee *(CVE–27) testify to the tremendous damage the little carrier received when hit by a Japanese suicide plane off Leyte Gulf, 25 October 1944. She made it back to the United States for repairs under her own power.*

*Crewmen aboard PT boats watch bomb explosions as Japanese planes dodge ack-ack fire.
The Liberty ship to the left was subsequently hit by a Japanese plane that was shot down.*

A direct hit by a Japanese bomber sets fire to a gasoline dump at 'White' beach, Leyte.

One of the great moments in history occurred when President Osmena and General MacArthur stood on the steps of the Tacloban City Hall, 23 October 1944, and proclaimed civil government reestablished in the Philippines.

had been sunk, and 7 CVEs, 1 DD and 2 DEs had been badly damaged.[4] If the Japanese kept coming, they could enter Leyte Gulf in a few hours and all that stood between them and the amphibious shipping in the harbor was Oldendorf's squadron. And Oldendorf's ships were low on armor-piercing ammunition and exhausted from the Surigao battle, which had ended but a few hours earlier.

MacArthur was deeply worried. His supply lines were in jeopardy. His former high opinion of Halsey underwent a drastic change. In an exchange of dispatches a few days previously he had stated his position.

RADIO: HALSEY to MACARTHUR (21 Oct 44)

MY PRESENT OPERATIONS IN STRATEGIC POSITION TO MEET THREAT OF ENEMY FLEET FORCES ARE SOMEWHAT RESTRICTED BY NECESSITY OF COVERING YOUR TRANSPORTS AND OTHER OVERSEAS MOVEMENTS X REQUEST EARLY ADVICE REGARDING WITHDRAWAL OF SUCH UNITS TO SAFE POSITION WHICH WILL PERMIT ME TO EXECUTE ORDERLY REARMING PROGRAM FOR MY GROUPS AND ALLOW FURTHER OFFENSIVE OPERATIONS.

RADIO: MACARTHUR to HALSEY (21 Oct 44)

THE BASIC PLAN FOR THIS OPERATION IN WHICH FOR THE FIRST TIME I HAVE MOVED BEYOND MY OWN LAND-BASED AIR COVER WAS PREDICATED UPON FULL SUPPORT BY THE THIRD FLEET X SUCH COVER IS BEING EXPEDITED BY EVERY POSSIBLE MEASURE BUT UNTIL ACCOMPLISHED OUR MASS OF SHIPPING IS SUBJECT TO ENEMY AIR AND SURFACE RAIDING DURING THIS CRITICAL PERIOD X . . . . . CONSIDER YOUR MISSION TO COVER THIS OPERATION IS ESSENTIAL AND PARAMOUNT X.[5]

---

[4] U.S. losses, Battle off Samar Island:

Sunk—		Damaged—	
	St. Lo (CVE-63)	*Sangamon* (CVE-26)	
	Gambier Bay (CVE-73)	*Suwannee* (CVE-27)	
	Hoel (DD-533)	*Santee* (CVE-29)	
	Johnston (DD-557)	*White Plains* (CVE-66)	
	Samuel B. Roberts (DE-413)	*Kalinin Bay* (CVE-68)	
		Fanshaw Bay (CVE-69)	
		Kitkun Bay (CVE-71)	
		Heerman (DD-523)	
		Richard M. Rowell (DE-403)	
		Dennis (DE-405)	

[5] From "Reports of General MacArthur."

However, Halsey, being independent of MacArthur's command, acted in accordance with his own ideas of his paramount mission. He left San Bernardino unguarded in favor of pursuing the Japanese decoy force.

Frantic signals were sent by Kinkaid to Halsey for help. Hoping to save some of the ships of my force, I arranged to concentrate all Seventh Amphibious Force ships in shallow, narrow San Juanico Strait, which separates Leyte from Samar, with the slight hope they would be out of reach of a raiding force. Nimitz queried Halsey as to his whereabouts. Oldendorf was pulled out of Surigao Strait and directed to guard the eastern entrance of the Gulf from the new threat.[6] And then a curious thing happened. The Japanese commander, Admiral Kurita, reversed direction about noon and headed for the entrance to San Bernardino, which he was able to enter without hindrance a few hours later. Some of the reasons for his decision to turn back, he said later, was his knowledge of the total defeat of Japanese naval forces in Surigao Strait, uncertainty as to the strength of Oldendorf's squadron, failure of his communications, lack of air coverage, and a belief that Halsey was on the way to cut him off.

One of the rich prizes that the Japanese Center Force would have encountered if they had continued on their way a few hours longer was a lumbering group of seventy-five ships, principally LCTs, APc's and LCIs, en route to Leyte, almost in sight of their goal and blissfully unaware of their danger. They were under the command of Commander B. C. Allen, Jr. This is his account of that trip:

> I had fifty LCTs and a few APc's I wanted to get to Leyte from an assembly point at Hollandia. The total distance was around 1,500 miles, with a possible stop at Biak after the first 300 miles. The LCTs were not made for that kind of work in the open sea, had no navigational facilities, and anyway it was beyond the limit of their cruising range, even with the refueling stop.

> I borrowed a frigate and some LCI gunboats for escort, a repair ship—which was invaluable and worked the entire voyage—and a group of LCIs to use as navigational escorts. The latter I deployed around the perimeter of the LCT formation and used them like sheep dogs, and to tow disabled LCTs. The trip would have been impossible without them, and their group commander did a wonderful job. We had a formation of around seventy-five ships and craft, without good communications, and occupying a lot of acres of salt water. Just changing course was a major evolution.

[6] Captain R. N. Smoot, who commanded Destroyer Squadron 56 in the battle of Surigao Strait, wrote that when his squadron was pulled off the job of chasing Japanese ships during the early morning hours of 25 October and told to prepare for an immediate attack against another Japanese force, he ordered his ships to replenish with ammunition from a merchant-manned ship in Leyte Gulf. The disreputable and very unpleasant skipper refused to order his men to open the hatches until after 0800. It was then about 0600. "I had no alternative but to send our own tired and sleepless sailors over the gunwhales and open the hatches ourselves. Meanwhile the ship's smirking crew sat around on deck drinking coffee and making disparaging remarks, and for a few minutes it looked as though we were going to have our own little war right there. I reported the incident to Admiral 'Oley,' my immediate boss, who was giving me 'what-for' for taking so long."

We stopped at Biak for refueling before starting the long over-water leg. Wind and sea were very adverse, and we had to push to the limit to maintain our schedule. The sheep-dog LCIs were in constant use preventing straying, and towing cripples, but did such a good job not one single stray became seriously separated from the formation. We encountered a great many engine casualties, particularly as I had to push them to their limit to maintain schedule. But the repair ship with help from the crews of the LCTs kept them going, though at one time all of the LCIs had an LCT in tow.

The one unfortunate incident was the foundering of *LCT-175* in angry seas one night off Palau, fortunately without casualties. The cause was gradual flooding of her wing tanks, followed by progressive breakdown of her internal watertight bulkheads.

The poor old *LCT-175* had been somewhat of a jinx ship throughout her career. She first got into trouble at Morobe during the early operations in support of the attack on Lae. During a heavy Jap air attack she took a bomb through her cargo deck which blew out most of her bottom. Almost unbelievably there were no casualties. After a temporary patch-up job she made the trip back to Milne Bay under her own power. There she remained for about six months before getting back in service. Later, while undergoing repairs at Admiralty Islands, her back was broken in drydock. Again she was repaired, but she had been put together in a slightly hogged condition, causing her bow to ride low. Anyway, her series of mishaps finally resulted in her loss.

We eventually arrived at Leyte about an hour and a half ahead of schedule, to be met by a young boarding officer who simply did not believe what he saw.

The only part of the naval battle off Samar in which ships of the Seventh Amphibious Force participated was in the rescue of survivors.

At 1500 on the day of the battle, Captain Charles Adair showed me an intercepted dispatch from a plane which reported groups of men hanging to rafts and debris in the waters off Samar. Apparently no ships were in the area. Adair proposed we organize a rescue group of our amphibious craft and suggested LCIs would be particularly suitable because of their bow ramps.

A priority dispatch was immediately sent to Commander Seventh Fleet (Admiral Kinkaid) requesting approval of our rescue mission. Adair assembled two PCs and five LCIs. Medical personnel and supplies were sent aboard. In an hour they were formed into a task group and ready to depart for the rescue area about 125 miles away. Lieutenant Commander James A. Baxter, U.S. Naval Reserve, commanded the task force.

No reply to our dispatch to Commander Seventh Fleet having been received by 1600, a second dispatch was sent off urging immediate approval and Captain Tarbuck was sent by boat to the Seventh Fleet flagship, the *Wasatch,* about a mile away to get action.[7]

[7] It was after dark when Tarbuck started his return from the Wasatch. His small boat, without a compass, became lost. Out of the blackness loomed a large merchant ship. There was no answer to their hail, so Captain Tarbuck boarded the ship and finally found a frightened seaman who was cowering in a cubbyhole. Asked about the whereabouts of the skipper and the rest of the crew he said that when the bombs started dropping everybody abandoned ship

An hour later the rescue plan was approved and Baxter's small task force was under way. They will always be gratefully remembered by the more than eleven hundred survivors they picked up. Extracts from the logs of all but one of these ships are used to tell the story. Unfortunately, the log of the *LCI-34* could not be found in the archives.

25 October 1944 (Wednesday)

1600 *PC–623* Task Group 78.12 formed consisting of *PC–623* (flagship), *PC–1119*, LCIs *34, 71, 337, 340* and *341* to search for survivors.

1806 *PC–623* One medical officer, Lieutenant (jg) Lucas, and one PHM, 1/c Wattengel, came aboard.

26 October 1944 (Thursday)

0400 *PC–623* Task Group proceeding to area to conduct search for naval survivors.

0550 *PC–623* LCIs *340* and *341* unable to make 10 knots and dropped back, best speed 9 kts.

0621 *LCI–341* Fanned out in line formation abreast with 1000-yard intervals between ships. Commenced search for survivors.

0625 *PC–623* Sunrise.

0810 *PC–623* Increased interval to 2000 yards. Better visibility.

0910 *PC–623* Sighted several planes and ships. Unable to contact due to sun and distance. Have received no, repeat no, information relating to survivors.

1049 *LCI–71* Passed through oil slick.

1400 *LCI–341* Three friendly seaplanes passed abeam two miles.

1440 *LCI–71* Sighted airplane belly tank off port bow, distance 50 yards.

1445 *LCI–71* Sighted three unidentified aircraft dead ahead.

1500 *PC–623* Passed through heavy oil slick.

1645 *LCI–340* Sighted object in water. It appears to be a survivor.

1659 *PC–1119* Sighted 50-caliber ammo box; also 2 belly tanks and numerous boxes.

1700 *LCI–340* Picked up Japanese survivor. He was kept afloat by holding on to a wooden box. Survivor was stripped for firearms but none were found. All papers and valuables were taken in custody by Commanding Officer. Survivor was then given medical attention, food, water, and placed under guard.

1700 *PC–623* Maneuvered to recover objects in water (Japanese).

1716 *LCI–341* All ships coming about to search area thoroughly.

1812 *LCI–341* General Quarters. Ack-ack off port bow.

1820 *LCI–341* Sunset. Darkened ship.

1848 *LCI–341* Secured from General Quarters.

2127 *LCI–337* Sighted much debris and heavy oil slick. Completed investigation of objects in water. No sign of life.

---

because the ship was loaded with ammunition. When asked why he didn't go with his buddies, he said, "They left before I got the word." And Tarbuck added, "On every ship there is always someone who never gets the word."

2220	PC–623	Sighted red, white and green flares bearing 270°T. Investigating flares.
2247	PC–623	Sighted several rafts of survivors from CVE–73.
2300	LCI–337	Arrived in survivor area, cruised and maneuvered as necessary to pick up men in water.
2335	PC–623	Lying to, to receive survivors.
2335	LCI–340	Received radio message to proceed to vicinity of PC–623 to pick up American survivors.

27 October 1944 (Friday)

0025	PC–1119	Sighted three life rafts containing U.S. Navy survivors.
0030	LCI–71	Sighted first survivors and picked them up.
0030	PC–1119	Commenced taking aboard U.S. Navy survivors.
0030	LCI–341	Survivors sighted in water, stopped engines. Hoisted out small boat.
0055	LCI–337	Survivor sighted and rescued on starboard hand.
0058	LCI–341	First survivors aboard from *Gambier Bay* (CVE–73).
0115	LCI–71	Continued picking up survivors, a few at a time.
0121	LCI–341	Steaming at slow speeds picking up survivors.
0122	LCI–340	Picked up lone survivor, American from CVE–73. He was given immediate medical attention, dry clothing, food, and drink.
0142	LCI–337	Survivor aboard.
0156	LCI–340	Pulled seven life rafts that were tied together alongside and started taking survivors of CVE–73 aboard.
0215	LCI–337	Sighted floating life raft. Rescued group of survivors.
0235	LCI–341	Life raft alongside. Taking aboard survivors. Sixteen men.
0247	LCI–340	Completed taking on survivors from the seven rafts. (Approximately 110 U.S. Navy survivors.) Some of the survivors were badly wounded and were given all the medical attention that this ship was able to give.
0335	LCI–71	Picked up 144 men from several life rafts.
0345	PC–1119	Finished taking aboard 183 Navy survivors. Names, rank, serial number as per list forwarded to SOPA [Senior Officer Present Afloat].
0348	PC–623	Detached PC–1119 to return to San Pedro Bay (Leyte Gulf) as they had 200 survivors aboard, instructing them to make full report to CTF 78 [Commander Seventh Amphibious Force].
0415	LCI–341	Reported number of survivors on board this time are 36, many of which have shrapnel injuries and suffering from exposure.
0622	LCI–340	Daylight came and we proceeded to continue the search for survivors.
0654	LCI–337	Four survivors sighted and rescued. One man apparently dead.
0745	LCI–337	Rescued approximately 58 survivors in a group from DD–533. Also one man from DE–413.
0800	PC–623	Standing by taking on survivors from DE–413. They were oil-covered.
0830	LCI–341	Life raft alongside, took aboard 36 men, survivors of USS *Hoel*.[1]
0839	PC–623	Sighted more survivors from DD–533. Some were taken aboard.

---

[1] The destroyer Hoel had made a gallant attack on a Japanese battleship. Most of the crew of 300 were killed by gunfire and explosions. The Commanding Officer, Commander L. S. Kintberger, was among the 36 rescued after 40 hours in the water.

0840	*LCI–337*	Maneuvering to pick up survivors.
0849	*PC–623*	Picking up survivors from *DD–557*.
0900	*LCI–337*	Rescued survivor from *DD–557*.
0904	*LCI–341*	Picked up life raft with 11 men aboard. Survivors USS *Johnston*. Continuing to pick up scattered survivors.
0905	*LCI–337*	Rescued five survivors from USS *Johnston* (*DD–557*).
0920	*PC–623*	Pumped 5,000 gallons fuel overboard to lighten ship. [The *PC–623* had aboard 260 survivors. The fuel was pumped overboard to compensate for the added weight of the survivors.]
0925	*LCI–71*	Eight more survivors picked up.
0930	*LCI–71*	Under way with 175 survivors aboard.
0930	*LCI–337*	Large group of survivors aboard, approximately 85 men.
0930	*LCI–340*	Rescued 13 men from life raft in position: Lat. 12°06′30″ N., Long. 125°42′ E. Men were given all the medical attention that this ship could render. Attempted to give all survivors dry clothing, bunks, warm food, and drink. A number of these men were badly injured and were from *DD–557*.
0936	*LCI–341*	Completed search. Total number reported aboard 90 men. Impossible to get complete list of names due to very crowded conditions and physical condition of men. Fell into column formation, course 150°T.
0945	*LCI–337*	Sounded General Quarters. Sighted one enemy plane off bow. Identified as "Betty" bomber.
0952	*LCI–341*	Enemy plane made run on ships strafing, but doing no damage. Secured from General Quarters.
1130	*LCI–341*	Fell out of formation to investigate debris.
1140	*LCI–341*	Returned to formation.
1200	*PC–623*	Steaming as before on course 150°T. Report was made that Capt. Viewig, Cdr. Thomas (*DD–533*), Lt. Comdr. R. Copeland (*DE–413*) had been picked up.
1806	*PC–623*	C/S to 9.2 knots. Count was made of survivors aboard—inaccurate. 260 men and one dead.
1840	*LCI–337*	Along port side of USS *DE–47*. Doctor came aboard.
1955	*LCI–341*	C/C 309°T. Standing into Leyte Gulf.
2000–2400	*LCI–340*	Five officers from the *CVE–73* picked up: Lt. Comdr. J. A. Samders, USNR, Lt. W. Stringer, USNR, Lt. (jg) A. S. Young, Ens. L. L. Epping, USNR, and Ens. A. W. Beisang, USNR. Also 98 men from the *CVE–73* and 18 men from the *DD–557*. List attached.

28 October 1944 (Saturday)

0150	*PC–71*	Dropped anchor near hospital ship.
0232	*PC–623*	Boats alongside for debarkation of survivors.
0345	*LCI–71*	Small boats began coming alongside to transfer survivors.
0350	*LCI–341*	Small boats alongside to transfer survivors to hospital ships.
0401	*LCI–340*	Transferred Japanese survivor to small boat with all his possessions for transportation to the USS *AGC–9*.
0645	*LCI–340*	Starting transferring American survivors to small boats for transpor-

tation to hospital ships for treatment. The hospital ships were the USS
LSTs *226* and *464*.

0850 *LCI–337* LCM alongside to transfer wounded men to hospital ship *LST–464*,
                a converted hospital ship. Stretcher cases only.
0942 *LCI–71*   Last of survivors transferred from this ship.

The sequence of events recorded in the abbreviated style of ships' logs gives no hint
of the drama that must have prevailed in the rescue area. The survivors were in
shark-infested waters, clinging to rafts and debris, some for periods of forty hours;
some were wounded; all were chilled at night and under a torrid sun during the day,
hoarding their Very's signal lights, seeing planes overhead but themselves unseen.

Through the daylight hours of 26 October, Baxter's small task force searched the
battle area without success. Current and wind had carried the survivors away. It was
the Very's signal lights, fired at night, that finally guided the task force in the proper
direction and to rescue 1,153 men. It was an outstanding search and rescue operation
which has received little recognition.

With the safe arrival of the slow resupply convoy for Leyte Gulf, I left in my
flagship for Hollandia. During the return trip I wrote to Vice Admiral R. Jacobs,
chief of Bureau of Naval Personnel, and summarized the thoughts that were then
uppermost in my mind. Here are some extracts:

> I am en route to Hollandia after some exciting days in Leyte Gulf. [Admirals]
> Wilkinson, Conolly, Royal, and Struble are ahead of me and Kinkaid is following.
> Fechteler has remained behind as Senior Officer Present Afloat in Leyte Gulf. In a few
> days Fechteler will undertake a minor landing in Surigao Strait, and Struble will follow
> with a medium-sized landing in the Visayas in about a month. The rest of us will plan
> at Hollandia for the big move to Lingayen in December.
>
> The landing at Leyte Gulf went off as scheduled. There were no man-made obstacles
> of any consequence and the supporting naval gunfire overwhelmed light beach opposi-
> tion and drove it back. As the troops drove inland their difficulties increased; however,
> they have such a preponderance in troop strength that the Japs can only offer temporary
> ground resistance. They, however, put on an almost continuous series of small day and
> night air raids over the transport area, which was surprising considering the severe
> working over their airfields had received in the preceding two weeks. Their naval
> reaction was more violent than expected, and the only one I know that properly
> appraised this situation in advance was Captain Tarbuck. He is the senior naval
> representative on MacArthur's staff. In the light of what has happened, his "estimate of
> the situation" on 4 October is almost uncanny.
>
> [Admirals] T. L. and C. A. F. Sprague, with their CVEs, DDs, and DEs, did a
> magnificent job. Their skill, courage, and determination got us out of a pretty difficult
> situation. The difficult situation may have developed because of the independent relation-
> ship between the Seventh and Third Fleets.
>
> A factor that has recently arisen is the Jap suicide dive. In this [Samar] battle with the

CVEs, he had such success with his few unorganized suicides that it may be assumed he will develop and organize considerable groups of fanatics for this purpose. It is a particularly effective weapon against large transports and CVEs. It is hard to combat on moonlight nights, or at the first break of light in the morning or at dusk when the air cover is least effective. I do not feel that we should discount the capability of these suicide attacks when operating within reach of his land-based airfields and believe that a determined attack of this nature on a dawn approach of transports might well break up the landing.

I am advocating, for our subsequent moves in the Philippines, we revert to the system which gave us so much success in the New Guinea landings. As you know, this provided for the initial assault waves to be landed from APDs followed by the LCIs and LSMs, and finally by the LSTs. The foregoing has the advantage of cutting down the time of getting assault troops and equipment on the beach, and in addition the dispersal of our landing force elements among smaller naval units reduces the hazards from air attacks. Large transport and cargo ships would be used for work in the rear areas and for later supply echelons.

Six LSIs—British designation for APAs—recently arrived from England and have been assigned to my force. They participated in the Normandy landing, but operating conditions there are far different from what they will find in the tropics. Their communication equipment is awaiting installation, their cargo handling facilities are inadequate, and their material condition poor. We are using them for training but doubt they will be helpful. Four are in use to train American divisions. Differences in landing force technique are bothersome, particularly as the troops will not be carried to the assault beaches in LSIs, but rather in our own APAs or landing craft. Two of the LSIs are being used to train Australian troops with some satisfaction. However, I doubt if the training value of these ships balances their absorption of our limited maintenance facilities. Their best use would be in the movement of troops around in the rear areas, but I do not suppose they would take kindly to that idea.

A few days later my flagship was at anchor in the peaceful, well-lighted harbor of Hollandia, and my activities became almost wholly involved with preparations for a new series of landing operations.

24:

Interim Operations

LEYTE WAS A BIG OPERATION, THE BIGGEST BY FAR OF ANY World War II operation in the Pacific. More importantly, it was the first time that all the forces of General MacArthur, Admiral Nimitz, and overseas bomber commands had been brought together. Although it was a joint operation, each command retained its independence of action.

But these independent commands did not operate in the Philippines for very long. Within a few days after the naval battles ended, Admiral Halsey withdrew the Third Fleet to Ulithi to replenish depleted fuel supplies and Vice Admiral Wilkinson withdrew the Fifth Amphibious Force to the rear to organize and await a next assignment. The heavy bombers from the Marianas and the China-Burma-India theater returned to their normal activities.

On the departure of the Central Pacific ships, the responsibility for the supply of troops on Leyte and the responsibility for their air and naval protection reverted to the shore-based air and ships of the Southwest Pacific, and they were hardly equal to the task. Air protection awaited the construction of bases on Leyte and that job was delayed by soggy ground, heavy rains, and frequent Japanese air attacks. And the shipping situation was equally serious. There were not enough amphibious ships to maintain the proper flow of supplies and at the same time carry out a number of small but essential landing operations before making the big move to Lingayen Gulf on the west coast of Luzon.

As a substitute for amphibious shipping, merchant-manned Liberty ships took over the greater part of the supply runs; and no one liked that at all. When it came to fighting off air attacks, merchant-manned ships had neither the gunfire, training, or discipline to properly protect themselves; and there were not enough escort ships in the Southwest Pacific to do it for them.

Hardly a supply convoy entered Leyte Gulf without tales of Kamikaze attacks and a cry for air protection. A typical report is that of Task Unit 76.4.7, en route from Hollandia to Leyte during the latter part of November. It was composed of transports, general cargo ships, three tankers, and an ammunition carrier—thirty-six ships in all. All were merchant manned. They were escorted by five small, Navy-manned craft.

For the twenty-four hours preceding their entrance into Leyte Gulf they were under almost continuous air attack from one or more planes, and on constant guard against submarines which were reported in the vicinity. This particular convoy was more ably handled than were some of the others; but even so, they lost one Liberty ship with its cargo, another was seriously damaged, and a few others suffered minor hits but were able to continue in formation. Fifty-three men were killed and forty-one were injured. The skill and courage of the master of the SS *Marcus Daly* saved his ship from foundering after being hit by a Kamikaze. Each convoy commander ended his voyage report with the same words:

> Too many ships in convoy, too few escorts, and too little air cover.

Everyone agreed with their conclusions, but was helpless to do anything. The aircraft carriers had departed from the area, the airfields at Leyte were inadequate, and the escort ships were spread too thin to do a proper job.

The fear of Kamikazes was not limited to the Merchant Marine. The medical officer of the *LST-470* had this to say:

> On bloody Sunday, 12 November 1944, while on the Leyte supply run, we had our first experience with Kamikazes. When the shooting started I went back to the liquor locker and selected a good quart of bourbon that I had hoarded, and reappeared on the deck. I did the best I could to give everyone a "nip." That's all they got, but it was a whale of a morale builder. Shouts all over the deck told me not to forget Jim, Frank, etc. The Executive Officer told me afterwards, "Doc, I was green until you came along with that bottle of booze. I was a man after one small snort. I could kill them all."

While the operations section of my staff was struggling with the problem of damaged ships, lost cargoes, convoys and their escorts, the planning section was struggling with preparations for the big landing in Lingayen Gulf on 20 December as well as smaller landings that demanded immediate attention.

Lingayen Gulf, like Leyte, would be a joint operation under MacArthur's direction, but an even larger one. The Japanese were in far greater strength on Luzon than on

Leyte and that meant more troops would be required, and that called for more ships to carry them. Fortunately, excess ships from the Normandy landing were now heading toward the Pacific and would eventually be ready for MacArthur's use. Most of these were APAs, although our preference was for LSTs and other beaching types.

The Lingayen landing had been scheduled for 20 December on the optimistic assumptions that the American troops would be in complete possession of Leyte prior to that time and that the Army airfields would be functioning in full strength and able to supply air cover for convoys as they headed towards Luzon. But neither of these assumptions worked out as had been hoped. Airfield development was slower and Japanese resistance more determined than had been expected.

The move to Lingayen would need to be delayed until another island had been seized which would be more suitable for the construction of airfields, and at the same time conveniently located to provide air protection along the sea route to Lingayen Gulf. General MacArthur decided upon the island of Mindoro. Intelligence information indicated it was weakly defended, the soil conditions were good, and its location ideal. Orders were issued for the seizure of Mindoro Island on 5 December and the Lingayen operation was postponed until 9 January.

What I felt at the time is expressed in a letter I wrote to Admiral Jacobs, on 24 November 1944:

> The situation at Leyte indicates that the Jap is far more determined in his defense than had been anticipated. What air he has is aggressive, his ground troops are stubborn, and his naval units are close enough and strong enough to be treated with respect. Unfortunately, on our side, Army air offered to take over the responsibility for all air support before they were prepared to do so. Their fields on Leyte are inadequate and their organization and pilots not trained for the job in hand. As soon as the carriers departed the bad news began. Jap troop reinforcements from Luzon were landed with little interference and his air hit our shipping too frequently. Fortunately, the fast carriers were recalled and made some effective strikes, with the results that the Jap air raids have decreased and Jap convoys are having trouble. When Army air gets firmly established and can work on Jap fields, which is their specialty, the Jap air over Leyte should go down fast. In the meantime, I hope the carriers stick around.
>
> Our big operation, M-1 [Code name for Lingayen Gulf] should not get under way until Jap air, sea and ground defense in the Central Philippines undergoes a definite change for the worse.
>
> All our ships plus those borrowed from CincPac [Admiral Nimitz] are busy pouring supplies and reinforcements into Leyte. At the moment I have 900 ships under my operational control. Of course many of them are little fellows such as LCTs and LCIs, but they also have their administrative problems.
>
> The planning for the M-1 show is almost completed, and all preparations have been made for executing some intermediate moves when the Leyte situation improves.
>
> My own routine has almost become a cycle: conferences, plans, execution of plans, then repeat. Only the geography changes.

The loss of ships from Kamikaze attacks was making it almost impossible to meet the problems of resupply and at the same time get our depleted outfit readied for the big operation. And then there were always a few small subsidiary landings that developed overnight and had to be done in a hurry. No matter how small, they required careful attention and, what was more important, drained off some of our amphibious craft. Two of these small operations took place on two groups of tiny islands of the Mapia and Asia groups during the third week of November.

These little-known islands on the sea route between Biak and Mindanao were of no strategic importance but they were wanted as weather stations and as sites for the establishment of the Loran navigation system. All the troops, transports, and escort ships assigned to this operation were American except H.M.S. *Ariadne*, a British destroyer commanded by Captain Lord Ashbourne, who also commanded the expedition. There were only about two hundred Japanese on the little islands, but they could be troublesome if not handled properly. In spite of the care that went into the planning and the preponderance of the forces that were made available, seventeen Americans lost their lives and thirty more were wounded in this lonely operation of transitory military importance.

In the report of these out-of-the-way and little-known landings there were only two items that might be worth recording. One of them concerned the assault on the tiny island of Pegun of the Mapia group. The following is quoted from the report of Captain Lord Ashbourne:

> The first assault wave reached the northern tip of Pegun Island at 1115 without having seen a single Japanese, but at 1130 there were a series of dull explosions behind our troops, and upon investigation, these proved to be the remains of thirteen Japanese soldiers, who had decimated themselves for the Glory of the Emperor by holding hand grenades to their stomachs. Prior to committing suicide the Japanese had destroyed a wireless set and all their rifles. For some inexplicable reason they had discarded their uniforms, and for the ritual of self-destruction had attired themselves in pyjamas. I was amazed at the size of the enemy who had killed themselves in this fashion; they were all between 5' 10" and 6' 0". They looked remarkably fit and did not appear in the slightest degree emaciated.
>
> It is difficult to understand the mentality of the enemy on Pegun Island. These thirteen men had committed suicide when there was an excellent opportunity of their occasioning our troops many casualties after the latter had passed by.
>
> In addition, three Japanese guns—a 37mm. antitank gun, and two 75mm. mountain guns—had been found intact, loaded, and without a shot having been fired through them on D-day.

If any conclusion may be drawn from this report it is that the Japanese garrisons on these isolated islands of the Pacific considered their cause a hopeless one.

The other item, unfortunately, followed the pattern of some others which had gone before. Eight members of a reconnaissance party had been landed from H.M.A.S. *Goulburn* on 26 September with the expectation they would be picked up a few days later with valuable information regarding enemy activity. But they were not picked up, because they had been captured. Ashbourne's assault force found two of the bodies on one of the islands but no trace was ever found of the other six men.

The next in the series of subsidiary operations was on a larger scale and took place on the west coast of Leyte. This landing had become necessary in order to speed up the ground war on Leyte, which was not going too well. A month had passed since Allied troops had been landed on Leyte's east coast in overwhelming numbers, but they were still meeting stubborn resistance. The Japanese had been pouring reinforcements into Leyte by way of a few ports they still held on its west coast. Army planes from the partially completed Leyte fields had hindered but could not stop the flow of reinforcements. Occasional raids by planes from Halsey's fast carriers had been helpful but they were too infrequent, and of too short duration, to completely stop the traffic. Destroyer and PT forays against the enemy convoys were tried but Kamikaze attacks drove them off.

Apparently the only way to break up the flow of reinforcements was to seize the town of Ormoc which was the principal Japanese port of entry for troops and supplies, but the U.S. Navy took some serious losses in doing it. Among the casualties were some destroyers which had participated in every previous landing of the Seventh Amphibious Force without serious damage, until the law of averages finally caught up with them. A graphic description of this small but important operation is contained in the report made by Lieutenant Dwight Shepler, a combat artist, who was aboard one of the destroyers as an observer. I quote him at length because of his stirring word picture of life aboard a destroyer under Kamikaze attack:

> The USS *Flusser,* flagship of Destroyer Squadron Five, stood out of Humboldt Bay, Hollandia, on the morning of 27 November at the head of a division of destroyers returning to Leyte after a short availability alongside the elderly destroyer tender *Dobbin.* Making twenty knots behind her were the *Shaw,* the *Smith,* and the *Lamson,* tin cans of the Mahan class whose names conjure up recollections of Pearl Harbor, Santa Cruz, and the countless actions and landings of the Southwest Pacific. Three days away was Leyte Gulf and the epidemic of Jap suicide planes, one of which had exploded so close to the *Flusser* as to shower the bridge of the ship with debris of the aircraft. So it was a wary if a fast passage, all hands searching the skies, unconcerned with the many fathoms of the Mindanao Deep. Two days out a Jap "Betty" made a twin-motored run on the destroyer division, but was driven off from her low-altitude attack by intense gunfire, telling tales to her base on her radio.
>
> Leyte Gulf was in a virtually continuous condition of "Flash Red." The four destroyers were assigned to antisubmarine work across the mouth of Leyte Gulf, and patrolled the "Ping Line" for several days with nothing but ephemeral contacts on the

echo ranging sound gear. The task force of old battleships and some cruisers patrolling the horizon south of Samar threw up flak into the squally, rainy season sky on several occasions, but for some reason none of the enemy pilots picked out the Mahans for a target. That was to come later.

Returning to San Pedro Bay of Leyte Gulf, on 4 December, the *Flusser* and several ships of DesRon Five were assigned to convoy an emergency supply echelon to Baybay immediately—a recently captured small port on the west coast of Leyte. We sailed with a convoy of ten LSMs and four LCIs, hugging the coast through Surigao Strait and along the west side of the island, arriving at Baybay about 11 P.M. It was urgent to discharge the equipment and get out under cover of darkness as soon as possible; but communications had been fouled up and there was nobody there to mark the landing beach. The resourceful LSM flotilla commander groped in through the pitch night and found his own beach. An amusing note was interpolated by an LSM skipper who drove firmly onto the beach and had half his cargo of trucks discharged before someone with cat's eyes discovered that he was on a small island just off the inky shore. This error was remedied with commendable speed.

Two Jap planes kept droning through the dark sky at low altitudes like vampire bats, but unlike bats couldn't tell where we were in the darkness close to shore. They strafed occasionally, hoping to draw our fire so that we would reveal our position, but the "trigger-happy" gunners all managed to control themselves. One of the enemy planes finally dropped a near miss which caused sprung plates on the fantail of our sister ship the *Drayton,* while the other ineffectually bombed a small island several hundred yards away, and probably went back to base claiming a cruiser.

The delay in not having an Army beach-marking and working party was costly for we sailed at 3 A.M., behind schedule, and with the Jap air force aware of our presence. Just before noontime, when we were passing Cabalian Bay in Surigao Strait, twelve Jap planes popped onto our radar from the cover of the mountains and almost as quickly were in mass suicide dive upon the task group. Four of them hit ships, four missed and hit the water, three were shot down, and one, possibly the supervisor of hari-kari, went home without doing anything. The small combat air patrol of Lightnings from the hard-pressed fields of Leyte fought well, accounting for one and a half of the planes shot down. *Flusser* caught one diving at her, in a converging pattern of tracers, to send the plane in an uncontrolled exploding crash two hundred yards off her quarter. When this almost instantaneous action was over one LSM was sinking in two pieces, another was on fire on her fo'csle where a crash-diver had hit a glancing blow that was to put her in the repair yard for a month. All ships rallied to pick up wounded and survivors.

The bulk of the wounded were tranferred to the *Flusser;* the fire on the burning LSM was finally extinguished and she was taken in tow by an LCI.

As we entered Leyte Gulf from Surigao Strait planes were overhead again. The destroyer *Mugford* turned from patrol to join our antiaircraft screen. A suicide plane managed to get through intense fire, which drove off two or three others, and came down in an inexorable shallow dive out of the sun to hit the *Mugford* squarely at the base of the single stack in a monstrous red explosion. This destroyer managed to get the resultant fire out, and took care of her own casualties, which were surprisingly small in number; but her engine rooms were out of commission and she had to be taken under tow.

On 6 December the *Flusser* sailed again from Leyte with the amphibious force commanded by Rear Admiral Arthur D. Struble, attacking Ormoc on the morning of 7 December. We had the close bombardment position near the beach and next to the assault lanes. This dawn landing of the 77th Division caught the Japs by surprise, with all their forces opposing the ground troops to the north and the south of the landing area.

The return from Ormoc to Leyte consisted of running a gauntlet of the aroused Jap air force. The amphibious force, covered only by destroyers in these narrow waters, fought off successive waves of planes, many of which got through. The Army and Marine Combat Air Patrol fought well, but the enemy was too numerous and his fields too many. Our sister ship the *Mahan,* radar picket, was hit three times by suicide planes and had to be destroyed in Ormoc Gulf. The APD *Ward* was also sunk before we left the Gulf. Both sinking ships left towering columns of smoke mushrooming into the sunny sky as we sailed on. Sporadic attacks came to a crescendo in mid-afternoon when planes began coming in low over the water. Three roared in astern of the convoy and the destroyer *Edwards,* in a magnificent bit of gunnery, picked off two of them which exploded above the water in great crimson flames. A Dinah came in on our quarter out of this melee as we "fishtailed" at thirty knots. The plane approached in a flat dive, all our guns firing madly. When it seemed inevitable that the sinister shape which loomed so big would certainly hit us the plane began to fall off to the right and began to smoke, crashing broad on our starboard bow at a thousand yards or more. British Lieutenant General Herbert Lumsden, who was on the bridge of the *Flusser,* calmly remarked, "Oh, he funked it, he funked it; he did not have the nerve." Lumsden, who was British representative with General MacArthur's headquarters, was later killed on the bridge of the *New Mexico,* in Lingayen Gulf. Lumsden had distinguished himself when his armored units covered the rear-guard action at Dunkirk, and later in Africa when his armor made long sweeping attacks in the desert, navigating by the stars.

As the screen maneuvered at high speeds through becalmed sailing canoes, a plane came in astern of our sister ship, the *Lamson,* and despite violent firing on her part, dove over the fantail strafing—and crumpling the stacks, crashed into her superstructure in an awesome explosion. *Lamson* lost headway and became dead in the water, and the *Flusser* as flagship of DesRon Five turned back to help her, arriving simultaneously with the rescue tug *ATR-31,* which had been tagging along at the end of the convoy. The tug nosed up through the survivors, who had both jumped and been blown off the destroyer, to pour three streams of water at close range into the flaming superstructure. The *Flusser* maneuvered to pick up survivors and put over her whaleboat. This process was interrupted several times by Jap planes which caused us to get underway and fight off attack. As the fate of the *Lamson* hung in the balance, the *Flusser* and the tug picked up and took off all survivors and wounded. The fire was finally extinguished and the tug took the *Lamson* under tow. The hours from mid-afternoon until nightfall seemed an eternity. As this trio crawled back towards Surigao from the Quatres Islands bombers kept coming over us, but by some twist of fate none of them crash dived, though one Tojo put a stick of two bombs astraddle us.

The combat air patrol and the *Flusser* shot down a couple of the attackers and drove off the rest.

When reluctant night finally came we were virtually out of all types of ammunition except star shells, our number one gun and our starboard forty millimeters were inoperative. The destroyer *Reid,* which was to be sunk in two minutes by suicide planes several days later, turned back from the convoy miles ahead to relieve us, and the *Flusser* sped at thirty knots through the roaring monsoon night of Surigao Strait to the hospital ships of Leyte Gulf.

All the bunks of officer's country, the wardroom, and until nightfall, even the galley passageway were full of casualties. The atmosphere of the ship long buttoned up for battle was incredibly hot and oppressive. The doctor, pharmacist's mates, and several others of us worked at top speed for twelve hours, sweat pouring out of us in gallons. All around were the grey faces of men in severe shock, and the pitifully burned bodies writhed with pain. A gunner's mate lay on one of the transoms, his right leg a mangled remnant. As the doctor cut it off I laid it aside in a pillowcase. The gunner's mate, feebly smoking a cigarette, kept saying through his morphine, "Won't somebody help me hold up my laig. I can't hold up my laig any longer. Doc, won't somebody just hold up my laig?"

On the opposite transom lay the body of a lad with almost all his body burned, swathed in bulky white ointment bandages. This poor burned lad's eyes and nose were protruding from a rim of cotton. The great bandaged arms began to flail and he went into violent convulsions which threw him off the transom onto a man with a broken leg lying in a litter. A hand had to be detailed to hold this burned lad down, for hours. He had everything in him the doctor dared administer. He died on the hospital ship, as did the boy with the leg and several others. Plasma flowed like water, the lights went out periodically as we opened the quick-acting doors to dispose of mangled clothes, the accumulation of plasma boxes, and other by-products of emergency dressing. In all the heat our clothes were soaked with cold sweat, it never dried out.

It is the opinion of all in this area that the decision against Jap military power in the Philippines was at Leyte, and that Ormoc finally called it. This "end run" caught the Japanese by surprise in the rear, and denied the enemy the use of Ormoc for the voluminous reinforcements they were pouring in from other parts of the islands. The operations described, and the resupply echelons which followed, had to sail into the heart of Japanese land-based air power throughout the Visayans, Southern Luzon, and Mindanao. This and the Mindoro operation were a bitter pill for the Navy, but in those weeks the outcome was decided.

The decision to land the troops of the 77th U.S. infantry division on the beaches of Ormoc was not made until 30 November. Hurried changes in schedules were made. Ships which had been scheduled for a landing on Mindoro on 5 December were rescheduled for Ormoc, and the Mindoro landing was postponed from 5 December to 15 December.

If there had been any question as to the effectiveness of Japanese air power, the results at Ormoc dispelled all that. They had developed a deadly weapon in the suicide plane. As long as their numbers held out, we could expect heavy losses of surface ships as they came closer and closer to Japanese bases.

Rear Admiral A. D. Struble had hardly returned with his battered ships from

Ormoc when he had to leave again on a bigger and equally hazardous job of landing another division of troops and airfield construction equipment on the southwest corner of the island of Mindoro, 250 miles in the direction of Manila and just that much closer to the heart of Japanese air power.

In Struble's task force were the usual miscellaneous assortment of amphibious ships, tugs, mine sweepers, cargo ships, a squadron of PT boats, and escorting destroyers—169 ships in all. A few miles ahead was a task force of cruisers, and ahead of them another task force comprising a division of battleships and a division of cruisers. These heavy ships preceded the convoy as a safety measure in case the Japanese decided to make a surface attack with the remnants of their fleet. In addition, two divisions of CVEs accompanied the battleships to provide air cover for the heavy ships as well as Struble's convoy. Their planes would augment the Army planes from Leyte which would be in the air to break up any enemy attack. As a further measure of security, air raids were stepped up on Japanese bases by Army long-range bombers and planes from the Navy's fast carriers. Even so, Japanese Kamikaze attacks could not be stopped in their entirety.

The day after Struble's ships left the comparative security of Leyte Gulf on their way to Mindoro their troubles began. A Japanese plane painted black came in low and almost before it was observed crashed into the deck of his flagship, the cruiser *Nashville*. One hundred and thirty-one men were killed and 158 wounded. Struble transferred his flag to a destroyer, the *Nashville* returned to Leyte, and the convoy continued on its way. A little later the destroyer *Haraden* was hit by a Kamikaze. Every hour from that time onward the ships of each task group were harassed by bogies. Dog fights went on intermittently between the air cover and attacking planes. Occasionally a Kamikaze would be brought down by antiaircraft fire. But the real effort of enemy plane attacks was saved until the ships were unloading on the Mindoro beaches; then they came in big numbers. They sank two LSTs and one LSM, and damaged one cruiser, one patrol boat, and two destroyers.

But the landing went off as planned. The troops and equipment were on the beach and there was little fighting ashore.

As long as the carrier planes remained in the vicinity of Mindoro, ships losses were kept within acceptable limits, but when the carriers left, the resupply echelons were mostly on their own.

When a new area such as Mindoro has been captured and the big ships withdrawn, there remains behind a small group of naval men who have the job of supervising the unloading of ships, expediting their turn-around time, and handling other purely naval activities in the beach area. Important decisions rest in the hands of these little-known men whose judgment and courage often affect the lives of those ashore as well as those afloat.

The first resupply echelon for Mindoro consisted of eight LSTs, twelve LSMs, and six Liberty ships, with a destroyer escort. All were attacked by Kamikazes. Of this group, two LSTs were sunk; one Liberty ship and one destroyer were damaged. In the next echelon, three of the four Liberty ships in the convoy were sunk, and three LSTs and two destroyers were damaged. Most attacks occurred while the ships were discharging cargo.

The heavy responsibilities that fell upon the shoulders of Reserve Commander Jack P. Bandy, who succeeded to the job of Senior Officer Present Afloat at Mindoro, are described in this report:

Because of serious injuries to Captain Mentz when the *Orestes* was attacked on 30 December 1944, I assumed the duties and responsibilities of SOPA MINDORO on 31 December.

At the time, the following conditions prevailed at Mindoro. The destroyer *Gansevoort* was anchored off White Beach with the after engine room and fireroom flooded and abandoned by the crew. The *Orestes* was beached at Caminawit Point, badly damaged. The crew were all ashore. The *Porcupine* was abandoned and burning off Blue Beach. The crew was ashore. Two Liberty ships had just been sunk, one off White Beach and one in Ilin Strait. One Liberty ship was missing. There was no naval base organization, so the duties of that group fell on the SOPA. Communications with General Dunkle of the Western Visayan Task Force were limited to a telephone, usually inoperative, at the PT Base. Various small naval units, such as FS and LCMs, were present but didn't know who they belonged to. Gasoline and food supplies were short.

I was also concerned with the evacuation of survivors, the hospitalization of the wounded, and the proper identification and burial of the dead. This was difficult because most bodies were severely burned. There are fourteen unidentified naval dead buried in the cemetery at Mindoro. Arrangements were made with the Army to salvage equipment from the *Gansevoort* as it was believed that the Japs would soon sink her.

On the night of 31 December–1 January five bombs landed in the PT Base area, killing eleven men and wounding sixteen. Most of these were survivors from the *Orestes*. The acting commanding officer of *FS-180*, a Coast Guard ensign, reported to me that his captain had been evacuated and that eighteen of the twenty-five men in his crew were wounded. He was loaded with gear from NABU 5. I made arrangements for the PT Base to unload the ship.

On 1 January the missing Liberty, the *Juan De Fuca,* was located on Baniago Reef. She had been bombed and run aground on the night of 31 December. The crew was living on Ambulong Island. I rescued the crew and brought them to the PT Base to await instructions.

There were heavy air attacks on the night of 1–2 January. The Liberty ship *Clayton* was hit in number 3 hold and had to be beached to prevent sinking. Two men were killed and eleven wounded. The crew abandoned the ship and most of them refused to return stating that their contract had expired on 30 December. On 2 January I received word that there was a salvage crew on board the *LST-749* located about 60 miles south of Mindoro and I was directed to recover them. I sent two PTs to find them but the LST could not be located. Several days later two of the party were rescued from Cuyo Island and they reported that the LST sank on the night of 26 December.

The ships at Mindoro continued to take the brunt of the enemy plane attacks until the great Lingayen Gulf convoys moved into range during the first week of January 1945, and presented closer and more important targets.

One of the little-known and tragic by-products of the attack on Mindoro was the reaction of the Japanese garrisons on the various islands of the Central Philippines toward their American prisoners. As Admiral Struble's ships headed toward their goal, each Japanese commander felt his own particular island was the probable point of attack, and each commander took his own precautionary measures. On Palawan, the American prisoners were forced to dig trenches, presumably to be their graves. Two of the prisoners escaped, hid in caves, and eventually made their way to Leyte, where they arrived in an emaciated and half-starved condition and told the story of their terrifying experiences.

The almost continuous use of the same ships day after day in waters subject to frequent bombing attacks had a serious effect on their crews. The men became jumpy and some were on the verge of a breakdown. The Navy Department had issued instructions to send men home after a year in the combat zone, but not enough replacements arrived to permit doing this, or even sending them to Australia for a breather. As an example of this tension, four men deserted from the destroyer *O'Brien* the night before the ship sailed on the Mindoro operation. Apparently they took a rubber life raft equipped with arms and provisions and disappeared into the jungle. Only men on the verge of a nervous breakdown would have undertaken such a senseless risk.

On the destroyer *Flusser,* the frayed nerves of the young officers in the wardroom were reported in these words:

Flusser and *Shaw* were scratched from the Mindoro operation, which was about to sail, and on an hour's notice sent to convoy four LSDs (Landing Ships Dock) from Leyte to Hollandia. Fire control on both destroyers was in sorry shape after all the shooting and near hits at Ormoc, and we were to tie up alongside the *Dobbin* again for several days of repair.

As we left Leyte, and until we were out of range of Jap air power, the *Flusser* complement was an uneasy and jumpy array of men after all the sleepless nights and constant action. A steward would drop a tray in the pantry, which would cause all in the wardroom to sit bolt upright, then collapse on the table and say, "My God, don't *do* that." The wardroom loud speaker would suddenly squawk, "Now sweepers, man your" —by which time everyone would be nearly to the ladder. Lieutenant Irving (Cactus) Tolzien, U.S. Naval Reserve, the antiaircraft gunnery officer, was having a very restless sleep in his bunk, moaning and mumbling in a frustrated way. He awoke suddenly and looked at his roommate with an expression of relief.

"What were you dreaming about, Cactus?"

"Well, there was a piece in the sky that just wouldn't get dark."

To ease the pressure on personnel, ships that had recently participated in one hazardous operation were not immediately assigned to another, whenever this was possible. But this was not always possible. Some types of ships—rocket LCIs, APDs, salvage tugs, and mine sweepers—were usually in such demand and so scarce that their crews had to take more than a fair share of combat action.

Supervising the operating requirements of more than nine hundred ships, in itself, was a massive undertaking, and yet it was but part of the routine work of the staff of the Seventh Amphibious Force in preparing for the movement to Lingayen Gulf.

Plans, assignments of ships, and schedules of amphibious ship movements were all made at Hollandia. Individual units were trained at such faraway places as Bougainville in the Solomon Islands and New Caledonia, where one of the Seventh Amphibious Force's mobile training units from Milne Bay was sent to train and indoctrinate the 25th, 37th and Americal Divisions in Seventh Amphibious Force procedures. Beach parties, medical cadres, minesweeping groups, construction battalions and all the other various types of unit activities that go to make up an invasion force were readied for departure from Milne Bay, Oro Bay, Finschhafen, the Admiralty Islands, and other Southwest Pacific ports that had served our needs so well during the past year. Soon after the departure of these units, station crews would fold up their temporary bases and move all activities to a new location, somewhere in the Philippines. Each time they left what had been thriving communities with good roads, piers, dry docks, recreation fields, movie theaters, and post exchanges; all the features of busy overseas military bases would be abandoned, and the jungle and the natives would take over.

Lingayen Gulf is a big, sheltered body of water a little more than one hundred miles north of Manila, with good anchorages for more than a thousand ships. Along much of the shoreline the LSTs would be able to unload directly to the beaches over dry ramps. The Japanese had used this area for their invasion of the Philippines just three years before.

Information from Philippine guerrillas led to the belief that the Gulf was heavily mined and that there were a number of coastal batteries in the area. As a result, the decision was made to send Vice Admiral Oldendorf's six old battleships, some cruisers, destroyers, and minesweepers into the Gulf three days in advance of the landing date, in order to take out the coastal batteries and sweep mines.

Other guerrilla intelligence information indicated there were 105,000 Japanese troops on Luzon, with 30,000 concentrated in the Lingayen area. The landing promised to be a bloody affair.

Japanese task force, on the horizon to the right, lands a salvo astern of the Kitkun Bay
*(CVE-71). Beyond the carrier, a smoke screen is being laid by destroyer escorts to cover
the carrier in her escape. Off Leyte Gulf, 25 October 1944.*

The general scheme of the operation was but little different from the one used at
Leyte. While Oldendorf was taking out the coastal batteries and clearing up the
mines in the Gulf, Halsey's heavy battleships and fast carriers would cruise north of
Luzon to guard against any raids of the Japanese fleet and at the same time launch
heavy air strikes on Japanese bases on Formosa and Luzon. Additional strikes would
be made by Allied land-based bomber planes against other Japanese air bases in the
Philippines and Netherlands East Indies.

At last all was ready. The plans had been distributed and preparations completed.
In order to reach rendezvous points on time the slow ships left distant bases during

the early part of December. For ships nearer the combat area, the jump-off time permitted some pre-Christmas festivities.

On 23 December 1944, a Seventh Amphibious Force farewell party was given on the beaches of Hollandia for those who were leaving, by those who would be left behind. It was a clear, warm, beautiful moonlight night. Big bonfires were built to light up the scene. Picnic suppers and surf bathing were part of the program. All the nurses, Red Cross workers, and WACs in the area were invited. Phonographs and an improvised orchestra blared Irving Berlin's "I'm Dreaming of a White Christmas." No one seemed to tire of it. Perhaps I remember it so vividly because it was my birthday. But there was a note of sadness in the air. Most of those who were leaving this lovely tropical setting would never return and those who were left behind would close out their activities and move elsewhere. Firm friendships which had been formed in the past few months would be broken and never reestablished.

At midnight the party was over and next morning the smaller ships sailed for Lingayen Gulf. The *Blue Ridge,* my flagship, being bigger and faster, could delay until the day after Christmas before heading for its loading port and again concentrating on the grim business of war.

25:

Luzon Landings

ACROSS THE WESTERN PACIFIC THROUGHOUT THE MONTH OF
December 1944, ships of all types stood out from many ports, large and small, to form
convoys in the greatest overseas expedition in history. My flagship, the *Blue Ridge,*
sailed on 28 December from the port of Aitape in one of these convoys. Other
convoys later joined us. This part of the expedition was transporting more than
100,000 troops and would land them on enemy beaches more than 2,000 miles away in
the heart of enemy country. Following in a few days was another convoy with
another 100,000 troops for use as reinforcements or for subsidiary operations.

The ships of the Seventh Amphibious Force, designated Task Force 78, steamed
past Wakde, Biak, Sansapor, and finally Morotai, each port arousing memories of
former anxious days. In passing Sansapor, our convoy was joined by the ships under
the command of Rear Admiral W. M. Fechteler, Task Group 78.2. Off the coast of
Mindanao we were to rendezvous with Amphibious Task Force 79 from the Central
Pacific, under command of Vice Admiral T. S. Wilkinson. Some of his transports
carried troops from as far away as Bougainville in the Solomon Islands.

Task Force 78, comprising 420 ships of all types, including 109 merchant-manned
Liberty ships, was in the van of this armada, followed by Task Force 79 with almost
two-thirds as many. These numbers did not include the escort carriers and cruisers
with their accompanying destroyers, which would provide air and surface protection
to the convoy while en route.

Ahead of the big ships went the little fellows, such as the *PC-623*, monotonously

291

patrolling back and forth on the lookout for submarines. Every few days their monotonous duty was broken as they dropped back to be refuelled by tankers or by their bigger sisters. Far behind them, for almost one hundred miles, stretched the main body of ships.

The journey to Leyte was one of watchful waiting, but little action. The sea was glassy in the equatorial calm. Escort planes from the CVEs would occasionally roar across the convoy. Once a Japanese plane, a Betty, appeared dead ahead of the *PC-623*, just skimming the water to evade radar. Hellcats from the CVEs took after her.

Entering Leyte Gulf with that great armada evoked far different thoughts and feelings from those uncertain days just two and a half months before. Now we entered the Gulf in daylight, with no fear of mines. The convoy was met by friendly ships. Among those which joined the convoy was the cruiser *Boise* with General MacArthur aboard.

The convoy did not stop in Leyte Gulf but sailed on out through Surigao Strait, made famous by Vice Admiral Oldendorf's smashing victory of 23–25 October, then through the waters that had proved so costly to Rear Admiral Struble's ships just two weeks before.

Three days ahead of the convoy sailed Vice Admiral Oldendorf with his bombardment force of six old battleships, six cruisers, and forty-one ships of various types. And ahead of these went a slower group of smaller ships, mainly minesweepers and salvage tugs, scheduled to reach the entrance to Lingayen Gulf simultaneously with the bombardment force.

It was expected that Kamikazes, to make better use of their nearby airfields, would let the convoys approach the west coast of Luzon before undertaking heavy attacks. In such case, the minesweeping group and the bombardment group would be their initial targets, rather than the troop-laden and weakly defended transports which were trailing behind by three days.

As it turned out, a small-scale Kamikaze attack was made on the ships of the minesweeping group on 2 January as they emerged from Surigao Strait. The oiler *Cowanesque* was hit and the *YMS-53* received minor damage from a near miss. Two days later, as they were nearing Manila Bay, this same group of ships was again attacked. The tug *Apache* and the *LCI-70* were hit, but the damage was not serious enough to prevent their continuing on to Lingayen Gulf. It was the last attack made on this advance contingent of small ships. Apparently the Japanese had decided to concentrate on the bombardment and escort carrier force a short distance astern.

Oldendorf's force received no air attacks until near the west coast of Luzon. Then on 4 January, the *Ommaney Bay* (*CVE-79*) was badly damaged by a Kamikaze and later had to be sunk by torpedoes from our own ships. From then on, Oldendorf's ships were under continual surveillance of Japanese planes and intermittent attacks

A flotilla of Coast Guard-manned LSTs ploughs through the China Sea, headed for Lingayen Gulf and the Luzon beaches.

Small beside the Iowa class battleship it is refuelling, this tanker of Service Squadron Six feeds the ship's power plant, saving the battleship a long trip back to a shore base.

USS Callaway (APA-35) throws up ack-ack as a divebomber attacks her off the coast of Luzon. She was hit immediately forward of the stack a few seconds later. In spite of casualties, damage was repaired and she returned to port.

Troops climb down the landing nets of a Coast Guard-manned invasion transport on their way to the assault beach at Lingayen Gulf, 9 January 1945.

Ablaze, this Japanese Kamikaze plane passes near the escort carrier after being hit by the ship's antiaircraft fire.

Coast Guard landing craft unload troops at Lingayen Gulf against light resistance.

by Kamikazes. Off Manila Bay on the afternoon of 5 January they were under attack for two and a half hours by more than fifty suicide planes. Seven ships were severely damaged—the escort carriers *Manila Bay* and *Savo Island*, the cruisers *Louisville* and H.M.A.S. *Australia*, the destroyers *Helm* and H.M.A.S. *Arunta*, and the destroyer escort *Stafford*.

As the bad news from the bombardment group reached us, we wondered whether the Japanese would hit the troop-laden convoys next, or continue to concentrate on Oldendorf's ships as they moved up the Luzon coast and into Lingayen Gulf.

Except for two ineffectual submarine attacks, the big transport convoys (Task Forces 78 and 79) had been left alone as they ploughed through the turbulent Sulu Sea three days in the rear of the advance force. On the afternoon of 5 January, about the time Oldendorf's ships were under attack, a midget submarine fired two torpedoes at the cruiser *Boise*, the ship in which General MacArthur was embarked. Both torpedoes missed. The unlucky submarine surfaced, was rammed by the destroyer *David W. Taylor*, and presumably sunk. A little later, another midget submarine fired two torpedoes which missed, but the submarine was luckier and escaped. That night a group of fifteen Japanese planes passed over the formation. With commendable restraint, all antiaircraft fire was withheld and the enemy apparently never knew the rich prize that lay beneath him.

In spite of submarine harassment and Kamikaze attacks, all task forces maintained the time schedule. Early on the morning of 6 January, Oldendorf's bombardment ships, escort carriers, minesweepers, and demolition teams entered Lingayen Gulf.

These groups had hardly started on their assigned jobs of knocking out coastal batteries, clearing out mines, and removing underwater obstacles when the Kamikazes attacked in great strength in a series of raids that lasted until sundown. Sixteen ships were hit.[1] Casualties were heavy. Among them were Lieutenant General Lumsden, British representative of Prime Minister Churchill, and Bill Chickering of *Time* magazine, both killed instantly on the bridge of the *New Mexico*. The survival chances of the troop transports when they entered the Gulf two days later looked dim, if the Japanese could keep up the intensity of their attacks.

That night Admiral Oldendorf advised Admiral Kinkaid of the seriousness of the situation and recommending that "drastic measures be taken to correct a condition which otherwise might require reconsideration of the current plans." The operation was too far along for any change of plans. The alternative was to request Halsey to move the Third Fleet to a position to the westward of Luzon so carrier planes could attack all Japanese airfields in the vicinity of Lingayen and

[1] Among them were the battleships *New Mexico* and *California*, cruisers *Minneapolis*, *Australia*, *Louisville*, and *Columbia* (hit twice), five destroyers, two minesweepers, an aviation tender and an APD.

provide cover for the transports when they entered the Gulf on the ninth. The Third Fleet did not move into those dangerous waters to the westward of Luzon but did intensify attacks on Japanese airfields.

Included in the preparations for entering Lingayen Gulf was the plan to fuel accompanying small craft and "short-legged" destroyers, at a rendezvous arranged with tankers from Mindoro. Fueling at sea within range of enemy planes is always a hazardous operation. There was the full expectation that before the fueling was completed planes or submarines would attack. But not until late that afternoon, after all refueling had been completed, did a small group of planes attack the formation. Only *LST-912* was unfortunate enough to be hit by a Kamikaze. Antiaircraft fire brought down two of the planes.

As the long convoy steamed past the high mountains of Mindoro, at whose base were the recently established U.S. airfields, we heard the Domei News Agency in Japan broadcast in English the course, length and breadth of our convoys, with exaggerated reports of what had happened to the ships already in Lingayen Gulf and warnings of what would happen to us.

According to the operations order the troop convoys should pass to the westward of Manila harbor some time that night. From intelligence information we had learned that among the ships there were two Japanese destroyers. It was reasonable to assume they would attempt to escape before the exit was bottled up, and perhaps make a forlorn desperate attack. There was also the possibility of a Japanese raiding force of surface ships from Camranh Bay, in Indochina, several hundred miles west of Manila across the South China Sea.

To take care of these contingencies, four destroyers were stationed on either flank of the task group and at five miles from the axis to cover probable escape or attack sectors. One destroyer steamed five miles in the van. The PCs and SCs dropped back.

The new disposition, which was made just before sunset, would weaken the antisubmarine screen, but it was a justifiable risk. A Catalina seaplane—better known as "Tom Cat"—with special radar equipment patrolled overhead and was advised of our expectations. Shortly after 2100, the "Tom Cat" reported a surface vessel approaching from the north. The aircraft was directed to circle and watch, while the four destroyers were ordered to close and destroy it. In a few minutes star shells, gun flashes, and tracers lighted the sky. The action was plainly visible from the bridge of the *Blue Ridge*. The Japanese destroyer never had a chance and the battle had hardly started before it was over. One of the enemy ship's magazines was hit and she sank amidst a tremendous explosion that firelighted the sky. The attacking destroyers were told to remain behind to pick up survivors—more to gain intelligence information than for humanitarian purposes—if they could do so without too much delay, and then rejoin the formation. No survivors, however, were recovered.

For the remainder of the night, the convoy was continuously snooped by enemy planes, of which our night fighters shot down four.

At dawn of the eighth, the convoy again came under air attack. The combat air patrol shot down six enemy planes and damaged several others, but not before a few got through and hit the *Kadashan Bay, Kitkun Bay, Callaway,* and *LST-912.* But there was no delay in the forward movement of the convoy.

Oldendorf's ships in Lingayen Gulf for 8 January indicated the Kamikaze attacks were continuing, but on a lessened scale. The unlucky cruiser *Australia* had received her third and fourth hit. The rest of the report was more cheerful. Most of the coastal batteries had been located and destroyed; there were no underwater obstacles; and very few mines had been found. It was learned later that many mines had been removed by guerrillas who had used their explosive charges for sabotage purposes.

On the last leg of the long voyage, the convoy received two reports with dangerous implications. That they were false was not known at the time. A strong Japanese naval force was reported to have left Singapore to intercept the convoy. Nerves had become frayed from loss of sleep and almost continuous standing-by at battle stations. Adding to the strain was the possibility that the Japanese had eased up in their air attacks on Oldendorf in order to mobilize for one overwhelming attack when the troop convoys entered the Gulf.

At last, during the early morning darkness of 9 January 1945, the troop convoy, led by the *PC-623,* entered Lingayen Gulf. This was the same *PC-623,* under Lt. Commander James A. Baxter, U.S. Naval Reserve, which did such an outstanding rescue job on 25 October 1944, after the battle of Leyte Gulf.

Every man was at his battle station as each ship headed for its assigned position—ships of Task Force 78 to the north, and Task Force 79 to the south. Troops from transports clambered down cargo nets into the ships' boats which when loaded circled about while awaiting the signal to head for the beach.

There was no time to worry whether the Kamikazes had a delayed punch awaiting us at daylight. Everyone was too busy with the immediate job of getting troops and equipment ashore at the right place and the right time. With the break of dawn, the Kamikazes came as expected, but not in the staggering strength of their previous attacks. Again they concentrated on the combat ships, unwisely from their point of view. The battleship *Mississippi* was hit, the cruiser *Australia* was hit for the fifth time, *Columbia* for the third time, and the destroyer escort *Hodges* suffered minor damage.

This air attack did not interfere with the landing schedule. Troops in amphibious tractors and small boats headed for the beach under a heavy covering bombardment by battleships, cruisers, and destroyers. As they neared the beach the big ships ceased their bombardment, and the LCI rocket ships on both flanks of the assault boats started their incredible rain of fire. The landing itself was anticlimactic. When the troops reached the beach at 0930, instead of meeting a hail of bullets, they went ashore standing up. Enemy troops had retreated to defensive positions in the nearby hills.

Filipinos emerged from everywhere, most waving white flags. This was the day they had been awaiting for three long, cruel years. Bed sheets, old shirts, anything white on a bamboo pole served as a signal for the pitiful little groups that greeted the American troops as they stepped ashore.

Within a few hours the first wave of troops had moved inland about a mile, meeting little opposition. More waves followed in a steady stream. Intermittent artillery fire from Japanese positions on the rear slopes of the hills took some toll of the landing craft unloading on the beaches. The *LST-127* received seven hits. The LSTs *463, 469,* and *470* each received one hit, as did the *LCI-72* and the LSMs *219, 269,* and *127.* But the disembarkations continued and that afternoon Corps and Divison commanders were able to establish their headquarters ashore.

About a thousand ships were now in the harbor and on each one there was feverish activity. As soon as the transports and freighters were unloaded they were formed into convoys for return to the rear areas. All the combat ships, except those required to escort departing convoys, remained in the harbor to provide local naval protection against surface raids.

Following the pattern established at Leyte, at sundown and sunrise the ships of Task Force 78, except those unloading at the beach, were anchored in a close circle and covered with a dense smog by LCI smoke layers. These evening and morning periods were the times the Kamikazes could be expected to attack, and they did, but each day on a lessened scale. When the air attacks were over, the business of unloading reinforcements and supplies would continue night and day, as before. No smoke-enveloped ship was ever hit.

At Lingayen the Japanese tried out a new type of attack. This time they used suicide boats, the seagoing counterparts of the Kamikazes, but far less successful. The midget boats were fifteen feet long with a speed of thirty knots. Each boat carried one man who steered it to the target; upon contact, a 500-pound explosive charge went off. We had no advance knowledge of the presence or capabilities of such craft, and were unprepared to meet their first attack on the night of 10 January, when a group of them came out of the darkness from nowhere and hit the transport *Warhawk,* the destroyers *Philip* and *Robinson,* the LSTs *925, 1025, 1028* and *610,* and the LCIs *974* and *365.* That was their first and last success in Lingayen Gulf. A night patrol screen of small craft was established which effectively met this local challenge. These enemy craft, however, did give us some trouble in other sections of Luzon.

The first step in the shore campaign was to seal off the Japanese in the surrounding hills and then commence the advance to Manila. Between Lingayen Gulf and the city of Manila lies the Central Luzon Plain—a flat, low area thirty to fifty miles wide and one hundred miles long. It is the richest agricultural section in the Philippines, with paved highways and railroads. On either side of the plain are rugged mountains in which the Japanese had set up strong pockets of defense. They avoided committing large bodies of troops to a major action, but resorted to delaying tactics such as mining highways and blowing up bridges. American troops advanced toward Manila along two parallel roads. They were helped by Filipino guerrillas who provided intelligence information and harassed the retreating Japanese.

MacArthur urged speed. In Manila and in other cities and camps throughout Luzon were thousands of internees and prisoners of war who were awaiting liberation. Fresh in the minds of everyone was the massacre of the prisoners of war at Palawan when the fanatical Japanese commandant learned of the approach of an amphibious assault force.

As part of the speed-up in the capture of Manila, the Seventh Amphibious Force was directed to land the XI Army Corps—44,400 men—on an undefended beach near San Antonio. This was just north of Subic Bay, on Luzon's west coast, about 50 miles to the northwest of the entrance to Manila Bay. Another 8,000 troops were to be landed at Nasugbu a few miles south of the entrance to the Bay. These two forces were to advance inland and join with the troops coming down from Lingayen to encircle the city of Manila.

The San Antonio landing was made on 29 January by an attack force under the command of Rear Admiral Struble, and two days later the one at Nasugbu was made by forces under Rear Admiral Fechteler. Additional landings were scheduled to be undertaken as fast as ships and troops could be made available.

Although Vice Admiral Wilkinson had returned to his duties in the Central Pacific, a major portion of those amphibious ships from the Pacific Fleet which had participated in the Leyte and Lingayen operations were temporarily assigned to the Seventh Amphibious Force. These ships were used to bring forward troop reinforcements to exploit MacArthur's advance down the Luzon Plain. Six divisions of troops —more than 100,000 men—were transported from New Guinea and Leyte in one month.

The availability of ships and personnel for the new series of amphibious operations was far different from the difficult days of 1943 when we were struggling along the New Guinea coast and members of my staff had to be assigned as task force commanders whenever simultaneous operations were undertaken, and when the loss of even a single ship might jeopardize a forthcoming operation. It was much easier now. The Seventh Amphibious Force had three competent group commanders: Rear Admirals A. D. Struble, F. B. Royal (on loan from the Central Pacific), and W. M.

Fechteler—later relieved by A. G. Noble. Each had his own staff and flagship, and enough transports, tankers, and supply ships to carry out independent and simultaneous operations—and Japanese resistance was crumbling everywhere.

At San Antonio and Nasugbu, the troops landed without opposition although a night attack by midget surface boats similar to those used at Lingayen sank *PC-1129* and indirectly led to the sinking of two PT boats, *PT-77* and *PT-79,* by our own destroyers because of mistaken identity.

Although the immediate objective of the Luzon landings was the capture of Manila, the early release of prisoners of war and internees was uppermost in everybody's mind. Three weeks to the day after the landing on the beaches of Lingayen, a small group of Filipino guerrillas and men from the 6th Ranger Infantry on the east flank of the main column, entered the prison camp at Cabanatuan twenty-five miles behind Japanese lines, overwhelmed the garrison, and returned to U.S. lines with five hundred internees.

As the troops in Lingayen approached Manila, Japanese resistance stiffened and the advance slowed. Fearful of the fate of the internees and prisoners of war within the city, a "flying column" of the 1st Cavalry Division entered a section of Manila on 3 February and headed down Rizal Avenue to Santo Tomas University. The gates were battered down by tanks, the guards were wiped out and more than 3,700 emaciated internees were liberated. The next day more than 1,000 American prisoners of war, broken in health and spirit, were rescued from Bilibid prison. Their jailers had fled at the approach of the troops. But three weeks of heavy fighting lay ahead before the Japanese could be cleared from numerous defensive pockets within the city and another large group of internees could be released from the Philippine General Hospital.

Mrs. William Greenbaum was an internee in Iloilo and in Santo Tomas. In her account of her experiences she stated,

> The women suffered privation and hardship rather than brutality. Some men prisoners, however, did suffer from terrible mistreatment. We had friends who died from beatings or who were permanently injured; others were shot; some decapitated. People of every class and character were crowded together. There were a number of known spies among the prisoners and there was always the danger of informers—despicable people who hoped to gain some small favor from the Japanese by giving information about another prisoner.
>
> We knew a group of sixteen missionaries and mining people who took refuge in the mountains not far from Iloilo. Eventually they were captured and the entire group beheaded. My husband and I with five other families—eleven adults and four children —were hiding out in the same general vicinity as the missionary group. We, too, were finally taken prisoners but by a more civilized group of soldiers. After four frightening and difficult days we arrive at an internment camp.

One of the more spectacular rescues of internees occurred at the prison camp at Los Banos on Laguna de Bay, forty miles south of Manila. The rescue was undertaken by a combined group of Filipino guerrillas, a company of paratroopers and some ground troops who crossed the bay in half a hundred amtracs—modernized mechanized versions of alligators and buffaloes.

The Los Banos stockade was fifty miles inside the Japanese lines, across swampy and difficult country. With split-second timing the rescue groups converged on the outskirts of Los Banos during the early morning hours of 23 February. The guerrillas broke down the stockade gates, the sentries and guards—about 250 of them—were killed, the 2,000 internees were hurried to the amtracs and all hands escaped across the bay. The fight and the escape lasted but an hour. It was all over before the several thousand Japanese in camps a few miles away knew what was happening. One of the internees was Sister Aimee, a Maryknoll nun and a relative of Lieutenant Commander O'Neil of my staff. In a cheerful manner she related her experiences as a captive of the Japanese since December, 1941. She had been moved from one prison camp to another until she finally ended up at Los Banos. The nuns in her group suffered no personal abuse, but they had little privacy. Guards were in their vicinity at all hours of the day and night. During the last six months of their internment, life grew tougher and food scarcer—so much so they were reduced to one meal a day of unpolished rice and a vegetable soup made of weeds growing in the countryside. She humorously told of guards making the women wear signs giving their age. The last night at Los Banos was frightening. Word had seeped in that a rescue would be attempted the following morning. The nuns were assembled in the chapel with the full expectation that they would be machine gunned before the rescue could be effected. When the fighting in the courtyard started, they lay down on the chapel floor while the bullets passed overhead. Within minutes they heard American voices telling them to get out fast and head for the water.

26: Liberation of the Philippines and Borneo

THE AMPHIBIOUS OPERATION AT LINGAYEN WAS A COMBINED EFfort of the Central Pacific and Southwest Pacific Forces. When the assault phase of the landing was completed, most of the Central Pacific ships were returned in preparation for operations in that area. A few were held over for a short time to participate in operations which had already started, but in the main all further landings leading to the complete liberation of the Philippines would be undertaken solely by the ships of the Seventh Amphibious Force. The Borneo landings would include Australian and Dutch ships temporarily assigned to the Seventh Amphibious Force for those operations.

The first in the series of new landings, and as essential as the capture of Manila itself, was the capture of a group of small islands guarding the entrance to Manila Bay. Corregidor, where U.S. forces under General Wainwright made their last stand in the early days of the war, was the largest of these islands and the most heavily fortified by the Japanese. The other three were Caballo, Carabao, and El Fraile, on which the monitor-like Fort Drum had been constructed by the U.S. Army many years before.

A few miles to the north and west of Corregidor, and within range of its guns, was the small harbor of Mariveles at the southern end of Bataan Peninsula, through which the main body of MacArthur's troops had escaped before retreating to Corregidor. The mountainous and heavily forested Bataan Peninsula had recently become a haven for isolated Japanese Army units.

Plans were prepared for the capture of each of the islands in succession as troops and ships became available. Corregidor was the first on the list. As part of this operation, the capture of the nearby harbor of Mariveles was necessary. It was scheduled for 15 February with an assault on Corregidor the following day.

The Navy's job during these operations was one of bombardment to keep the Japanese in their hilltop caves, to sweep the waters of the heavily mined area, and to land the assault troops on the Mariveles beach. Small landing craft manned by the Army would be used for the assault on Corregidor.

MacArthur's intelligence section estimated Japanese troop strength on Corregidor at about eight hundred. This proved to be wide of the mark although it was based on information from many sources including prisoners of war,[1] intercepted messages, captured documents, and guerrillas.

The landing at Mariveles went off as scheduled. First came the bombardment and then the troops went ashore from landing craft without opposition. The few defenders had retreated to the hills. It all looked too easy. Even the guns on Corregidor did not interfere with the Mariveles landing, probably because cruisers and destroyers circled around firing at every gun flash. Minesweepers were busy doing what they did best. While the LSTs unloaded in Mariveles harbor that night and the LCSs (armored LCIs) were anchored in a protective screen around them, a group of midget suicide surface craft, armed with high-explosive bombs, came out of the darkness and sank three LCSs.

About a hundred of these midget suicide boats had been hidden in the caves of Corregidor but not all their pilots relished the idea of dying for the Emperor. Prisoners reported that the pilots of most of the thirty boats that had set out for the Mariveles attack were drunk. Some of the boats were intercepted by American destroyers and sunk. Ten more returned to Corregidor with various excuses for not continuing on to Mariveles.

The next day the Corregidor operation was undertaken. It was spectacular and costly. Lying athwart the entrance to Manila Bay, the fortress of Corregidor, from seaward, presents bold cliffs which drop sharply from the flat dome of a high plateau, its rock core filled with tunnels and gun positions. From the air it looks like a big tadpole, the curling tail pointing eastward towards Manila. The light cruisers *Cleveland, Denver, Montpelier, Boise,* and *Phoenix,* accompanied by destroyers, had been bombarding the island for three days and the minesweepers had been operating in the surrounding waters. For the previous two weeks Army bombers had been hitting the island steadily, but there was no visible evidence of the punishment it was taking. Finally, on 14 February, a battery on the northwest side of the fortress opened up on the minesweepers. They replied feebly with their three-inch guns until joined by

[1] Japanese prisoners usually talked quite freely after capture.

destroyers and cruisers who took up the battle. With her superstructure aflame, the minesweeper *YMS-48* took a half dozen hits and sank. The *YMS-8*, the leader of the group, although herself hit, succeeded in countermarching the formation, a difficult maneuver because of the awkward sweep wires. Before the coastal battery was silenced, the destroyers *Hopewell* and *Fletcher* had been hit.

On the southern side of the island another group of sweepers was cutting chemical horn-type mines at the rate of one a minute. This time the batteries on Corregidor, aided by guns from the small island of Caballo and Carabao to the south, joined in and were bracketing the sweepers repeatedly with near misses. Following the mine-sweepers were two LCI gunboats, busily engaged in exploding the many floating mines with gunfire as they were cut loose from their moorings. The hazardous and important work of these small ships with their resourceful and youthful skippers paved the way for many a successful landing.

Beginning at dawn on 16 February, the naval and air bombardment of preceding days again got under way. When the bombardment stopped and the smoke and dust cleared away, the planes carrying the 503rd Parachute Regiment started coming in like a great migration of waterfowl. Flying low over the island's small plateau, plane after plane spewed forth its cargo at 300 feet and the multicolored chutes of men and material drifted down like confetti as the hidden machine guns of the enemy took their toll.

Several of the fast PT boats had been assigned to air-sea rescue, in anticipation of some paratroopers missing the small target. As the first battalion jumped, many of the white chutes, carrying men, were swept out over the cliffs by the wind, as well as the bright red, blue, and yellow ones carrying equipment.

Some of the paratroopers attempted to regain the top of the plateau, while others worked their way to the bottom where they were taken aboard rubber rafts from the PT boats.

An hour after the first parachute battalion had dropped its load, an amphibious landing was made with ground troops at the base of the pollywog's tail. To keep the enemy within his caves, Army planes continued dropping napalm bombs and strafing every flat bit of ground and tunnel opening.

Shortly after noon, planes dropped the second battalion of paratroopers, and most of these seemed to make it; simultaneously several men slid down a steep gully, leaving long streamers of dust behind. The PTs took them aboard, and they proved to be men from the first drop who had laboriously climbed the tough slopes only to find themselves isolated by a superior number of Japanese who finally forced them over the edge as their ammunition gave out. They were carried to a control vessel. White chutes covered the sides of the island like an enormous Monday morning wash gone astray. Because of heavy losses sustained in the first two parachute drops, the third drop was cancelled and these men went ashore the next day ingloriously—as far as they were concerned—with the infantry.

Although U.S. troops occupied the open spaces on the island, the remnants of the Japanese garrison remained holed up in its maze of interconnecting caves and tunnels. For the next ten days shore-based artillery and destroyers kept firing into all visible cave entrances. Finally, there was a massive explosion in the magazines of Malinta Hill, probably of suicide origin, which effectively sealed up nearly all the remaining defenders. For all practical purposes, on the twelfth day of the attack the island was in American hands, but American losses were far heavier than had been expected, with more than 200 men killed and more than 400 wounded. Of the enemy, 4,500 dead were counted; only 20 were captured.

The fall of Corregidor opened the way for intelligence officers aboard fast PT boats to examine the wreckage in the harbor, but, because of mines and other island defenses, several weeks would pass before larger ships could move about the harbor in safety.

Manila Harbor is only a small part of Manila Bay, which is thirty miles across. Two main breakwaters fork out from the mouth of the Pasig River protecting the anchorages from the seasonal monsoons. Rusted superstructures of many Japanese ships were visible evidence of the effectiveness of the raids of carrier planes during the preceding three months. Over sixty major hulks were visible within and outside the breakwaters, and many more were known to be resting on the bottom.

Flames from a burning Manila, and gunfire explosions, formed a chaotic background as PT boats roamed among these sunken ships. Guerrillas had cautioned that Japanese snipers might be hiding in some of the wrecks. No ship was boarded until it had been liberally sprayed by machine guns. On most ships only dead Japanese were found, but occasionally some defensive rifle fire was encountered. On these occasions, an LSM equipped with flame throwers would be brought into play. One of the ships boarded was the cruiser *Kiso*, sunk by U.S. carrier aircraft on 13 November 1944. Her decks were awash and crumpled, her misshapen smoke stacks at all angles.

Commodore W. A. Sullivan, the Navy's expert on salvage operations who had shown his ability at Casablanca, Naples, Cherbourg, and elsewhere, was flown from Europe to tackle the job of clearing Manila Harbor. It proved to be, so he said, far tougher than anything he had yet attempted.

The capture of Corregidor made it possible for MacArthur's dream of a return to the "Rock" to come true. Three years before, on 11 March 1942, he had left Corregidor aboard the *PT-41*, a defeated general, accompanied by a few of the staff who had suffered with him during the disastrous days of Bataan and Corregidor. The report of this visit was given by Lieutenant Dwight Shepler, an observer aboard the PT boat which carried General MacArthur on his triumphant return:

On the afternoon of 1 March, Vice Admiral Barbey set forth from Subic Bay to escort General MacArthur back to Corregidor the following morning. Four PTs had evacuated the General and his key personnel from the island, and he wanted to return the same way. The quartet of torpedo boats, from the Subic Bay squadrons commanded by Lieutenant H. Stillman Taylor, USNR, negotiated the two-hour trip to Cavite at the customary 35 knots, tied up there for the night at the ramshackle docks.

The General, five stars set in a circle on the open collar of his khaki shirt, stepped aboard *PT-373* from Dock 2, Manila, on the morning of the second, as Admiral Barbey met him. He strolled across the fo'csle, informally greeting all hands, and remarked:

"So this is the 373. I left on the 41. It has been a long time."

Lieutenant Joseph A. Roberts, USNR, backed his boat out into the channel as the General stood on the bow talking with Admiral Barbey, General Krueger, Lieutenant General Sutherland, Brigadier General Carlos Romulo, and others of his party. Astern the three other PTs formed in port echelon, carrying other Army personnel who had fought in the Bataan-Corregidor nightmare of '42.

The Commander Southwest Pacific Area has about as impressive and easy presence as one is liable to see, despite prejudices that have been formed with reason in local naval circles by the nature of the communiques emanating from his headquarters. Once the PTs were on their course he hardly took his eyes off the blue silhouette of the island, lighter in color than the thirty miles of water ahead. As the echelon swung in towards the remnants of the dock below Malinta Hill he became intensely animated, pointing out landmarks to the Admiral and talking volubly.

In a convoy of jeeps the party toured the island as far as the residual fighting on the eastern end. We passed numerous prone Japs and the air over the whole wreck of the island was redolent of death. It was much worse than being to the leeward of the Brighton slaughterhouse when a scorching August breeze is coming down the Charles. At intervals along the route serious, bronze-faced soldiers guarded the way, their rifles at salute.

After an inspection of Malinta tunnel and other points the entourage wound up to "Topside" and the high plateau of the main body of the island where the General cited the paratroopers for their spectacular and successful attack, and the Stars and Stripes went up the flagpole.

Although Corregidor had been the main guardian of the entrance to Manila Harbor, entrance for merchant ships would be blocked as long as the islands of Caballo, Carabao and El Fraile remained in Japanese hands. As in Corregidor, the defenders were holed up in caves and tunnels. Bombardment from the air and sea could not root them out.

A small amphibious force was landed on Caballo on 27 March, and met with very little resistance as they spread out and occupied all the flat ground. But they could neither stay there nor get the defenders out until some ingenious person figured out a method of pumping diesel oil uphill into the caves and igniting it with phosphorous shells. That worked.

Next on the list was the small island of El Fraile on which the U.S. Army had built, many years before, the imposing Fort Drum with 18-foot-thick concrete walls, 14-inch guns, and many interconnecting underground passages. U.S. warships had knocked out the big turret guns, but the Japanese garrison with smaller guns, plenty of ammunition, and adequate food and water were in a good position to withstand a long siege. Plane bombardment and naval gun fire could keep the defenders within the fort but couldn't pierce its interior. A landing force could get on top of the fort, somewhat like being on top of a turret, but at nightfall the garrison could emerge from some unexpected opening.

An extension of the idea used so successfully on Caballo was tried out. Under cover of planes and naval bombardment an LSM worked its way to one side of the fort and was held there by two landing craft. A specially constructed ramp was dropped from the superstructure of the LSM to the fort's top side. Men poured across it to stand guard at all the openings. Other men placed hose nozzles in ventilator openings and through them pumped 1,800 gallons of an explosive mixture of gasoline and diesel oil, with a time fuse. To keep the Japanese from emerging to see what was going on, planes kept buzzing the fort and destroyers made a lot of gunfire noise. When all was ready, and that was only a matter of minutes, the LSM with all its men and six accompanying landing craft withdrew to a safe distance. The time fuse was expected to function in about twenty minutes, and it did. But it was evidently a dud—the resulting explosion was but little more than a good-sized firecracker.

A conference was called aboard my flagship to determine what went wrong and what to do next. While we were assembling, perhaps an hour later, a terrific roar went up from El Fraile, followed by a fiery black cloud. It seemed as if the whole top of the fort must come off. Two days later a small party attempted to land, but it was still too hot for a reconnaissance. It was almost two weeks before the tunnels could be entered.

We learned later that the initial explosion had set off a fuse-like oil slick which, like a delayed timing device, had finally entered the fort's magazine with devastating results.

Apparently the suffocating death of the defenders on Caballo and El Fraile was too much for the Japanese garrison on Carabao, for they abandoned the island a few days later.

Paralleling the fighting in the harbor was the vicious block to block fighting in the old part of the city of Manila. Few buildings were left intact. The city was paralyzed.

During this period of rooting out the last pocket of Japanese resistance and clearing the rubble from the streets, making temporary repairs to sewage systems and other municipal services, raising sunken ships and making piers operable, MacArthur maintained his headquarters in Leyte, and in order to be nearby, my flagship was anchored in Leyte Gulf.

As fast as ships and troops could be released from activities at Luzon, hard-hitting amphibious landings were made on all the other islands of the Philippines where the Japanese were still in control. The amphibious shipping which had been borrowed from the Central Pacific Forces was returned on 15 February for use in the Iwo Jima and Okinawa campaigns. From a logistics standpoint it was just as well, for the Service Force of the Southwest Pacific did not have the needed number of repair ships, provision ships, ammunition ships or tankers to take care of any overload. Except for the three Australian transports, the Seventh Amphibious Force was again restricted to LSTs and smaller craft in their landing operations.

Even so, fourteen major and twenty-four minor landings were made by ships of the Seventh Amphibious Force in a period of forty-four days. At some of the landings the Japanese fought desperately. At others, they made but token resistance at the shore line, then retreated to the hills to be hunted down by guerrillas.

Each landing, regardless of size, was as meticulously planned and executed as if it were another Lingayen Gulf. In general, the attack format was similar to the one used so successfully in the hop, skip, and jump operations along the New Guinea coast. But now there were advantages not enjoyed in those earlier days. The Allied Air Force controlled the skies and the U.S. Navy controlled the seas. Occasionally enemy planes would snoop and attack and there was always a threat from stray submarines or a suicidal raid from Japanese cruisers and destroyers. But the only real danger in all these subsidiary operations was from mines, coastal batteries, and the local ground troops.

Excellent intelligence information was obtained from low-flying reconnaissance planes and guerrillas concerning enemy defenses, troop strength, and character of beaches. But there was one vital bit of intelligence of which we were never quite sure, and that pertained to the character of the Japanese troop commander. Was he stubborn and willing to fight at the water line, would he be prudent and withdraw to defensive positions in nearby hills, or would he timidly seek shelter in the mountains until starvation and guerrillas drove him out? Of the many landings made during this period, a few unusual incidents have remained in my memory.

One of these was the landing on 28 February, near the town of Puerto Princesa, on Palawan. There was more interest than usual in this operation; earlier two escapees from the prisoner of war camp on this island had described their terrifying escape from the fiery death that the other prisoners had met there in December. Strong opposition was probable as there were about 2,700 troops on the island and 1,800 of them were in the vicinity of Puerto Princesa. The Japanese had good reason to expect an attack and had sufficient strength to put up a strong defense if led by an able and determined commander. Beach approaches were difficult and the area readily lent itself to mine laying.

U.S. ships bombard Corregidor prior to the assault that retook the island, 13 February 1945.

The capture of Corregidor made General MacArthur's dream of returning to the "Rock" come true. On 2 March 1945, Admiral Barbey escorted General MacArthur back to Corregidor. Left to right: Vice Admiral Barbey, Lieutenant Commander Mailliard, Colonel Lloyd Lehrbas, General MacArthur, Brig. General Carlos Romulo.

In an impressive ceremony, General MacArthur and various senior officers stand at attention while the United States flag is again raised on Corregidor, 2 March 1945.

Ferocious fighting and resistance by the Japanese characterized the battle of Manila. Some of the city's finest buildings were destroyed, among them the once-beautiful Legislative Building.

Using a specially built ramp from the bridge of a Seventh Amphibious Force LSM to the top of the wall of Fort Drum, men poured 1,800 gallons of an explosive oil and gasoline mixture into the fort to capture it.

Coast Guard boats land Australian troops at Balikpapan, Borneo, after a heavy bombardment, 1 July 1945, the last assault for the Seventh Amphibious Force.

But surprisingly, there were practically no defense preparations nor any defense. The minesweepers happily reported, "No mines." Under cover of cruiser, destroyer, and rocket bombardment the troops landed without opposition. Not until they reached the foothills did they encounter any resistance, and then it was perfunctory, for the Japanese simply retreated into the heavily forested mountains in the center of the island.

Our forces gave a military burial to the charred remains of the 150 American prisoners of war. They had been burned to death on orders of the panic-stricken Japanese commander, on 14 December, when Admiral Struble's task force had been sighted in the Sulu Sea and was assumed to be headed for Palawan.

Another incident concerns an unsuspected trait of Japanese character which was brought to light as a consequence of the landing on Panay on 18 March 1945. The two landing beaches chosen were approximately twelve miles to the west of the provincial capital, Iloilo. There was little evidence of defense preparations. There were no mines or beach obstacles. A short prelanding bombardment was stopped when big signs appeared, NO JAPS HERE. When the troops of the landing force reached the beach they were greeted by uniformed guerrillas drawn up in dress parade style.

The 2,000 Japanese who had been stationed in Iloilo had set fire to the town and then retreated to their hideouts in the mountains. They had taken with them all the male members of a colony of 200 Japanese immigrants who had been brought to the island to take over the lush sugar plantations of the dispossessed foreigners. The unusual and horrifying aspect of this retreat was that the colonists had abandoned their wives and children, and in some cases murdered them to avoid their falling into the hands of the guerrillas or Americans. A few of the children were rescued and given shelter by the nuns of a local convent.

After Panay, came operations on the islands of Negros, Cebu, Bohol, and Mindanao. On the larger islands two or more widely separated landings would often be necessary.

As the series of operations in the Philippines drew to a close, a new series was planned which involved the capture of the rich oil ports of Borneo. Their capture would serve the dual purpose of reducing Japanese sources of oil and providing airfields for use against targets in Southeast Asia. As it turned out these operations were different from those that had gone before.

The mine fields were heavier and, for the first time in any Pacific campaign, man-made obstacles had been laid off the beaches. Also, the composition of our attacking forces was more international in character than it had been in the Philippine operations. The Allied Air Force was composed of units from New Zealand,

Australia, and the United States; the assault troops were Australian; and the naval force included Dutch as well as Australian and U.S. ships.

Tarakan, a small island rich in oil lying in a delta on the east coast of Dutch Borneo, was the first objective in the new series. No attempt was made to achieve surprise. For four days a group of minesweepers under cover of naval and air bombardment engaged in the hazardous job of clearing the area of mines. Two sweepers were damaged. Admiral F. B. Royal, U.S. Navy, with his task force of amphibious ships carrying 18,100 Australian troops, arrived off Tarakan during the early morning hours of 1 May 1945. The unusual features of the operation were the extreme tidal range encountered and the fact that LSTs beached in mud instead of sand. Seven LSTs were stranded in silt for 11 days. Another unusual feature was the beach obstacles, made of iron rails set upright in the mud and connected by heavy wire. At that time the Seventh Amphibious Force had no underwater demolition teams to remove them; however, a unit of the Royal Australian Engineers undertook the job and cleared a path for the assault boats.

Although there were 2,300 Japanese troops in the garrison, they made no effort to oppose the landing at the beachhead, but instead retreated to defensive positions in the hills. A small well-hidden coastal battery managed to sink the minesweeper *YMS-481* and damage *YMS-334* and *YMS-364* before it was finally taken out by cruiser gunfire. The *YMS-363* was damaged by a mine. It was another six weeks before the island was free of Japanese and the civil administration of Tarakan could be taken over by Dutch officials.

Next on the schedule was Brunei Bay, a fine harbor in North Borneo. Again Admiral Royal commanded the task force and again Australian troops comprised the assault force, but this time with twice as many troops. Two simultaneous landings were planned, one on the mainland and one on the nearby island of Labuan. The attack procedure was similar to that used at Tarakan. For one week prior to the landing, minesweepers under protection of naval bombardment had swept the adjacent waters, but this time an underwater demolition team was available to clear and buoy a path through the beach obstacles.

The attacking force arrived during the early morning hours of 10 June, and after the usual heavy naval bombardment the troops were able to go ashore without opposition. As had happened in all the recent operations, the defenders had retreated to defensive positions in the nearby hills.

One week later, Admiral Royal left in his flagship for Leyte Gulf to prepare for the next amphibious assignment. The strain and responsibility of commanding one amphibious operation after another with little rest finally took its toll. He died from a heart attack the next day. The Navy lost one of its finest officers.

The Australians had some bitter memories regarding North Borneo. Upwards of 2,000 of their countrymen who had been captured in the Malayan campaign had been confined in prison camps in that area. When Allied landings commenced in the Philippines, late in 1944, the prisoners were moved into the interior for better security. Six of them escaped and were saved by friendly natives. All the others died from starvation and brutal treatment.

The savagery of war was not limited to one side. About 20,000 Japanese were in North Borneo at the time of the Allied landing on 10 June. They continued to hold most of the back country until the emperor ordered their surrender a few months later. They were marched, unarmed, toward the small port of Beaufort where ships were waiting to transport them to Japan. Without proper protection en route, they were attacked by native tribesmen and all but a few hundred were massacred.

The third and—as it proved later—final amphibious operation in the Borneo series was scheduled for 1 July 1945 at Balikpapan, the oil center on Borneo's southeast coast.

The Balikpapan operation was an unusually important one, not because of its size —for it was no larger than many others—but because of the belief that the Japanese intended to use it as a tryout of new defense techniques which would be employed to resist the Allied invasion of Japanese home islands. This was widely heralded as scheduled to take place in the fall of 1945.

There was no question but that the Japanese were going all-out in their defense preparations. Reconnaissance planes reported deep, wide trenches parallel to the beaches connected by ditches to oil tanks buried in the surrounding hills. There was the possibility that oil would be run into the trenches and set afire to present a wall of flame to any assault force, or perhaps the trenches would be deep enough and wide enough to provide sand traps for troops and tanks. It was evident that bulldozers would be needed in the first assault waves to dig a path through the trenches.

The beach approaches were known to be heavily mined—including magnetic mines which had been laid earlier by the Allies, the hardest type to remove—and it was suspected that land mines had been planted among the pillboxes. Natives supplied intelligence information on a series of parallel underwater obstacles in shallow water a few hundred yards offshore. These consisted of hardwood pilings connected by chain or heavy wire.

A channel would have to be cleared and buoyed before any assault force in landing boats could make its way to the beaches. And this job would be far more difficult than the ones at Tarakan and Brunei Bay because of the very shallow waters offshore, which did not permit fire support ships within five miles of the beach line. To add to the support difficulties, the nearest Allied air base was over four hundred miles away.

Fortunately, we were able to borrow a division of escort carriers from the Central Pacific to provide the needed close air support.

The plans called for Rear Admiral Noble to command the amphibious task force and I to be the overall naval commander. The Seventh Australian Division would furnish the ground troops, and U.S. naval forces would be augmented by Netherlands and Australian cruisers, destroyers, and transports.

Balikpapan was an easy place to defend. In addition to the shallow water, obstacles and mines, in the area immediately back of the shore line were low hills that provided excellent positions for coastal guns and antiaircraft batteries.

More than the usual amount of attention was given to clearing out the defenses before the arrival of the landing forces. For sixteen days Allied planes bombarded the area—probably the longest bombardment of the Pacific war. For two weeks, minesweepers under distant cover of cruisers and destroyers swept the shallow waters of the area while undergoing fire from the coastal batteries and an occasional attack from planes. Eleven minesweepers of a rapidly diminishing force were either sunk or damaged by mines and shellfire.[1] While engaged in their dangerous business they beat off an air attack, shooting down three planes.

For one week prior to the landing two underwater demolition teams worked every day on the difficult job of beach reconnaissance and clearing a boat passage through the obstacles while under machine-gun fire from the shore. The teams— 91 men in each team—were carried to the area in two APDs. When ready for their demolition job, the "frogmen" would climb into landing boats, wearing their swim suits and flippers and carrying explosives and other obstacle clearing equipment. The boats would head for the beach until 400 yards offshore, then change course to parallel the shore line. The frogmen would go over the side toward the barricades, fasten the explosive charges with timing mechanism to the obstacles, then swim back to the boat. A gap of about 40 yards could usually be made on each sortie. It was a dangerous business that required exact timing. When the job was completed a boat passage 1600 yards wide had been cleared and buoyed to the primary beach and a passage 800 yards wide had been cleared and buoyed to two secondary beaches. In addition, the frogmen had provided valuable information regarding depth of water, beach gradients, and character of bottom—all accomplished without the loss of a single man. It seemed incredible.

On 1 July 1945, just as the sun came over the horizon, the amphibious task force with 33,000 Australian troops embarked, anchored off Balikpapan. Just two years and one day before, a few ships operating on untried principles had inaugurated the type of amphibious warfare that was used thereafter in the Southwest Pacific. It had been

[1] *YMS-50, YMS-364, YMS-335, YMS-339, YMS-47, YMS-10, YMS-39, YMS-49, YMS-368, YMS-365,* and *YMS-314.*

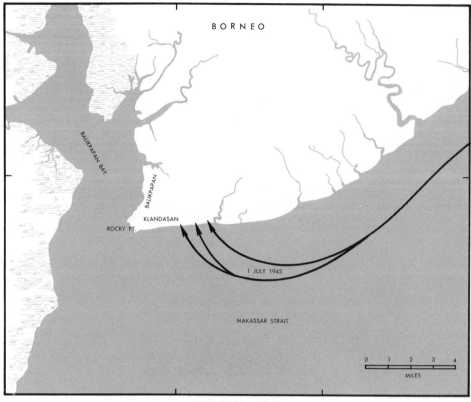

BALIKPAPAN, BORNEO

a shoestring operation carried on at night on the small islands of Woodlark and Kiriwina, 2,500 miles to the eastward. Since then, 55 successful landings had been made. Now more than 200 ships were in the amphibious task force assembled in the waters off Balikpapan. It was broad daylight. There was no sneaking in and out at night as we had to do at Woodlark and Kiriwina for fear of enemy planes and ships. Now there was an air of confidence. The Seventh Division of Australian troops was embarked in the transports, General MacArthur was aboard the cruiser *Cleveland,* and I was in the cruiser *Phoenix.*

There was no element of surprise in the Balikpapan operation. The concentrated air and naval bombardment of the past two weeks and the work of the minesweepers and the frogmen was enough to inform the defenders of the place of landing. To them, only the date was uncertain. Tokyo Rose had broadcast what would happen to the attackers when they headed for the beach. There was no question but that the Japanese intended to put up a stiff fight.

Air bombardment, naval gunfire, and rockets concentrated on the well-marked Japanese positions as the landing boats loaded with Aussies headed for the shore through the openings in the beach obstacles. Artillery and machine-gun fire splashed around the boats, but the enemy made few hits. Their gunners were smothered by Allied gun power. When the troops rushed ashore they met little opposition. There was not a single tree or palm left standing. The bulldozers which were landed with the first waves to dig a path through the big ditches were unneeded. The heavy bombing and gunfire had caved in the sides. Although the enemy had built a series of well-constructed concrete machine-gun nests and strong points that fronted the landing beaches, overwhelming Allied gunfire had either destroyed most of them or forced the enemy to abandon them. Two dazed Japanese were found in a pillbox and only 8 more wounded were found in the first 500 yards, but 460 bodies were lying in the immediate vicinity.

After leaving the flat beach area and moving to the foothills, resistance became tougher. The enemy had taken good defensive positions in caves and in the hills, but the Aussie troops kept expanding their front lines in all directions.

About an hour after the first wave of troops hit the beach, I received a signal from General MacArthur that I join him for an inspection of the fighting ashore. I suggested a slight delay as the troops were still fanning out from the beaches and the front lines were not far away, but he wanted to go right away. I picked him up in a landing boat with a few of his staff, some war correspondents and a camera crew.

As usual, MacArthur was immaculately dressed with well-pressed khaki trousers and carrying light tan gloves. The rest of us looked shopworn and "perspiry." It was hot. MacArthur led the group along the swampland and parallel to the beach. He stopped at a little creek to speak to a group of Australian troops struggling to get a small artillery piece across the stream. They were a tough-looking lot, bare from the waist up, sweat and dirt clinging to their faces. The men paused in their work, and MacArthur, wishing to be friendly, asked, "How goes it, gentlemen?" There was a sudden silence and an immediate sense of hostility. If he had used a few epithets, the "Diggers" would have understood, but to be addressed as "gentlemen" smacked of something they didn't like. After a few more seconds of embarrassing silence, MacArthur moved on.

With his party he climbed a small shale hill, dotted with Australian foxholes, which was less than 200 yards from the enemy front lines. There he started looking over some field maps while the camera crew ground away. An Aussie major came running up and warned everybody to take cover as there was a machine-gun nest in a nearby hilltop. Before he had finished, there was the rat-tat-tat of machine-gun bullets. In a few seconds the firing had stopped, apparently smothered by the Australians, but not before all of us had dropped. But not MacArthur. He was still standing there looking over his map, quite unperturbed as I and the others took a more upright position.

I shamefacedly said something about fighting ashore being no place for the Navy, and supposed I was the first one to hit the dirt. "No," said Lee Van Atta, INS war correspondent, "I was looking up as you came down." As he turned toward me, MacArthur in a very matter-of-fact manner said, "You did exactly right," but he added no comment regarding his own actions. He gave the impression that no Japanese bullet had been made that could bring him down. Undoubtedly, there was some fine film footage showing an erect and well-groomed General looking over a battlefield while those about him were dropping to the ground. As far as I know, however, the film was never shown.

Although we didn't realize it at the time, the Balikpapan operation on 1 July 1945 was the last for the Seventh Amphibious Force. We had completed a two-year combat record of fifty-six amphibious assault landings involving the overwater movement of more than a million men. On 14 August, the Japanese accepted the provisions of the Potsdam Declaration and agreed to surrender.

27:

Korea and North China Operation Troops

WITH THE CAPTURE OF BALIKPAPAN ON 1 JULY 1945, FURTHER operations in the Philippines and Borneo suddenly seemed unimportant. The word was now out that the Joint Chiefs of Staff had authorized a landing on the Japanese home island of Kyushu on 1 November, and that MacArthur would be the overall commander.

Every ship, every man, and every bit of equipment in the Pacific would be needed for this mammoth undertaking which would dwarf into insignificance any overseas attack that had ever been attempted in all history.

As a first order of business, most of the rear bases would be closed down and men and equipment moved to staging positions in the forward area.

The movement of the ships and planes and men of the Southwest Pacific along the coast of New Guinea and then into the Philippines had left in its wake a chain of bases extending from Australia to Manila. The speed of advance had been so great that some of these bases were far in the rear long before they were completed. All had served a purpose as stepping-stones in the march to the Philippines, but with the capture of Manila much of their usefulness had passed and, more importantly, each required a complement of combat troops as protection against the large bodies of Japanese troops which had been bypassed and remained behind as a threat in the nearby jungle. These thousands of Allied troops and thousands of tons of supplies in the rear areas were now urgently needed at the new jump-off bases in readiness for the assault on Japan.

More than 150 LSTs, LCIs and LSMs took part in this roll-up movement in the Southwest Pacific. To meet a roll-up deadline of 15 September, two squadrons of large transports and Navy-manned freighters were obtained on loan from the Central Pacific, and the Army provided large numbers of civilian-manned freighters. It was the first time that the beaching ships of the Seventh Amphibious Force were engaged solely in the type of noncombat operations for which they had been especially designed.

Ships of the Central Pacific had their own problems and deadline dates. Usually, they carried their roll-up cargo to the Marianas and to Okinawa, while those of the Seventh Amphibious Force offloaded their cargo at Leyte and other bases in the Philippines.

The coordination of the movement of all these ships was a tremendous job. In the Southwest Pacific the two officers with the responsibility of this undertaking were Captain S. G. Barchet who handled the distribution within the Philippines and Commander L. J. Manees, the Commander of LST Flotilla 15, who handled the movement of the ships from the rear. There is little glory in jobs of this type, but a lot of tact and executive ability is required.

In the roll-up work, no doubt some things were overlooked. In the years to come, natives prodding the jungles of New Guinea and adjacent islands may still find rich caches of drums of gasoline and other usable equipment left behind by the Americans in the hurried closing of their bases.

In addition to the planning for the invasion of Kyushu on 1 November, a second landing was scheduled to be made near Tokyo a few months later. Also, a less well-known plan—code named "Blacklist"—was in the making at MacArthur's headquarters in Manila. It provided for the peaceful occupation of Japan and Korea in case the Japanese should suddenly surrender. A preliminary draft of "Blacklist" was submitted to the senior commanders at Guam on 20 July.

"Blacklist" would require the use of all the available armed forces in the Pacific to carry out a peaceful occupation. Even though the Japanese Government formally surrendered, there was always the uncertainty whether the military commanders in Japan and in other areas throughout the Pacific would meekly submit to unconditional surrender terms. Any weakness in the strength of the occupation forces might encourage recalcitrant commanders to resist. About 1,700,000 combat troops were estimated to be in Japan proper, and perhaps double that number of civilian defense volunteers. In Korea there were about 270,000 regulars and a much smaller number of civilian volunteers that would need to be disarmed. China was another spot that required close watching.

Amidst all this fevered planning and guesswork a world-shaking event took place which in itself was enough to bring the war to a swift and sudden end. On 6 August the U.S. dropped the world's first atomic bomb on Hiroshima. So little was known about the atom bomb that when the news reached our forces, very few understood its significance. There was a tendency, at first, to think of it as just another, albeit more powerful, bomb. Not until the terrible destructive details were made known did we begin to comprehend what had taken place. On 9 August another atomic bomb was dropped on Nagasaki. On that same day the Russians declared war on Japan and invaded Manchuria and North Korea. They met little resistance for the famed Japanese Kwantung Army had been skeletonized in providing reinforcements for their hard-pressed garrisons throughout the Pacific. Japan was stunned by these developments and on 15 August President Truman was able to announce the unconditional surrender by the Japanese Imperial Government. Orders were sent out for the occupation of Japan and Korea, and shortly afterwards orders were issued for the 1st and 6th Marine Divisions to be moved into North China to assist the government of Chiang Kai-shek in returning that part of China to Nationalist control.

It is difficult now, over twenty-five years later, to realize the overnight change in the attitude of the men in the combat zone from one of war to one of peace. Suddenly everybody wanted to go home. No one was interested in becoming a member of the occupation forces, but no one could be released. Every ship, plane, and man that had been mobilized for the invasion of Japan would be needed for its occupation, as well as other Japanese occupied territories, until it was known whether the hundreds of thousands of well-armed Japanese scattered throughout the Pacific would obey their Emperor and surrender without a struggle.

The change in the orders for the Seventh Amphibious Force was immediate and drastic. Instead of landing assault troops on the shores of Kyushu, the Force would transport the 24th Army Corps from Okinawa to Korea where it would accept the surrender of all Japanese forces in that area. Following that move, the 1st Division of Marines would be embarked at Okinawa for the trip to Tientsin, and as soon as ships became available the 6th Division of Marines would be transported from Guam to Tsingtao and Chefoo. When the new orders arrived, I was aboard my flagship, the *Catoctin,* in Manila Harbor. Most of the Amphibious Force ships were on various roll-up jobs, some as far away as New Guinea.

There was the same feverish activity in assembling the ships and getting their supplies aboard as in the old hurry-up combat days, but the tensions were no longer with us. Lights were now on in all the harbors and on the ships. There was less secrecy and passengers could come and go.

Just before leaving Manila I had the pleasure of meeting Archbishop Spellman of New York, who had been designated by his Holiness, Pope Pius XII, as Catholic Military Vicar of the U.S. Armed Services. My flagship was sailing that night for Okinawa and I invited him to ride with me. Since he was celebrating an important mass in Manila the following morning, arrangements were made for him to be flown to Okinawa where he could join the ship when we stopped to pick up Lieutenant General J. R. Hodge and the 24th Army Corps.

En route to Okinawa we ran into a series of typhoons that were sweeping along the Philippine coast and heading northward toward Japan. On arrival at Buckner Bay, the big fleet port of Okinawa, we found the harbor a shambles. Small boats had been washed ashore and big ships had been ripped from their moorings. Almost a week was lost in getting the troops and supplies of the 24th Army Corps loaded and ready, but finally at 1100 on 5 September the convoy was under way.

Instead of using combat-loaded LSTs—which had served our need in the Southwest Pacific—the 24th Corps was embarked in large transports. The convoy included eighteen APAs, one AKA, some APDs, a minesweeping group, and miscellaneous support craft. In the offing were some carriers and cruisers ready for action in case they were needed. No one knew whether troops would be permitted to land on the beaches peaceably, and the transports were loaded accordingly. We were particularly wary of mines. Our destination was the port of Inchon on the west coast of Korea.

Little was known about the harbor of Inchon other than its reputation for a great range in the rise and fall of tides, the greatest in that part of the Far East. Unloading of ships, we understood, could only be done at high tide alongside the sea wall for a few hours each day. At low tide even the small shallow draft boats would become stranded in mud flats some hundreds of yards offshore. There was reported to be a small inner basin where round-the-clock unloading operations could be carried out, but we were not sure of its capacity or even if it was in working condition.

As the convoy approached the harbor during the early morning hours of 8 September, uncertain of its reception, a few floating mines were sighted, but none gave us trouble. While steaming slowly toward the anchorage, my flagship was approached by a small boat carrying some Koreans. With considerable suspicion we permitted them to come aboard. One of them stated he was a graduate of Brown University and that he had some information he thought we would be pleased to have. A member of my staff, Lieutenant Joseph O'Neil, also a graduate of Brown University, questioned the Korean to verify his statement. When our suspicions were satisfied we were glad to get the news he brought. He told us there were very few Japanese in Inchon; that there would be no opposition to our arrival in Korea; that General Abe, the governor general, would cooperate in the surrender of all Japanese troops in Korea and was sending a delegation of officers to the flagship to make the preliminary arrangements. Our guest supplied reasonably accurate data regarding prisoners of war, tides, roads, and available transportation to Seoul, the capital of Korea and the headquarters of the governor general. In spite of these assurances we were greatly relieved when the Inchon signal tower hoisted, "Welcome United States

Archbishop Spellman conducting services aboard Admiral Barbey's flagship, the U.S.S. Catoctin, *September 1945, en route to Korea.*

The Americans receive a warm welcome in Jinsen (now Inchon), Korea, September 1945.

The Rising Sun comes down and the American flag is raised while the formal surrender takes place at the palace, Seoul, Korea.

The Japanese generals sign the surrender documents in the governor's palace, 9 September 1945.

Fleet." A few minutes later a Japanese harbor pilot came aboard, followed by a small Japanese delegation headed by a major general.

Later that day an advance group of Americans went ashore, met with representatives of the Japanese, and completed arrangements for the surrender of all Japanese forces in Korea south of the 38th parallel to take place at the governor's palace at Seoul at 1600 the next day. Groups of planes from U.S. carriers were in the air all day, flying over most of Korea to discourage any thoughts of resistance on the part of isolated units.

While details were being worked out for the military surrender at Seoul, Lieutenant O'Neil, as the representative of Archbishop Spellman, was arranging for the opening of the impressive cathedral in Seoul. He had a difficult job and little time to do it. The cathedral had not been used for a long time and the people who had been attached to it were scattered. Finally he was able to locate some Belgian priests and nuns who "turned to" enthusiastically for a grand opening and mass to be held on the following day under the sponsorship of Archbishop Spellman. To give as much publicity as possible to this historic event in the lives of Korean Christians, leaflets were dropped over the city and countryside notifying the citizens of the cathedral opening and the hour that mass would be celebrated.

The following afternoon the official party of American officers assembled on the dock at Inchon. Transportation from Inchon to Seoul for the surrender ceremony presented some problems. The passenger cars offered by the Japanese were in such poor condition that it seemed advisable to make the trip in the jeeps carried aboard each of our ships.

It was quite a caravan that took off from Inchon for Seoul, a few miles inland. Besides General Hodge, Admiral Kinkaid and myself—each in his own jeep—most of the Army and Navy unit commanders were in the long convoy. In addition, the convoy carried a security guard as a precaution against some possible fanatics. But there were no unpleasant incidents.

Archbishop Spellman rode with me. The narrow paved highway was in poor condition. During our slow drive we noticed a few shelters built in some of the trees that bordered the roadway. The shelters were primitive things, somewhat similar to the huts that young boys build in the trees in the United States. At one of the caravan stops, Archbishop Spellman left the jeep to stretch his legs and as he stood there the occupants of one of the nearby trees climbed down. They bowed deeply in deference to the clerical robes and listened carefully as though they understood the slowly spoken words, "Put your trust in God, buy Liberty Bonds, and vote for Clancy."

On arrival at the governor's palace in Seoul, Archbishop Spellman and his temporary aide, Lieutenant O'Neil, left the military group and headed for the cathedral.

The formal surrender of the Japanese in the governor's palace was an impressive occasion. The Americans entered first and seated themselves on one side of a long, narrow table. On the other side were a row of chairs where the Japanese would be seated. The surrender document with pen and ink was placed on the table in front of the seats that would be occupied by the senior Japanese of the Army, Navy, and Air Force. When all was in readiness, the Japanese were asked to enter the room. Each stood behind his designated chair until given the word to be seated. Their faces were expressionless. General Abe looked over the surrender documents—written in both English and Japanese—and started to sign. Although he could control the muscles of his face, he could not control the muscles of his stomach, and midway in the signing he pulled out his handkerchief to catch its contents. Twice the same thing happened, but the document was finally signed by General Abe and his associates and then passed across the table to the Americans who also signed. When all signatures were properly affixed, a signal was given to men waiting in the courtyard. The Japanese flag was lowered and the flag of the United States was hoisted in its place.

While the formal surrender was taking place in the palace, in another part of the city Archbishop Spellman was celebrating mass at the cathedral. Because of the short notice regarding the opening of the cathedral, he hardly expected more than a handful of the faithful to be present, but to his surprise the cathedral was overflowing and it became necessary to celebrate the mass on the adjacent hillside to accommodate the great crowd.

Upon the completion of the formal surrender ceremonies, General Hodge and his troops took charge. Allied prisoners of war and internees were cared for. For the next few days regiment after regiment of well-armed Japanese troops stacked their arms at designated places and awaited repatriation to their homeland.

Under less pressing conditions, the job of getting supplies ashore at Inchon for General Hodge's men would have presented no particular problem in spite of the small amount of unloading time due to the great rise and fall of tides. But again the same old shortage of ships and "hurry-up" situations came into being as in our former combat days. This time it was the urgent need to move the Marine 3rd Amphibious Corps, consisting of the 1st and 6th Marine Divisions, to North China where the Allied military and political situation was getting out of hand. The problem was made more difficult because of the separation of the 3rd Corps elements. Corps headquarters was in Guam. The 1st Division was at Okinawa awaiting transportation to the Tientsin-Chinwangtao area and the 6th Division—less one regiment which was in Japan—was standing by at Guam for transportation to the Tsingtao-Chefoo area.

The situation in China was a delicate one. During recent months most of the Japanese troop strength—close to a million of them with an additional group of perhaps eight hundred thousand puppet troops—had been withdrawn from the South to North China and to Manchuria. The bulk of the Nationalist troops of Chiang were in the south of China, some hundreds of miles away. Although the Chinese Communist 8th Route Army of Mao Tse-tung was operating in North China, their loyalty to Chiang was doubtful. Because of the wartime destruction of most bridges and many rail lines, the quick movement of large bodies of loyal Nationalist troops from the south could only be undertaken by sea or air transport, and Chiang had very little shipping and almost no planes under his control. With the capitulation of the Japanese, American troops would be needed to police the area until loyal Chinese troops of Chiang's own choosing became available. The 3rd Marine Corps was but a small part of the number of troops Chiang and his American Chief of Staff, Lieutenant General A. C. Wedemeyer, had urgently requested.

Although the Japanese and their puppet troops controlled most of the big cities of North China and the main arteries of communication, the Chinese Communist troops of Mao Tse-tung controlled the countryside. Their numbers were not great but they had the loyal support of the peasants because of their program of giving them land to farm.

Mao Tse-tung and his army commanders had given grudging loyalty to Chiang during the war years, but now that the war was over it was probable they would take a more independent stance.

President Chiang must have felt that such was the case, for as soon as he received word of the Japanese government's surrender, he directed all Japanese and puppet army commanders to hold their positions and surrender only to representatives of his choosing. He also directed General Chu Teh, Commander of the Communist 18th Group Army (formerly the 8th Route Army)—whose troops were in North China— to hold his troops at present posts and await further instructions.

But General Chu Teh had other ideas. He refused to accept the order and directed his troops to undertake the surrender of Japanese and puppet troops and occupy any territory which had been under their control. On 24 August they moved in and occupied the weakly held port of Chefoo.

Fortunately for Chiang, in most areas the Japanese ignored the orders from the Chinese Communists and decided to hold their present positions. It was a peculiar situation. A few weeks before the Japanese troops were engaged in fighting the Nationalist troops of General Chiang. Now they were carrying out his orders and holding off Chinese Communists. It was a matter of self-interest. Surrendering to the Nationalists would be the first step in repatriation to their homeland. Surrendering to the Communists meant an uncertain future, probably in labor camps.

To ease the worsening rift between the Nationalist government and the Communists, United States Ambassador Patrick Hurley arranged a conference between Mao and Chiang on 18 August at the Nationalist capital of Chungking. But Mao was suspicious of Chiang and would not leave his Communist headquarters at Yenan unless personally escorted by Hurley, which was done. The conferences accomplished very little. The major disagreement was over control of the armies. Chiang insisted that the Communist armies be integrated into those of the Nationalist forces. Mao insisted they remain as units under his personal control.

Chiang's troubles were not limited to North China. Soviet armies were swarming over Manchuria, accepting the surrender of Japanese troops and then shipping them off to labor camps in Siberia. To add to his woes they were stripping the area of industrial machinery, estimated as worth three-quarters of a billion dollars, and arming the Chinese Communists with Japanese weapons. As if this were not enough, at war's end Chiang had been forced—by pressure from the United States—to enter into an agreement with the Russians on 14 August which provided, among other obnoxious things, that the Soviet government retain special privileges in the two most important ports of entrance into Manchuria, Port Arthur and Dairen. This provision eliminated those ports from military use by Nationalist troops and would seriously hamper them in any effort to re-occupy Manchuria. In return for these concessions, the Russians recognized the Nationalist government of China as the legitimate government and agreed to refrain from interference in China's internal affairs. Russia also agreed to commence withdrawing its troops from Manchuria within three weeks of the end of the war and to complete the withdrawal within three months.

The policy of the U.S. government as it filtered down to the commanders on the spot was to assist the Chinese Nationalist government of President Chiang in some urgent and temporary needs that he was unable to handle at the moment. Among these was the need to rescue Allied prisoners-of-war and internees from the camps scattered throughout North China, to accept the surrender of Japanese troops, to transport all Japanese to their home islands, and to assist in the transportation of limited numbers of Nationalist troops from the south of China to the north. Although Chiang was the recognized head of the Chinese government and our wartime ally, there was no desire on the part of our government to become involved in any civil war that might break out between the Nationalists and the Communists. Indeed, there were many crosscurrents of opinions in the United States, including some in responsible positions in government who did not think of Mao Tse-tung and his followers as Communists in the accepted meaning of the term, but rather as agrarian reformers who wanted to free themselves from a corrupt Nationalist government.

It was into this confusion of political and military opinion that the 3rd Amphibious Corps of Marines was to be launched. To speed up joint planning and transportation arrangements, my Chief of Staff, Commodore Ray Tarbuck, was flown to Corps Headquarters at Guam.

If all went as planned, large ships would transport the 1st Marine Division to the mouth of the Pei Ho River and from there small shallow-draft amphibious craft would move them up the river to Tientsin. From Tientsin they would fan out to Peking and Chinwangtao. As soon as ships could be turned around they would pick up the 6th Marine Division and land them at Chefoo and Tsingtao, two ports on the Shantung peninsula.

Alternate plans were made for the Marines to be transported to Shanghai if there was danger of their being caught in the middle of a fratricidal war in carrying out their North China landings.

Nationalist troop movement from the south of China to the north was delayed until the Chinese armies could be assembled at embarking ports and American ships were freed from the job of transporting Marines.

The convoy of transports carrying the 1st Division of Marines got under way from Okinawa for North China on the afternoon of 26 September. It was not what the Marines had hoped for. They had hoped for the honor of leading the parade of victorious troops down the main streets of Tokyo. They had started the amphibious war in the Pacific with the landing at Guadalcanal and had taken part in many a bloody and heartbreaking campaign until war's end. But it wasn't the Marines who led the triumphal march down the Ginza. That honor went to the First Cavalry Division, which had been with General MacArthur during his struggling campaign along the New Guinea coast and into the Philippines. Although the Marines had missed the victory march in Tokyo, they were happy to settle—as an interlude before going home—for North China as being a great improvement over backward Okinawa.

While under way, the convoy was notified that the Japanese were carrying out the orders of the Generalissimo and had retained control of Tientsin, Peking, Chinwangtao and the communications lines connecting those places, and were anxiously awaiting the arrival of the Marines in order to surrender to them and get started on their way home.

Before daylight on 30 September the convoy anchored in the bay off the mouth of the Pei Ho River. Shortly afterwards the Marines were transferred to shallow draft amphibious ships—LCIs, LCMs and LCTs—and the run up the river commenced. The small coastal town of Tanku was first occupied and then came the river movement to the great industrial city of Tientsin. After all these years the one thing that stands out in my memory was the enthusiastic welcome of the Chinese. The river banks were lined with people and thousands of them were waving American flags. Where these poor people got the materials to make those flags will always be a mystery to me.

There were no unpleasant incidents during the landing or for the first few days of the occupation. The Japanese were well organized, well disciplined, and almost subservient in their desire to please. Their sole interest was to be on their way home. But the Marines were in no hurry to have the Japanese withdraw, for they were useful allies. They protected the bigger cities and guarded the bridges and rail lines from Communist-led guerrillas. However, the Generalissimo wanted the Japanese out of the country as soon as possible as their great numbers posed a potential threat to Chinese security.

On 6 October, just one week after his arrival, Major General Rockey, the Marine commander, on behalf of the Allies, accepted the surrender of Japanese General Uchida, commander of the 50,000 troops in the Tientsin area. The Japanese were directed to give up all arms and equipment of every description—artillery, rifles, ammunition, grenades, automobiles—everything with one exception. Every tenth man was allowed to keep his rifle and five rounds of ammunition to temporarily assist in guarding the storehouses, bridges, and rail lines until the Marines were in a position to take over these duties by themselves or turn over this job to the Chinese Nationalists.

28:

Final Operations

DURING THE FEW WEEKS THE 6TH MARINE DIVISION WAS waiting at Guam to be sea-lifted to the important ports of Chefoo on the north coast of the Shantung Peninsula and to Tsingtao on the Peninsula's south coast, Chiang's situation in North China had steadily worsened. He had few loyal troops in the area and the Communists were becoming stronger. They had captured Chefoo and were spreading their influence throughout the countryside. The 1st Division of Marines was being harassed by an increasing number of guerrilla attacks, all of them being Communist inspired. Japanese Major General Nagano with 10,000 troops was holding Tsingtao and a few other nearby cities, and also keeping open some of the main rail lines while awaiting the arrival of the 6th Marines. But it was a situation that could not last much longer. The peasants hated the Japanese who had treated them cruelly during the war years. They were sympathetic to the Communists, mostly because of the promises of much-needed land reform, and partly from fear. Chiang was distrusted. He had little to offer. His main support came from the war lords, the landlords, and a privileged few; and they preferred the "status quo."

Alternate plans had been prepared for the transportation of the 6th Marine Division to Shanghai if the landings at Chefoo and Tsingtao proved impractical—presumably because of opposition from the Communists; as it turned out, by the time the Division was embarked, the only ports in North China under the control of the Communists were those of Chefoo and Wei Hai Wei, both on the north coast of the Shantung Peninsula.

Although the Communist armies of Generals Mao Tse-tung and Chu Teh were presumably a part of the Nationalist Army and would carry out the orders of President Chiang Kai-shek and welcome the arrival of the Marines at Chefoo, there was no assurance that this would be done.

Accordingly, while the Marines were under way from Guam, the Seventh Fleet commander, Admiral Kinkaid, sent a note to the Communist commandant at Chefoo, notifying him of the proposed landing and requesting the orderly with-drawal of his troops and the removal of mines and beach defenses. The note was delivered to the mayor, who was also the commandant, on 4 October by Rear Admiral T. G. W. Settle who had arrived off Chefoo in his flagship, the cruiser *Louisville*. The mayor informed Settle that no action would be taken on the note pending instructions from Yenan—the Communist headquarters of Mao Tse-tung and Chu Teh—and that if the Marines should land without his permission they would be held accountable for any unpleasant incidents that might develop.

It was in this atmosphere of uncertainty and possible involvement in a civil war that I was directed to proceed to Chefoo and make recommendations as to further action.

I arrived off Chefoo in my flagship, the *Catoctin,* on 7 October with Major General Rockey aboard. Shortly after anchoring, the Communist mayor of Chefoo, Mr. Yu Ku-ying, came aboard to discuss the purpose of our visit. General Rockey and Admiral Settle participated in the conference.

The substance of the mayor's comments was that he had been advised of the proposed landing by the Marines and that he had asked Yenan for instructions, but as yet none had been received. He repeatedly referred to the Americans as his friends and could see no reason for the landing of their troops as there were no Japanese troops in the vicinity nor any prisoner-of-war camps. He said that Chefoo had been taken from the Japanese by Chinese Communist troops after some hard fighting and he let us know that they intended to keep control of the port and repeated what he had already told Settle. If any unpleasant incidents developed out of the proposed landing of the Marines, the Americans must assume full responsibility. He was particularly interested in knowing if any Chinese Nationalist troops were included in the proposed landing. He stated, somewhat bitterly, that Generalissimo Chiang had been using Japanese troops to attack those of the Communists. The mayor invited us to visit his headquarters ashore at 1600.

That afternoon, when we arrived at the dock, we found cars awaiting us. We were driven down the main street to the mayor's office. Most of the stores were closed, and the street was lined with armed soldiers standing at attention, as we drove between them from the dock to the mayor's office.

On the wall behind the mayor's desk were pictures of Stalin and Mao Tse-tung,

The Communist mayor of Chefoo, Yu Ku-ying (left), confers with Admiral Barbey, Major General Keller E. Rockey, and Rear Admiral T. G. W. Settle.

Admiral Barbey meets Madame and Generalissimo Chiang Kai-shek in Chungking, November 1945.

but none of Chiang. Tea was served. The conversation was merely a repetition of the thoughts that had been expressed aboard ship earlier in the day. The mayor was still awaiting instructions from Yenan.

On our return to my flagship, General Rockey, Admiral Settle and myself sent off a joint dispatch with our recommendations and the reasons for them. It was noted that there were no prisoners-of-war camps nor any Japanese in the area, that the Communists were in full control and would probably resist any landing of the Marines, that the Marines could capture the port without too much trouble, but doing so would involve us directly in the first steps of a probable civil war. We therefore collectively recommended that those Marines who were then headed for Chefoo be diverted to Tsingtao.

Within a matter of hours our recommendations were accepted and the convoy was diverted to Tsingtao.

The decision regarding landing or not landing Marines at Chefoo was unusually important as it would have a direct bearing on the future military actions of the United States in China and particularly on the extent to which our country would aid President Chiang Kai-shek if full-scale civil war developed.

The next important transportation job for the Seventh Amphibious Force was the movement of three Chinese armies from Haiphong (Indochina) and Kowloon (near Hong Kong) to the north of China. My orders were to transport three armies from these ports—no more, no less. Chiang was bitterly disappointed at these orders. He confided to me that three armies (about 30,000 men in a Chinese army) were not enough to take over the North China area being policed by the Marines and also to occupy Manchuria in the vacuum created by the withdrawal of the Russians. A few Nationalist divisions had been air-lifted by American planes into Nanking, Shanghai, and Peking, but nowhere near enough to meet all of Chiang's requirements. He feared a take-over of Manchuria by the Chinese Communists, aided and abetted by the Russians. Although the Communists were not in open rebellion against him, there was always the possibility they would set up an independent state whenever they were in a position to do so.

Finding the ships to move even three Chinese armies involved more than the usual difficulties. Owing to public demand in the United States for prompt demobilization of the Armed Forces, many men were on their way home because they had met the Navy Department's requirements for immediate discharge and as a consequence some of the ships that were still with us were operating with skeleton crews.

In addition to finding the shipping for the movement of Chinese armies was the need for ships to transport the hundreds of thousands of Japanese troops and civilians who had been assembled at North China ports and were impatiently awaiting repatriation. A few available Japanese transports helped out a little, but it was the LSTs that did most of the work. The larger ships, the APAs, were assigned to the movement of Chinese troops.

The repatriation job was a comparatively simple one, principally because the Japanese were well organized and well disciplined. And this applied not only to the combat troops, but to the civilians as well.

One afternoon on the docks of Tsingtao, through which 75,000 civilians were repatriated, curiosity brought me to the spot where a thousand Japanese civilians in two parallel lines were standing or sitting awaiting embarkation on an LST. All the personal belongings that they were allowed to take with them were neatly stacked alongside. As I approached they jumped to attention, and on signal from each squad leader opened their bags or suitcases for inspection. Even the little children conformed to the pattern of their elders. And this particular group was no different than the others, I was told. All an LST skipper had to do was to appoint squad leaders, mark off the space in the ship assigned to each squad, notify them of the ship's regulations, and the squad leader did the rest.

Even the surrender of the Japanese troops was made simple because of their organization and discipline. The Marines, as representatives of the Nationalist government, laid out the rules and the Japanese commanders did the rest.

A typical surrender ceremony took place at Tsingtao at the race course on the outskirts of the city. Flags of the United States and China flew from the surrender platform. The audience was a cosmopolitan group including Nationalist Chinese, Allied military officers, and internees who had been released a few days previously from their prison camp. Twelve thousand Marines stood at attention in the oval race course. Major General Eiji Nagano signed the surrender document on behalf of the 10,000 Japanese troops in the immediate area. Marine Major General Lemuel Shepherd and Lieutenant General Chen Pao-tsang of the Chinese Nationalist Army signed on behalf of the Allies. Ten copies of acceptances had been prepared in Japanese and English. Immediately after the signing, the Japanese general and his staff unhooked their samurai swords and laid them on the surrender table. The Marine band then played the American National Anthem followed by the Chinese National Anthem. General Rockey and myself were present but not participants in the ceremony.

Shortly after the surrender the repatriation of this particular group of combat troops began. They would be debarked in ports in metropolitan Japan where they would be demobilized and sent to their homes. Chinese Nationalist prisoners and Korean laborers would be brought back on the return trip.

The transportation of the Chinese armies from the south to the north was not so simple a matter. With the Japanese we knew where they would be embarked and where disembarked. There were no disciplinary problems nor any health problems. But with the Chinese it was different. We knew where their troops would be embarked but not where they would be disembarked. Generalissimo Chiang wanted them landed at Manchurian ports to take over that area before the Chinese Communists moved into the vacuum created by the withdrawal of the Russians. His American advisers preferred the Chinese be disembarked in North China ports in order to relieve the Marines of their peace-keeping responsibilities.

The U.S. Theater Commander—who was also Chiang's Chief of Staff—had recommended to the Joint Chiefs of Staff that the Marines be relieved of all their duties on 15 November and returned to the States. This action, if approved, would require the Nationalist forces to move additional armies from the south or abandon Manchuria to the Communists.

U.S. policy at that time was to assist the Nationalist government but not to the extent of armed involvement with the Communists. There was a growing feeling in the administration that a coalition government of Nationalists and Communists was essential to the development of a united China and the avoidance of civil war.

The Generalissimo's decision to have the Japanese surrender only to loyal Nationalists or to United States forces—but not to Communist troops—led to the suspicion, in Communist eyes, that American troops and ships would be used to support Chiang in any domestic struggle that might develop.

During the closing months of 1945, the Marines had been subjected to an increasing number of harassing attacks on the railways, cutting of communications, and the establishment of numerous roadblocks. The railway between Peking and Tientsin had frequently been blocked and under fire.

These attacks were admittedly carried out by units of the Communist 8th Route Army for the purpose of preventing the expansion of the Nationalists into areas of Red control. In at least two cases where Marines were wounded—at Tientsin and Tangshan—Communist leaders formally apologized, and in the other instances reiterated a desire to avoid hostilities with the Americans, but at the same time expressed determination to maintain their present holdings.

Although the Marine-guarded trains were getting through to Peking and Tientsin despite the roadblocks and firing, the larger cities were actually islands in the Communist sea.

Such uneasy peace as did exist in North China appeared to depend almost entirely on the continuance of the negotiations at Chungking between Generalissimo Chiang and Mao Tse-tung and the Communist reluctance to force a situation which might turn United States military strength against them.

Should negotiations at Chungking fail, or should the Communist leaders eventually decide to openly challenge the influx of the Nationalist troops either by air, rail or sea, the last chance for a peaceful settlement would be gone.

There was no accurate estimate of the number of Communist troops in North China and Manchuria. The Reds claimed one million uniformed men. They had probably about one-half that number. In case of an outbreak of hostilities, the Communists were unlikely to be opposed by any residents of the rural areas. Most of the shopkeepers and peasants who gave either real or opportunistic loyalty to Chiang, were already in the cities, thus leaving the Reds a relatively clear field elsewhere.

In an attempt to keep abreast of a very fluid political and military situation, at least one U.S. ship was stationed at each of the larger Chinese ports. One day a surprising report was received from the ship on duty at the port of Chefoo. The report stated that eight small steamers and four junks, some of them flying the United States flag, had arrived off Chefoo and were disembarking fifteen hundred poorly equipped troops on a barren island about a mile and a half offshore. The troops were supposedly a unit of the Nationalist forces under the command of General Wang Chuh-shan who had come from Taku with the intention of capturing Chefoo from the Communists. He asked for U.S. naval gunfire support. His official status seemed a bit uncertain. There was a suspicion that Wang's little army was a bunch of freebooters who were hoping to exploit to their own advantage a troubled and confused situation. Some of his men were identified as former collaborators of the Japanese occupation forces. When Wang found out there would be no gunfire support from American ships, his little armada sailed away.

Wang's little diversionary effort at Chefoo did not appear to be part of the Nationalist campaign, whose purpose was to keep the 53,000 U.S. Marines in North China while Chiang's loyal armies moved into Manchuria.

Since the Manchurian ports of Port Arthur and Dairen were not available as unloading points for Chinese Nationalist troops, Chiang requested that his 13th Army be debarked at Hulutao and his 52nd Army at Yingkow. He also advised that both of these Manchurian ports were under Russian control and that they had agreed to assist in the debarking of the troops. The first contingent of the 13th Army had already left Kowloon for Hulutao in Seventh Amphibious Force ships, and the 52nd Army was standing by at Haiphong awaiting transportation.

Statements from the Nationalists, the Communists, and the Russians were often so contradictory that it seemed advisable to obtain on-the-spot information before the arrival of the armies at their destination.

The first port of call in my flagship was Hulutao. I sent a small boat ashore to find out who was in charge of the port and to arrange for the exchange of official visits. As the boat neared the pier—with the U.S. flag prominently displayed—it was fired upon. The boat returned to the flagship.

Shortly afterwards, Lieutenant General Lau Shek Hai, Communist commander, came aboard and apologized for the shooting incident. He said his troops had been under orders—presumably from Yenan—to prevent any boat from entering the harbor unless previous orders had been given for its passage and that this order had been issued after Chinese puppet troops, calling themselves Nationalist soldiers, had tried to approach Hulutao.

General Lau charged that while details of an agreement between Generalissimo Chiang and Mao Tse-tung were being worked out at Chungking, the Nationalists were using the time to consolidate their positions in North China. He indicated that, unless instructions were received from Yenan to the contrary, he was prepared to oppose the landing of Nationalist troops.

Subsequent visits ashore located a small detachment of Russians, but they had no local authority. Enough information was obtained, however, to indicate the Russians were actively aiding the Communists in spite of their assurances and agreements with the recognized Chinese government of President Chiang.

It was assumed that any attempt to put the 13th Army ashore at Hulutao would result in bitter fighting with the probable involvement of U.S. naval ships. To avoid this possibility, the transports carrying the 13th Army were diverted to Chinwangtao, a port near the southern end of the great Chinese wall separating North China from Manchuria.

The next reconnaissance stop of the flagship *Catoctin* was the port of Yingkow. The following day, Nationalist General Tu Li-ming came aboard. He had arrived off the port in a small Chinese ship to arrange for the landing of the 52nd Army. He told us that at a conference at Hsinking on 29 October with Marshall Marinofsky—the commander of Russian Manchurian forces—the Nationalist representatives had been assured the Russians controlled Yingkow and that the troops of Chiang Kai-shek would be welcomed. My Chief of Staff, Captain S. G. Barchet, was sent ashore to look over the situation.

The visit to Yingkow was a futile one. There were only a few hundred Russians in the garrison but they were in complete control of the port, although there appeared to be several thousand Chinese Communist soldiers busily engaged in erecting beach defenses against the proposed landing of Nationalist troops. The Russian commandant seemed unaware of any agreement between Marshall Marinofsky and the Chinese government, but stated he would get in touch with Russian headquarters at Mukden and bring the information to the flagship the following day. Instead of calling at the flagship the next day, the commandant and presumably most of the Russian garrison had departed Yingkow during the night and left the Chinese Communists in control of the port. The scheduled landing of the first echelon of the Nationalist 52nd Army—then on the high seas—was canceled, and at the request of the Chinese high command was diverted to Chinwangtao.

Trying to assist the Chinese government without becoming directly involved in any fratricidal conflict was becoming more difficult every day, and the Russians were adding to the difficulties. The negotiations at Chungking were showing little progress in bringing together the Communists and the Nationalists, but the Joint Chiefs of Staff were still hopeful of avoiding a complete break between the two forces.

Perhaps it was just as well the 52nd Army did not attempt to land at Yingkow, especially against determined opposition. The units that landed at Chinwangtao did not look much like an effective fighting force. They were poorly equipped, had little artillery—perhaps because they were dependent on animal transport which had been left behind—wore motley uniforms and carried a heterogeneous collection of rifles including European, American, and Japanese. However, they had been battle-tested and had seen action in South China and Indochina, and might have performed better than their appearance indicated. Their principal weakness was in their deplorable physical condition. Captain Emmett D. Hightower, the Force medical officer, reported that about three-fourths of them had diseases of one type or another ranging from scabies, ulcers, trachoma, chronic malaria, diarrhea, and venereal infection, to cholera. Eighteen Chinese died on the trip, thirteen were suspected cholera cases. One little seven-year-old soldier was given a cheer by the ship's company as he proudly marched ashore carrying a full knapsack.

Before the troops had embarked at Haiphong, they were screened by medical officers who culled out the worst physical cases, including those who had not been inoculated against cholera.

Virtually every Chinese suffered from seasickness on the trip. To add to the woes of the ships' officers and crews, the troops were not accustomed to the modern plumbing found aboard the transports. Dark corners seemed preferable to toilets, and urinal troughs, wash basins, and shower stalls were used interchangeably. But the troops were docile and willing to learn. However this transporting job was a distasteful one with the ever present danger of an outbreak of cholera among the ships' personnel in spite of the unusual precautions that were always taken.

The 13th Army which had landed at Chinwangtao about a week previously—it had been originally scheduled for Hulutao—was known as a sponsored army. This meant they were among the elite few who had been trained and equipped by the Americans, but even so their equipment, training, and health was far below U.S. standards. When they landed in the freezing midwinter cold of Chinwangtao they were still wearing their light tropical uniforms, with no replacement in sight.

After the troops debarked, they marched toward the town of Shanhaikwan, a few miles inland, and joined the other Nationalist troops that were concentrated in the area. Shanhaikwan was of strategic importance because of its location in a gap of the great wall of China and astride the Peking-Mukden rail line. The Nationalists had decided to move their troops into the heart of Manchuria along this rail line, fighting their way against the Communists if necessary. They had no choice since all Manchurian ports were closed to them.

As soon as the first echelon of Chinese troops was debarked at Chinwangtao and the transports fumigated and made ready, they were sent south again for their next load. It was a discouraging business. The ships were operating with skeleton crews because of the demands for immediate release of the men who had accumulated the necessary discharge "points." The personnel situation had become so acute that I had recommended certain ships be turned over to the Chinese and Japanese to permit them to do their own transporting of personnel. No action was taken on this recommendation while I was in the Orient.

In this business of transporting Chinese, the matter of using the ships' plumbing facilities was one of vital concern. The troops were willing and even eager to master the intricacies of shipboard life. As often happens in situations that need a practical solution, a chief petty officer came forward with a suggestion that was brilliant in its simplicity. He proposed the formation of demonstration teams on each transport. As each company of Chinese came aboard they would be guided in single file past each bit of ship's plumbing which would be in use by a member of one of the demonstration teams.

The Chinese are great imitators and they did their best to conform to western standards, not only in regards to plumbing, but in other matters. It was difficult for them to accept the fact that women should not accompany the troops, and a few were brought aboard surreptitiously. Records were few and life was cheap. If a man died aboard ship he was tossed overboard. The men were counted when they came aboard and again when they debarked. Any difference in numbers was presumed to be because men had died at sea.

As commander of the Seventh Amphibious Force, my duties in China were concerned primarily with transportation problems, but on 19 November I relieved Admiral Kinkaid as Commander of the Seventh Fleet and transferred to my new flagship, at Shanghai. My old flagship, the *Catoctin,* was ordered to the States for decommissioning. Before leaving she was loaded down with short-timers who were scheduled for early discharge.

At the farewell party given for the departing officers of the *Catoctin* at a Shanghai hotel by those who were left behind, an amusing incident occurred that illustrates the mixed-up situations that seemed to pop up throughout China at that time, and also that loyalty takes many forms. En route to the reception I was introduced to a Russian lady who said she was married to a Frenchman named Barbey, but at the moment he was in a Shanghai jail—if I remember rightly—where he was being held by the Americans as a former collaborator with the Japanese. Feeling that some of the young officers were doing a bit of spoofing, I asked to see her passport, which she promptly produced. When I stepped out of the hotel elevator at the proper floor with my accidental companion, I introduced her as Mrs. Barbey to two ensigns who formed the reception committee. They both looked a bit startled, but later one sidled up to me and whispered, "Don't worry, Admiral, your secret will be safe with us."

Like everyone else in the Far East, I too was anxious to go home, but some of us had to stay a little longer. Because of my own longings, I remember in particular a letter from a little girl, Maurine Roesken. It was an appealing letter. She said she was but eight years old and hadn't seen her daddy for a long, long time and was so anxious for him to be home at Christmas. And then she added that she had seen a picture of me and that I had such a kind face she knew I would help her.

In checking into the matter, I found that her father had left on the *Catoctin* for San Diego a few days previously, and barring some red tape delay could be home for Christmas. I sent a dispatch to the ship with a summary of the little girl's letter, and then forgot about the matter. Sensing a human interest story, Joe Hearst, an enterprising war correspondent for the Chicago *Tribune,* sent in a short feature article about the kind admiral. It hit the Sunday editions. And then my troubles started. I was deluged with mail from congressmen, mothers, wives, and little girls. One of the more angry letters came from a woman in the Middle West whose son, she said, was on my flagship. She didn't tell me her name, she said, because I was the kind of a man who would put him in the brig if I knew who he was, but she knew her son had more "points" than Maurine's daddy who got sent home because of some blarney from a little girl, but she intended to write her congressman about it. And, for no apparent reason, she added, ". . . MacArthur is a dirty dog."

Retaining enough men to keep the ships functioning had become a more difficult problem than the repatriation of the Japanese or the movement of Chinese troops. In the hope that the recommendations to transfer some LSTs to China would be accepted and partially relieve an acute personnel situation, arrangements were made for the establishment of an LST training school for Chinese at Tsingtao. It was a simplified three-months' course. Two Chinese were stationed with each U.S. officer or seaman to learn one particular job, such as navigator, helmsman, heaving the lead, tending the anchor, or acting as engineman. Some of the LSTs that were turned over to the Nationalists many months later became manned by sailors who were the product of this first elementary training project.

My days in China were drawing to a close, for I had requested duty in the States after three years of overseas duty. There were a few trips to Chungking and Nanking as the house guest of the Generalissimo and Madame Chiang Kai-shek where I had the pleasure of sleeping between silken bed sheets, and then there was the freezing trip from Hulutao to Changchun—fifty miles inland—as the train guest of Nationalist General Tu Li-ming. The armies of General Tu had moved along the Peking-Mukden railroad to Changchun and finally had branched out to the port of Hulutao. As the Chinese advanced, the Communists retreated, but the Manchuria that General Tu captured was a wasteland. All usable equipment had been moved out with the Russians.

General Tu, like all the other senior Nationalist leaders, considered the Chinese

Communists as their enemies, but the U.S. government preferred to consider them as agrarian reformers and sent General George C. Marshall to China during the last week of December 1945. I was one of the group that met him on his arrival at the Shanghai airport. His mission was plain. He hoped to convince Generalissimo Chiang and General Mao Tse-tung that a peaceful and unified China could only be obtained by a coalition government of Nationalists and Communists. The negotiations had barely gotten under way when I left China in mid-January 1946. The Marines were still in North China guarding the railroads and the large cities; the Japanese were still being repatriated in American ships with American crews; the Russians were slowly withdrawing from Manchuria; large bands of well-armed Japanese troops were refugees in the Manchurian hills, refusing to surrender except to the Americans; and General George C. Marshall—the personal representative of President Truman—was attempting to reconcile the opposing views of Generalissimo Chiang Kai-shek and General Mao Tse-tung.

It was a situation that I was happy to leave.

Epilogue

WITH THE END OF WORLD WAR II AND THE DEMOBILIZATION OF much of the armed strength of the United States, the Joint Chiefs of Staff set about the job of reorganizing the military forces to meet current requirements and to lay plans for the future.

Unfortunately, there was a feeling among some influential military leaders that amphibious warfare as known in World War II need no longer become part of future planning. Indeed, the chairman of the Joint Chiefs of Staff testified before the Armed Services Committee of the House of Representatives, in October 1949, that it was doubtful if there would ever again be large-scale amphibious operations.

In this atmosphere of doubt, the specialist in amphibious warfare was relegated to the "has been" group with the battleship sailor and the cavalryman. Less than one year after the statement by the chairman of the Joint Chiefs of Staff, a major amphibious landing was made by the troops of General MacArthur at Inchon, Korea,[1] and the whole cycle of amphibious thinking underwent a change.

But the change in thinking came too late to save the careers of many fine officers who suffered for the unlikely reason that they had become too expert in the field of amphibious warfare. Most of them had been retained in the battle zone far beyond their allotted time because the pressures had become too great to permit their

[1] The landing was made 15 September 1950. Immediately afterwards General MacArthur sent a message to Admiral Barbey who was then Commandant of the Thirteenth Naval District: "The landing was made in the best Barbey tradition."

replacement by less experienced personnel. Understandably, the Navy promotion system did not look kindly on those who had become too specialized in a type of warfare that was believed to be outmoded.

Among the fine regular officers who joined my staff at its beginning and who remained with me far beyond their allotted time, and may have suffered thereby, were two with whom I was particularly closely associated during our steady advance along the New Guinea coast and into the Philippines.

One was Captain Francis W. Benson, an amphibious combat veteran of the Guadalcanal campaign who carried the load of operations officer from our jump-off in Australia until our arrival in the Philippines more than a year later. He controlled the movement of thousands of ships. He knew the capability of every big transport, every beaching craft, and every skipper—and understood the combinations that must be brought together to get the best results for every operation.

Then there was Commander Charles Adair, whose prior jungle experience proved invaluable in plotting the movement of beaching ships through uncharted waters and onto hostile tropical shores. He had been in Manila during the attack on Pearl Harbor, and later joined a small group that escaped in the diesel-powered schooner USS *Lanikai*. Cruising at six knots at night, dodging Japanese ships and planes, and hiding in the jungle in the daytime, he had become quite expert in small craft operations around uncharted isles by the time he arrived in Australia almost three months later.

There were others on the early staff who carried a heavy burden in developing the new technique in amphibious operations and became specialists in the art, a technique that did not rely on superior air power or superior naval power to cover landing operations. Among them was Commander B. B. C. Lovett, staff aviator, who had the frustrating and sometimes fruitless task of trying to obtain adequate air cover for our operations from the shore-based Fifth Air Force. Also, Captains Bern Anderson and K. J. Christoph, and Commander M. T. Farrar, who carried out a multitude of jobs from training, to planning, to control of amphibious craft in the steaming jungle ports of New Guinea. Their ingenuity in getting ships and craft discharged across surf-bound beaches and swamplike terrain in the face of enemy bombers and hostile troops entitle them to a special place in the review of unsung heroes of the regular Navy.

I look back with admiration on the difficult task of Commander Sherry Betts, our able aerographer, and the impatient demands made upon him for accurate weather forecasts and his need to rely on sketchy reports from coastal stations in China and other faraway places to supply us with the data we so urgently needed.

Not only officers of the regular Navy suffered promotion stagnation because of prolonged assignment to the staff of the Seventh Amphibious Force—there were others as well. Two in particular I recall because of their heavy responsibilities and the unquestioned reliance that was placed upon their work. One was Major J. S. Blais, U.S. Marine Corps. He had been temporarily assigned to our early staff—presumably for a few weeks—by the Commanding General of the 1st Marine Division, but he remained with us until the occupation of the Philippines. He prepared all bombardment plans and supervised their execution. It sounds like a simple enough job, but it wasn't. The gunfire of every ship had to be coordinated with that of the planes. Cruisers, destroyers, rocket craft, and beaching ships—each had their own type of ammunition and range of fire. Blais became an expert in the matter of shore bombardment.

The other member of this duo was Lieutenant Russell J. Schmidt, U.S. Naval Reserve. He had been a repair supervisor for the Bell Telephone Company before joining our staff. As staff communication officer it was his job to convert a destroyer with a fairly simple communication system into one that could serve as a temporary flagship for our beaching operations which required simultaneous communication systems with other ships, planes overhead, and troops ashore. There was no one to turn to for help in these matters and he had little to work with. His results were a maze of ingenuity. He loved his work and at the end of the war he transferred to the regular Navy. But he, too, was caught in the same prejudices as many others. Amphibious warfare was a thing of the past and when promotion time came, there was no need for specialists in his field.

Later, this group was joined by veterans from other areas and they too were kept on overseas duty far beyond their allotted time simply because they became too valuable in the arduous mopping-up campaign in the Philippines and in the delicate postwar handling of Chinese and Korean problems. Among the many in this group I will mention but two, Captains S. G. Barchet and J. D. Hayes, because these two were closely associated with me as members of my personal staff.

Every important naval operation since World War II—and that includes worldwide refugee activities as well as warlike operations in the Mediterranean, the Caribbean, and more recently in Southeast Asia—has been amphibious in character. And it is likely to remain so as long as United States military might is projected into areas without adequate port facilities.

As long as we have a Navy, it is doubtful if the Joint Chiefs of Staff will ever again relegate our amphibious ships and the men who man them to the "Port of No Return."

Appendixes

A:

Naval Commanders, Landing Force Commanders, and Major Landing Units

WOODLARK

Rear Admiral Barbey, USN.
Brigadier General Cunningham, USA.
112th Cavalry Regimental Combat
Team (Reinforced)

LAE

Rear Admiral Barbey, USN.
Major General Wooten, A.I.F.
9th Australian Infantry Division,
A.I.F. (Australian Imperial Forces)

FINSCHHAFEN

Rear Admiral Barbey, USN.
Major General Wooten, A.I.F.
9th Australian Infantry Division,
A.I.F.

ARAWE

Rear Admiral Barbey, USN.
Brigadier General Cunningham, USA.
112th Cavalry Regimental Combat
Team (Reinforced).

CAPE GLOUCESTER

Rear Admiral Barbey, USN.
Major General Rupertus, USMC.
First Marine Division (Reinforced).

SAIDOR

Rear Admiral Barbey, USN.
Brigadier General Clarence Martin,
USA.
126th Infantry Regimental Combat
Team (Reinforced) (32nd Division)

ADMIRALTY ISLANDS

Rear Admiral Fechteler, USN.
Brigadier General Chase, USA.
First Brigade (Reinforced), 1st
Cavalry Division.

AITAPE

Captain A. G. Noble, USN.
Brigadier General J. A. Doe, USA.
163rd Regimental Combat Team (Reinforced) (41st Division)

HUMBOLDT BAY

Rear Admiral Fechteler, USN.
Major General Fuller, USA.
41st Infantry Division (less 163rd
Regimental Combat Team) (Reinforced).

TANAHMERAH BAY

Rear Admiral Barbey, USN.
Major General Irving, USA.
24th Infantry (Reinforced) (less 1
Regimental Combat Team)

WAKDE

Captain A. G. Noble, USN.
Brigadier General J. A. Doe, USA.
163rd Infantry Regimental Combat
Team (Reinforced) (41st Infantry
Division).

BIAK

Rear Admiral Fechteler, USN.
Major General Fuller, USA.
41st Infantry Division (less 163rd
Regimental Combat Team) (Reinforced).

NOEMFOOR

Rear Admiral Fechteler, USN.
Brigadier General Patrick, USA.

158th Infantry Regimental Combat
Team (Reinforced)

SANSAPOR

Rear Admiral Fechteler, USN.
Major General Siebert, USA.
6th Infantry Division (Reinforced).

MOROTAI

Rear Admiral Barbey, USN.
Major General Hall, USA.
XI Corps

Rear Admiral Fechteler, USN.
Major General Persons, USA.
31st Infantry Division (Reinforced),
126th Infantry Regimental Combat
Team of 32nd Division

LEYTE

Vice Admiral Kincaid, USN.
Lieutenant General Kreuger, USA.
Sixth U.S. Army.

1. NORTHERN ATTACK FORCE

Rear Admiral Barbey, USN.
Major General Siebert, USA.
X Corps

A. *Palo Attack Group*
Rear Admiral Barbey, USN.
Major General Irving, USA.
24th Infantry Division (less 21st
Regimental Combat Team)
(Reinforced)

B. *Ricardo Attack Group*
Rear Admiral Fechteler, USN.
Major General Mudge, USA.
1st Cavalry Division.

C. *Panaon Attack Group*
Rear Admiral Struble, USN.

21st Infantry Regimental Combat Team of 24th Infantry Division.

D. *Dinagat Attack Group*
Rear Admiral Struble, USN.
Lieutenant Colonel Mussie, AUS.
6th Ranger Battalion.

2. SOUTHERN ATTACK FORCE

Vice Admiral Wilkinson, USN.
Major General Hodge, USA.
XXIV Corps.

A. *Able Attack Group*
Rear Admiral Connolly, USN.
Major General A. V. Arnold, USA.
7th Infantry Division.

B. *Baker Attack Group*
Rear Admiral Royal, USN.
Major General Bradley, USA.
96th Infantry Division.

MAPIA-ASIA

Captain Lord Ashbourne, RN.

Elements of the Eighth Army.

ORMOC

Rear Admiral Struble, USN.
Major General Bruce, USA.
77th Infantry Division (less 1 Regimental Combat Team) (Reinforced).

MINDORO

Rear Admiral Struble, USN.
Brigadier General Dunkel, USA.
19th Regimental Combat Team from 24th U.S. Infantry Division. 503rd Parachute Regiment.

LINGAYEN

Vice Admiral Kincaid, USN.
Lieutenant General Kreuger, USA.
Sixth U.S. Army.

1. LINGAYEN ATTACK FORCE

Vice Admiral Wilkinson, USN.
Major General Griswold, USA.
XIV Corps.

A. *Able Attack Group*
Rear Admiral Kiland, USN.
Major General Beightler, USA.
37th Infantry Division

B. *Baker Attack Group*
Rear Admiral Royal, USN.
Major General Rapp Brush, USA.
40th Infantry Division.

2. SAN FABIAN ATTACK FORCE

Vice Admiral Barbey, USN.
Major General Swift, USA.
I Corps.

A. *White Beach Attack Group*
Vice Admiral Barbey, USN.
Major General Wing, USA.
43rd Infantry Division.

B. *Blue Beach Attack Group*
Rear Admiral Fechteler, USN.
Major General Patrick, USA.
6th Infantry Division.

3. RESERVE GROUP

Rear Admiral Connolly, USN.
Major General Mullins, USA—
Brigadier General McNider, AUS.
25th Infantry Division—158th Regimental Combat Team.

ZAMBALES

Rear Admiral Struble, USN.
Major General Hall, USA—Brigadier
General Chase, USA.
XI Corps Troops—38th U.S. Infantry
Division. 134th Regimental Combat
Team of 24th Infantry Division.

NASUGBU

Rear Admiral Fechteler, USN.
Major General Swing, USA.
11th Airborne Division (less Parachute Regimental Combat Team).

BATAAN-CORREGIDOR

Rear Admiral Struble, USN.
Brigadier General Chase, USA—Colonel Jones, AUS.
38th Infantry Division—503rd Parachute Regiment.

PALAWAN

Rear Admiral Fechteler, USN.
Major General J. A. Doe, USA.
186th Regimental Combat Team of
41st Infantry Division.

LUBANG

Captain H. F. McGee, USN.
1st Battalion, 21st Infantry of 24th
Division.

ZAMBOANGA

Rear Admiral Royal, USN.
Major General J. A. Doe, USA.
41st Infantry Division.

PANAY

Rear Admiral Struble, USN.
Major General Rapp Brush, USA.
40th Infantry Division (less 1 Regimental Combat Team).

CEBU

Captain A. T. Sprague, USN.
Major General W. A. Arnold, USA.
American Division (less 164th Regi-
mental Combat Team).

CABALLO

Rear Admiral Struble, USN.
Brigadier General Chase, USA.
Elements of 38th Division.

NEGROS

Captain A. T. Sprague, USN.
Major General W. A. Arnold, USA.
American Division (less 164th Regi-
mental Combat Team).

LEGASPI

Captain H. F. McGee, USN.
Brigadier General McNider, AUS.
158th Regimental Combat Team (Reinforced)

SANGA SANGA

Captain J. D. Murphy, USN.
Colonel Moroney, AUS.
One Battalion Landing Team of 163rd
Regimental Combat Team of 41st
Infantry Division.

MASBATE

Captain H. B. Hudson, USN.
Colonel Stratta, AUS.
108th Regimental Combat Team of
40th Infantry Division.

JOLO

Captain J. D. Murphy, USN.
Colonel Moroney, AUS.
Elements of 41st Infantry Division.

BUSANGAS

Commander L. R. Neville, USN.

Elements of the 186th Regimental Combat Team of 41st Infantry Division.

BOHOL

Captain W. V. Deutermann, USN.

1 Battalion Landing Team of 164th Regimental Combat Team of Americal Division.

EL FRAILLE

Commander S. H. Pattie, USN.
Lieutenant Colonel Lobit, AUS.
1st Battalion of 151st Regimental Combat Team of 38th Division.

PARANG, MINDANAO

Rear Admiral Noble, USN.
Lieutenant General Siebert, USA.
X Corps (24th and 31st Infantry Divisions)

MACAJALAR

Rear Admiral Struble, USN.
108th Regimental Combat Team of 40th Infantry Division.

TARAKAN

Rear Admiral Royal, USN.
Brigadier General Whitehead, A.I.F.
26th Australian Infantry Brigade Group (Reinforced) A.I.F.

BRUNEI BAY

Rear Admiral Royal, USN.
Major General G. F. Wooten, A.I.F.
9th Australian Division (less 26th Brigade), A.I.F.

BALIKPAPAN

Rear Admiral Noble, USN.
Major General Milford, A.I.F.
7th Australian Division, A.I.F. (plus Corps Artillery).

KOREAN OCCUPATION

Vice Admiral Barbey, USN.
Lieutenant General Hodge, USA.
XXIV Corps.

A. *Initial Lift*
Commodore T. H. Brittain, USN.
Major General A. V. Arnold, USA.
7th Infantry Division.

B. *Initial Follow-Up*
Commodore J. H. Palmer, USN.
Brigadier General D. J. Meyers, USA.
40th Infantry Division.

C. *Final Follow-Up*
Commodore J. H. Palmer, USN.
Major General C. E. Hurdis, USA.
6th Infantry Division.

CHINA OCCUPATION

Vice Admiral Barbey, USN.
Major General K. E. Rockey, USMC.
III Marine Amphibious Corps.

1. TIENTSIN, CHINA
Commodore T. H. Brittain, USN.
Major General De W. Peck, USMC.
1st Marine Division.

2. TSINGTAO, CHINA
Commodore E. T. Short, USN.
Major General L. C. Shepherd, USMC.
Sixth Marine Division.

B:

Troops and Cargo Transported in Major Assault Operations

Troops and Tonnage Carried by SEVENTH AMPHIBIOUS FORCE in Amphibious Assault Landings |30 June 1943—1 July 1945

AMPHIBIOUS SHIPPING LIFTS

OPERATION	ASSAULT		FOLLOW-UP		TOTAL	
	Pers.	Tons of Equip. & Supplies	Pers.	Tons of Equip. & Supplies	Pers.	Tons of Equip. & Supplies
WOODLARK ISLAND	2,600	2,400	9,500	32,700	12,100	35,100
KIRIWINA ISLAND	2,500	1,400	2,200	6,400	4,700	7,800
LAE	7,800	3,300	8,700	8,900	16,500	12,200
FINSCHHAFEN	5,300	3,000	5,000	5,000	10,300	8,000
ARAWE	2,200	2,200	2,600	6,000	4,800	8,200
CAPE GLOUCESTER	12,500	8,700	11,500	14,300	24,000	23,000
SAIDOR	7,200	3,000			7,200	3,000
ADMIRALTY ISLANDS	1,000		8,300	14,500	9,300	14,500
AITAPE	6,300	4,700	10,100	12,800	16,400	17,500
HUMBOLDT BAY	8,400	4,800	13,400	18,800	21,800	23,600

OPERATION	ASSAULT		FOLLOW-UP		TOTAL	
	Pers.	*Tons of Equip. & Supplies*	Pers.	*Tons of Equip. & Supplies*	Pers.	*Tons of Equip. & Supplies*
TANAHMERAH BAY	10,400	4,500	21,500	17,500	31,900	22,000
TOEM-WADKE	7,800	4,400	18,000	18,000	25,800	22,400
BIAK	7,500	5,600	21,000	20,300	28,500	25,900
NOEMFOOR	7,100	5,900	13,400	18,500	20,500	24,400
SANSAPOR	7,300	4,800	20,900	40,300	28,200	45,100
MOROTAI	17,000	9,000	39,800	96,800	56,800	105,800
LEYTE	39,800	38,400	44,400	48,000	84,200	86,400
ORMOC	3,800	3,600	3,000	9,000	6,800	12,600
MINDORO	16,600	27,600	5,100	16,800	21,700	44,400
LINGAYEN	43,500	41,300	91,200	108,800	134,700	150,100
LUZON REINFORCEMENT			90,600	78,500	90,600	78,500
SUBIC BAY	44,400	53,400			44,400	53,400
NASUGBU	8,000	4,200			8,000	4,200
CORREGIDOR	4,300	6,400			4,300	6,400
PALAWAN	8,500	12,300	7,700	13,200	16,200	25,500
ZAMBOANGA	14,500	11,500	5,900	15,100	20,400	26,600
SULU ARCHIPELAGO	6,600	4,700	900	1,800	7,500	6,500
PANAY	9,800	10,500	3,400	7,100	13,200	17,600
CEBU	10,800	11,200	3,800	9,400	14,600	20,600
BOHOL-NEGROS	5,600	3,300			5,600	3,300
PARANG MINDANAO	24,500	27,300	34,800	49,600	59,300	76,900
DAVAO MINDANAO			4,100	8,000	4,100	8,000
MACAJALAR BAY, MINDANAO	4,100	3,600	1,500	3,000	5,600	6,600
LEGASPI	4,500	1,700	1,600	2,000	6,100	3,700
MINOR PHILIPPINE OPER.	6,000	6,000			6,000	6,000
TARAKAN	13,500	15,200	4,600	7,700	18,100	22,900
BRUNEI BAY	25,400	26,200	8,100	23,300	33,500	49,500
BALIKPAPAN	25,000	26,800	8,600	26,800	33,600	53,600
TOTALS	432,100	402,900	525,200	758,900	957,300	1,161,800

C:

Landing Craft Plans

LSD—LANDING SHIP, DOCK

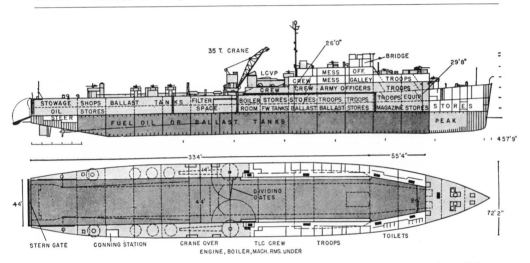

The LSD is designed to transport loaded landing craft to the landing area, where the well is flooded and the craft move out under their own power. Landing craft up to the size of LCI(L)s may be stowed in the well. It has a capacity of two LCTs, each with 12 medium tanks, or 14 LCMs, each with one medium tank or 1,500 long tons of cargo. Troops: 22 officers, 218 men. Dimensions: length, 457'19" o.a.; beam, 72'. Speed: 15 knots.

APD—HIGH-SPEED TRANSPORTS (DESTROYERS)

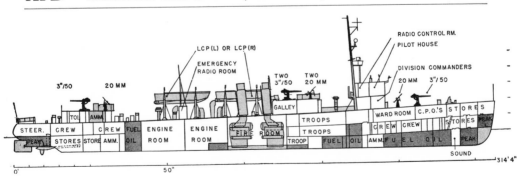

Converted "flush-deck" destroyers designed to accommodate raiding parties and land them by small craft. An APD has a capacity of four LCP(L)s or LCP(R)s and one Marine rifle company. Over 200 men have been successfully accommodated. Dimensions: 314'4" o.a.; beam, 31'8"; 11'11" plus 4' sound dome (maximum draft). Speed: 23 knots maximum.

LST—LANDING SHIP, TANK

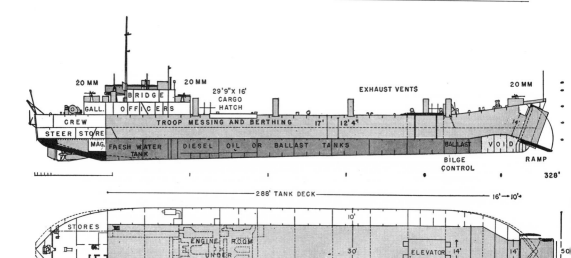

An oceangoing ship designed to land waterproofed tanks or vehicles over a low ramp onto a beach slope. For inaccessible landings, sectional pontoons are used or earth causeways are built. The oceangoing load is limited to 2,100 tons on LST(1) class and 1,900 tons on LST-542 class. Dimensions: length, 328'0" o.a.; beam, 50'0". Speed: 10.8 knots maximum.

LSM—LANDING SHIP, MEDIUM

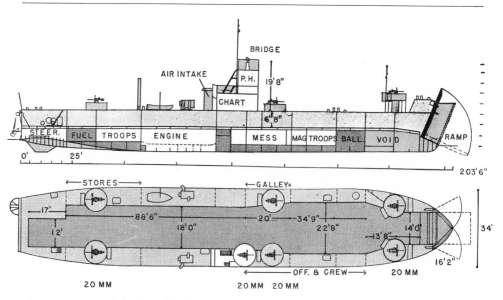

An oceangoing tank landing ship designed to operate with LCI(L)s. An LSM can carry five medium or three heavy tanks, or six LVTs, or nine DUKWs, as well as two officers and 52 men. Dimensions: 203'6" o.a.; beam, 34'0". Speed: 13.3 knots.

LCI(L)—LANDING CRAFT, INFANTRY (LARGE)

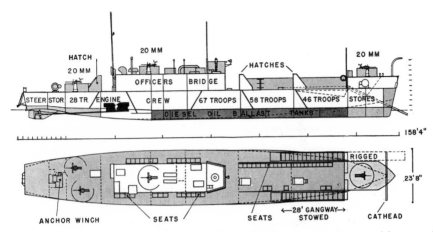

An oceangoing infantry carrier designed for direct unloading onto the beach, with a capacity for six officers and 182 enlisted men. It carries four 20-mm. guns. Dimensions: length, 158'5½" o.a.; beam, 23'3". Speed: 14 knots maximum.

LCT(5)—LANDING CRAFT, PERSONNEL (RAMP)

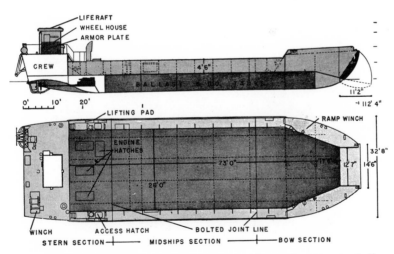

An LCT(5) is constructed in three watertight sections and may be transported disassembled on decks of larger vessels. An LST can carry five of these sections or an assembled LCT, which is launched over the side by listing. An LCT(5) has no troop accommodations, but can carry 150 tons of cargo. It carries two 20-mm. guns. Dimensions: 117'6" o.a.; beam, 32'. Speed: 8 knots.

LCM(3)—LANDING CRAFT, MECHANIZED (MARK 3)

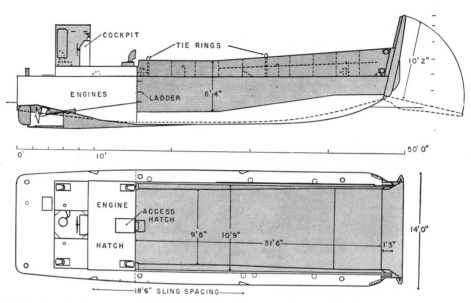

Designed to land motor vehicles or one medium (30-ton) tank directly onto the beach. Also capable of carrying 60,000 pounds of cargo or 60 troops. It is equipped with two 50-caliber machine guns. Dimensions: length, 50'0" o.a.; beam, 14'1". Speed: 11 knots.

LCVP—LANDING CRAFT, VEHICLE, PERSONNEL

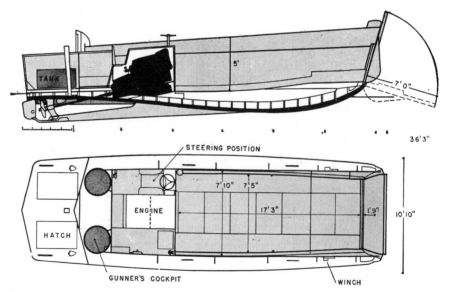

An improved LCV with steering control and gunners' cockpits in the hold, with a capacity of 36 troops, a 6,000 pound vehicle, or 8,100 pounds of general cargo. It carries two 30-caliber machine guns. Dimensions: length, 36' o.a.; beam, 10'5¼". Speed: 9 knots.

LCV—LANDING CRAFT, VEHICLE

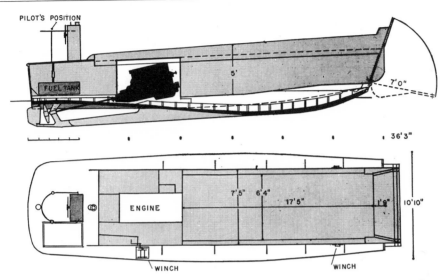

A small, wood-hulled vehicle carrier for initial and subsequent landing waves. Also used as personnel and cargo carrier. It can be transported on the deck of an APA, AKA, or LST, or in the hold of an LSD or LCT. It has a capacity of one 1-ton truck, 36 troops, or 10,000 pounds of cargo. Dimensions: length, 36'3" o.a.; beam, 10'10". Speed: 9 knots (loaded).

LCP(R)—LANDING CRAFT, PERSONNEL (RAMP)

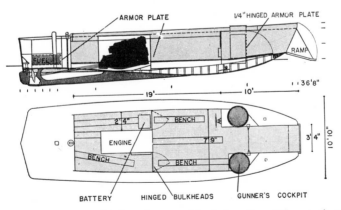

A personnel carrier with a ramp added to decrease debarkation time. These craft may be carried on APA, AKA, or APD davits, from which they may be lowered fully loaded. Dimensions: 36'8" o.a.; beam, 10'10".

D: Miscellaneous Data

SEVENTH AMPHIBIOUS FORCE OPERATIONS
30 June 1943—1 July 1945

OPERATIONS	TIMES H-Hour	Sunrise	CARRIER AIR SUPPORT AVAILABLE	STAGING AREA	DISTANCE FROM STAGING AREA
WOODLARK	2100(K)	0630(K)	No	Milne Bay	150
KIRIWINA	0630(K)	0611(K)	No	Townsville, Australia.	710
LAE	0630(K)	0612(K)	No	Buna	150
				Milne Bay	320
FINSCHHAFEN	0445(K)	0558(K)	No	Lae	60
				Buna	140
ARAWE	0630(L)	0646(L)	No	Goodenough Is.	245
GLOUCESTER	0715(L)	0653(L)	No	Buna	210
				Goodenough Is.	270
				Milne Bay	385
SAIDOR	0650(K)	0605(K)	No	Goodenough Is.	340

SEVENTH AMPHIBIOUS FORCE OPERATIONS (*continued*)

30 June 1943—1 July 1945

OPERATIONS	TIMES H-Hour	*Sunrise*	CARRIER AIR SUPPORT AVAILABLE	STAGING AREA	DISTANCE FROM STAGING AREA
ADMIRALTY ISLANDS	0815(L)	0820(L)	No	Buna	430
AITAPE	0645(K)	0626(K)	Yes	Finschhafen	430 *
HUMBOLDT BAY	0700(K)	0634(K)	Yes	Finschhafen	520 *
TANAHMERAH BAY	0700(K)	0636(K)	Yes	Goodenough Is.	820 *
TOEM-WADKE	0800(K)	0640(K)	No	Aitape	225
BIAK	0715(K)	0651(K)	No	Humboldt Bay	300
NOEMFOOR	0800(K)	0703(K)	No	Toem	265
SANSAPOR	0700(K)	0715(K)	No	Toem	440
MOROTAI	0830(I)	0622(I)	Yes	Aitape Toem	905 690
LEYTE	1000(I)	0630(I)	Yes	Hollandia Manus Finschhafen	1240 1565 2075
ORMOC			Yes	Leyte	160
MINDORO		0709(I)	Yes	Leyte	480
LINGAYEN	0930(I)	0730(I)	Yes	Aitape Sansapor	2135 1835
LUZON REINFORCEMENT			Yes	Leyte Morotai Biak	810 1380 1770
ZAMBALES SUBIC BAY	0830(I)	0730(I)	Yes	Leyte	640
NASUGBU	0815(I)	0728(I)	No	Leyte	560
CORREGIDOR	0900(I)	0721(I)	No	Subic Bay	25
PALAWAN	0845(I)	0719(I)	No	Mindoro	285
ZAMBOANGA	0915(I)	0701(I)	No	Mindoro	335
SULU ARCHIPELAGO	0800(I)	0649(I)	No	Zamboanga	175

* Direct. A devious route was used by assault echelons.

30 June 1943—1 July 1945

OPERATIONS	TIMES		CARRIER AIR SUPPORT AVAILABLE	STAGING AREA	DISTANCE FROM STAGING AREA
	H-Hour	*Sunrise*			
PANAY	0830(I)	0655(I)	No	Lingayen	525
CEBU	0830(I)	0646(I)	No	Leyte	235
PARANG MINDANAO	0800(I)	0635(I)	No	Mindoro	490
				Morotai	470
DAVAO		0622(I)	No	Parang	270
MACAJALAR BAY, MINDANAO		0623(I)	No	Ormoc	150
LEGASPI	1000(I)	0642(I)	No	Subic Bay	360
TARAKAN	0815(I)	0700(I)	No	Morotai	650
BRUNEI BAY	0915(I)	0705(I)	No	Morotai	950
BALIKPAPAN	0900(I)	0715(I)	Yes	Morotai	800

Index

Edited by Louise Gerretson
Designed by Gerard A. Valerio
Composed, printed, and bound by Kingsport Press, Inc.
Composed in eleven point Granjon text and Goudy Old Style display
Printed offset on sixty pound Mohawk Ravenna smooth
Bound in G.S.B. S/522 khaki